Finance and Occupa

C000102890

About the Author

Charles Sutcliffe is a professor of finance at the ICMA Centre, Henley Business School, University of Reading, where he teaches a course on occupational pensions. Previously he was a professor of finance and accounting at the University of Southampton, and the Northern Society Professor of Accounting and Finance at the University of Newcastle. In 1995-96 and 2003-04 he was a visiting professor at the London School of Economics. Between 2001 and 2007 he was a member nominated trustee of the Universities Superannuation Scheme (USS), and from 1981 to 1985 a trustee of the Berkshire Local Authorities Superannuation Fund. He has published in a wide range of refereed journals, and is also the author of ten books. He has acted as a consultant to the Financial Services Authority, the Securities and Investments Board, H.M. Treasury, the Cabinet Office, the Corporation of London, the United Nations, the London Stock Exchange and the London International Financial Futures and Options Exchange.

Contents

List of Figures

List of Tables

1

Introduction to Pension Schemes

Attitudes towards old people have shown a very marked change over the past 100 years. In 1914 Ignatz Leo Nascher wrote the following in the preface to one of the first gerontology textbooks: *'We realise that for all practical purposes the lives of the aged are useless, that they are often a burden to themselves, their family and the community at large. Their appearance is generally unaesthetic, their actions objectionable, their very existence often an incubus to those who in their humanity or duty take upon themselves the care of the aged.'* However, during the last century there has been a substantial change in attitudes towards the elderly, and a more optimistic view of being old was provided by the French entertainer Maurice Chevalier who said that *'Old age isn't so bad, when you consider the alternative'* (Morris and Palmer 2011). Over the 100 years since Nascher wrote his preface, pension systems have been developed around the world to provide for the retired.

Pension schemes have become important economic institutions both in the UK, and globally. (In the USA pension *schemes* are known as pension *plans*.) Total UK pension liabilities in 2010 were £7 trillion, which was almost five times UK Gross Domestic Product (GDP) in that year, and represented assets worth over £2 trillion. Therefore pension schemes play an important role in capital markets as major institutional investors. They also have liabilities that are substantially larger than their assets. While western countries have created their pension systems over the past century, developing countries such as China and India face a substantial challenge, and have the potential for an enormous expansion of their pension systems.

Pension systems throughout most of the world are in a state of long-term crisis. This is a very slow-moving crisis, which is creeping up on us decade by

© The Author(s) 2016
C. Sutcliffe, *Finance and Occupational Pensions*,
DOI 10.1057/978-1-349-94863-5_1

decade, and any remedies will take decades to have a material effect. So we cannot wait until serious problems are obvious to all before taking remedial action. Pensions policy is very long term – 20 year old workers can expect to be drawing a pension 65 years later, partly based on contributions made when they were 20 years old. Therefore the effects of changes in pensions policy only appear slowly, and the pension system is always in transition, with different sets of rules applying to contributions made in different years, and this inevitably creates complexity.

There is great variety in pension arrangements, and so what follows in this book is true in most countries, most of the time; but may not be true in all countries all of the time. This book focuses on the important financial features of occupational pensions, and does not cover the institutional and regulatory details in any depth. Where relevant, the institutional details are mostly based on those in the UK, although there are many references to other countries.

1.1   The Three Pillars

The aim of a pension scheme is to provide an income for those who have stopped working – usually due to their advanced years or ill-health. It was only in the twentieth century that significant numbers of people had lived long enough for the provision of income during the retirement period to be of importance. In most countries the pension system has three pillars or legs – state pensions, occupational pensions and private pensions (see Fig. 1.1).

a. State Pensions
The first state pension scheme was introduced by Otto von Bismarck in Germany in 1889 for workers aged over 70. It was contributory, compulsory and targeted at skilled male workers (Schieber 2012, p. 27; German Empire, 1889). There was no need to retire to receive this pension, which covered 40 % of the workforce and was below the subsistence level (Arza and Johnson 2006). Denmark introduced a state pension scheme in 1891, as did New Zealand in 1898 (Rogers and Millar 1903). In June 1893 Octavia Hill, a

PENSIONS

STATE PENSIONS	OCCUPATIONAL PENSIONS	PRIVATE PENSIONS

Fig. 1.1 The three pillars

leading nineteenth century social reformer and founder of the National Trust, gave evidence to the Royal Commission on the Aged Poor, set up to consider establishing a non-contributory state pension scheme in the UK. She argued strongly against such a step on the grounds that it would: (a) discourage thrift, (b) be inadequate, (c) destroy the responsibility of relatives, (d) cruelly raise expectations and (e) apply to everyone including the well-off. The final report rejected the idea of a state pension (Royal Commission 1895). However, in 1908 David Lloyd George introduced the first general old age pension in the UK. This was a *non-contributory* pension from age 70, paid from 1 January 1909 – 'Pensions Day'. Life expectancy at birth in 1908 was only 48 years, while UK male life expectancy at age 70 was about six years. This UK state pension was subject to a means test as well as a test of moral character (e.g. no drunkards, criminals or those who habitually failed to work); and recipients of poor law relief and aliens were also excluded. Pensioners with an annual income of less than £21 received the maximum rate of 5 shillings (25pence) per week (Morris and Palmer 2011). In 1908, 40 % of those over 70 qualified, and in 1909, 680,000 people received this pension. By 1911 this had risen to over one million pensioners (Salter et al. 2009).

Following its proposal by Lord Beveridge, in 1946 the National Insurance Act introduced a mandatory *contributory* state pension in the UK. This was paid from age 65 for men, and age 60 for women; effective from 1948. While these retirement ages remained unchanged for many decades, they have recently been harmonised, with the female retirement age rising in stages to 65. The retirement age of 65 will rise in the future, and there is debate about raising this age towards 70 for both men and women by the middle of this century. In August 2012 the UK pensions minister, Steve Webb, said of the UK state system that '*the current system is so complex, it would baffle even Einstein*'.

b. Occupational Pensions

A few employers (who are known as sponsors of the pension scheme) have offered pensions to some of their employees for hundreds of years. The first organised UK pension scheme was for Customs and Excise staff in 1671, although from 1590 the Chatham Chest provided pensions for the Royal Navy (Morris and Palmer 2011, p. 124). The first corporate occupational pension scheme in the USA was created by American Express in 1875 (Schieber 2012, p. 24). Widespread occupational pension schemes are a more recent arrival, with substantial growth occurring after the Second World War. The Universities Superannuation Scheme (USS) is a very large UK occupational pension scheme that will be used as example later in this book.

c. Private Pensions

Individuals deliberately choose to make contributions to a pension scheme which is separate from their employer, and not run by the state. These have names such as personal pensions and stakeholder pensions.

These are the three pillars or legs of the pension system, and each pillar has a different motivation. State pensions are provided as part of the welfare state, and help to ensure that old people are not left destitute. Contributions to state pensions (called National Insurance in the UK) are compulsory in the UK. There are three main motives for state pensions (Banks and Emmerson 2000). First, market failure may be preventing individuals from efficiently providing a pension for themselves; for example missing markets, high transactions costs, monopolistic markets and adverse selection (see Sect. 5.5b for details of adverse selection). Second, paternalism may be the motive because individuals unwisely choose not to provide for themselves, even though the opportunities for such provision exist. This failure by individuals may be due to the complexity of the problem, or to a lack of self-control. Finally, the motive may be to redistribute income to those not rich enough to provide adequate pensions for themselves. Occupational pensions are voluntary in the UK, although they were compulsory until 1986, and are offered by some employers as a way of recruiting and retaining good staff. They can be viewed as deferred wages, and so offering a good pension enables employers to pay lower wages. Section 2.1 discusses the reasons for the provision of occupational pension schemes. Private pensions allow workers to voluntarily save for their retirement and top up their state and occupational pensions. The self-employed, who are not members of an occupational scheme, may also choose to contribute to a private pension.

Two additional pillars were identified by the World Bank in 2005 (Holzmann and Hinz 2005), although they are not pensions. The zero pillar is where the state guarantees a minimum income paid for out of taxation, for example a welfare state; and the fourth pillar covers personal savings, informal family support and non-financial assets such as houses. The Geneva Association identified a different additional pillar, in addition to the three pensions pillars, making a total of four. Their additional pillar is the part-time employment of pensioners (Geneva Association).

d. Ranking of National Pension Systems

In recent years national pension systems, which include all three pillars, have been ranked in 2015 by the Melbourne Mercers Global Pension Index. The ranking is subjective, but gives some idea of those countries with well-regarded national pension systems (see Table 1.1). These countries have been scored on adequacy (benefits, savings, tax support, benefit design and growth assets),

Table 1.1 Melbourne Mercers Global Pension Index 2015 (Mercers 2015)

Rank	Country	Score	Rank	Country	Score
1	Denmark	81.7	14	USA	56.3
2	Netherlands	80.5	15	Poland	56.2
3	Australia	79.6	16	S. Africa	53.4
4=	Switzerland	74.2	17	Brazil	53.2
4=	Sweden	74.2	18	Austria	52.2
6	Finland	73.0	19	Mexico	52.1
7	Canada	70.0	20	Italy	50.9
8	Chile	69.1	21	Indonesia	48.2
9	UK	65.0	22	China	48.0
10	Singapore	64.7	23	Japan	44.1
11	Ireland	63.1	24	S. Korea	43.8
12	Germany	62.0	25	India	40.3
13	France	57.4			

sustainability (coverage, total assets, contributions, demography and government debt) and integrity (regulation, governance, protection, communication and costs). Table 1.1 shows that there is a considerable range between the scores of the best (Denmark) and the worst (India) countries.

1.2   Replacement and Coverage Rates

When someone retires they are concerned about the extent to which their income will drop. One measure of this is the replacement rate, which is their pension divided by their pre-retirement income. The replacement rate can be computed using either net or gross income and pension. The net replacement rates for the mean earners in the OECD countries in 2014 appear in Table 1.2, where pensions and incomes are after tax and social security contributions, and pensions include mandatory and voluntary private and state pensions. Table 1.2 shows there is considerable variation in replacement rates, and some countries have a net replacement rate of over 100 %, so that the mean earner experiences a rise in his or her net income on retirement! In the UK the net replacement rate is 61 %, which is below the OECD average of 68 %. In contrast to most other countries, where almost all of a pension comes from mandatory state and private pensions, in the UK the net replacement rate for mandatory state and private pensions is only 28 %. Therefore those in the UK who do not have a voluntary pension face a dramatic drop in their net income on retirement.

Another feature of a pension system is the coverage rate, i.e. the proportion of the population who are members or pensioners of a pension scheme. Most UK workers are enrolled in the mandatory state pension scheme. But in 2003 almost half of those of working age in the UK were not covered by

Table 1.2 Some net replacement rates for the mean earner 2014 (OECD 2015a)

India	109.7 %	France	67.7 %
Turkey	104.8 %	Denmark	66.4 %
Canada	96.1 %	Saudi Arabia	65.4 %
Netherlands	95.7 %	Germany	64.7 %
Austria	91.6 %	Czech Rep.	63.8 %
Hungary	89.6 %	Finland	63.5 %
Portugal	89.5 %	UK	61.2 %
Spain	89.5 %	Norway	60.2 %
Luxembourg	88.6 %	Estonia	59.8 %
Argentina	87.5 %	Australia	58.0 %
Russia	86.4 %	Slovenia	57.4 %
USA	81.9 %	New Zealand	56.8 %
Slovak Rep.	80.6 %	Sweden	55.8 %
China	80.5 %	South Africa	54.8 %
Italy	79.7 %	Poland	52.8 %
Iceland	76.7 %	Switzerland	46.9 %
Brazil	76.4 %	Korea	45.0 %
Greece	72.9 %	Japan	40.4 %
Belgium	72.1 %	Chile	37.7 %
Ireland	72.1 %	Mexico	28.4 %
Israel	68.8 %	Indonesia	13.8 %
OECD (34) average	68.4 %		

Table 1.3 Membership of UK occupational pension schemes 2003

Contributing to an occupational scheme	42 %
Not contributing but covered by partner's contributions	11 %
Not covered by an occupational scheme	47 %
Total	100 %

an occupational pension scheme, as shown in Table 1.3. However the recent introduction of auto-enrolment in the UK is changing this situation (see Sect. 1.9).

1.3   Funded Versus Unfunded Schemes

Figure 1.2 shows that during their adult lives people wish to consume roughly a constant amount per year. Their income rises as they age, but ceases when they retire. Since they have no income in retirement, but wish to keep on consuming, people save during their working lives. Figure 1.2 includes their wealth, which increases over time due to additional saving, and returns on previous savings. The period of saving for retirement is called the accumulation phase, and the period when wealth is used to finance post-retirement consumption is called the decumulation phase. Figure 1.3 shows that a person

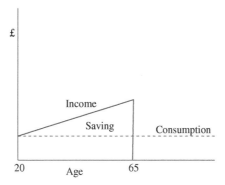

Fig. 1.2 Income and consumption

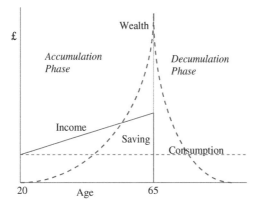

Fig. 1.3 Accumulation and decumulation

may live so long that their wealth is eventually exhausted. This problem will be considered in Chap. 5.

Pension schemes receive inflows of contributions during a person's working life (the accumulation phase), and provide pensions after retirement (the decumulation phase). They can be divided into those that have accumulated a fund of money from which to pay pensions (funded schemes), and those that do not have any accumulated funds and use current cash inflows to meet pension payments (unfunded or pay-as-you-go (PAYG) schemes).

a. Funded Schemes

The creation of a legally separate funded pension scheme from which the sponsor (employer) cannot remove funds helps to reassure scheme members that the sponsor will deliver on its pensions promise to the scheme members, even if the sponsor goes into liquidation. Funds are accumulated to pay for the pensions promise, i.e. pay the pensions, and this money is called a pension

Table 1.4 Occupational and personal pension assets in European countries in 2014 (Investment and Pensions Europe 2015)

UK	€2190 bn	46 %	Norway	€30 bn	½ %
Netherlands	€1050 bn	22 %	Belgium	€20 bn	½ %
Switzerland	€677 bn	14 %	Austria	€19 bn	½ %
Germany	€193 bn	4 %	Iceland	€19 bn	½ %
Denmark	€125 bn	3 %	Portugal	€17 bn	½ %
Ireland	€109 bn	2 %	Sweden	€16 bn	½ %
Italy	€106 bn	2 %	France	€10 bn	0 %
Spain	€100 bn	2 %	Total	€4774 bn	100 %
Finland	€93 bn	2 %			

fund. It is usually invested in financial and real assets until needed to pay pensions. Investing the money will be considered in detail in Chap. 3. Figure 1.3 shows that, as a scheme member gets older, the size of their associated pension savings grows during this accumulation phase until they retire. On retirement they enter the decumulation phase during which the funds saved in the accumulation phase are depleted.

In the UK all private sector occupational pension schemes and private pensions are funded. If the scheme sponsor (employer) of an occupational scheme goes into liquidation, the accrued pensions will still be paid using the assets in the pension fund, making the pension more secure. Table 1.4 shows that in 2014 the pension assets in Europe are dominated by the UK, with approaching half the total assets, the Netherlands with over one fifth of the total assets, and Switzerland with over one seventh. On the other hand, some large countries such as France, Spain, Italy and Germany have very low levels of pension funding.

This difference between countries in the extent to which they fund their pensions systems is further revealed in Table 1.5. This shows the ratio of pension assets to GDP for OECD countries, and since most countries do not pre-fund state pensions, the assets covered in Table 1.5 are largely for occupational and private pensions. Table 1.5 reveals very considerable differences between countries which might be expected to have roughly similar ratios. For example the Netherlands has pension funds equivalent to 159 % of GDP, while France has pension assets of only 0.5 % of GDP, and Germany has assets of just 6.7 % of GDP.

Table 1.6 shows the ratio of pension assets to GDP for non-OECD countries, and reveals the very large potential for a growth in pension assets in many countries. For example, the ratio of pension assets to GDP for Pakistan and Albania is 0 %, 0.6 % for India, 1.2 % for China and 5.5 % for Russia.

Table 1.5 Pension fund assets relative to GDP for OECD countries 2014 (OECD 2015b)

Rank	Country	Assets/GDP (%)	Rank	Country	Assets/GDP (%)
1	Netherlands	159.3	18	Portugal	10.1
2	Iceland	146.8	19	Spain	9.5
3	Switzerland	120.3	20	Sweden	9.3
4	Australia	110.0	21	Norway	8.8
5	United Kingdom	96.0	22	Poland	8.8
6	United States	83.0	23	Czech Republic	8.0
7	Canada	76.2	24	Korea	7.3
8	Chile	68.3	25	Germany	6.7
9	Ireland	58.1	26	Italy	6.7
10	Israel	54.9	27	Austria	5.8
11	Finland	51.0	28	Belgium	5.6
12	Denmark	48.6	29	Turkey	5.5
13	Japan	30.2	30	Slovenia	4.2
14	New Zealand	20.0	31	Hungary	4.1
15	Mexico	15.7	32	Luxembourg	3.2
16	Estonia	11.3	33	Greece	0.6
17	Slovakia	10.6	34	France	0.5

Table 1.6 Pension fund assets relative to GDP for non-OECD countries 2014 (OECD 2015b)

Rank	Country	Assets/GDP (%)	Rank	Country	Assets/GDP (%)
1	South Africa	94.8	23	Thailand	6.9
2	Liechtenstein	78.4	24	Macedonia	6.4
3	Namibia	77.3	25	Maldives	6.1
4	Botswana	47.3	26	Russia	5.5
5	Hong Kong	37.8	27	Lithuania	5.3
6	El Salvador	31.6	28	Nigeria	5.1
7	Malta	26.9	29	Zambia	3.4
8	Papua New Guinea	24.8	30	Romania	3.0
9	Jamaica	22.1	31	Mauritius	2.2
10	Croatia	21.4	32	Egypt	2.0
11	Uruguay	20.8	33	Indonesia	1.8
12	Trinidad & Tobago	20.6	34	Gibraltar	1.8
13	Peru	19.9	35	Latvia	1.7
14	Kosovo	19.8	36	China	1.2
15	Colombia	19.8	37	Panama	0.9
16	Kenya	14.0	38	Serbia	0.6
18	Malawi	13.7	39	India	0.6
17	Lesotho	13.7	40	Armenia	0.3
19	Brazil	12.0	41	Ukraine	0.1
20	Costa Rica	11.8	42	Albania	0.0
21	Dominican Rep. Rep.	11.0	43	Pakistan	0.0
22	Bulgaria	10.0			

Table 1.7 UK pensions liabilities December 2010, £ trillion (Levy 2012)

	£ trillion	% GDP
Government		
State pensions (unfunded)	3.843	263
Public sector (unfunded)	0.852	58
Public sector (funded)	0.313	21
	5.008	342
Private sector		
DB (funded)	1.340	92
DC workplace (funded)	0.386	26
DC individual (funded)	0.326	22
	2.052	140
Total UK pension liabilities	7.060	482

b. Unfunded or Pay-As-You-Go (PAYG) Schemes

State pensions are generally unfunded, i.e. paid out of current tax revenues (PAYG). In the UK the schemes for employees of the state (public sector workers) are also unfunded, and this includes school teachers, civil servants, National Health Service employees, the armed forces and so on. In this case, if the scheme sponsor (the government) goes bankrupt, the pensions will probably also disappear. But the government has the power of taxation, and so pensions sponsored by the government are very secure, even though they are unfunded. Table 1.7 shows UK government and private sector pension liabilities in 2010. The total pension liability was 482 % of UK GDP in 2011, while Table 1.5 revealed that pension assets were only 96 % of GDP in 2012. This large gap between the assets and liabilities of the UK pension system is principally due to the £3.8 billion unfunded state pension liability. UK local government pensions, and some quasi-governmental schemes are funded, as are all defined contribution pensions. DB (defined benefit) and DC (defined contribution) pension schemes will be explained in Sect. 1.6.

1.4   Macroeconomic and Inter-generational Considerations

Funding a pension scheme just means that money has been saved and invested. The goods and services consumed by pensioners must be produced by the pensioner's home economy at the time they are consumed, unless people stockpile tins of food, bottles of wine, shirts, cars, TV sets and so on, for consumption when they retire; or import goods and services from other countries during their retirement. Therefore pensioners require the economy to be able to produce most of the goods and services they consume in their retirement at the time of consumption. Funding (saving) ensures that consumption has previously been foregone and the resources invested. Hopefully this investment enables the economy to grow faster, thereby increasing the resources available in future to provide for pensioners. Funding also gives the owners of the pension assets a claim on the available resources at a time of their choosing.

There is an inter-generational aspect to pension provision irrespective of whether or not schemes are funded. PAYG and funding are just different ways of organising claims on future output, and it is each generation that provides goods and services to the previous generation. Therefore pensions are a mechanism for inter-generational redistribution. If no more children were born anywhere in the world, what would happen to the pension system? Even though the UK population has saved over £2 trillion in financial assets, these will be of little use in a world where everyone is a pensioner, and no-one is producing the goods and services pensioners require. As the number of people of working age drops and production declines there would be massive inflation, as a wall of money (pension savings) chases fewer and fewer goods and services. Many people will continue to work beyond the normal retirement age as they cannot afford to retire (and wage rates are now much higher), despite having adequate savings before the dramatic decline in the birth rate.

The real world situation is less dramatic, but in many countries there has been a substantial increase in the proportion of the population who are pensioners. This increase is due to factors such as increased longevity (see Sect. 1.8) and lower fertility, and leads to an increase in the price of labour, relative to the prices of goods and capital. This change in relative prices results in a shift in factor input proportions from labour to capital, and an increase in the imports of consumption goods from countries without such an increase in pensioners. For France, Italy and Germany, Börsch-Supan et al. (2014) have estimated that this automatic macroeconomic response will offset about half the decline in consumption per head due to increasing longevity and the higher proportion of pensioners which will occur over the 2005–50 period. The demands made by pensioners on the economy in 2009 varied considerably between countries. Table 1.8 has the ratio of annual pensions payments (of which state pensions are a major component) to GDP. This reveals that pensions are a major burden for the Italian economy, but much less important for Mexico.

Table 1.8 Public and private pension benefit expenditures, % of GDP in 2009 (OECD 2013a)

Italy	17.0	Spain	9.3
Austria	14.2	Czech Republic	8.8
France	14.1	Denmark	8.6
Greece	13.4	Canada	8.2
Japan	13.3	Luxembourg	8.2
Portugal	12.8	Estonia	7.9
Germany	12.1	Slovak Republic	7.3
Switzerland	12.1	Turkey	6.8
Poland	11.8	Ireland	6.2
Belgium	11.5	Norway	6.0
Slovenia	10.9	Australia	5.5
UK	10.8	Iceland	5.5
Sweden	10.7	Israel	5.0
Netherlands	10.7	Chile	4.9
United States	10.7	New Zealand	4.7
Finland	10.2	Korea	2.2
Hungary	9.9	Mexico	1.7
OECD	9.2		

Table 1.9 Percentage membership of UK pension schemes by socio-economic group and sex 2008–10

Socio-economic group	Men	Women	Difference
Large employers and higher managerial	83	78	5
Higher professional	74	76	−2
Lower managerial and professional	69	72	−3
Intermediate occupations	63	60	3
Lower supervisory and technical	55	43	12
Semi-routine occupations	40	36	4
Small employers and own account workers	40	25	15
Routine occupations	36	20	16

1.5   Pension Scheme Membership

The membership of occupational pension schemes increases with socio-economic group and salary, as demonstrated in Table 1.9. Men are also more likely to be pension scheme members, particularly for those in lower socio-economic groups, although the gap is closing. Balasuriya et al. (2014) used a sample of 20,000 people who started working for a new employer within the past year. They found the probability of participating in an occupational pension scheme (i.e. joining the scheme) was increased if the employee was a financially pessimistic, female, non-smoking, high income, university graduate, with a permanent contract working for a large employer in a finance related job. (See Sect. 2.3d for the factors determining participation in just DC schemes.)

1.6   Main Types of Occupational Scheme

We now move from considering the entire pension system, and focus on occupational pension schemes. There are two main types of occupational pension scheme – defined benefit (DB) schemes and defined contribution (DC) schemes (other types of pension scheme will be considered in Sect. 2.9a). Table 1.10 shows that in 2015, 6.8 million people were active members of funded DB and DC schemes, and 3.4 million were in unfunded DB schemes. Active members are those currently contributing to the scheme. DB was the dominant form of pension scheme with 7.0 million active members, as against 3.2 million active DC members. The public sector had 5.4 million active members (all in DB schemes), and the private sector had 4.8 million active members. There has been a big increase of 2.3 million in the active membership of DC schemes since 2011 due to the introduction of auto-enrolment, and the number of active DC members will soon exceed that of DB active members.

Table 1.11 shows that over 30 million people are, or will, receive an occupational pension. The large numbers of pensioners and deferred pensioners, relative to active members can be seen in this table. There are over 20 million deferreds and pensioners, against only 10 million actives. A deferred pensioner is someone who has left the scheme, and the benefits they have accrued during their active membership of the scheme are called a preserved pension. Deferred pensioners receive this preserved pension when they retire.

Table 1.10 Active members of UK occupational pension schemes, million (ONS 2013a, 2015c)

	2011	2014
Public sector unfunded DB	3.3	3.4
Public sector funded DB	2.0	2.0
Private sector funded DB	1.9	1.6
Total DB	7.2	7.0
Private sector funded DC	0.9	3.2
Total DB and DC	8.1	10.2

Table 1.11 Membership of UK occupational pension schemes in 2014, million ONS (2015a)

	Active	Deferred	Pensioner	Totals
Private	4.8	6.8	5.0	16.6
Public	5.4	3.8	4.6	13.8
Totals	10.2	10.6	9.6	30.4

Most people who are not members of a DB pension scheme still have an economic interest in DB schemes. They may be shareholders, possibly indirectly via their DC pension, in companies which sponsor DB schemes, or have a spouse who is a member of a DB scheme. They may also pay taxes (local and national) which are used to fund public sector DB schemes.

a. DB Schemes

DB schemes are managed by a board of trustees. Most DB schemes in the UK base the pension on the worker's *final salary*. The sponsor (employer) promises to pay a pension of a specified size which is usually related to the years of employment (accrued years) and final salary. The accrual rate is the proportion of the final salary that accrues as additional pension for each additional year of service (employment).

Example. If the scheme's accrual rate is 80ths, and the scheme uses final salary, then the pension is:

Annual Pension = (No. of Years of Service/80)×(Final Salary)

For someone who has worked for the company for 40 years, and retires on a salary of £30,000, their annual pension is (40/80) × £30,000 = £15,000. Both the sponsor and scheme member usually make payments into the pension scheme to meet the pension promise. For the USS (which is described in Sect. 3.2a) final salary section, the sponsors paid 16 %, and the members paid 7.5 %, so the total contribution rate was 23.5 % of salary. Accrual rates can be expressed as percentages. For example an 80ths scheme corresponds to an accrual rate of 1/80 = 1.25 % per year, while a 60ths scheme has an accrual rate of 1/60 = 1.67 % per year.

The assets held by the scheme in order to pay pensions is called the pension fund, and is invested in a pooled manner, i.e. all contributions are paid into a single pension fund. On retirement, the pension scheme makes the agreed payments to the pensioner until they die, and may then pay a pension to any widow, widower or dependants. In effect, on retirement DB scheme members acquire an annuity whose value is determined by the computation of their annual pension. (Annuities are discussed in Chap. 5.)

The risk that the pension fund will be insufficient to meet the pensions promise is usually assumed by the sponsor. Most UK DB pension schemes are 'balance of cost' schemes, where the members pay a fixed percentage of pensionable salary, and the sponsor pays the remainder of the uncertain cost of providing the benefits. This exposes the sponsor to a range of risks:

1. Investment risk – returns on the pension fund investments are risky.
2. Longevity risk – the life expectancy of pensioners is risky.
3. Salary growth risk – the final salary is risky.
4. Inflation risk (for index linked pensions) – the inflation rate is risky. In the UK, sponsors are only required to inflation index pensions up to some specified lower limit (e.g. 2.5 %), and so pensioners face inflation risk for values above 2.5 %, or whatever higher number is specified by their scheme.
5. Interest rate risk – the liabilities are valued by discounting at an interest rate which is risky.
6. Regulatory risk – the regulations and their interpretation may be changed.

Usually every three years, the pension scheme is valued by the scheme actuary, and a surplus or deficit computed. Of necessity, such valuations involve many forecasts of events far into the future, and so actuarial valuations are only estimates, and different actuaries can produce very different valuations of the same pension scheme. Actuaries used to value scheme assets using a dividend discount model, where the expected stream of dividends is discounted back to the present using a chosen discount rate. As market values are available for the vast majority of assets, these days the current market values of the assets are usually used. The liabilities are not traded on a market and do not have a readily available current market value, and so it is in the valuation of the liabilities where there is the greatest scope for different valuations of the same scheme. In recent years a buyout market has developed (see Sect. 2.5) where insurance companies charge a price for 'buying' a scheme's liabilities, but these prices are not used by actuaries when valuing schemes. If the scheme is 'balance of cost' the actuarial surplus or deficit may cause the trustees to increase or decrease the sponsor's contribution rate, while the members' contribution rate usually remains unchanged. Thus, provided the sponsor does not default, the risks of under-funding fall on the sponsor. The next section considers different ways of valuing the liabilities of a pension scheme in the absence of a market in liabilities.

b. Valuation of DB Pension Liabilities

Before the liabilities can be valued they need to be defined. Then the appropriate discount rate(s) need to be chosen to value the liabilities, and finally the scheme valuation is used in setting the contribution rate.

i. Definition of Pension Liabilities

Should the liabilities be valued on the assumption that all scheme members immediately leave the sponsor's employment? Or should the valuation take account of the implicit contract with members for continued employment and membership of the scheme, which will lead to future pay rises that revalue the years of service they have currently accrued? The second view is supported by the implicit contract of employment which recognises that sacking workers is difficult, and that most workers will continue as employees and scheme members for many years. The choice made between alternative definitions of the liabilities has a large effect on the value placed on the liabilities, and in the USA this distinction has led to three different definitions of the pension liability.

ABO

The Accumulated (or Accrued) Benefit Obligation (ABO) is just the value of the benefit payments that have been accrued to date, and ignores any future salary growth. If pensioners have a contractual right to cost of living increases, or if deferred pensioners have a right to have their pensions up-rated, these expected costs are also included in the calculation of the ABO. The ABO assumes the scheme is terminated immediately, which is generally unrealistic. Since an increase in salary revalues the accrued liability for all previous years, the ABO rises at a rate that increases with the number of years a worker has accrued, and if the age distribution of scheme members is uneven, the use of the ABO may create funding problems. For example, the average accrued years and salaries of the members of a scheme closed to new members will increase over time, leading to a steadily increasing contribution rate.

PBO

The Pension Benefit Obligation (PBO) not only includes benefits accrued to date (the ABO), but also an allowance for expected future salary increases for existing members until their expected date of separation (retirement or stopping employment prematurely). This salary growth revalues these accrued benefits upwards by the time a member retires or leaves. The PBO represents an estimate of the present value of the expected cost of paying the pensions that have been accrued to date, assuming the members continue in employment and receive pay rises during their future employment with the sponsor. Use of the PBO produces a fairly constant rate of increase in the pension liability for an individual.

PVB

The Present Value of Benefits (PVB) is a third, largely unused, measure of the liabilities. This is the PBO plus the cost of the additional years that existing members are expected to accrue before they leave or retire.

At retirement the ABO, PBO and PVB liabilities for an individual will be identical. The ABO and PBO valuations tend to be used for different purposes, for example the PBO for the financial statements, and the ABO for regulatory and funding purposes. The most popular actuarial valuation method in Europe is the projected unit method which allows for projected increases in salary, and so is similar to the PBO.

In the UK actuaries use a range of different actuarial models for valuing the liabilities. There are five different ways of valuing the liabilities, and actuaries may simultaneously produce five alternative valuations for the same scheme:

1. Scheme specific funding. This was introduced in 2005. The liabilities are valued using the scheme's 'technical provisions', which are set by the scheme. The resulting surplus or deficit is used by The Pensions Regulator (TPR) when considering whether the scheme needs a recovery plan.
2. Buyout. This is the full cost of transferring all the scheme's liabilities to an insurance company (See Sect. 2.5b).
3. Section 179. This valuation is used to compute the Pension Protection Fund (PPF) levy (see Sect. 2.8b). It is roughly the sum that would have to be paid to an insurance company to take on the obligation of paying the PPF levels of compensation, which are about 90 % of the promised pension. So a Sect. 179 valuation is more likely to show a surplus than is a buyout valuation.
4. Financial Reporting Standard (FRS) 17. This accounting standard specifies how the liabilities must be valued when producing the published accounts of the sponsoring company.
5. Actuarial valuation. The basis for valuing the liabilities is chosen by the scheme and the scheme actuary, and they have considerable latitude.

ii. Discount Rates

Having decided on the definition of the liabilities (e.g. ABO or PBO), the next step is to choose the appropriate discount rate in the absence of default risk. Because pensions may be paid many years in the future, small changes in the discount rate have a substantial effect on the value of a scheme's liabilities, and there has been a long-running debate over how to choose an appropriate discount rate. The traditional actuarial solution in the UK and USA is to use the expected return on the scheme's investments, but this is incorrect if the aim is to produce the economic value of the liabilities. Novy-Marx (2013a) explored three logical implications of using the expected return on the scheme's assets as the discount rate, showing that it can have ridiculous results. First, literally destroying an investment in bonds can increase a scheme's funding ratio as the average expected return on its assets rises, reducing the value of its liabilities by more than the decrease in the value of the assets. Second, merging two schemes can worsen their aggregate funding ratio; and third the use of the expected return on assets is equivalent to discounting the liabilities at the riskless rate and valuing equities at more than twice their current market value.

Economic theory is clear that the appropriate rate for discounting cash flows such as pension liabilities is the rate of return on assets with the same risks, expected return and maturity as the liabilities, i.e. a replicating portfolio. While the correct discount rate is easily defined, it is much harder to identify in practice. Merton (2014) has pointed out that the replicating asset for a pension promise of a given amount is a single premium deferred annuity (SPDA, see Sect. 5.20), but the market in such assets is largely non-existent. Therefore SPDAs cannot be used in practice to value the liabilities. The fixed income market can be used to provide the returns on a series of zero-coupon government bonds maturing each year, corresponding to the annual projected cash flows of the pension liability. This assumes there are government bonds with a sufficiently long maturity to discount the most distant liabilities, and this is generally not the case. While such a yield curve supplies a different discount rate for each maturity to allow for differences over time in interest rates, a common simplification is to use a single discount rate, i.e. a flat yield curve. Rather than use the returns on different maturities of government debt as proxies for the discount rates, stochastic discount factors (SDF) can be used (Chapman et al. 2001; Hoevenaars and Ponds 2008; Hoevenaars et al. 2009; Hoevenaars et al. 2010; Hoevenaars 2011; Draper et al. 2014). These are discount rates estimated from market data, and should give similar answers to those provided by the returns on government debt.

The risks and liquidity of zero-coupon bonds and pension liabilities are different. Government bonds are liquid, while pension liabilities cannot be traded, and for this reason returns on government debt are lower than on pension liabilities. Conversely, the returns on nominal government bonds include an inflation risk premium, while UK pension liabilities are inflation indexed and, if fully indexed, do not include an inflation risk premium. In practice these two offsetting adjustments tend to cancel out. The ABO is exposed to inflation risk, while the PBO is subject to inflation risk, salary growth risk and separation risk. This suggests the ABO is valued at a discount rate that reflects the riskless interest rate plus an inflation risk premium, less an illiquidity premium, while the additional cash flows implied by the PBO definition of liabilities, i.e. (PBO–ABO), are valued at a higher discount rate that also allows for salary growth risk and separation risk (Novy-Marx 2013b).

There is also the risk of default by the sponsor, which has so far been excluded. Should the pension liabilities be seen as a promise that must always be met, with possible default ignored? Or should the risk that the sponsor will default on part, or all, of the liabilities be recognised by valuing only the payments that are actually expected to be made by the sponsor? This choice leads to substantially different discount rates, and therefore to different values of the liabilities. Inkmann et al. (forthcoming) distinguish between the benefits *promised* to members, where default risk is ignored when setting the discount rate; and the benefits that are *expected* to be paid, where default risk is recognised and the discount rate increased accordingly. Brown and Pennachi (2015) make a similar distinction.

A scheme should be funded on the basis that its liabilities will be met in full without default, and so the promised benefits are the appropriate liability measure for setting the contribution rate and a buyout valuation. This leads to a low discount rate with no allowance for default risk, and a high valuation of the liabilities. If default risk is recognised, the discount rate is increased to reflect this possibility, leading to a reduction in the size of the liabilities, i.e. the present value of the cost of paying the expected benefits. But the value of the expected benefits should not be used to set the contribution rate as this can lead to a vicious circle, with the contribution rate tending towards zero. If default risk is recognised when setting the contribution rate the presence of default risk increases the discount rate. This reduces the size of the liabilities, leading to a lower contribution rate, which then increases the default risk, leading to a further rise in the discount rate etc. However, from the point of view of the shareholders, default is a possibility which should be recognised when valuing the company, and so they should use a higher discount rate to produce a value for the expected benefits. The expected benefits, which allow for default risk, may also be useful to employees when comparing the remuneration offered by two different employers, or choosing between DB and DC schemes. Therefore allowance for default risk, and hence the value of the liabilities, depends on the purpose for which the value of the liabilities is needed, and the value of the liabilities when valuing a company for investment will probably be lower than for an actuarial valuation of the scheme.

Inkmann et al. (forthcoming) propose that schemes should publish two liability values: the promised liability where the discount rate ignores default risk, and the expected liability where the discount rate is increased to allow for default risk. The difference between these two liability valuations reflects the scheme's default risk, and alerts members to the likely size of the reduction in their promised benefits. In practice the discount rate for liabilities that actuaries use is usually slightly higher than the riskless rate, for example the rate on AA corporate bonds, but this is an approximation. There are substantial differences between schemes regarding the risk of default, salary growth risk and separation risk, in addition to inflation risk and illiquidity risk; and an ad hoc adjustment to the discount rate (or rates) is required. However making such an adjustment is more art than science at the moment.

iii. Setting the Contribution Rate

When setting the contribution rate the actuary and trustees need to value the assets and liabilities, and decide how to change the contribution rate and asset allocation in response to the resulting surplus or deficit. Each of these steps can be done in different ways, and the two main approaches will be characterised as the traditional actuarial approach and the economic approach.

The traditional actuarial approach is to value the assets using a dividend discount model, where judgement is needed in forecasting future dividends and selecting a discount rate to value this dividend stream. Therefore the value of the assets is subjective and actuaries often use this freedom to smooth asset values over time. Under this traditional actuarial approach the liabilities are discounted at the expected rate of return on the scheme's assets. Since a major portion of the assets is probably invested in equities, this expected return is generally well above the risk-free rate, and is affected by the actuarial judgements used to value the assets, for example the dividend stream and the assumed future asset allocation. The result is a substantial under-valuation of the liabilities, and surpluses and deficits that are largely determined by actuarial judgements. Due to the use of a high discount rate, the surplus is biased upwards (compared to current market value), and the deficits and surpluses are smoothed over time with little connection to current market values. A simple mechanical rule is then applied to compute the required change in the contribution rate. For example, if the scheme has a deficit of £225 million, and uses a spread period of 15 years over which to eliminate the deficit, the contribution rate needs to rise by an amount that will generate an additional £225 million in contributions over the next 15 years, for example 225/15 = £15 million per year, where this simple calculation ignores the time value of money. Since the values of the assets and liabilities are smoothed, changes in the contribution rate are also smoothed when using the traditional actuarial approach.

The economic approach is to value the assets at their current market value, and to use the rate of return on assets with the same risk, expected return and maturity as the liabilities as the discount rate to value the promised benefits. Subjectivity is minimised and the valuation of both the assets and liabilities is determined by current market values, rather than actuarial judgements, and the resulting surplus or deficit is an unbiased estimate of the current market value of the scheme. Valuing both assets and liabilities according to the same economic principles (market value) ensures that the comparison of assets and liabilities is not comparing apples with oranges (i.e. assets valued on one basis, and liabilities valued on another). The users of scheme valuations generally assume a valuation represents the current market value of the scheme, rather than some abstruse actuarial concept such as scheme specific funding, buyout, Sect. 179, Financial Reporting Standard (FRS) 17 or actuarial valuation. So an economic valuation means what users expect it to mean. Because market values are volatile, the resulting scheme surpluses or deficits are also volatile. Economists adopt a different approach to actuaries when setting the contribution rate, and construct an asset liability model (ALM) (see Sect. 3.2e). This involves estimating the future cash flows of the scheme under a range of different contribution rate and asset allocation strategies, and then discounting them back to the present. The ALM needs to be stochastic to allow for the risk involved in future cash flows, and this can be accomplished using Monte Carlo analysis. This involves generating a very large number (say 5000) different future scenarios (e.g. different asset returns, contributions received, pension payments made etc.) and produces (say) 5000 outcomes for each contribution rate and asset allocation strategy, providing an estimate of the riskiness of that strategy. The trustees are then presented with the outcomes of the ALM, and they make a judgement about their most favoured risk-return trade-off and inter-generational redistribution when setting the contribution rate and asset allocation.

iv. Actuarial or Economic Approach?

The traditional actuarial approach generates a scheme valuation that is subjective, probably biased towards a surplus, and with little economic meaning. A mechanical rule is then applied to this subjective valuation to produce a contribution rate. This is an economically flawed procedure. The economists' approach is to value the assets and liabilities at their current market value, and so the scheme valuation is not subjective, should be unbiased, and does have economic meaning. Economists then build a stochastic ALM using forecasts of future cash flows made using various statistical procedures. This is essentially an objective process, although inevitably some methodological choices will have to be made. The trustees are presented with the output from the ALM and make explicit risk versus return judgements in order to set the contribution rate and asset allocation for the scheme.

In recent years actuaries have moved in the direction of economists by valuing assets at their current market values and using a discount rate that is a gilt rate plus some subjective number, giving a rate which is probably a lot lower that the expected return on the assets. This leads to a markedly larger valuation of the liabilities, and can lead to reporting a large deficit. This deficit is then fed into the actuaries mechanical procedure for raising the contribution rate to remove the deficit over a chosen spread period, and this can generate very large contribution rate increases. This volatility in the contribution rate is exacerbated if the scheme has a large proportion of its assets invested in equities. Such a mixture of the traditional actuarial approach and the economic approach involves little judgement, is becoming increasingly common and is flawed.

As well as using scheme valuations for setting the contribution rate, one or more of the actuarial valuations is also reported externally. There is empirical evidence that schemes seek to manipulate their discount rate to manage the reported value of their liabilities. Kisser et al. (2014) analysed the liability valuations of 11,963 US DB schemes and found them to be understated by roughly 10 % due to the use of a high discount rate. This effect was particularly pronounced for under-funded schemes. They also examined the effect of Moving Ahead for Progress in the 21st Century Act (MAP-21) passed by the US Congress in 2012 on the discount rates used by 5218 US DB schemes. Schemes adopting this rule were able to use a higher discount rate, and in 2012 the average discount rate rose by 2.13 %, particularly for under-funded schemes, thereby reducing their liabilities. Such manipulation of the discount rate raises fears that this leads to schemes setting unrealistically low contribution rates.

c. DC (or Money Purchase) Schemes

The 401(k) investments in the US are essentially DC schemes. For a description of the US DC system see Choi (2015). The contribution rates of the sponsor and members are a fixed proportion of salary, and each member accumulates their own pot of money. In the UK when a member of a DC scheme retires the balance in their account is paid out to them tax-free. A quarter of this sum can be used for whatever purpose the pensioner wishes. Until April 2015 the remaining 75 % had to be used to buy an annuity before they were age 75, although some exceptions existed. Since April 2015 the requirement to buy an annuity with this 75 % has been dropped, and any money not used to buy an annuity or invested in drawdown (see Sect. 5.2) is taxed at the person's marginal rate of income tax. Now that the pension pot can be used to 'buy a Lamborghini', DC schemes are no longer pension schemes as they do not provide a pension; they are tax-exempt savings schemes for retirement.

Example. Holly Davis is a member of a DC pension scheme and pays pension contributions of 5 % p.a. Her employer pays pension contributions of 9 % p.a., making a total contribution rate of 14 % p.a. For simplicity, contributions are assumed to be paid at the end of each year. Her annual salary and the annual returns on her pension pot are shown in Table 1.12. The contributions are invested according to Holly's wishes, and when she retires after five years her pension pot is worth £24,728. She can use a quarter (£6182) for whatever purpose she wishes. Until April 2015 the remaining £18,546 had to be used to buy an annuity before she reached the age of 75. Now she can take the remaining 75 % as cash, although this will be subject to tax.

Each member of a DC scheme has three crucial decisions to make:

(a) How to allocate the money in their pensions pot between different asset classes when investing their pot of money, which will be considered in Sect. 3.1a.
(b) Which annuity to buy (if any) with their lump sum (See Sect. 5.14).
(c) When to buy this annuity, which will be considered in Sect. 5.13.

i. DC Administration
In the UK, DC schemes can be administered in one of two ways. With a trust-based scheme a trustee board manages the scheme, as for DB schemes. For contract-based schemes an insurance company is contracted to supply a DC pension to each of the company's employees. A contract-based scheme is essentially a collection of individual personal pensions and includes what are called group personal pensions and stakeholder pensions. There are no trustees, although from April 2015 contract DC schemes were required to set up an independent governance committee. For the sponsor, a contract-based

Table 1.12 DC example

	Earnings	Contribution	Op. fund	Return	Cl. fund
1	£30,000	£4200	0	–	£4200
2	£31,000	£4340	£4200	5 %	£8750
3	£32,000	£4480	£8750	6 %	£13,755
4	£33,000	£4620	£13,755	6 %	£19,200
5	£34,000	£4760	£19,200	4 %	£24,728

DC scheme is easier, quicker and cheaper to set up and run than a trust-based DC scheme. With a contract-based scheme, pension provision is entirely outsourced, but the sponsor has little control.

ii. DC Risks

The risks concerning investment returns, longevity, salary growth and inflation rest with the member until they buy an annuity, when they pass to the annuity provider (salary growth risk is no longer relevant). The sponsor does not bear any of these risks, except for some salary growth risk. An increase in salary leads to a higher absolute sponsor contribution, although it is an unchanged proportion of salary.

iii. Small Self Administered Schemes (SSAS)

SSAS are small occupational pension schemes where the members can take a major part in running the scheme. They are targeted at company directors and allow the scheme to lend 50 % of the assets to the sponsor, and to invest in a very wide range of assets. The total funds under management in SSAS in 2013 were about £15 billion, and so they form only a small part of the pension industry. They are broadly similar to defined contribution schemes, and will not be considered further.

Four ways of classifying occupational and private pension schemes in the UK are shown in Table 1.13. Schemes may be second pillar (occupational or personal) or third pillar (private), occupational or non-occupational, DB or DC, and funded or unfunded.

Table 1.13 Private pension system in the UK (ONS 2013a)

	Occupational salary related	Occupational money purchase	Group personal pensions	Individual pensions
Occupational v personal	Occupational		Personal – contract-based	
Workplace v non-workplace	Workplace – employer sponsored			Non-workplace
DB v DC	Defined benefit	Defined contribution		
Funded v unfunded	Unfunded	Funded		

1.7   The Tax Benefits of Pensions

An important incentive for making pension contributions to occupational and private pensions in the UK is the tax benefits. The state provides these benefits to encourage people to lock up their savings in pension schemes, which helps them to avoid falling back on the state for assistance when they retire. The UK system for taxing pensions is called exempt-exempt-taxed (EET) and is also used by the Netherlands, France, Germany, Estonia and Spain, (Oxera 2013). Under an EET system:

(a) Pension contributions are exempt, and so the pension contributions of the sponsor and the members are tax deductible.
(b) Pension scheme returns are exempt, and so dividends, capital gains and interest on the DB pension fund or the DC pension pot are tax exempt. This is of direct benefit to the sponsor in DB schemes, and the member in DC schemes.
(c) Pension payments are taxed, and so pension income received by pensioners is subject to the normal income tax rules. When a member retires in the UK they can also choose to take a tax-free lump sum. For DC schemes this is up to 25 % of their pensions pot. For DB schemes there is also an upper limit of 25 %, although the scheme rules may set a lower limit, for example three or four times their annual pension.

Other countries have different tax systems for pensions (e.g. ETT (exempt-taxed-taxed) in Sweden and Italy), TEE (taxed-exempt-exempt) and TTE (taxed-taxed-exempt) where, for example, ETT means contributions are tax deductible, the investment income of pension funds is taxable, and pension payments to pensioners are taxable (Börsch-Supan and Lührmann 2003; Bateman et al. 2001). The EET system broadly corresponds to an expenditure tax, where income is taxed when it is consumed; while the TEE system broadly corresponds to a comprehensive income tax where income is taxed when it is earned. It will now be shown that, given some assumptions or questionable realism, the TEE and EET systems lead to identical tax payments.

a. Comparison of the EET and TEE Taxation Systems

Consider a DC pension scheme that operates, for the moment, under a TTT tax regime. For simplicity, this analysis assumes a simple model with all the contributions made at time zero. These contributions are then invested for one period, and the pension pot is paid out and taxed at the end of this period. In reality contributions to a scheme and their investment occur over several decades, as do the withdrawals from a pension pot, but the conclusions are unaltered. For a more detailed comparison of EET and TEE see Armstrong et al. (2015).

Let the wages out of which members pay their pension contributions be taxed at the rate of w%, the sponsor's contributions to the scheme be taxed at x%, the pension scheme's investment income be taxed at the rate of y%, and the tax rate on pension payments received by members in retirement be z%. If a member's gross pensionable income is £Y, the member's contribution rate is m%, the sponsor's contribution rate is s%, and the gross rate of return on the pension scheme's investments is r%, then the after-tax value of a member's pension pot (P) is given by:

$$P = YBD(1-z)$$

where $B = m(1-w)+s(1-x)$, and $D = 1+r(1-y)$, and the total tax paid on the pension (T) is:

$$T = Y[wm + xs + B(ry + zD)]$$

For EET $w = x = y = 0$ because the member is exempt from these taxes, and so

$$P_{EET} = Y[m+s](1+r)(1+z), \text{ and } T_{EET} = Y[m+s](1+r)z$$

For TEE $y = z = 0$ because the member is exempt from these taxes, and so

$$P_{TEE} = YB(1+r), \text{ and } T_{TEE} = Y[mw+sx]$$

If the rate of tax on wage income equals the rate of tax on the sponsor's contribution (i.e. $w = x$); and the rate of income tax when a member retires is equal to that today (i.e. $w = z$), then for EET: $P_{EET} = Y[m+s](1+r)(1-w)$, and $T_{EET} = Y[m+s](1+r)w$. For TEE: $P_{TEE} = Y[m+s](1+r)(1-w)$, and $T_{TEE} = Y[m+s]w$. Therefore the value of pension pots under both EET and TEE are equal to $Y[m+s](1+r)(1-w)$, and the present value of taxation under EET, discounting at the rate of r%, is $PV(T_{EET}) = Y[m+s]w$, which is the same as for TEE. So, given the various assumptions, the EET and TEE taxation regimes result in identical pension pots, and identical tax burdens.

Table 1.14 has an example which compares the operation of the EET and TEE tax systems, and shows that the net value of the final pension pot and the present value of the taxes paid are identical at £1716 and £1040 respectively. The overall tax rate in each case is 1040/(1716 + 1040) = 37.736 %. This rate is not 40 % because the investment income is tax exempt for both EET and TEE. If the pensions contributions had been paid into a savings account

Table 1.14 Example of the EET and TEE tax systems

		EET		TEE
Gross income		£10,000		£10,000
Member's contribution (8 %)	£800		£800	
Less tax at 40 %	0	£800	£320	£480
Sponsor's contribution (18 %)	£1800		£1800	
Less tax at 40 %	0	£1800	£720	£1080
Pre-investment pension pot		£2600		£1560
Gross investment return at 10 %	£260		£156	
Less tax on returns	0	£260	0	£156
Gross final pension pot		£2860		£1716
Less tax on pension pot at 40 %		£1144		0
Net final pension pot		£1716		£1716

where the investment income is tax exempt, for example an individual savings account (ISA), the taxation would be exactly the same as the TEE system for pensions. Given the above assumptions, the taxation for an ISA would also be identical to the EET system.

The present value of the tax on the EET pension pot paid out as pensions, discounted at the investment rate of return, is £1144/(1.10) = £1040.

Tax on member's contribution	0	£320
Tax on sponsor's contribution	0	£720
Tax on investment returns	0	0
Tax on final pension pot	£1040	0
Present value of the total tax	£1040	£1040

However, in reality the EET and TEE systems are not equivalent. The rate of income tax on a member's contributions may not be equal to the tax rate on the sponsor's contributions, and the member's tax rate when retired may not be equal to their tax rate when working due to a progressive tax system. In addition, the appropriate discount rate may not be equal to the rate of return on the investments. There are advantages and disadvantages to the EET system, relative to the TEE system (Boeri et al. 2006):

1. With TEE the tax is collected up-front, rather than when the member is retired, which ensures that the tax is collected from those who emigrate on retirement, which may not be the case for EET. In this way TEE prevents people benefiting from tax arbitrage which occurs when people move on retirement from a low-tax country with poor public services to a high-tax country with good public services. By emigrating they are taxed at a low rate, but receive high-cost public services in retirement.

2. TEE raises more tax revenue from those who are higher-rate taxpayers when working, but who pay a lower rate when retired, while the EET system raises more revenue from those who are taxed at a higher rate when retired than when working. Most tax systems are progressive and most people have higher incomes when working, so TEE generally raises more revenue that EET.

3. EET spreads the payment of taxes across each person's life as they pay tax on their salary (excluding the portion that is deferred salary and goes into a pension scheme) when working, and on their pension when retired. In a progressive tax system this is argued to be fairer as TEE includes pension contributions as part of salary, and this may push people into a higher tax bracket.

4. TEE carries the risk for members that tax policy may change and their investment income and pensions may be taxed as well, which may discourage saving in pension pots, although EET is also vulnerable to an increase in the taxation of pension pots, as shown by recent UK experience.

5. EET includes pensioners in the tax base, while they are excluded under TEE, and being part of the tax base helps to preserve political support for public spending on services for pensioners.

6. Some people see pension contributions, not as deferred pay, but as a form of taxation. TEE then appears to involve double taxation, while EET does not.

7. TEE does not influence the riskiness of the assets in which the pension pot is invested, while under EET the government shares the investment risks with the member as taxation occurs after, rather than before, the investment of the assets. This risk sharing may lead to investment in riskier assets than does TEE, and this will tend to increase both the size of pension pots and tax revenues.

8. For DB pensions there is only an indirect connection between contributions and the size of the pension pot at retirement. In this case it is fairer to use EET and tax members on the income they actually receive, and not their contributions. Similarly DB members receive their pensions for a different number of years before they die, and so taxation based on the income actually received is fairer, i.e. EET.

9. With EET the receipt of tax revenue by the government is delayed until after retirement, and so current tax rates will need to be higher than otherwise to finance current government expenditure; while future tax rates can be lower. The reverse is true for TEE.

10. Because tax is only paid when the pension income is received, EET pension pots are larger than TEE pension pots throughout the accumulation phase. The behavioural effect of this difference in the size of pension pots is unclear.

11. Armstrong et al. (2015) constructed a general equilibrium overlapping generations model to compare the EET and TEE tax systems using UK data. They show that, because TEE shifts the tax burden to those of working age, there is a reduction in their after-tax income. This leads to a reduction in their savings and consumption; and to lower investment, GDP, productivity and real wages; as well as a rise in real interest rates.

National Insurance Contributions (NICs)

NICs are effectively a tax on earned income that accrues UK state pension benefits. For employees their NIC payments are based on their gross income before any occupational pension scheme contributions. So their occupational pension scheme contributions are subject to a NIC 'tax'.[1] No NICs are payable when a member receives a pension. So employees' NICs follow the TEE model. There are some exceptions to the TEE model, as sponsor contributions to an occupational pension scheme are exempt from NIC payments, as is pension investment income received by the scheme. Therefore, for sponsors this form of taxation (NICs) follows an EEE model so far as pension contributions are concerned. Employers must also pay NICs on the gross salary they pay to their employees.

b. Magnitude of Tax Relief on Pension

Under the EET system all the contributions to pension schemes and all investment returns on this money are eventually subject to income tax when the pension payments are received by the pensioner. Therefore contributions to a pension scheme are not tax exempt, just tax deferred. The UK has five main exceptions to a pure EET system: (a) employers receive corporation tax relief on their NIC to the state pension, (b) members can opt to receive a tax-free lump sum of up to 25 % of the value of their pension pot, (c) pension funds pay stamp duty (a form of taxation) when they buy UK equities or property, (d) the dividends received by pension schemes are paid out of income that has been subject to corporation tax and (e) contributions in excess of the annual allowance, and pot values in excess of the lifetime allowance, are taxed. This has led some people to comment that the UK is moving to a TET system. Some

---

[1] Members can opt into salary sacrifice whereby their salary is reduced by their pension contribution, which is paid directly to the scheme by their employer. The result is that a member's salary for NIC purposes is reduced, and so both the member and the employer avoid paying NIC on the member's pension contribution.

Table 1.15 Tax relief enjoyed by pensions in 2011–12, billion (Emmerson 2014)

(a) Employers' NIC relief received	£10.8
(b) Tax-free lump sum received	£2.5
	£13.3
(c & d) *Less* Stamp duty and corporation tax paid	£2.0
(e) *Less* Annual and lifetime allowance taxes	n/a
Total relief	£11.3

estimates of the annual magnitude of these tax reliefs that are exceptions from a pure EET system appear in Table 1.15. The total amount of the taxes on those exceeding the annual and lifetime allowances have not been quantified.

Table 1.15 shows that the lion's share of the tax relief (i.e. exceptions to a pure EET system) goes to employers, as they are able to charge their NIC contributions against their taxable income, which is not the case for scheme members. The exemption of employers from paying NIC on their pension contributions creates an incentive for employers to offer remuneration to members in the form of pensions rather than salaries, as this reduces the net cost to the employer. The example in Table 1.16 shows an example of the benefits to the sponsor of reducing salaries and using this money (£750,000) to contribute to a pension scheme. This results in an increase in the sponsor's net profit of £52,250 from offering a pension scheme.

To quantify the cost of tax relief on pensions the UK tax authorities effectively compute the difference in tax revenue between the TTE and EET taxation systems (HMRC 2014), and this approach leads to much larger estimates of the amount of tax relief. Usually the NIC relief is also included in the total relief figure, as shown in Table 1.17. Johnson (2014a) not only includes NICs, but also a tax-free lump sum of £4 billion, while ignoring the tax paid on pensions received, so that he arrives at a total cost of tax relief on pensions of £54,000 million for 2012–13.

The corresponding HMRC total reliefs figure for 2011–12 at £37,800 million is slightly lower than for 2012–13, and is more than three times bigger than the figure computed for the same year by Emmerson in Table 1.15. The main cause of this big difference is that the HMRC computations are for pension contributions, NIC, investment income and tax on pensions paid in the *same* year. In a steady state where the level of pension contributions, NIC, investment income, pensions paid, longevity and tax rates remain constant over time there is no problem, but this is not reality. The computation needs to compare the tax paid and reliefs received by a particular age cohort over the course of their lives. If the number of pensioners, wage levels or tax rates increase over time, the HMRC calculation will overstate the tax relief. Since the number of pensioners, wage rates and longevity show strong upward

Table 1.16 Example of the benefits to the sponsor from offering a pension

	Pension	No occupational pension
Company trading profit	£10,000,000	£10,000,000
Less Salaries	£5,000,000	£5,750,000
Less Employer's NIC at 10 % of salary	£500,000	£575,000
Less Employer's pension contribution at 15 % of salary	£750,000	–
Taxable profit	£3,750,000	£3,675,000
Less Corporation tax at 30 %	£1,125,000	£1,102,500
Net profit	£2,625,000	£2,572,500

Table 1.17 Pension tax reliefs computed by the HMRC for 2012–13 (HMRC 2014)

Income tax relief on pension contributions by members and sponsors	£27,900 m
Income tax relief on investment income on pension pots	£6,900 m
Total tax reliefs	£34,800 m
Less tax paid on pensions received	£12,000 m
Total	£22,800 m
Relief on employers' NIC	£15,200 m
Total reliefs	£38,000 m

trends, the Treasury figures grossly over-state the amount of tax relief. This was pointed out by Sinfield (2000), who described the Treasury figure as giving '*a false impression*', while Armstrong et al. (2015) said the Treasury figure '*could be a substantial overstatement*', and Dilnot and Johnson (1993) described these figures as '*not useful as estimates of tax expenditures on pension schemes. It is in fact rather hard to think of any useful purpose to which these figures might be put*'. According to the US Government (2015), figures such as those used by the Treasury '*do not accurately reflect the true economic cost of these provisions*', and the US government provides estimates of the cost of pension tax relief using a present value methodology. It should also be remembered that in 2011–12 UK pensioners paid £45.6 billion in direct (£18.8 billion) and indirect (£26.8 billion) taxes (Prudential 2014).

In a critique of the HMRC numbers, Robbins and Roberts (2015) argue that the employer contributions used by HMRC include additional contributions made to remove deficits accrued in previous years, and that the tax relief on these in 2013–14 was at least £4 billion. In addition, the HMRC figures include employers' NIC relief of over £3 billion on these deficit contributions. Therefore, the HMRC figures for 2013–14 overstate the total reliefs by over £7 billion. This suggests that, if a similar adjustment for deficit contributions is made to the HMRC figures in Table 1.17, total reliefs for 2012–13 drop to about £31 billion, and the total relief estimated by Emmerson in Table 1.15

Table 1.18 Bankers' pension pots (*Financial Times* 1 May 2013)

		Pension pot
Spain		
Francisco González	CEO, Banco Bilbao Vizcaya Argentaria	£67,210,000
Alfredo Sáenz	CEO, Santander	£74,290,000
USA, UK, Germany		
Lloyd Blankfein	CEO, Goldman Sachs	£22,000
Jamie Gorman	CEO, Morgan Stanley	£47,000
Mike Corbat	CEO, Citigroup	£62,000
Anthony Jenkins	CEO, Barclays	£232,000
Anshu Jain	CEO, Deutsche Bank	£347,000

would drop to about £8 billion. In which case the total relief estimate of £8 billion is only one fifth the size of the HMRC estimate of total relief in Table 1.17. There is also the issue that, if tax relief on pensions were abolished, there would be an increase in other forms of tax-privileged saving (e.g. ISAs), thereby reducing the reduction in tax relief.

Various commentators have also made the point that most UK tax relief on pension contributions (e.g. over £50 billion has been mentioned) goes to the higher paid, and argued that this massive tax relief should be both reduced and distributed more equally. But under an EET system much of this tax relief is not tax relief, but just tax deferral. Eventually the tax will be paid, and it is a foregone conclusion that most of the tax deferral will affect those who are eventually more highly taxed because they are highly paid.

Taxation is a powerful influence on occupational pensions, providing an incentive to lock money away for several decades. Since taxation systems differ between countries, this leads to differences in the incentives to put money into pensions. Examples of the pension pots of some leading bankers and their dramatically different size, appear in Table 1.18. The pension pot of Alfredo Sáenz (Santander) was worth over 3300 times more than that of Lloyd Blankfein (Goldman Sachs), and taxation is an important reason for these enormous differences between Spain and the other countries.

1.8   Life Expectancy

Life expectancy is a crucial aspect of pension provision. Longevity has been increasing for centuries, and in recent decades the rate of increase has accelerated. In 1950 the life expectancy of a UK male aged 65 was 12 years (i.e. 77 years). By 2004 this number had increased by 58 % to 19 years (i.e.

84 years). It is forecast to increase to 21 years by 2030 (i.e. 86 years). Thus, by 2030 existing scheme members may work for 45 years, and draw a pension for 21 years, i.e. they work for roughly twice as long as they received a pension (45/21 = 2.1). But in 1950 a member may have worked for 45 years and drawn a pension for only 12 years, i.e. they worked for almost four times as long as they received a pension (45/12 = 3.8). In 1950 workers had four years of contributions to build up their pension for each year of retirement, but by 2030 this will have dropped to only two years, suggesting that members need to double the proportion of their salaries that go to provide their pension. If the UK state retirement age in 2013 was set to give the same expected time drawing the state pension as in 1908 when the UK state pension was introduced, men would have to retire at 80 years old (Longevitas 2013).

Not only does increasing longevity raise the cost of providing pensions, but uncertainty over the rate at which longevity will increase in the future leads to considerable long-run risk in the value of the liabilities. While variations in interest rates have a major effect on the value of liabilities in the short run, interest rates tend to be mean-reverting in the long run, leading to much smaller long-run effects on liabilities. In contrast, changes in longevity have a modest effect on the value of liabilities in the short run, but are not mean-reverting in the long run, and so can lead to very large long-run changes in the value of the liabilities.

Table 1.19 has forecasts of the increase in the population aged over 60 expected in a number of countries, and shows that by 2050 41 % of the Japanese population are expected to be over the age of 60, while only 7 % of the Nigerian population will be over 60. It also shows some very large increases, for example that in Iran the population aged over 60 will rise from

Table 1.19 Percentage of the population over 60 years of age (%) (*Financial Times* 6 July 2013)

	2012	2050	Increase (%)		2012	2050	Increase (%)
Iran	8	33	25	India	8	19	11
S. Korea	17	39	22	Japan	32	41	9
China	13	34	21	Australia	20	29	9
Brazil	11	29	18	USA	19	27	8
Turkey	10	26	16	UK	23	30	7
Mexico	10	26	16	S. Africa	8	15	7
Indonesia	9	25	16	Sweden	25	31	6
Russia	19	31	12	Kenya	4	9	5
Egypt	8	20	12	Nigeria	5	7	2

Table 1.20 Number of people aged 90 and over per 100,000 population in 2013 (ONS 2014a)

Country	No. per 100,000	Country	No. per 100,000
India	77	USA	707
China	146	Canada	708
Russia	212	Denmark	721
Brazil	253	Finland	731
Poland	299	Germany	778
Croatia	305	UK	822
Bulgaria	368	Spain	875
Czech Republic	422	Norway	882
Republic of Ireland	457	Italy	979
Slovenia	501	France	995
Iceland	546	Sweden	1004
New Zealand	561	Japan	1266
Australia	655		

8 % to 33 %. As the population aged over 60 rises, this will make pensions more costly.

There are substantial differences between countries in the number of very old people (i.e. aged 90 and over), as shown in Table 1.20. Japan has 79 % more people aged over 90 than does the USA, and over eight times as many over 90s as China.

There is some evidence that being in receipt of a pension increases longevity, supporting the assertion made by Jane Austen in 1811 (Austen 2013) that '*people always live forever when there is an annuity to be paid them*'. In 1907 and 1912 the US Army started paying pensions to all US Army veterans, and this increased their longevity by 0.82 years and 2.35 years respectively. The biggest effect was a drop in deaths from infectious diseases, suggesting that improved nutrition may have been responsible for the increase in longevity (Salm 2011). Philipson and Becker (1998) argue that pensions alter the trade-off between the quality and quantity of life by providing an incentive to live longer. This encourages pensioners to spend more on their health, diet and sanitation, and to change their lifestyle choices, for example give up smoking and drinking, and so live longer. Here are four examples of extreme longevity associated with pensions.

Example 1. William Martin fought in the American Civil War, which ended in April 1865 when he was 20 years old. In 1921, aged 76, William was awarded a Confederate pension for his military service. In 1927, when he was 81, William married Alberta Stewart, who was then 21 years old. William died in 1931, and Alberta married William's grandson. She continued to receive a

Confederate pension until she died on 31 May 2004 at the age of 97. So her pension was being paid 139 years after it was accrued.

Example 2. John Janeway fought for the Union in the American Civil War. In 1927 he married Gertrude Grubb Janeway when he was 93 and she was 18. Gertrude continued receiving a federal pension until she died in January 2003 at the age of 94 (Schieber 2012, p. 16). So her pension was paid until 138 years after it was accrued.

Example 3. In 1941 Spanish volunteers joined the Blue Division to fight for the Germans against the Russians in the Second World War. Over 73 years later in November 2015 the German government was still paying pensions to 41 wounded veterans, eight widows and one orphan.

Example 4. The world's longest lived person that has been verified is Jeanne Calment of Arles, France. She was born on 21 February 1875, and died in August 1997 aged 122 years old. '*In 1965, André-François Raffray, a (47 year old) lawyer in the southern French city of Arles, made a deal with a 90 year old local woman. In a contract relatively common in France, he agreed to pay her an income for the rest of her life in exchange for inheriting her house upon her death.*' (An early form of housing equity release.) '*Unfortunately for Mr. Raffray, the woman was Mme. Jeanne Calment, who went on to be the longest-lived person in the world at 122 years. She outlived the luckless M. Raffray* (who died from cancer in 1995), *who paid more than* (twice) *the value of the house before pre-deceasing her.*' Raffray's widow continued making the monthly payments until Calment died in 1997. '*In life, one sometimes makes bad deals*', said Mme. Calment (Richards and Jones 2004).

There are substantial differences in life expectancy between various groups. In Table 1.21 the TUC (2013) has reported the forecast differences in longevity in 2016 for people aged 65. Table 1.21 indicates that a woman living in

Table 1.21 Forecast differences in longevity in 2016 for people aged 65 (TUC 2013)

1	Gender	Women > Men	2.3 years
2	Class – men	Managerial & professional > routine & manual	2.8 years
3	Class – women	Managerial & professional > routine & manual	3.0 years
4	Location – men	E. Dorset > Manchester	5.9 years
5	Location – women	E. Dorset > Corby	6.2 years

East Dorset with a managerial or professional job has a considerably longer life expectancy than a man living in Manchester with a routine or manual job (i.e. 5.9 years). In 2012–14 life expectancy at birth for boys in Kensington and Chelsea was 8.6 years greater than for boys born in Blackpool; and life expectancy at age 65 for women living in Camden was 5.8 years longer than for women living in Manchester, (ONS 2015b). Between 1985 and 2005 life expectancy for the least deprived (based on an index of income, employment, health, education, housing, environment and crime) in England rose at a faster rate than for the most deprived (Lu et al. 2014), leading to a widening of the gap in their life expectancies.

People tend to spend their final years in ill health, and in recent years a distinction has been drawn between life expectancy and healthy life expectancy. UK healthy life expectancy is considerably shorter than life expectancy, and for those aged 65 in 2008–10 there was a 7.7 year difference for men, and an 8.8 year difference for women (Sinclair et al. 2014). There are also some large differences in healthy life expectancy between UK local authorities. For 2009–11 women at birth in Richmond upon Thames had a healthy life expectancy that was 18 years greater than for those born in another part of London – Tower Hamlets. These differences are probably due to lifestyle, diet, accommodation and so on.

Dependency Ratio
Over time the number of workers per non-worker has declined, and is forecast to decline sharply in the future. In 2003, 13.8 % of the UK population was aged 65 or higher, and this is forecast to increase to 18.1 % in 2015 (or almost one in five persons). This is due to the declining birth rate, longer periods of education, early retirement and increased longevity, and means that each worker has to support more pensioners. The dependency ratio is used to quantify the relationship between the size of the working and non-working populations, and is defined as: *Dependency ratio = Non-workers/ Workers*. (See Sect. 2.14c for a discussion of Chinese dependency ratios.)

1.9   Auto-Enrolment

Given the emerging problems for UK pensions, the government set up the Turner Commission to investigate the problems and recommend solutions. In 2005 the UK Turner Commission identified six main options for state pensions: (a) allow pensions to get lower, relative to wages, (b) increase the retirement age so that people must work longer, thereby increasing the number of workers and decreasing the number of pensioners, (c) workers must pay higher taxes to support pensioners, (d) workers must save more to free up resources to be consumed by pensioners, (e) increase the growth rate to provide more goods and services for pensioners and (f) encourage immigration to provide more workers – this final option was not recommended. In 2005 the Turner Commission proposed that all workers be automatically enrolled in an occupational pension scheme meeting specified minimum standards. At the same time the Commission recommended the establishment of a National Pensions Savings Scheme (NPSS, subsequently renamed the National Employment Savings Trust, NEST). This is a government run not-for-profit scheme offering DC pensions that meet the auto enrolment standards.

Auto-enrolment began operation in October 2012 in the UK and every sponsor must automatically enroll its employees in a DC pension scheme such as NEST, or one of its private sector rivals, unless the employee specifically chooses to opt out, or the sponsor offers a superior pension scheme. The employer's contribution rate is 4 %, and the employees' contribution rate is also 4 %. Over time the total amount of money in these auto-enrolment schemes will grow to a considerable size. By the end of 2014, 5,134,000 employees had been auto-enrolled, and it expected that it is will eventually lead to an extra nine million DC scheme members, increasing DC contributions by £15 billion per year by 2019–20 DWP (2015b).

In the 1990s a number of other countries introduced new DC occupational pension systems. There are a couple of examples, with a more in-depth analysis of the Chinese reforms, in Sect. 2.14. In 1992 the Australian government required payments of a percentage (now 9 %) of salary into approved DC schemes. This led to a big increase in Australian pension fund assets under management. Since the late 1990s Sweden has had six National Pension Funds (AP1, AP2, AP3, AP4, AP6 and AP7). The total mandatory contribution rate is 18.5 %, of which 2.5 % goes into a DC scheme where the employee has to choose from a menu of over 700 approved, privately managed, investments. About 90 % of members fail to make an investment choice, and end up in the default fund (AP7). The remaining 16 % of each member's contribution goes to a Notional DC scheme (see Sect. 2.9a(iv)).

References

Armstrong, A., Davis, E. P., & Ebell, M. (2015, September). *An economic analysis of the existing taxation of pensions (EET) versus an alternative regime (TEE)* (NIESR discussion paper no. 455), 44 pages.

Arza, C., & Johnson, P. (2006). The development of public pensions from 1889 to the 1990s. In G. L. Clark, A. H. Munnell, & J. M. Orszag (Eds.), *Oxford handbook of pensions and retirement income*. Oxford: Oxford University Press.

Austen, J. (2013). *Sense and sensibility.* Solis Press, Chapter 2, page 10. Tunbridge Wells, England.

Balasuriya, J., Gough, O., & Vasileva, K. (2014). Do optimists plan for retirement? A behavioural explanation for non-participation in pension schemes. *Economics Letters, 125*(3), 396–399.

Banks, J., & Emmerson, C. (2000). Public and private pension spending: Principles, practice and the need for reform. *Fiscal Studies, 21*(1), 1–63.

Bateman, H., Kingston, G., & Piggott, J. (2001). *Forced saving: Mandating private retirement incomes*. Cambridge: Cambridge University Press.

Boeri, T., Bovenberg, L., Coeuré, B., & Roberts, A. (2006). *Dealing with the new giants: Rethinking the role of pension funds* (Geneva reports on the world economy 8). Centre for Economic Policy Research.

Börsch-Supan, A., & Lührmann, M. (2003). Retirement benefit and pension taxation principles. In O. Castellino & E. Fornero (Eds.), *Pension policy in an integrating Europe* (pp. 152–173). Northampton: Edward Elgar.

Börsch-Supan, A., Härtl, K., & Ludwig, A. (2014). Aging in Europe: Reforms, international diversification and behavioural reactions. *American Economic Review, 104*(5), 224–229.

Brown, J. R., & Pennachi, G. G. (2015, June). *Discounting pension liabilities: Funding versus value* (Working paper). National Bureau of Economic Research, no. 21276, 49 pages.

Chapman, R. J., Gordon, T. J., & Speed, C. A. (2001). Pensions, funding and risk. *British Actuarial Journal, 7*(part 4, no. 33), 605–662.

Choi, J. J. (2015). Contributions to defined contribution pension plans. *Annual Review of Financial Economics, 7*, 161–178.

Department for Work and Pensions. (2015a). *Creating a secondary annuity market.* Department for Work and Pensions, Cm 9046, March, 29 pages.

Department for Work and Pensions. (2015b). *Workplace pensions: Update of analysis on automatic enrolment.* Department for Work and Pensions, September, 10 pages.

Dilnot, A., & Johnson, P. (1993). Tax expenditures: The case of occupational pensions. *Fiscal Studies, 14*(1), 42–56.

Draper, N., Van Ewijk, C., Lever, M., & Mehlkopf, R. (2014). Stochastic generational accounting applied to reforms of Dutch occupational pensions. *De Economist, 162*(3), 287–307.

Emmerson, C. (2014). Taxation of private pensions. In C. Emmerson, P. Johnson, & H. Miller (Eds.), *The Green Budget 2014* (pp. 221–239). London: Institute for Fiscal Studies.

Empire, G. (1889). An act concerning insurance in case of disability and old age. *Quarterly Journal of Economics, 4*(1), 103–128.

Geneva Association. https://www.genevaassociation.org/programmes/life-and-pensions

Hannah, L. (1986). *Inventing retirement: The development of occupational pensions in Britain.* Cambridge: Cambridge University Press.

HMRC. (2014). PEN 6 cost of registered pension scheme tax relief. Her Majesty's Revenue and Customs, February.

Hoevenaars, P. M. M. (2011). Pricing embedded options in value-based asset liability management. In B. Scherer & K. Winston (Eds.), *The Oxford handbook of quantitative asset management* (pp. 449–469). Oxford: Oxford University Press.

Hoevenaars, R. P. M. M., & Ponds, E. H. M. (2008). Valuation of inter-generational transfers in funded collective pension schemes. *Insurance, Mathematics and Economics, 42*(2), 578–593.

Hoevenaars, P. M. M., Kocken, T., & Ponds, E. (2009). Pricing risk in corporate pension plans: Understanding the real pension deal. *Rotman International Journal of Pension Management, 2*(1), 56–63.

Hoevenaars, P. M. M., Molenaar, R. D. J., & Ponds, E. H. M. (2010). Public investment funds and value-based generational accounting. In A. Berkelaar, J. Coche, & K. Nyholm (Eds.), *Central bank reserves and sovereign wealth management* (pp. 328–348). New York: Palgrave.

Holzmann, R., & Hinz, R. (2005). *Old-age income support in the 21st century: An international perspective on pension systems and reform.* Washington, DC: World Bank.

Inkmann, J., Blake, D., & Shi, Z. (forthcoming). Managing financially distressed pension plans in the interest of beneficiaries. *Journal of Risk and Insurance.*

IPE. (2015). Top 1000 pension funds 2015. *Investment & Pensions Europe.*

Johnson, M. (2014a). Retirement saving incentives: The end of tax relief and a new beginning. Centre for Policy Studies, April, 22 pages,

Johnson, S. (2014b). Longevity swaps market shows signs of life. *The Financial Times,* 9th February.

Kisser, M., Kiff, J., & Soto, M. (2014). *Do pension plans manipulate pension liabilities?* (Working paper). Norwegian School of Economics, 43 pages.

Levy, S. (2012). Pensions in the national accounts – A fuller picture of the UK's funded and unfunded pension obligations. Pensions Analysis Unit, Office for National Statistics, April, 23 pages.

Longevitas. (2013). *Insurance or right?* Longevitas, January.

Lu, J., Wong, W., & Bajekal, M. (2014). Mortality Improvements by Socio-Economic Circumstances in England (1982 to 2006), *British Actuarial Journal,* vol. 19, no. 1, March, pp. 1–35.

Mercer. (2015). *Melbourne Mercer global pension index*. Melbourne: Australian Centre for Financial Studies.

Merton, R. C. (2014). The crisis in retirement planning. *Harvard Business Review, 92*(7&8), 43–50.

Morris, P., & Palmer, A. (2011). *You're on your own: How policy produced Britain's pensions crisis*. London: Civitas.

Nascher, I. L. (1914). *Geriatrics: The diseases of old age and their treatment*. Philadelphia: P. Blakiston's Son & Co.

Novy-Marx, R. (2013a). Logical implications of the GASB's methodology for valuing pension liabilities. *Financial Analysts Journal, 69*(1), 26–32, 261–275.

Novy-Marx, R. (2013b, September). *Economic and financial approaches to valuing pension liabilities* (Working paper). Pension Research Council, WP2013-09, 12 pages.

OECD. (2013a). *Pensions at a glance 2013, OECD and G20 Indicators*. Paris: OECD.

OECD. (2015a). *Pensions at a glance 2015, OECD and G20 indicators*. Paris: OECD.

OECD. (2015b). *Pension markets in focus 2015*. Paris: OECD.

Office for National Statistics. (2013a). *Pension trends*. Chapter 6, Private Pensions, 2013 Edition. London: ONS.

Office for National Statistics. (2014a). Estimates of the very old (including centenarians) for England and Wales, United Kingdom, 2002 to 2013. London: ONS, 16 pages.

Office for National Statistics. (2015b). *Life expectancy at birth and at age 65 by local areas in England and Wales, 2012 to 2014*. London: ONS, November, 24 pages.

Office for National Statistics. (2015c). Active members of occupational pensions: Employer contribution rates and characteristics by pension benefit structure, 2014. ONS, December, 11 pages.

Oxera. (2013). Study on the position of savers in private pension products. Oxera, January, 305 Pages.

Philipson, T. J., & Becker, G. S. (1998). Old-age longevity and mortality-contingent claims. *Journal of Political Economy, 106*(3), 551–573.

Prudential. (2014). *Tax takes a 30% bite out of pensioner income*. Prudential.

Richards, S., & Jones, G. (2004, October). *Financial aspects of longevity risk*. Paper presented to the Staples Inn Actuarial Society.

Robbins, D., & Roberts, D. (2015). *Ending higher rate relief on pension savings – Not as obvious as it seems, Towers Watson perspectives* (Technical paper no. 2015–0003), 30 pages.

Rogers, F., & Millar, F. (1903). *Old age pensions – Are they desirable and practicable*. London: Isbister and Co Ltd.

Royal Commission. (1895). *Royal Commission on the aged poor*. HMSO, Cd. 7684, volume 3, Minutes of Evidence, paras. 10466, 10513 and 10702.

Salm, M. (2011). The effect of pensions on longevity: Evidence from Union Army veterans. *Economic Journal, 121*(552), 595–619.

Salter, T., Bryans, A., Redman, C., & Hewitt, M. (2009). *100 years of state pensions: Learning from the past*. Oxford: Faculty of Actuaries and Institute of Actuaries.

Schieber, S. J. (2012). *The predictable surprise: The unravelling of the U.S. retirement system*. Oxford: Oxford University Press.

Sinclair, D., Moore, K., & Franklin, B. (2014). Linking state pension age to longevity – Tackling the fairness challenge. International Longevity Centre-UK, 30 pages.

Sinfield, A. (2000). Tax benefits in non-state pensions. *European Journal of Social Security, 2*(2), 137–167.

TUC. (2013). *Life expectancy inequalities and state pension outcomes*. Trades Union Congress, August, 23 pages.

US Government. (2015). *Fiscal year 2016 analytical perspectives of the US government*. US Government Printing Office.

2

Selected Pension Scheme Topics

This chapter goes into greater depth on a range of topics. Two fundamental questions relate to why employers choose to offer pension schemes and why they have switched to offer defined contribution (DC), rather than defined benefit (DB), schemes. After considering these two questions, this chapter analyses the problems with DC schemes, which this switch to the widespread use of these schemes will amplify. Next this chapter looks at ways the sponsors of DB schemes can shed responsibility for their DB schemes, and ways they can deal with rising longevity. This is followed by details of national insurance schemes to protect the members of DB schemes in the event of sponsor default. As well as DB and DC schemes, many other pension scheme designs are possible, and some of the alternatives are presented. This leads on to a consideration of the widespread use of uniform contribution and accrual rates, and the redistributive effects of pension schemes. Economies of scale are an important feature of pension schemes, and after analysing their nature there is a description of the pension system in a major emerging economy – China.

2.1   Why Do Employers Provide Pension Schemes?

Where the provision of occupational pensions is voluntary, employers need to justify why they provide a pension. This sub-section, which relies on McCarthy (2006), considers reasons why the provision of an occupational pension is of benefit to both the employees and the employer. A survey of 166 UK companies by the Confederation of British Industry (2015) found that

© The Author(s) 2016   **43**
C. Sutcliffe, *Finance and Occupational Pensions*,
DOI 10.1057/978-1-349-94863-5_2

96 % thought there is a good business case for providing a pension scheme, with 92 % agreeing that it helps to retain and motivate staff, and 89 % thinking that a pension scheme enhances the reputation of the sponsor.

To the extent that pensions provide a benefit to employees, they also benefit the employer, as salaries can be correspondingly reduced, i.e. a compensating wage differential. The following studies have estimated the size of this trade-off between pension benefits and wages: Allen et al. (1986), Clark and McDermed (1986), Disney et al. (2009), Ehrenberg (1980), Ehrenberg and Smith (1981), Freeman (1985), Gerakos (2010), Gunderson et al. (1992), Haynes and Sessions (2013), Gunderson, Hyatt and Pesando (1992), Inkmann (2006), Montgomery and Shaw (1997), Montgomery et al. (1992), Moore (1987), Pesando (1984), Schiller and Weiss (1980), Smith (1981) and Smith and Ehrenberg (1983). In related studies, Bulow and Landsman (1985), Dorsey et al. (1998), Even and MacPherson (1990) and Gustman and Steinmeier (1995) have estimated the effect on wages of being covered by a pension scheme, i.e. the effect of being offered a pension, rather than the size of the pension benefit offered. However attempts to quantify the wage-pension trade-off have encountered substantial econometric and data problems (Allen and Clark 1987). Subject to these reservations, the evidence suggests the trade-off is well below the one-for-one trade-off predicted, and this may be due to the associated benefits and costs to the sponsor and the members, which are considered below. It is also possible that members and sponsors suffer from 'pensions illusion' or wage rigidities and do not require an offsetting increase in wages when pension rights are reduced, or a decrease in wages when pension rights are increased.

Pensions are often described as deferred wages, and instead of being paid out as wages now, the money is paid later as a pension. If wages were a perfect substitute for pensions, only the total size of a person's remuneration package (wages plus pensions) would matter; the form of this remuneration would be irrelevant. Therefore offering a pension would be irrelevant, as would its design, and there is no reason why employers should offer pension schemes. However, wages and pensions are not perfect substitutes because of incomplete markets, taxation etc., and so offering a pension matters. There is no market where individuals can buy and sell pension obligations, For example, pensions due to be paid in retirement cannot be traded for more consumption now – they are highly illiquid assets (although see Sutcliffe 2015). Therefore the presence of pension schemes and their design matters.

There are a number of ways in which sponsors and members benefit from offering remuneration via pensions in a world with incomplete and imperfect markets. The first four of these benefits apply to both DB and DC schemes, the next four apply only to DB schemes, the ninth applies principally to DB schemes, and the last two benefits only apply to DC schemes. Since any benefit to the members also represents a benefit to the sponsor due to compensating wage differentials, all the items listed below benefit both the members and sponsor, except for the fourth, seventh and eighth which benefit only the sponsor.

1. Tax benefits. Under the EET tax system members do not pay income tax on income used to pay their pension contributions, while sponsors charge their pension contributions against profits, and so receive tax relief. Members also receive a tax-free lump sum. In addition, pension funds do not pay tax on the income from their investments (see Sect. 1.7).

2. Transactions costs and economies of scale. The sponsor benefits from economies of scale in collecting and investing the pension money. Large funds can invest much more cheaply than individuals, particularly in more unusual assets, allowing them to achieve greater diversification. They can also hedge some of the risks. Pensions can give workers privileged access to the annuity market via a DB pension provided by the scheme, or discounted access to an annuity provider. However, while claimed, this benefit for DC schemes may not exist as annuity providers generally offer annuities to their existing DC customers at the same rates as they offer them to open market customers (Financial Conduct Authority 2014).

3. Expertise. Many individual members lack the expertise to invest and manage their pension funds, and sponsors have greater access to such expertise.

4. Savers and non-savers. Offering a pension scheme (DB or DC) attracts workers who place a value on saving for their retirement. A pension scheme tends to attract workers who are 'low discounters', i.e. willing to take the long view, such as investing in their pension over a 40-year period (Ippolito 1997). Economically correct discounting uses compound (or exponential) discounting, i.e. $PV = A_t/(1 + r)^t$. High or 'hyperbolic discounters' undervalue money in the future leading to time-inconsistent decisions (i.e. what is preferred at one point in time is inconsistent with what is preferred at another point in time). Low discounters tend to make better employees as they consider the long-term consequences of their decisions. While any pension scheme tends to sort workers into savers and non-savers, i.e. low and high discounters, there are differences in the degree of sorting achieved by DB, DC and US 401(k) schemes, with DB schemes tending to achieve greater sorting.

5. Risk bearing. DB pensions involve a range of risks – longevity, investment, salary, inflation, interest rates and regulation. If sponsors are less risk adverse than members, for example because the sponsors' shareholders' portfolios diversify the risks of the companies in which they are invested, it is preferable for sponsors to provide a DB pension, bear the risks, and charge the members an implicit insurance premium via a reduction in their remuneration, given the market imperfections which stop a third party providing such insurance at a lower price.

6. Mortality discount or credit. Like annuities, the pensions provided by DB schemes benefit from the mortality credit (the mortality discount or credit is considered in Sect. 5.6). The mortality discount or credit occurs because some pensioners die young, and the money that would have been used to pay their pensions can be used to increase the pensions of those who survive.

7. Retirement age. DB schemes can be designed to encourage workers to retire at a specified normal pension age (NPA). This removes older employees who may be higher paid, lower productivity individuals who cannot have their wages reduced because wages are generally rigid downwards, and who cannot be easily sacked due to age discrimination and other laws. For example, a DB scheme may offer additional accrued years to encourage workers to take early retirement, while stopping accrual after the NPA is reached. Offering additional years is not possible with a DC scheme.

8. Under-funding. A DB scheme allows under-funding by the sponsor, while a DC scheme does not. Such under-funding has a number of advantages for the sponsor, but some disadvantages for members (see Sect. 4.8b).

9. Pension capital loss (PCL). Leaving a DB scheme involves a PCL for the member, while leaving a DC scheme (or a 401(k) scheme) has smaller costs for members. On moving to another employer, a member can either transfer their accrued benefits to the pension scheme of their new employer, or become a deferred pensioner of the scheme of their old employer. If a member choses to transfer their accrued benefits, DB schemes generally do not give full credit for accrued years, for example the cash equivalent transfer value (CETV) may be less than the actuarially fair value of the accrued years. For those who chose to become deferred pensioners of a DB scheme their accrued benefits are not uprated by salary increases, but only by inflation (or not uprated at all in the USA). Over the 30 years to 2010 UK national average earnings grew by 382 %, while the retail price index grew by 230 %, i.e. 1.3 % less per year (Salt 2012). For US workers the average PCL for DB schemes has been estimated at half a year's salary (Gustman and Steinmeier 1993). The presence of the PCL can make employees reluctant to change jobs, and this is illustrated in the following example.

Example. Nadine Boynton earns £30,000 per year, and has accrued 25 years of service with the pension scheme of her current employer. She expects a significant promotion before she retires in 15 years and this is expected to raise her final salary to £60,000. Martsad Ltd offer her a job which is expected to produce a final salary of £65,000. Both sponsors offer a final salary DB scheme with 80ths accrual, and uprate deferred pensions (i.e. the member ceases accruing benefits, and will receive a pension when they retire based on the benefits accrued to date) by 2.5 % per year. If Nadine stays with her current employer she will receive a pension of (£60,000)(40/80) = £30,000 p.a. If she leaves (becoming a deferred pensioner) and joins Martsad Ltd. she will receive a pension from Martsad Ltd. of (£65,000)(15/80) = £12,188 p.a. In addition she will receive a pension from her current employer of £30,000(1.025)^{15}(25/80) = £13,578 p.a., giving Nadine a total pension of £25,766 p.a., or £4234 less than if she had stayed with her current employer. This pension reduction has a present value of roughly £100,000.

For DC schemes there are losses on quitting, but these are generally substantially smaller than for DB schemes. A survey of UK DC schemes in 2015 found that between 84 and 90 % of the money in DC schemes is not subject to an exit charge (FCA 2015). Where there is an exit charge it is generally less than 5 % of the value of the pension pot, although in a very small number of cases it is over 40 % of the pension pot. However those who cease contributing to a DC scheme may face other costs. The annual charges for deferred pensioners of a contract-based DC scheme may double, as they change from being wholesale to retail customers, (Harrison et al. 2012). An Office of Fair Trading (2013) investigation found that the additional annual charge was, on average, 0.47 %. Which? reports that, while only a small percentage of the pension pot in any one year, these extra charges for deferred pensioners can reduce the size of the final pension pot by 25 % (House of Commons Work and Pensions Committee 2013). These active member discounts (or deferred member penalties) have become widespread in recent years, but were banned from April 2016.

The PCL leads to a number of benefits from offering a DB scheme, and to a much lesser extent, a DC scheme. Workers will be more productive because they do not want to be sacked and suffer the PCL. In addition, there will be less labour turnover because quitters also suffer the PCL. This penalty for leaving attracts workers who expect to stay a long time, and discourages workers from quitting. The lower labour turnover then encourages the employer to invest in training the workers, making them more productive. Being better trained and more productive may enable the members to earn higher wages. Final salary DB schemes bring an additional advantage, which is not provided by DC schemes. They attract workers who expect to stay with the company and end their career on a high salary, i.e. would-be high fliers who expect to remain with the company.

10. Access to the pension pot. In the USA workers get access to their DC (or 401(k)) pension pot when they cease working for the sponsor, which is not the case for DB schemes. So DC and 401(k) members who are non-savers are incentivised to quit their employment (Ippolito 2000). Over time, as their pension pot gets bigger, this incentive to quit increases. Therefore, if low discounters are employed, subsequently they are incentivised to quit, while this is not the case for members of a DB scheme. In the UK as from April 2015, members of DC schemes have had access to their pension pot after the age of 55.

11. Choice of contribution rate. Members of 401(k) schemes in the USA can choose their contribution rate, and the employer can make a matching employer's contribution. Workers who are savers will tend to choose to make higher contributions, resulting in higher employer contributions to their pension pot (Ippolito 2000). Therefore the total compensation of savers is higher than for non-savers, which will tend to encourage savers not to quit. Like DC scheme members, 401(k) scheme members also have an incentive to quit to get access to their pension pot, but this incentive is reduced for low savers because they will tend to choose a lower contribution rate and therefore have smaller pension pots.

2.2   The Death of DB Schemes

In January 2015 the PPF 7800 index showed an aggregate deficit of £367.5 billion for UK DB schemes. There have been three main responses by sponsors to the recent pensions crisis: (a) close the DB scheme to new members (called a soft freeze in the USA) and introduce a DC scheme with a markedly lower sponsor contribution rate; (b) close the DB scheme to future accruals (called a hard freeze in the USA) and introduce a DC scheme with a markedly lower sponsor contribution rate; and (c) reduce the benefits and increase the contribution rate for scheme members. There are also some other reactions, and the detailed response to large deficits has taken many different forms, and these will now be considered.

a. Responses to a Large DB Pension Deficit

There are many ways in which a DB scheme can respond to a large deficit, besides hoping that in time the deficit will disappear without the scheme taking any explicit corrective action.

1. The sponsor injects funds (or assets) into the scheme. For example the John Lewis Partnership gave their pension scheme some shares in Ocado,

Philips contributed its stake in NXP Semiconductors, and Costain and Interserve each gave a portfolio of public finance initiative (PFI) holdings to their schemes. A sponsor can also fund a deficit by borrowing the money, eliminate the deficit immediately, and gradually repay the loan over subsequent years; rather than by increasing contributions to the scheme over a number of years. Eliminating the deficit immediately has the advantage that the scheme avoids higher PPF (Pension Protection Fund) or PBGC (Pension Benefit Guarantee Corporation) levies, which increase with the size of any deficit (see Sect. 2.8).

2. The sponsor engages in asset-backed funding (ABF) where business assets are used to generate cash which is paid to the scheme, or funds are placed in an escrow account.

Asset-backed funding (or asset-backed contributions, ABC) occurs when the sponsor transfers an asset into a special purpose vehicle (SPV), see Fig. 2.1. The first ABF was executed by Marks and Spencer in 2007. The assets of the SPV remain the property of the sponsor, and revert back to them on termination of the SPV. Some or all of the income from the assets in the SPV is paid to the pension scheme as an income stream (or lump sum). This may involve the sponsor paying rent to the SPV for the use of the property transferred, or royalties for the use of brand names. Appendix 1 has a list of UK companies that have funded their pension scheme using an ABF. This shows that property is usually the asset involved, although trademarks, TV licences, maturing whisky, brands and bonds have also been used. ABFs reduce the PPF scheme levy, extend the time allowed by the Pensions Regulator to complete a recovery plan, and give the scheme greater security because the SPV will continue in the event of the liquidation of the sponsor. Usually the value of the assets transferred to the SPV exceeds that necessary to generate the projected income stream to the pension scheme. In many cases the

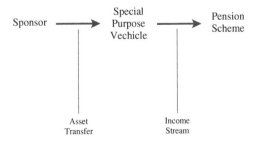

Fig. 2.1 Asset-backed funding

value of assets transferred to the SPV exceeds 5 % of the scheme's assets as the 5 % limit on self-investment does not apply.

If an escrow account is used the sponsor pays money into it (Bush et al. 2014). The assets in the escrow account are held by a third party and released to the scheme or sponsor according to pre-determined rules. The advantages of an escrow account are that: (a) the sponsor can recover any surplus pension funding because the money is not locked inside a pension scheme, (b) the assets can remain on the sponsor's balance sheet: and (c) the sponsor retains control of the assets in the escrow account. The disadvantages are that: (a) the sponsor only receives tax relief on the money paid into the escrow account when the money is transferred to the scheme; and (b) corporation tax is payable on investment returns on the money in the escrow account.

Other possibilities for dealing with an under-funded DB scheme are also available. (a) The sponsor could give the pension scheme the security of a prior claim on some company asset such as real estate. (b) The sponsor's parent company may also guarantee some or all of the sponsor's responsibilities for the scheme. (c) The sponsor may buy protection for the scheme from a third party (e.g. a surety bond from an insurance company or a letter of credit from a bank).

3. The contribution rates for both the sponsor and the members are raised. A variant of this is to introduce tiered contribution rates to make high paid members contribute more, and the issue of uniform contribution and accrual rates is analysed in Sect. 2.10.

4. Cap and share. An upper bound is specified for the sponsor's contribution rate and if there is any need for increases in contributions above this level to cover the anticipated cost of future service, this cost will be shared between the sponsor and the members in some agreed proportion, or benefit reductions introduced. The Universities Superannuation Scheme (USS) introduced cap and share in 2011.

5. An increase in the retirement age (e.g. 60–65). This has been a widespread response.

6. There is a reduction in the benefits flowing from *future* accruals, for example remove full inflation indexation, remove the widows' pension, remove the lump sum, and cap increases in pensionable pay to (say) a maximum of 3 % per year.

7. The investment policy of the pension fund is altered, for example the equity-bond balance is changed (see Chap. 3).

8. The sponsor starts a DC scheme with a low sponsor contribution rate, closes their DB scheme to new members (a soft freeze), and offers new employees this DC scheme; or closes the DB scheme to future contributions

and accruals (a hard freeze), and offers this DC scheme to present and future employees. This policy has been adopted by many sponsors.

9. The pension scheme is switched from final salary to career average (see Sect. 2.9a(i)), and there is a reduction in the sponsor's contribution rate for the career average scheme (e.g. USS in 2011).

10. Hybrid. The DB scheme remains open, but only the first x% of salary is pensionable in the DB scheme. For salary above this level a DC scheme is offered (e.g. USS in April 2016).

11. Enhanced transfer values (ETV). Deferred pensioners can transfer out of the scheme in exchange for a cash transfer sum that is in excess of the cash equivalent transfer value (CETV).

12. Retirement transfer option (RTO). Some schemes offer members the ability to take a transfer value on retirement. This gives members the flexibility to reconfigure their pension to their own circumstances and preferences (e.g. a single person will not benefit from survivor benefits). With their transfer value members can take a lump sum, buy an appropriate annuity, go into a drawdown arrangement or just spend the money less any tax.

13. Pension increase exchanges (PIE). Any member or pensioner in the scheme can exchange some of their non-statutory rights to a pension that increases with inflation, for a pension that is initially higher, but where inflation increases are reduced to the statutory minimum. For example, in 2014 38 % of BAE Systems pensioners accepted a PIE, and TUI Travel had a 28 % take-up rate for a PIE from its pensioners (LCP 2015a). But there are dangers for pensioners in accepting a PIE. The real value of a pension that has capped indexed linking will show a substantial drop over a few decades. For example, if the initial value of a level pension is £10,000 p.a. and the inflation rate above the statutory minimum is 3 % p.a., after 30 years the real value of the pension will have dropped to only £4120 p.a. (i.e. a 59 % reduction). In addition, inflation indexation removes inflation risk.

b. Reasons for the Closure of DB Schemes

In recent years many sponsors have closed their DB schemes, either to new members (a soft freeze), or to future accruals (a hard freeze). While the large deficits are a major reason for closure, there have been a host of additional negative factors for UK DB schemes.

1. Deficits. The substantial deficits on DB schemes have been caused by:

   A. The fall in interest rates due to quantitative easing by the UK government, leading to a lower discount rate for valuing the liabilities.

Quantitative easing occurs when the central bank uses newly created money to buy financial assets, thereby injecting money into the economy and lowering interest rates. In the UK £375 billion was injected in this way between 2009 and 2012. However the Bank of England (2012) has argued that, although it lowered interest rates, quantitative easing raised the prices of the other assets held by pension funds, making its overall effect on deficits broadly neutral.

B. The major stock market decline when the FTSE 100 index more than halved in value after its peak in December 1999. The closing FTSE 100 index fell from 6806.50 index points in December 1999 to 3287.00 index points in March 2003, a fall of 3519.50 index points, or 52 %.

C. Many UK DB schemes had large surpluses in the 1990s, and the sponsors took extended contribution holidays (i.e. zero contribution rate) or contribution reductions.

D. The conversion of discretionary benefits into non-discretionary benefits by new regulations, thereby increasing the liabilities of DB schemes.

E. Increases in DB benefits, encouraged by the large surpluses of the 1990s.

F. The use of DB pension schemes to finance early retirement on very favourable terms (e.g. offering additional accrued years).

G. The tax limit on scheme surpluses motivated surplus reduction in the 1990s via sponsor contribution holidays, increases in benefits and financing early retirement.

2. Financial Reporting Standard (FRS) 17 and market volatility. Until the introduction of FRS 17 in 2003, company published accounts were not much affected by the surplus or deficit on the pension scheme. FRS 17 requires companies to account for pension scheme surpluses and liabilities in their financial statements, and so volatility in pension scheme funding levels feeds through to the published accounts. This increased volatility in reported results was unwelcome, and the closure of the DB schemes of BA (British Airways) and Dixons has been attributed to FRS 17 (Morris and Palmer 2011, p. 52). This also caused a switch from equities to fixed income investment which are less volatile (Amir et al. 2010).

3. Inflation. The effective move from *limited* price indexation to *fully* indexed pensions. Under limited price indexation a cap is placed on the size of any inflationary increase in pensions (i.e. x%). If price inflation is higher than x%, the increase in pensions is x% plus a proportion (often set to zero) of any excess over x%. So in times of high inflation (i.e. inflation

exceeds the cap) pensions are capped and increase by less than inflation. When there is low inflation (i.e. inflation is less than the cap) pensions increase by the full amount of inflation. Until it was reduced to 2.5 % in April 2005, 5 % was the statutory minimum for limited price indexation. So the fall in annual increases in the retail price index (RPI) to below 5 % since July 1991 has meant that pensions have been fully indexed, rather than partially indexed.

4. Relative size. The increased size of pension liabilities, relative to the size of the sponsor. At one point the BA (British Airways) pension schemes were nine times bigger than the company's market capitalisation. In 2003 BA's chief executive Rod Edderington said: *The way I see it, there are two elephants in British Airways' rowing boat. One of them is the pension, the other is the debt.* If the pension scheme is large relative to the sponsor, the sponsor may be unable to bear the burden of funding the scheme, and such perceptions increase the sponsor's difficulties in raising capital.

5. Market volatility. The increase in stock market volatility created big swings in the actuarial valuations of pension scheme assets and liabilities, and hence their surpluses or deficits. Therefore the reported risks of sponsoring a pension scheme were higher.

6. Dividend tax relief. The abolition in July 1997 of tax relief for UK pension schemes on dividends. Until then UK pension schemes could reclaim the 20 % Advance Corporation Tax paid on UK company dividends, and this made every £1 of dividend income worth £1.25 to a UK pension scheme. Table 2.1 has estimates of the annual amount of tax relief lost by UK pension schemes due to this change. Ignoring the time value of money, the estimated total loss of tax relief across these 18 years is £128 billion, which represents a very considerable loss to UK pension schemes that every year continues to increase in size.

7. Actuarial techniques. Changes in actuarial technique led to more volatile surpluses and deficits. Assets were more commonly valued using current market prices rather than a dividend discount model; and the discount rate used to value the liabilities was lowered, instead of using the expected rate of return on the assets (see Sect. 1.6b).

8. Voluntary wind-up. Before 11 June 2003 solvent sponsors could wind up a UK DB scheme so long as it was fully funded according to the minimum funding requirement (MFR). MFR full funding was substantially short of meeting the pensions promise (e.g. it could lead to a shortfall of 40 %), and so winding up a scheme enabled the sponsor to avoid a substantial liability. Since pensions in payment have priority, on a voluntary wind-up very little money might be left for active and deferred members. After 11 June 2003 the MFR funding requirement was

Table 2.1 Abolition of tax relief on dividend income (Office for Budget Responsibility 2014)

1997–8	£2300 m	2006–7	£7756 m
1998–9	£3950 m	2007–8	£8197 m
1999–0	£5400 m	2008–9	£8165 m
2000–1	£5667 m	2009–0	£8108 m
2001–2	£5890 m	2010–1	£8505 m
2002–3	£6217 m	2011–2	£8759 m
2003–4	£6592 m	2012–3	£8862 m
2004–5	£6961 m	2013–4	£9308 m
2005–6	£7334 m	2014–5	£9741 m

replaced, and sponsors had to ensure their scheme had sufficient funds for a full buy-out, i.e. to buy a bulk annuity from an insurance company for the all the scheme's members and pensioners that would replicate their accrued benefits (see Sect. 2.5b). This clearly increased the potential burden of a DB scheme for the sponsors, as they could no longer walk away from an under-funded scheme.

9. Regulation. The increased regulatory burden of administering DB schemes due to the considerable increase in compliance requirements and regulation.
10. Risk of new legislation. The risk that new legislation or decisions by the law courts will further increase the liabilities of pension schemes.
11. Rising longevity. The increased cost due to rising life expectancy. Kisser et al. (2012) have estimated that an increase of one extra year in life expectancy increases the pension liabilities of US DB schemes by 3–4 %, and total US pension liabilities by $84 billion. In the UK an increase of one year in life expectancy has been estimated to cost private sector DB schemes an additional 3 % or about £60 billion (Lu 2015).
12. Longevity risk. The risk that life expectancy will increase substantially in the future, possibly due to a medical breakthrough.
13. Risks to the sponsor. The risks that pension schemes impose on the sponsors for example the risk that the pension fund will be insufficient to pay the pensions and the sponsor will have to make additional contributions, and the risk that the credit rating of the sponsor may be reduced because of the possibility of pension shortfalls. In 2003 Standard and Poor's cut the credit rating of Rolls Royce from *A–* to *BBB* because of its large pension scheme deficit of £1.4 billion (Richards and Jones 2004).
14. Trade unions. Trade unions support and defend DB pension schemes, but their strength has declined since the 1970s, leaving DB schemes vulnerable to sponsors wishing to end this form of pension provision (Dixon and Monk 2009).
15. Herding. Bridgen and Meyer (2005) have argued that companies have copied each other in closing their DB schemes. The economic case for

closure was not rigorously investigated, but after a few large firms closed their DB schemes the idea of closure spread around networks of company directors and trustees. Only a few consultants offer advice to trustees and sponsors, and they tended to offer uniform advice. This created a self-reinforcing process of closing DB schemes, and this has been called herding, a contagion, a fashion or a fad.

16. Staff retention. DB schemes help to retain staff, but a lower priority is now given to retaining staff.
17. DC schemes. Closure of a DB scheme offers the opportunity to replace it with a DC scheme with a lower sponsor contribution rate, lower administration costs and almost no risk to the sponsor.
18. Portability and control. The much greater portability of DC schemes is attractive to workers, and some workers value the additional personal control that DC schemes offer to members. They are also easier for members to understand. Since April 2015 pensioners over the age of 55 have been able to take their entire pension pot in cash, which is not legally possible with DB schemes.

For many years actuaries have generally under-estimated the value of the liabilities, and this led to contribution rates for the sponsor and the members that have been too low. This under-pricing was finally exposed in the early 2000s when a perfect storm of low interest rates and low asset values, together with the range of exacerbating factors mentioned above, resulted in the realisation that DB schemes have been chronically under-funded. Merton (2008) has written that '*the simplest explanation for what happened to defined-benefit plans is that they were mispriced, not three or five years ago but from the outset*', and that '"*defined-benefit plans have been underpriced from the beginning*'. In addition: '*Defined-benefit plans have some admirable features, and they may be used again, but we will not return to them with these benefits at this price.*' It is ironic that one of the major reasons for the decline of DB schemes is that shareholders dislike the costs and risks to which DB schemes expose the sponsor, as DB pension schemes themselves represent a substantial proportion of shareholders. Thus DB schemes are indirectly contributing to their own demise.

2.3   The Shift from DB to DC Schemes

a. Details of the Shift

DC schemes have become dominant in the USA, and a big switch from DB to DC is underway in the UK by private sector employers. By 2013 no firms in the FTSE 100 index had a final salary scheme open to new members (LCP 2014), and in 2014 only four FTSE 100 schemes provided new recruits with any form of DB pension: Diageo, Johnson Matthey and Morrisons with cash balance schemes, and Tesco with a career average revalued earnings CARE scheme (LCP 2015a). However, DB schemes still persist, and in 2014 only 14 FTSE 100 companies had no DB scheme, and 63 FTSE 100 DB schemes were allowing DB accrual (LCP 2015a). Like most things concerning pensions, the switch from DB to DC is unfolding over a very long timescale. This sub-section provides more details of the DB to DC switch, and the reasons for this switch will be considered in the following sub-section.

There are about 160,000 contract-based DC schemes in the UK, roughly 45,000 trust-based DC schemes (Harrison et al. 2012), and approximately 11,000 DB schemes, most of which are very small. The following statistics in Tables 2.4, 2.5 and 2.6 are based on the largest 7800 UK DB schemes. Table 2.2 shows the accelerating trend of closing DB schemes to both new members (soft freeze) and future accruals (hard freeze) that began in the early 1990s and continued into the early part of this century. This closure trend continued post-2007 (see Table 2.3) with just 13 % of DB schemes still open to new members in 2015. These open schemes accounted for 22 % of DB scheme membership, with these members of open DB schemes being concentrated in the public sector. In the UK the public sector (teachers, National Health Service, armed forces, local government, civil service, police force, etc.) is still very largely DB, while much of the private sector has switched to DC.

Between 2008 and 2015 the total number of UK DB scheme members declined by approaching 1.5 million people, and this decrease was principally in the active members (see Table 2.4). This table also shows that in 2015 only 16 % of the members of DB schemes were actives, indicating that in aggregate these schemes are mature.

Table 2.2 Closure of UK DB schemes to new members and to future accruals

Year	Closed to new members	Closed to future accruals	Total
1992 & 93	37	13	50
1994 & 95	80	12	92
1996 & 97	274	44	318
1998 & 99	250	50	300
2000 & 01	611	128	739
2002 & 03	937	227	1164
2004 & 05	569	281	850
2006 & 07	498	395	893
Totals	3256	1150	4406

Table 2.3 Status of UK DB schemes and DB members in 2006 and 2015 (PPF 2015b)

	DB schemes		DB members	
	2006 (%)	2015 (%)	2006 (%)	2015 (%)
Open	43	13	66	22
Closed to new members	44	51	32	62
Closed to future accruals	12	34	2	16
Winding up	1	2	0	0
Total	100	100	100	100

Table 2.4 Breakdown of UK DB membership in 2008 and 2015 (PPF 2015b)

	2008		2015	
Active members	22 %	2.74 m	16 %	1.75 m
Deferred pensioners	42 %	5.23 m	45 %	4.95 m
Pensioners	36 %	4.43 m	39 %	4.27 m
Total	100 %	12.40 m	100 %	10.97 m

Table 2.5 Active membership of public and private sector UK occupational pension schemes (million) (ONS 2012, 2013b, 2014b, 2015a)

Year	Public sector	Private sector	Total
1953	3.1	3.1	6.2
1967	4.1	8.1	12.2
1983	5.3	5.8	11.1
1995	4.1	6.2	10.3
2011	5.3	2.9	8.2
2012	5.1	2.7	7.8
2013	5.3	2.8	8.1
2014	5.4	4.8	10.2

Table 2.6 Membership of occupational pension schemes in 2013 (% of the workforce) (ONS 2014c)

	Men (%)	Women (%)
Public sector	87.6	83.8
Private sector	39.7	30.5
All sectors	49.3	50.3

The closure of DB schemes has been accompanied by the growth of DC schemes. In 2007 the numbers of active members of DB and DC schemes in the UK were roughly equal, but by 2020 it is predicted there will be twice as many active members of DC schemes than of DB schemes, due in part to the switch from DB, but mainly due to the introduction of auto-enrolment in 2012.

As Table 2.5 shows, the active membership of UK occupational pension schemes hit a peak in 1967, with 12.2 million active members, but by 2012 this had declined to 7.8 million actives. Active membership in the public sector (where DB schemes predominate) rose to a peak of 5.4 million in 2014; while in the private sector (where DC schemes predominate) active membership plummeted from 8.1 million in 1967 to 2.7 million in 2012, chiefly due to the closure of DB schemes. However, with the recent introduction of auto-enrolment the number of active DC members rose to 4.8 million in 2014, and will continue rising for the next few years as auto-enrolment is rolled out to smaller employers.

Finally, Table 2.6 shows that the proportion of the workforce who were members of an occupational pension scheme in the public sector in 2013 was more than double the rate in the private sector, particularly for women. The introduction of auto-enrolment is closing this gap between the public and private sectors, as shown in Table 2.5.

In the USA there has also been a big shift from DB to DC (401(k)) schemes. In 1980, 38 % of US private sector employees were members of a DB scheme, but by 2008 this had dropped to only 20 %, while the proportion who were DC members rose from 8 to 31 %. Some of this shift from DB to DC in the USA is due to changes in the pattern of employment, and the increasing administrative and regulatory costs of DB schemes (Ippolito 1995). Workers in large unionised manufacturing firms are more likely to be in a DB scheme, while workers in small non-unionised service firms are more likely to be in a DC scheme. It is the latter than have experienced the greatest growth over the past 30 years, partly explaining the shift from DB to DC in the USA. Ostaszewski (2001) has proposed a different reason for the switch from DB to DC in the USA. He pointed out that accrued DB pensions increase with salary growth, as they are based on the final (or average) salary. Since US Treasury bill returns have exceeded US salary growth, money contributed to a DC pension and invested in Treasury bills has grown faster and with lower risk than has the equivalent accrued DB pension promise. This created a motive for US scheme members wishing to switch from DB to DC schemes.

b. Some Reasons for the Shift from DB to DC

There are a number of reasons why schemes have decided to shift from DB to DC pensions.

1. Risk bearing. With a DB scheme almost all the risks are born by the sponsor: investment risk, inflation risk, interest rate risk, longevity risk, salary risk and regulatory risk. The member only bears the risk that the sponsor defaults on their obligations, and the UK, the USA, Japan, Sweden, Germany and Finland have pension insurance schemes to protect members in a DB scheme whose sponsor defaults (see Sect. 2.8). Therefore even default risk is largely

removed from DB members by this insurance paid for by the scheme. With DC schemes, the sponsor is not exposed to any investment risk, inflation risk, interest rate risk, longevity risk or final salary risk, while regulatory risk is also much reduced. These risks are borne by the member, and then, on retirement, by the company providing the annuity, or by the member if they do not buy an annuity. Therefore by switching from DB to DC the sponsor transfers almost all the risk to the active members, who may then transfer the decumulation risks to an insurance company via an annuity.

2. Changing employment. This has become an important issue as people change jobs more frequently than in previous generations. Changing employers generates difficulties and costs for a member's accrued pension benefits, particularly when the employee is a member of a DB scheme. Since each person in a DC scheme has their own pension pot, transferring between employers is more straight-forward for DC schemes. For DB and DC schemes the member can either leave a deferred pension with their former employer, or obtain a transfer to the pension scheme of their new employer. In either case they suffer a pension capital loss, although this will very probably be larger for those in a DB scheme (see Sect. 2.1). Therefore DC pensions are more portable than DB pensions, making them more attractive in this respect to members.

3. Contribution rates. Average sponsor contribution rates for UK private sector DB schemes are over four times larger than those for DC schemes, making DC schemes much cheaper for the sponsor. The average member's contribution rate for DC schemes is also much lower than for DB schemes (Table 2.7), making them attractive to short-sighted members. The much lower total DC contribution rates obviously raise questions about the adequacy of DC schemes to provide a decent pension, although there is no reason why DC contribution rates should be much lower than those for DB schemes. It is simply that DC schemes have chosen to set very low contribution rates. In a study of 616 large US companies, most of which had both a DB and a DC scheme, Brander and Finucane (2007) investigated the link between the percentage of the total pension assets in a company's pension schemes accounted for its DC scheme, and the returns on the company's equity. They found a positive association, and attributed this to

Table 2.7 Average UK private sector contribution rates in 2014 (ONS 2015a)

	Employer		Member		Total	
	Open	Closed	Open	Closed	Open	Closed
DB (%)	14.5	16.6	4.9	5.4	19.4	22.0
DC (%)	2.9	4.2	1.7	2.8	4.6	7.0

labour market effects leading to higher worker productivity for those in DC schemes. However this explanation is unlikely, and the result could also be due to markedly lower sponsor contribution rates for DC schemes, allowing the sponsor to generate higher profits.

4. Under-funding. With a DC scheme there is minimal risk to members from sponsor default, as their money is held in a separate trust, although fraud is always possible for any scheme. It is not possible to under-fund a DC scheme, although bad investments may result in a much smaller amount of money than expected in a member's DC pension pot, leading to an inadequate pension.

5. Heterogeneous preferences. In a DC scheme each member can select their own asset allocation and risk-return trade-off according to their own preferences and circumstances, and benefit or suffer from this decision. In a DB scheme a common asset allocation is made for all members. Unless there is a cap and share agreement under which the sponsor and DB members share the risks, the consequences of this decision fall largely on the sponsor.

6. Credibility. DB pensions are not contractual obligations, but promises managed by trustees who decide on such matters as the contribution rate, investment of the assets and the benefits (Besley and Prat 2005). This raises doubts about the credibility of the DB pensions promise, as it relies on agents (trustees) acting in the interests of the members. In contrast, the members of a DC scheme control their own asset allocation, might be able to adjust their contribution rate, and are not vulnerable to the benefits being altered by trustees. Therefore the credibility of DC schemes is higher than that of DB schemes.

7. Lump sum. From April 2015 members of UK DC schemes over the age of 55 have been able to take out their entire pension pot in cash, with the first 25 % being tax free. Members of DB schemes can only take out up to 25 % of their pension pot tax free when they retire, which may be well after they are 55 years of age. The remaining 75 % must remain in the scheme to provide a DB pension. Early access to the tax-free lump sum, and the ability to convert the entire pension pot to a lump sum, increase the liquidity of DC schemes, and therefore their attractiveness to members.

c. Members Preferences for DB Versus DC

Sometimes employees have a choice between a DB and a DC scheme, and there have been a range of research studies, principally in the USA, investigating the factors which determine this choice. In the US public sector, offering new members a choice between a DB and a DC pension scheme is common, particularly in higher education. Clark et al. (2006) studied the selections made by 7035 people employed by the University of North Carolina. The DC scheme was more likely to be chosen by younger white males employed by higher-level educational establishments. Florida allowed its school teachers to choose between DB and DC pensions, and 27 % of the 76,000 teachers studied by Chingos and West (2015) chose the DC scheme. Those opting into the DC scheme were white (rather than black or Hispanic), had higher degrees, taught maths or science, did not teach in special education, and left the scheme within six years. Clark et al. (2015) investigated the choice between a DC scheme and a hybrid scheme (DB and DC) offered to new members by the Utah Retirement System. Of the 6773 members who made an active choice, 48 % chose the DC scheme, and they tended to be aged under 30 years, female, and more highly paid, with a higher education. Washington State teachers were offered the choice between a DB scheme and a hybrid DB and DC scheme. Analysing the choices made by 27,355 members, Goldhaber and Grout (2016) found that selection of the hybrid DC and DB scheme was more likely for male, white members aged under 30 with a higher degree who are effective teachers on a higher salary. The US state of Michigan gave its 13,170 correction workers the choice of switching from DB to DC. Those who decided to switch to DC tended to have higher incomes, vested benefits, and be eligible for early retirement (Papke 2004b).

Brown and Weisbenner (2009) studied the DB versus DC decisions made by 45,000 members of the Illinois State Universities Retirement System (SURS). They found that the DC scheme was chosen by high earners who are well educated, married, in their thirties and who expect to stay with the scheme for a long time. This is a puzzling result because these choices appear to be suboptimal, as the DB scheme would probably have been a better choice for the majority of high earners. This may be due to the complexity of the decision, a lack of information to facilitate a sensible choice, over-confidence in the returns they will achieve on their DC investments, the political risk of under-funding the DB scheme, and a desire to be able to control their investments. In a subsequent study of the SURS, Brown and Weisbenner (2014) analysed the DB versus DC choices made by 1441 SURS members. They found that, while the relative generosity of the scheme to the person concerned was an important determinant of the choice, plan attributes (e.g. the safety of the scheme, having experts make the decisions, personal control over the investments, the ability to invest in equities) were even more important. Other important variables were risk preferences, education, income and beliefs about the scheme rules (even though these beliefs may be incorrect). This shows that the DB versus

DC choice depends on a variety of personal characteristics that are not usually available to researchers from administrative records.

A somewhat different question concerning the DB versus DC choice has been researched by Brown et al. (2015a). Their sample was 6055 participants in the SURS who had to choose between a traditional DB scheme, a DB scheme that is better for early leavers, and a DC scheme. Those who failed to make an active choice were defaulted into the traditional DB scheme. Brown et al. found that participants who were female, more highly educated, with higher levels of income and wealth, higher investment skills and a greater knowledge of the schemes were more likely to make an active choice, and less likely to be defaulted into the traditional DB scheme. The only non-US study is for Australia. Gerrans and Clark (2013) analysed 122,690 members of UniSuper, which covers Australian universities and offers a choice between DB and DC schemes. They found that members who were more likely to select the DC scheme were younger males with a higher income.

These studies of the choice between DB and DC schemes are very largely of US public sector schemes, where such choices are common. Most of these studies have found significant results for four common explanatory variables; indicating that DC schemes are more attractive to white, young, highly educated and well-paid members.

d. The Demand for DC Participation

In a study of participation in DC schemes, as opposed to the choice between DB and DC schemes, Munnell et al. (2001–02) found that the demand for DC membership increases with age, income, net worth, job tenure, sponsor matching contributions and the ability to borrow from the pension pot before retirement. Membership of DC schemes decreases if the person is already a member of a DB scheme, has a higher pension wealth and if they have a short planning horizon. Sethi-Iyengar et al. (2004) studied the effects on DC scheme participation rates of the number of investment choices offered to members. Using data on 899,631 employees in 647 firms with DC schemes, they found that, as the number of funds in the investment menu offered to members is increased, the participation rate of employees in the DC scheme is reduced, dropping from 75 % for a choice of two funds, to 60 % for a choice of 60 funds. This indicates that too much choice deters people from even joining the scheme. In a study of ten US schemes under a system of automatic enrolment, Beshears et al. (2010) found that matching sponsor contributions have a modest positive effect on DC participation rates, which is consistent with the results of Munnell et al. (2001–02).

2.4 Problems with DC Schemes

Apart from the decision to join, individuals do not have to make major decisions regarding their DB pension as the key decisions, such as the investment of the assets and the level of the contribution rate, are made by the trustees. However for DC schemes things are different, and members have to decide such matters as how to invest the money, possibly how much to contribute, and how to decumulate their pension pot—via an annuity, drawdown, or simply to take the cash. Pension decisions differ from most other economic decisions made by individuals as the consequences are manifest only in the long term, possibly decades later; so people cannot learn from their own experience until it is too late. Therefore they need to learn from the experience of their predecessors. There is also the problem for individuals of getting accurate data on which to base a decision. This lack of rapid feedback on the consequences of a pension decision means competition to provide value-for-money pensions is weak, and pension providers have little incentive to improve their pension products (Morris and Palmer 2011).

Merton (2014) has argued that the purpose of a DC scheme should not be to generate a large pot of money at the retirement date, but to maximise the probability of achieving a specified level of real income in retirement. These objectives differ because a rise in longevity, a drop in interest rates or a rise in inflation reduces the retirement income a pension pot can buy. Although it is straightforward to measure and report the current value of a member's pension pot, what members really need to know during the accumulation phase is the income from a real annuity their current pension pot could buy now, i.e. the inflation-indexed pension they will receive in retirement. This is given by the income from a single premium deferred annuity (SPDA, see Sect. 5.20) whose current price equals the current value of their pension pot. Members will then need to consider the size of the additional contributions to their pension pot before retirement. This will give members a much clearer idea of the adequacy of their pension provision to date. Therefore a DC pension pot should not be valued at its market value, but at the index-linked income it will provide in retirement. Reporting the real retirement income that a DC pension pot will provide may also encourage retirees to choose an annuity on retirement. Some further problems with DC schemes will now be considered.

a. Investment Risk

A number of studies have investigated the extent to which DC schemes can produce very different pensions for the same contributions. Burtless (2009a, b) have shown that the same contributions and asset allocation over a 40 year period during 1872–2008 produced very different pension pots. For example, assuming the DC pot was invested in equities, the highest replacement rate was 89 % (in 1999), which is 7.4 times higher than the lowest replacement rate of 12 % (in 1920), Burtless (2009a, b). This represents a very substantial difference in outcomes, illustrating the potential riskiness of DC schemes. A similar conclusion was reached by McFarland and Warshawsky (2010). They considered a life cycle fund starting at 88 % equities and ending at 34 % equities. Using US returns for 1875–2010, after 40 years of contributions the member was assumed to have retired each year between 1915 and 2010. On retirement the member purchased a nominal annuity at the prevailing annuity rate, but using 2010 life expectancies. The resulting replacement rates varied from about 15 % in 1922 to about 42 % in 1972. This analysis was repeated, but with the annuity purchased in a phased manner between the ages of 55 and 65, i.e. by purchasing a deferred annuity each year to come into payment on retirement (see Sect. 5.20). From 1970 onwards the purchase of phased annuities was superior in every year to buying an annuity only at retirement (Schieber 2012, pp. 357–360). These studies reveal the considerable investment and annuity rate risk to which different cohorts of DC member are exposed. Some cohorts will be lucky and their pension pots will enjoy high returns, and annuity rates when they retire will be high. However, other cohorts will be unlucky and endure low investment returns and then face low annuity rates.

b. Asset Allocation Decision

The members of DC schemes have to decide how to allocate their pension pot between different assets, managed by external fund managers (see Sect. 3.1a).

c. Management Fees

Each DC member's pension pot is invested with the external fund managers selected by that member from the menu on offer, and these external managers can make substantial charges and fees. The funds from which members can choose are selected by the scheme and its advisors, and they will not bear the fees and charges associated with these investments. While these management fees may appear small, they can lead to a substantial reduction in the final pension. Wood et al. (2014) found that in 2013 UK trust-based DC schemes had an average annual management charge (AMC) of 0.75 %, and contract based DC schemes had an average AMC of 0.84 %. They found the determinants of the AMC to be the number of scheme members, the scheme's age, the total value of the contributions to the scheme and whether a commission-based advisor was used. These charges appear modest, but over many years they can lead to a sizable reduction in the value of the final pension pot. A study found that over 25 years, the reduction in the final value of the DC pension pot due to investment charges and fees was an average of 19.0 %. The lowest reduction was 9.8 %, while the highest was 27.8 %, showing that charges and fees have a substantial effect on the size of the final pension pot. In a few cases these charges are considerably higher. A large study of UK DC schemes by the Independent Project Board (2014) found that in 2014 £42 billion of DC funds was subject to annual charges of above 1 %, of which £0.9 billion was subject to an annual charge of over 3 %. In addition, £3.4 billion was in DC schemes with exit charges of 10 %. From April 2015 the charges of DC default funds in auto-enrollment schemes have been capped at 0.75 %. The annual investment costs of large DB schemes are about 25 basis points per year, leading to a reduction in the size of a DB fund of only about 5.7 % after 25 years, which is appreciably lower than for DC schemes.

d. Limited Choice

Some DC schemes offer members an inefficient menu of possible investments, and this can result in lower returns or higher risk. Elton et al. (2006) analysed the investment choices offered by 401(k) schemes, and discovered that only 53 % offer a menu which permits the formation of an efficient portfolio. For example, DC schemes may not offer private equity, hedge funds, infrastructure or direct property. After 40 years the average value of the portfolios formed from the inefficient portfolios is 57 % lower than would have been the case if an efficient menu had been available. In a study of 7975 US DC schemes, AitSahlia et al. (2015) found that, based on their spanning properties, only between 28 and 46 % of schemes offer an efficient investment menu. Ayres and Curtis (2015) considered over 3500 401(k) schemes and found that after 40 years the restricted menus offered to members resulted in a 27 % reduction in the final pension pot. Angus et al. (2007) looked at the investment menu of TIAA-CREF, which is a very large US public sector scheme. They found that, because it omits a value index, a small-capitalization index, an international index, and a real estate index; it does not permit members to form efficient portfolios. After 20 years this led to a reduction in terminal wealth of between 20 and 40 %. Therefore, even if members know how to form efficient portfolios, or receive advice on how to achieve such an outcome; it may be impossible to select a portfolio that is efficient with respect to the universe of all assets, and their portfolio will necessarily be sub-optimal. In contrast to these results, a spanning test by Tang (2008) and Tang et al. (2010) of the menus of over 1000 US DC schemes with a median menu size of 13 funds found that 94 % of the menus were efficient portfolios.

As a general rule, a larger investment universe permits the selection of a more efficient portfolio, and so, ignoring any behavioural effects, large menus are better than small menus for rational fully informed investors. But Goldreich and Halaburda (2013) have shown that this proposition does not apply to DC pension investment menus. Using data on 191 401(k) schemes they found that, since there are differences in the ability of those who choose the assets included in the investment menus, and due to the low marginal cost of including additional assets in these menus, small menus permit the formation of more efficient portfolios than do large menus. This result applies, even if every member is rational and fully informed because high ability menu selectors choose a small number of high quality assets, while low ability menu selectors choose a large menu of low quality assets.

e. Annuity Rate Risk

Annuity prices vary with expected longevity and long term interest rates (see Sect. 5.1). Increases in expected longevity, coupled with a fall in interest rates led to UK annuity rates falling from 16.2 % in 1981 to 8.2 % in 2002 (Cannon and Tonks 2004); and by 2012 they had declined further to about 5.9 %. This reduction in annuity rates greatly reduced the size of the annuities that could be purchased by members of DC schemes with a given size of pension pot to far below what was expected when they joined the scheme. A new member of a DC scheme may wish to estimate the size of the pension pot they need on retirement to buy an annuity with a chosen income level, and this requires them to engage in the difficult task of forecasting the annuity rate in (say) 40 years time. Since the main drivers of annuity prices are interest rates and longevity expectations, Dowd et al. (2011) quantified the effect of these risks on forecasts of annuity prices in 40 years time. They suggest that individual members have an incentive to hedge these risks, but at present the requisite instruments do not exist.

f. Choice of Annuity
(See Sect. 5.14).

g. Timing of Annuity Purchase
(See Sect. 5.13).

h. Contribution Rate
The level of contributions to DC schemes is much lower than for DB schemes, and this will very probably result in substantially smaller pensions. In 2014 the average UK sponsor and member contribution rates for open DB schemes

were 14.5 % and 4.9 % respectively, while for open DC schemes they were only 2.9 % and 1.7 % respectively (see Table 2.7). So the total contribution rate for DB schemes was over four times that for DC schemes.

Some DC schemes, particularly in the USA, allow each member to choose their contribution rate, which offers a further area for mistakes by members, i.e. seriously under-contributing. A substantial number of sponsors tie their contribution rate to that chosen by the member, and so a low member contribution rate often leads to a low sponsor's contribution rate, exacerbating the problem. Where a scheme allows members to choose their contribution rate, it is necessary to have a default contribution rate for those who fail to make a choice. Choi (2015) gives seven behavioural reasons why members may fail to make an active choice of contribution rate: (a) the time and effort involved in departing from the default rate, (b) the default rate is seen as the recommended rate, (c) loss-aversion (or the endowment effect) and so they stick with the status quo, (d) the default rate serves as an anchor, (e) bounded rationality so they do not consider other rates, (f) cognitive dissonance so they come to prefer the status quo (the default rate), and (g) ignorance that they can choose their contribution rate. Choi et al. (2011) looked at seven 401(k) schemes and found that 30 % of older members chose to under-contribute to their pension, even though an arbitrage profit was available from higher contributions, resulting in a loss equivalent to up to 6 % of their salary each year. Cui (2008) argued that the choice of contribution rate is more important than the asset allocation, and that age-dependent default contribution rates are clearly preferable to a single default contribution rate.

As longevity increases, if the contribution rate and investment returns do not change, the value of the annuity that can be purchased by DC scheme members declines. In order for DC members to maintain their expected annual pension, they need to work longer to accumulate a larger pension pot and/or retire later. Making various simplifying assumptions, Madsen and Tans (2012a, b) have shown that, for the same pension to be received, an increase in life expectancy of five years requires an increase of two years in the retirement age. They also found that a 1 % decrease in interest rates and investment returns can lead to an increase of four years in the retirement age needed to maintain the value of the pension.

i. Inadequate Pensions

Although DC schemes cannot have deficits; low contribution rates, poor investment returns and low annuity rates at retirement can result in an inadequate pension. Since DC pensions are generally much lower than DB pensions, there is an increased risk of pensioner poverty. As the large scale adoption of DC schemes is recent, it will be many decades before the inadequacy of DC contribution rates is widely realized. The Pensions Policy Institute (2014) has estimated that, for a person on median earnings with total contributions of 8 % to their DC scheme, the probability of achieving their target replacement income on retirement are only 49 %. For those who start contributing later, or who take a career break the probabilities are lower. MacDonald and Cairns (2007) have simulated the effects on the dependency ratio of a situation where the entire pension system is DC, and members delay their retirement until their pension pot is big enough to provide an adequate pension. The result is a dependency ratio that fluctuates with the stock market, and this volatility in the size of the workforce will have negative implications for the economy such as amplifying business cycles (see Sect. 3.3b).

2.5   Pensions Buy-outs and Buy-ins

Companies with DB pension schemes have been seeking to shed responsibility for their accrued pension liabilities. This can be done by a buy-out or a buy-in, and in each case the deal is irreversible. As well as the UK, which is the world leader, buy-outs and buy-ins have also been taking place in the USA, Canada, Ireland and the Netherlands. The total value of buy-outs, buy-ins and longevity swaps (see Sect. 2.7a) in the UK by June 2015 was £105.4 bn., where just under half of these deals were longevity swaps (PPF 2015b).

a. Buy-ins
When there is a buy-in the DB scheme continues with all its liabilities and assets as before. In addition, an insurance company insures all the risks for a specified group of scheme members, and in return the sponsor makes a payment to the insurance company—the insurance premium. Rather than use a buy-in to insure all the risks for a specified group of members, a pension scheme can insure just one type of risk. This can be done using swap contracts to hedge longevity, investment or inflation risks. The most popular are longevity swaps (see Sect. 2.7a) and inflation swaps. If a scheme combines longevity, inflation and asset return swaps, it can create a synthetic buy-in. See Appendix 2 for a list of some large buy-ins, buy-outs and longevity swaps.

b. Buy-outs
A buy-out occurs when the DB scheme buys annuities for some or all of its members (i.e. a bulk annuity). On retirement each scheme member now

receives an annuity from the insurance company, rather than a pension from the sponsor. There are two types of buy-out—full and partial. (a) *Full Buy-Out.* The DB scheme is wound-up and all its assets are transferred to the insurance company in exchange for the annuities. The sponsor will probably also have to make a substantial payment to the insurance company to make up the difference between the price of the bulk annuity and the value of the assets transferred. This is not possible for very large schemes, as the buy-out market lacks sufficient depth. (b) *Partial Buy-Out.* The DB scheme continues and only the liability for the pensions of a specified group of scheme members (usually pensioners) is transferred to the insurance company, along with a matching transfer of assets. The scheme (and the sponsor) continue to be responsible for the pensions of the remaining members. Schemes seeking to reduce the cost of a buy-out should ensure their member records are in a good state, and their investments are in assets which are acceptable to the insurer. By the end of 2012 buy-outs and buy-ins covered about £30 billion of UK pension liabilities, (Hymans Robertson 2013).

Partial buy-outs, buy-ins and longevity swaps (see Sect. 2.7) mainly involve pensioners, rather than actives and deferreds, for three main reasons. (a) Lower Longevity Risk. Since the longevity of pensioners is shorter, it can be more accurately predicted than the longevity of actives and deferreds, leading to lower risk. (b) Fewer Events. Pensioners have already made various choices, such as their retirement date and lump sum decision. They are also no longer eligible for early retirement, ill-health early retirement, death-in-service benefit, transfers to or from another scheme, etc. Therefore it is easier to predict the value of the liabilities, resulting in less risk. (c) Shorter Duration. Due to their shorter longevity, pensioner liabilities extend over a shorter period of years, making it easier to find hedging instruments, such as bonds, to match their duration. Again there is less risk.

c. Regulatory Arbitrage

A buy-out by an insurance company means the deal is governed by insurance regulations, not pension regulations. As a result, the insurance company must maintain a large buffer of regulatory capital, and invest mainly in long term fixed interest securities. Neither of these restrictions apply to pension schemes, although the EU is introducing Solvency II which sets out capital requirements for insurance companies, and some have argued that these regulations should also apply to DB pension schemes. Cazalet Consulting (2014) have estimated that Solvency II will require insurance companies to hold roughly 10–15 % of their annuity liabilities in regulatory capital. Alternatively, the insurance regulations can be avoided by changing the deal into a non-insurance buy-out. The sponsor is restructured so that the sponsor of the DB scheme becomes a shell company. This DB sponsor, and its associated pension scheme, is then taken over by a financial company, which then becomes the scheme sponsor. This means that the pension scheme is governed by pension, rather than insurance regulations. Alternatively the financial company can take over the sponsor, and then sell off its operating assets, leaving just the DB pension scheme. Non-insurance buy-outs include Threshers and the Pension Corporation (June 2007), Thompson Regional Newspapers and Citigroup (August 2007), and Telent (formerly GEC-Marconi) and the Pension Corporation (September 2007). There was an outcry after the takeover of Telent by the Pension Corporation in September 2007, and the UK government imposed independent trustees on the Telent scheme. This discouraged any more non-insurance buy-outs.

2.6   Closed or Frozen Schemes

DB pension schemes can be closed (which is called frozen in the USA), and this can be done in two main ways. The more extreme choice is to close the scheme to further contributions (a hard freeze in US terminology). Not only can no-one join the scheme, but existing members cannot make any further contributions, and so do not accrue any additional benefits. The scheme will eventually cease to exist when all the members die. The less extreme choice is to close the scheme to additional members (sometimes called a soft freeze in the USA). Existing members continue making contributions and accruing additional benefits, but no-one is allowed to join. Again the scheme will cease to exist when all the existing members die. In the USA a soft freeze sometimes means that existing members accrue additional benefits from salary increases, but cannot accrue additional years of service, while a thawed scheme is one that has been unfrozen. A partial freeze occurs when the freeze applies to only some of the members of a US scheme.

A sponsor wishing to deal with the costs and risks of a DB scheme may consider winding-up the scheme. However in the UK this will trigger a requirement for the sponsor to fully fund the scheme immediately, and they may not wish, or be able, to inject this sum into the scheme. An alternative is to close (or freeze) the scheme. Once a scheme is closed its risk (salary, longevity, inflation, interest rate, and regulatory) reduces over time as no new members join; with no further accruals if it is hard frozen. Therefore the liabilities will be smaller than if the scheme had remained open. If a scheme is closed to further accruals (hard frozen), regular sponsor contributions cease, although the sponsor remains responsible for making good any under-funding. Therefore closing a scheme reduces the costs and risks for the sponsor. The scheme is now in 'run-off', and over time the liabilities will get smaller and smaller as pensioners and members die. Section 2.10 argues that, if the scheme has uniform contribution and accrual rates, each year the young members usually contribute more than the cost of the benefits they accrue. Closing a scheme ends this inter-generational cross-subsidy as there will not be any new young members, creating a tendency for the funding ratio of closed schemes to worsen over time, Campbell et al. (2006).

Closed schemes will probably have a negative cash flow as payments to pensioners exceed income from investments and contributions, and so need to hold highly liquid investments, and avoid long term illiquid investments. Due to the loss of the inter-generational cross-subsidy and the small size of contributions, relative to the liabilities, a soft freeze may lead to the contribution rate becoming more volatile, Campbell et al. (2006). For a hard frozen scheme, since all contributions have ceased, the contribution rate cannot be used to control the funding ratio, and UK legislation prevents accrued benefits being reduced. When all of the active members of a soft frozen scheme have retired, it faces the same problems as a hard frozen scheme in controlling the funding ratio. To reduce the risk of the sponsor having to make special contributions to rectify a deficit, a closed scheme may seek to hedge its risks (e.g. inflation, longevity and interest rates) using buy-ins, swaps etc., and to adopt a low-risk asset allocation. For example, in a simulation study, Butt (2011) found that closing a scheme led to a reduction of 30 % in investment in equities. Because the scheme looses economies of scale as it gets smaller and smaller, at some point it may be preferable to buy-out the scheme with an insurance company, replacing the DB pensions with annuities supplied by an insurance company (see Sect. 2.5a). Merger with another scheme is an alternative exit route, as is a wind-up (see Sect. 4.5a).

a. Determinants of the Closure Decision

The determinants of the decision to close (freeze) US schemes have been investigated by a number of researchers. Using a sample of 1802 US schemes, Munnell and Soto (2007) found that freezing was more likely for schemes where the sponsor had a higher credit risk, a larger market capitalization and was in an industry with a higher percentage of DC schemes. A high ratio of pensioners to total scheme participants also increased the probability of a freeze, while a unionised workforce and a high ratio of actives to total employees decreased the probability of a freeze. Under-funding of the scheme increased the probability of a hard freeze. In another study, Comprix and Muller (2011) analysed 17,560 US schemes and concluded that the probability of a hard freeze was higher for loss making sponsors that were small companies with small schemes, a low operating cash flow deflated by total assets, and a non-unionised workforce. Beaudoin et al. (2010) studied a sample of 147 US companies who froze their pension schemes, together with a matched sample of 147 companies which did not. The potential impact of the introduction of Statement of Financial Accounting Standards no. 158 on the sponsor's balance sheet led to an increase in freezes, as did a non-unionised workforce and a low average return on the sponsor's assets. For 93 US firms, Atanasova and Hrazdil (2010) found that freezing a scheme was associated with sponsors who had a small proportion of intangible assets and a non-unionised workforce; and small schemes with a small proportion of non-vested members. All four studies have found that sponsors with a non-unionized workforce are more likely to freeze their scheme, and there is some evidence that small schemes sponsored by unprofitable firms are also more likely to be frozen.

b. Effects of Closure

The hard freeze of a DB scheme is often accompanied by replacing it with a DC scheme, and Rauh et al. (2013) have found that in the USA this leads to a reduction in pension costs for the sponsors. The effects of hard freezing a US DB scheme have been investigated by Choy et al. (2014). They argue that a hard freeze has two effects which act in opposite directions on the riskiness of the sponsor. Hard freezing a DB scheme means the risk to the sponsor of funding the scheme declines as no further benefits will be accrued, and so the sponsor becomes less risky. But this also means that the sponsor's management are no longer accruing DB pension benefits, and may well be investing in the firm's shares via a replacement DC scheme. As a result the management are now less concerned about the sponsor defaulting on its DB pension obligations, and their interests are more aligned with those of the shareholders. Because of this the sponsor's management are more willing to make risky investments to secure higher returns, which increase the sponsor's risk exposure (see Sect. 4.5f). Choy et al. found that the second effect is dominant, and sponsors who have hard frozen their DB scheme tend to invest in risky research and development, rather than less risky capital expenditure; and to increase the sponsor's leverage, increasing the riskiness of the sponsor's equity returns and credit risk.

Four US studies have investigated the effects of a freeze on the sponsor's share price, and obtained mixed results. Milevsky and Song (2010), who analysed data on 75 US firms, found that a freeze leads to a rise in the sponsor's share price of 0.35 %. For sponsors with a high beta there was a rise of 1.9 %, and for low beta firms it was a fall of 1.7 %. This suggests that, for risky companies a freeze is good news as it reduces risks and costs, while for low risk firms it may be a signal of bad news. For 93 US firms, Atanasova and Hrazdil (2010) found that, after freezing their pension scheme, the sponsor's equity returns rose, and their credit rating improved. Using data for 13 US firms, Rubin (2007) showed that after closing a scheme the sponsor's share price rose by 25 % over the next 250 days. Finally, a study by McFarland et al. (2009) of 82 US firms concluded that freezing a pension scheme had no effect on the share price.

A study of 48 UK DB schemes that were hard frozen between 2006 and 2013 by Gardner et al. (2014) found no evidence of a share price response. This lack of response may be because the hard freeze had little effect on the sponsor's risks, was already incorporated into the sponsor's share price, was misunderstood by the market, or because the closure was motivated by the poor financial performance of the sponsor and this offset the positive effect of the scheme closure. Moving in the opposite direction (i.e. creating schemes), Yoshida and Horiba (2003) studied the effect of converting informal pension arrangements into formal pension schemes in Japan, and found it has a positive effect on the share price. This is attributed to signalling positive expectations about future profits.

2.7   Dealing with Rising Longevity

Longevity presents two problems—the cost of the actual and forecast increases in longevity, and the risk of unexpected increases in longevity in the future. First, longevity is increasing rapidly, which leads to a substantial additional cost for DB pension schemes, although Carnes and Olshansky (2007) have argued that life expectancy at birth is unlikely to exceed about 85 years. Second, the rate of increase in longevity is highly uncertain, which generates risk for DB schemes. Boyer et al. (2014) examined the effects of longevity risk on the Royal Canadian Mounted Police DB scheme. If the scheme wished to have sufficient assets to meet an increase in longevity 95 % or 99 % of the time, they needed to hold and additional 6 % or 9 % of assets. Michaelson and Mulholland (2014) have pointed out that global pension liabilities are well in excess of $60 trillion, while the global insurance industry has assets of only $4.2 trillion, and so cannot bear more than a small amount of the longevity risk of these obligations. However the global capital markets are large enough to absorb longevity risk, and researchers are searching for an attractive way of trading this risk on these markets. For a survey of ways of dealing with longevity risk see Blake et al. (2013a).

a. Longevity Swaps

One approach to dealing with longevity risk is to use longevity swaps. The DB pension scheme agrees the expected mortality of a group of scheme members (usually pensioners) with an insurance company. To the extent that actual pensioner mortality is lower (higher) from that in the swap agreement, payments are made to (from) the pension scheme. There are two types of longevity swap:- index-linked longevity swaps and named-life longevity swaps. Index-linked longevity swaps are based on the longevity index for some standard population, and this introduces basis risk which will be larger for schemes with few members. Named-life longevity swaps are linked to the actual membership of the scheme, and this removes the basis risk.

In the UK most longevity swaps have been named-life longevity swaps which have the advantage of removing basis risk for the scheme, and cost only a little more than index-linked longevity swaps because the companies providing longevity swaps have a well-diversified portfolio of longevity risks (Madsen and Tans 2011). However, a liquid secondary market is more likely to develop for standardized index-linked swaps than for named-life longevity swaps. The first longevity swap for a pension scheme was in May 2009 between Babcock International and Credit Suisse, covered some of the scheme's pensioners, and had a liability value of £750 million. Some subsequent large longevity swaps appear in Appendix 2. Unlike bulk annuities, swaps have the advantage of not requiring a big up-front payment.

Longevity has a very low correlation with the stock market index, giving it a very low CAPM beta. With this advantage, longevity may become a new asset class that is traded on the capital markets. For example, the correlations between US longevity (as measured by the QxX index) and indices of various US asset classes were computed by Rosenfeld (2009) as:- S&P 500 index 0.09; bond index –0.35; real estate index –0.16; and commodities index 0.21. There has been research on a wide variety of financial instruments allowing longevity to be traded on the capital markets such as longevity bonds, longevity futures, longevity options and so on; but despite the major advantage of a very low beta, a market in longevity has proved difficult to start.

The most successful instruments have been longevity swaps, and by the end of 2012 longevity swaps covered about £20 billion of liabilities (Hymans Robertson 2013) see Appendix 2. However longevity swaps cover just a tiny fraction of pension liabilities, and a number of obstacles to their use have been identified by Johnson (2014b). First, providers of longevity swaps want the pension scheme to have good data on its members to enable them to accurately price the deal, removing the information asymmetry between the scheme and the insurance company. If not, the price is higher. Second, there is a lack of competition amongst those providing longevity swaps. Initially, the banks were heavily involved in this market, but they have retreated due to fears about capital adequacy requirements. Third, capital market participants want to invest in a simple, liquid and tradable product, and this requires the swap to be based on an index. But most pension schemes want a longevity swap based on the mortality of their own members i.e. a named-life longevity swap. Finally, if the scheme subsequently wants a buy-out or buy-in, the presence of a longevity swap can complicate matters.

b. Increase the Normal Pension Age
An approach used by many schemes to reduce the cost of longevity is to increase the normal pension age (NPA) (e.g. from 60 to 65 years. This increases the age at which people retire, and so members contribute to the scheme for an additional (say) five years, and their pension will be paid for (say) five years less. Some schemes have changed their rules so that the NPA increases in future according to a pre-specified schedule (e.g. rises from 63 to 65 in 2017, from 65 to 66 in 2025, and from 66 to 68 in 2045. However this approach relies on the longevity increases forecast when the schedule of NPA increases was set, and so does not allow for the risk of future unexpected increases in longevity. When increasing the retirement date, care should be taken not to introduce sudden changes near retirement that are perceived as being unfair. In 2006 the Netherlands increased the retirement age for public sector workers born after 1 January 1950 by 13 months, which led to a strong deterioration in both the mental health and job motivation of those born in 1950, De Grip et al. (2012), and Montizaan et al. (2016).

c. Life Expectancy Adjustment Factors (LEAF)
An alternative to increasing the NPA is to adopt a life expectancy adjustment factor (LEAF). This automatically allows for the risk of unexpected increases in longevity, and once implemented avoids the need for decision makers to face the opposition that inevitably accompanies each decision to increase in the NPA. A LEAF transfers the risk of future changes in longevity to scheme members by automatically adjusting the accrued pensions for each age cohort by a factor which is set each year to reflect changes in expected longevity. It does this by reducing (increasing) the pension for a given retirement age, rather than delaying the date from which the pension is paid, i.e. the NPA. LEAF factors are used by a few UK corporate schemes (e.g. John Lewis, BAE Systems, RS Components), and by some state schemes (Sweden, Finland, Italy, Latvia, Poland, Switzerland, Germany, Portugal and Denmark). When longevity rises, individual members can decide whether to accept a lower pension, or to work longer and maintain the level of their pension.

d. Top Slicing Bulk Annuities

A recent development in dealing with longevity risk is the purchase of bulk annuities only for those members with the highest accrued benefits, as they represent the highest concentration of longevity risk. These bulk annuities are medically under-written, i.e. each potential annuitant undergoes some form of heath check before the price of the bulk annuity is set.

2.8 Pension Scheme Insurance

For there to be default by a DB scheme, the joint occurrence of two events is necessary—the scheme is under-funded, and the sponsor is unable to make good this deficit. To protect the scheme members and pensioners in such a situation some countries have solvency requirements for DB pension schemes (e.g. Netherlands), while other countries have pension insurance to protect members. The following countries have created pension insurance schemes (together with their establishment dates):- Sweden 1961, Finland early 1960s, USA 1974, Germany 1974, Ontario, Canada 1980, Switzerland 1986, Japan 1989, and UK 2005. Pension insurance companies provide benefits to the scheme members of failed schemes in three different ways:- (a) pay pensions (USA, UK and Japan), (b) buy annuities (Germany, Japan, Sweden and Switzerland), or (c) make payments to the pension scheme (Ontario). The schemes in four countries (USA, UK, Germany and Ontario) will be briefly outlined, with at least one country from each of the three different ways of providing insurance benefits.

Pension scheme insurance faces a number of problems which make it difficult for the private sector to provide such insurance, and these problems may explain why pension scheme insurance is provided by agencies created by the state. First, the benefits of pension insurance largely accrue to the members whose pensions are under-written by the insurer. Therefore, unless pension insurance is compulsory, schemes may not insure voluntarily. Legislating such compulsory insurance makes DB pension insurance part of the political arena, and that can lead to distortions in the market. For example, there may be restrictions preventing an actuarially fair levy (i.e. insurance premium), where financially weak firms are required to pay higher levies, making them even weaker. Second, pension insurance faces adverse selection (see Sect. 5.5b for details of adverse selection) if the levy does not correctly reflect the risk of default, and firms with a low default risk cross-subsidise those with a high default risk. To avoid paying these cross-subsidies, strong firms may seek to close their DB scheme and establish a DC scheme. Third, moral hazard (where one party exposes themselves to risk knowing that another other party will bear the cost) means that, if the levy does not reflect the scheme's investment risk, firms will increase their investment in equities, so increasing their expected returns, but also their default risk. In addition, financially weak firms may increase staff remuneration by increasing their pension benefits and the potential claim on the pension insurer, rather than increasing their wages. Finally, since there is a strong positive correlation between the financial strength of all the insured schemes within a country, the insurer is exposed to systematic macro risk which they cannot diversify away.

The adverse selection and moral hazard problems can be dealt with by correctly pricing the insurance to reflect the default risk of each scheme. This requires basing the levy on the scheme's asset allocation, funding status, and strength of the sponsor's covenant. However, it is a challenging task to compute actuarially fair prices for each scheme, and this objective may meet political opposition. In the absence of actuarially fair pricing, there are some other ways in which the insurer can seek to protect themselves. They can cap individual benefits to limit the insurance claim for any individual member, seek some connection between the risk of default and the levy, impose restrictions on the asset allocation, require a minimum funding level, and require collateral from the sponsor if default risk is high, (Cotter et al. 2012). In the light of these difficulties, the characteristics of the insurance schemes for four counties will now be examined.

a. USA—Pension Benefit Guarantee Corporation (PBGC)

The PBGC was set up in the USA in 1974 to pay pensions to those whose DB scheme had defaulted. In 2014 the PBGC covered 41 million workers and pensioners in over 24,000 US DB pension schemes. Each US DB scheme paid a compulsory fee of $57 per participant, plus $24 for each $1000 of unfunded liabilities. The sponsor is liable for a scheme's deficit up to a limit of 30 % of the sponsor's net asset value, with the PBGC paying the remainder of the deficit. Note that the levy does not vary with the scheme's asset allocation, nor with the insolvency risk of the sponsor, leading to moral hazard. Moral hazard occurs because pension schemes may take bigger investment risks, knowing that the resulting increase in the risk of default falls on the PBGC, while any higher returns benefit the scheme. This behaviour promotes adverse selection, with well-funded schemes closing their DB schemes to avoid the resulting actuarially unfair insurance premia. Funding for the PBGC comes from three sources:- (a) insurance premiums paid by the sponsors of DB schemes, (b) assets held by the DB pension schemes the PBGC takes over, and (c) investment income on its assets. In 2014 the PBGC had a deficit of $61.8 billion and assets of $89.8 billion. The bankruptcies by US airlines and motor companies greatly increased the PBGC deficit. The PBGC pays pension benefits up to a maximum of about $54,000 a year per person, depending on age, and in 2014 paid retirement benefits of $5.6 billion to 813,000 retirees of 4600 terminated US DB pension schemes.

b. UK—Pension Protection Fund (PPF)

The PPF began operating in the UK in 2005 when it covered 12.4 million DB scheme members, and by 2015 it covered 11 million people, (PPF 2015a). Previously, when a DB pension scheme was under-funded and the sponsor became insolvent, the members stood to lose part, or all, of their pension. Because pensions in payment have priority, a member who retired just before an insolvency might receive their full pension, while someone who retired just after an insolvency could lose their entire pension if there were no funds left after providing for the pensioners.

The PPF is essentially an insurance company and charges a compulsory levy to all UK DB schemes which is composed of two parts—a scheme levy and a risk-based levy. The scheme-based levy is a proportion of scheme liabilities and forms about 11 % of the total levy. The risk-based levy depends on the level of under-funding of the scheme, the asset allocation and the probability of the sponsor becoming insolvent over the following year as quantified by Experian credit rating scores. The risk-based levy is about 89 % of the total levy. Note that until 2012–2013 the PPF levy did not depend on the asset allocation of the scheme, leading to moral hazard. The PPF was the first national pension scheme insurer to introduce a risk-based levy (Clarke 2013). In a simulation of the PPF rules with and without the rule that bases the levy on the asset allocation, Butt (2013) examined the effects of the moral hazard created by ignoring the asset allocation when setting the levy. He discovered that, as schemes get closer to default, the equity allocation rises and the deficit increases.

When the sponsor defaults, the PPF takes over the assets remaining in the scheme and invests them (together with the levies) to pay the pensions. In 2015 the PPF had assets of £27.6 billion, a surplus of £3.6 billion, and in 2014–2015 the PPF levy was £574 million. Like the PBGC, funding for the PPF comes from three sources:- (a) the levies paid by the sponsors of UK DB schemes, (b) assets acquired from the DB pension schemes it takes over, and (c) investment income. The PPF aims to become self-sufficient (i.e. zero levy) by 2030 (Clarke 2013). If the sponsor becomes insolvent and the scheme is under-funded pensioners continue to receive 100 % of their pension from the PPF. Members who have not yet retired receive roughly 90 % of their pension (when it is due) from the PPF, subject to a cap of about £36,000 per year, depending on age. By 2015 799 schemes had transferred to the PPF, and by 2015 it had paid out a total of £1.8 bn. (PPF 2015a). In 2015 the PPF was paying pensions to 112,392 pensioners, and committed to making payments to 109,102 deferred pensioners. In 2015 the PPF also paid out a total of £186 million to 42,284 people under the Financial Assistance Scheme, which preceded the PPF.

c. Germany—Pensions-Sicherungs-Verein (PSVaG)

In 2015 the PSVaG protected the pensions of 10.9 million people in 94,000 German schemes. The compulsory levies of the PSVaG are based on each pension scheme's annual cost, and are not risk adjusted, leading to moral hazard. The PSVaG does not pay pensions, but buys annuities from insurance companies when a pension comes into payment. The PSVaG is funded on a PAYG basis, and so levies are the PSVaG's only source of funds. This makes the annual levy volatile. The maximum pension in 2004 was about £74,000 per year.

d. Ontario, Canada—Pension Benefit Guarantee Fund (PBGF)

In 2010 the PBGF protected 1580 schemes with over 1.1 million members in the Canadian state of Ontario. It charges a compulsory levy, largely based on the level of under-funding, which leads to moral hazard as the asset allocation and strength of the sponsor covenant are ignored. In 2012 the PBGF paid pensions of up to only $12,000 p.a. Rather than pay the pensions itself, it pays the money to the defaulting pension scheme. In 2015 it had assets of $543 million, and a surplus of $371 million. Crossley and Jametti (2013) compared the asset allocation of pension schemes in Ontario which are insured, with those of pension schemes in the rest of Canada which are uninsured. They found that the moral hazard created by this insurance led to an additional 2 % of the assets being invested in equities by Ontario schemes.

2.9   The Design of Pension Schemes

If markets are complete, pension scheme design is irrelevant (McCarthy 2005). In such a world, whatever the design of the pension scheme, sponsors and scheme members can always rearrange their portfolio of assets and liabilities and the division of compensation between wages and pension to give them the same desired outcome. This is because markets can be used to reconfigure any initial allocation into the desired allocation, and the design of the pension scheme is irrelevant. However, the real world does not offer complete markets because there are transaction costs, constraints, missing markets, moral hazard, etc.; and so pension scheme design, such as the choice between defined contribution and final salary schemes does matter. There is no single 'correct' pension scheme design—it depends on the characteristics and preferences of the company and its employees.

Pension schemes can be designed to perform one or more of the following main functions (Bovenberg and Van Ewijk 2012): (a) Consumption smoothing, i.e. people save while working, and dis-save when retired, so that their consumption remains roughly constant throughout their adult life (see Fig. 1.2). While a fairly smooth level of consumption is what most people prefer, pension schemes could also be designed to deliver other time patterns. (b) Pooling intra-generational risks, i.e. the diversification of unsystematic risks such as increased longevity or low annuity rates between people of the same generation. Imperfect insurance markets make it difficult or costly for individuals to insure such risks themselves, but this can be achieved via pension schemes. (c) Sharing inter-generational risks such as macro shocks, i.e. the pooling of systematic risks between different generations. Markets are limited or do not exist which allow different generations to trade items such as economic cycles or human capital.

a. Some Types of Pension Scheme

So far only the two main types of pension scheme design have been considered—final salary DB and DC. However a very range of pension designs is possible, and four additional designs will now be investigated—career average revalued earnings, cash balance, collective DC, and notional DC.

i. Career Average Revalued Earnings (CARE)

(This section is based on Sutcliffe (2010b).) CARE pensions are a type of DB scheme, but instead of being based on *final* salary, they are based on the *average* salary over a member's career with the sponsor. In a final salary scheme each annual salary is uprated each year using that member's actual rate of salary increase, including promotional increases. In a CARE scheme the annual salaries for all members in a particular year are uprated by a common revaluation rate that is specified in the scheme rules. The UK government has switched the Civil Service scheme to CARE from final salary, and in 2015 CARE was extended across the UK public sector to the NHS, local government, and teachers. In October 2011 USS switched from final salary to CARE for new members, and in April 2016 to CARE for all members. In the Netherlands many DB schemes have switched from final salary to CARE.

An important choice when designing a CARE scheme is the rate used when revaluing (or uprating) accrued benefits. Some possible revaluation rates are:-

1. Inflation. This is the most popular revaluation rate.
2. Limited Price Indexation (LPI). In the UK there is a legal obligation to revalue deferred benefits by inflation, subject to a cap of 2.5 %; and this cap can also be applied to revaluing the benefits of active members in a CARE scheme.
3. Average Earnings. This can be either national average earnings, or the average earnings of the company's employees.
4. Member's Wage Rate. The member's actual wage rate, i.e. a final salary scheme.
5. Riskless Rate of Interest.
6. Investment Return. This is the rate of return achieved by the pension fund on its assets. In this case the investment risk is passed to the members.
7. Zero. No revaluation.
8. Conditional Indexation. Three quarters of Dutch pension schemes are CARE, where the revaluation of accrued benefits by the inflation rate only occurs to the extent the scheme can afford it (see Sect. 2.9a(iii)).

Actuaries argue that salaries generally increase faster than inflation (1.3 % p.a., Salt 2012), and so a CARE scheme revalued using inflation, the most popular choice of revaluation rate, gives lower pensions than a final salary scheme if the accrual rates are the same.

Example. A CARE scheme has an accrual rate of 60ths and a revaluation rate of RPI. Havelock Sweeting joins this scheme for five years, and then retires. His annual pensionable salary is shown in Table 2.8, along with the increase in RPI for each year. The revalued average salary is 113,579/5 = £22,719. With five accrued years, Havelock's pension is (5/60)22,719 = £1893 per year. His corresponding final salary pension would have been higher at (5/60)23,000 = £1917 per year.

Table 2.8 Example of a CARE scheme

Year	Salary	RPI (%)	A	B
1	20,000	3	£20,000	£20,600
2	21,000	4	£41,600	£43,264
3	22,000	2	£65,264	£66,569
4	22,000	1	£88,569	£89,455
5	23,000	1	£112,455	£113,579

A = Salary + (Total revalued salary for previous years i.e. B for the previous year)
B = Closing total revalued salary [A × (1 + RPI)]

Advantages to the Sponsor of Switching to a CARE Scheme

1. In a final salary scheme a large pay rise revalues all accrued years. This does not happen with a CARE scheme, as accrued years are only uprated by the revaluation rate. Therefore pay rises are much more expensive with a final salary scheme.

Example. Suppose a sponsor has a £10 million pension liability for the past service of active members, and an annual wage bill of £1 million. This sponsor now grants an unexpected wage rise of 10 %, which is 7 % above inflation. With a final salary scheme the cost in the first year to the sponsor is the revaluation of past service (£10 m. × 0.10), plus the increase in annual salary costs (£1 m. × 0.10), or £1.1 million, ignoring the extra pension cost of the higher wages in the current year. Under a CARE scheme with RPI revaluation, the extra cost to the sponsor is the increase in salary cost for the current year of £0.1 m., plus the revaluation of the past service liability using RPI of (£10 million × 0.03) = £0.3 m., giving a total additional cost of only £0.4 m. In general, for every extra 1 % granted as a pay rise, the extra cost for a final salary scheme of the revaluation of past service plus the higher salary in the current year is (0.01×Liabilities) higher than for a CARE scheme for example (7 × 0.01 × £10 million) = £0.7 million = (£1.1 million – £0.4 million). In this example, the marginal cost for a final salary scheme of an extra 1 % pay rise is £110,000, not the £10,000 for a CARE scheme.

2. Since a large pay rise has a much smaller effect on CARE pensions, members of CARE schemes have less incentive to seek large pay rises.
3. If inflation is used as the revaluation rate, a CARE scheme replaces final salary risk with inflation risk, which is easier for the sponsor to hedge. It is also easier to forecast inflation risk rather than final salary risk.
4. If the CARE scheme uses the same revaluation rate for both deferred pensioners and active members, members leaving the firm and becoming deferred pensioners have no cost implications for the pension scheme. This makes it easier to forecast future pension liabilities.
5. Some members of a final salary scheme may delay retiring, hoping for a large pay rise that will revalue all their accrued benefits. This is not the case with CARE schemes.
6. CARE is a fairer scheme than final salary as it does not favour 'high flyers' and disadvantage 'low flyers'. The Cabinet Office wanted an equality-proof

scheme for the Civil Service, and the gave fairness of CARE as a reason for switching to a CARE scheme.

7. Because they involve substantial redistribution between members, final salary schemes can be unsuitable for use by multi-employer schemes such as USS.

8. CARE schemes offer the flexibility to change the revaluation rate and the definition of pensionable pay without creating the administrative problems of tranches of past service that occur with a final salary scheme.

9. CARE schemes do not generate a PCL for members, so removing the need to pay higher wages to compensate members for potentially suffering a PCL.

Advantages to Members of Switching to a CARE Scheme

1. Since CARE reduces the effect of a large pay rise on pension costs, it becomes easier for trade unions to negotiate larger pay rises.

2. It is easier to predict the size of a CARE pension than a final salary pension.

3. A CARE scheme is more attractive to risk averse workers, as revaluation rate risk is usually less than final salary risk.

4. If the revaluation rate is inflation, then the accrued CARE pension is fixed in real terms.

5. A cost neutral switch to a CARE scheme makes joining the scheme more attractive to staff without good career prospects ('low flyers').

6. CARE schemes benefit members whose earnings peak in mid-career (e.g. manual workers, or who wish to step down to a lower paid, less demanding, job.

7. Final salary schemes often exclude fluctuating emoluments (overtime, variable time employment, special payments, etc.) from pensionable pay because they are difficult to deal with in the benefit calculation. However CARE schemes have no difficulty with fluctuating pay, and so are popular in the retail sector with its many variable time employees. For example Tesco has a CARE scheme. Increasing what is included in pensionable pay increases pensions.

8. In CARE schemes the same revaluation rate can be applied to both active members and deferred pensioners, so eliminating the PCL suffered by deferred pensioners.

9. In a final salary scheme the sponsor has an incentive to sack long serving members just before awarding a large pay rise, but this is not the case with a CARE scheme.

Disadvantages to the Sponsor of Switching to a CARE Scheme

1. The sponsor has direct control over the salaries used in final salary schemes, but they do not control CARE revaluation rates such as inflation.
2. If the expected revaluation rate for deferred pensioners in a CARE scheme exceeds that for active members, workers have an incentive to quit because the PCL becomes a gain.
3. With a CARE scheme that uses the same revaluation rate for active and deferred accrued service, the PCL cannot be used to encourage members not to shirk or to quit. The absence of a PCL also means that a CARE scheme does not attract potential 'high flyers' who are low discounters.
4. A cost neutral switch to a CARE scheme increases the pensions of 'low flyers', and reduces the pensions of 'high flyers'. So high flyers will require an increase in their salaries to compensate for the drop in their total remuneration, while 'low flyers' need to have their salaries cut to offset the rise in their total remuneration. These changes in salaries will be difficult to implement as they relate to salary progression (salary increases throughout their career), not current salary levels.

Disadvantages to Members of Switching to a CARE Scheme

1. With a final salary scheme, for a given number of accrued years, the replacement ratio is fixed at (Accrued Years/Final Salary). For a CARE scheme, there is some uncertainty over the replacement ratio.
2. Unless the accrual rate is increased, a CARE scheme will very probably decrease pensions, particularly for 'high flyers'.

ii. Cash Balance
This is a hybrid between DB and DC schemes that is classified for legal purposes in the UK as DB. Cash balance schemes are popular in the USA, and in 2003 over 20 % of employees in US DB schemes were in cash balance schemes. Every year the employer and member pay x% of the member's current salary into the member's account with the scheme. In addition, each year the sponsor increases the member's account balance by an ' interest credit'. This is typically some pre-specified market rate of interest, such as the Treasury bill rate,

or it may be a constant amount such as 5 %. The benchmark chosen for use as the pre-specified interest credit rate may be changed from year to year. Many schemes provide higher increases in the account balance for workers who are older or have longer service. The account balances are invested by the scheme in a pooled manner. Decumulation is usually by means of the member buying an annuity, or receiving a lump sum in the USA. Since market rates of interest can change over time, the interest credit is risky, and this risk is shared by the sponsor and members. Cash balance schemes are easy to understand, and usually have no penalty for changing employer, making them portable. Three companies in the FTSE 100 offer cash balance schemes—Johnson Matthey, Diageo and Morrisons (LCP 2014). Here is an example of the operation of a cash balance scheme.

Example. Suppose Lilly Dillon starts work for Oceanic Airlines, and her annual salary is £20,000 in 2010, £21,000 in 2011, and £22,000 in 2012 when she retires. Oceanic has a cash balance pension scheme with a member's contribution rate of 5 %, and a sponsor's contribution rate of 8 %. For simplicity, pension contributions are only paid into the scheme at the end of each year. The rate for setting the interest credit is the Treasury bill rate, which is 5 % in 2010, 4 % in 2011 and 3 % in 2012. On retirement Lilly either receives a lump sum, or buys an annuity with the £8457 in her cash balance account (see Table 2.9).

iii. Conditional Indexation and Policy Ladders
In a traditional DB scheme the contribution rate of the sponsor is adjusted to keep the funding ratio (i.e. assets/liabilities) roughly around one, while pension benefits are revalued by salary growth. As a modification to this model, many Dutch schemes have made the revaluation of benefits and the indexation of pensions in payment conditional on the funding position of the scheme. Therefore Dutch schemes only promise a pension in nominal terms, as price indexation is not guaranteed, while UK schemes promise a pension in real terms, subject to any limited price indexation. This has resulted in Dutch schemes producing policy ladders, which are an explicit set of rules to be followed by the scheme when making decisions about funding and benefit revaluation. These policy ladders help scheme members understand the risks to which they are exposed.

1. Traditional DB
In Fig. 2.2 L_R is the value of the liabilities, allowing for the revaluation of accrued liabilities due to salary growth. The revaluation rate (the rate of increase

Table 2.9 Lilly Dillon example of a cash balance scheme

2010	Opening balance		0
	Interest credit		0
	Contributions	£20,000.00×0.13	£2600.00
2011	Opening balance		£2600.00
	Interest credit	£2,600.00×0.04	£104.00
	Contributions	£21,000.00×0.13	£2730.00
2012	Opening balance		£5434.00
	Interest credit	£5,434.00×0.03	£163.02
	Contributions	£22,000.00×0.13	£2860.00
	Closing balance		£8457.02

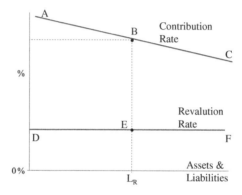

Fig. 2.2 Traditional DB scheme

in salaries) is fixed along the line DEF, and whatever the size of the assets and liabilities, there is full revaluation. The contribution rate is increased when the value of the assets (As) is less than the value of the liabilities, i.e. $As < L_R$, and reduced when $As > L_R$ along the line ABC. With the increased maturity of pension schemes, the accrued liabilities are usually large in relation to the annual contributions by active members. Therefore large increases in the contribution rate are required to deal with any deficits. This is illustrated in the following example.

Example. A pension scheme has a contribution rate of 20 % and a deficit of £10 million. The immature version of this scheme has mostly active members, and £20 million per year is paid in contributions. The mature version has mostly pensioners, and with few active members contributions are just £2 million per year. In order to remove the £10 million deficit within five years, what is the required increase in the contribution rate for the two different versions of this scheme? This requires contributions to rise by £2 million per year, which implies an increase in the contribution rate of (22/20) = 10 % for the immature scheme, i.e. a contribution rate of 22 %; and (4/2) = 100 % for the mature scheme, i.e. a contribution rate of 40 %.

Because it reduces all the liabilities, for most schemes a reduction in the revaluation rate has a bigger effect on the deficit than does a similar increase in the contribution rate. This is the rationale for conditional indexation and policy ladders, where scheme funding is controlled by varying the revaluation rate. While the contribution rate can be varied, it is usually a much less powerful tool for controlling the funding ratio.

2. Hybrid DB-DC

In Fig. 2.3 L_N is the value of the liabilities before any revaluation of the accrued benefits of active and deferred members, and the inflation indexation of pensions in payment. As for traditional DB schemes, the contribution rate is adjusted along the line ABC as the scheme moves between surplus and deficit—and the extra contributions are called a 'recovery premium'. In addition, when $As < L_R$ (i.e. a deficit) the revaluation rate is reduced along the line GL_NEF, and if $As < L_N$ there is no revaluation of the accrued benefits. There will also be a reduction to the indexation of pensions in payment. If $As > L_R$ there is unreduced revaluation. If A_S is between L_R and L_N (i.e. $L_R > As > L_N$) the revaluation rate is reduced to $(As - L_N)/(L_R - L_N)$ times the unreduced revaluation rate. Subsequently when $As > L_R$ (i.e. a surplus), catch-up revaluation can be given to offset any earlier under-revaluation by moving along the dotted line EH (Ponds and Van Riel 2009). After some years with a deficit, Dutch schemes may have to cut benefits.

De Haan (2015) analysed data on 213 Dutch schemes that submitted a short term recovery plan between 2008 and 2013. He found that these recovery

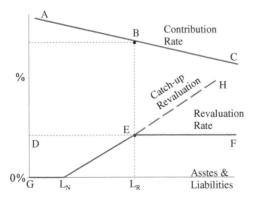

Fig. 2.3 Hybrid DB-DC scheme

plans followed a hierarchy. First, schemes increased their total contribution rate, then they moved to zero indexation, and finally, as a last resort, they cut benefits. Bikker et al. (2014) investigated the relationship between scheme funding ratios and their accrued liabilities. Using data on 500–600 Dutch schemes, they found that scheme accrued liabilities fall by 4 % when the funding ratio drops below about 105 %; and increase by 2 % when their funding ratio rises above about 125 %. These results are consistent with scheme policy ladders that comply with Dutch regulations. These require schemes with a funding ratio below about 105 % to draw up a recovery plan and not to index benefits, while a funding ratio above about 120 % is required before full indexation is allowed. In between these upper and lower funding ratios, partial indexation is permitted.

3. Collective DC (CDC)

In the Netherlands a scheme with conditional revaluation (indexation), but no adjustment of the contribution rate is called collective DC (or CDC). Definitions of CDC differ, and some authors define CDC as shown in Fig. 2.4. Others define it with conditional revaluation that is adjusted up or down according to the current surplus or deficit with no limits (see Fig. 2.5) (Hoevenaars and Ponds 2008). In this case when a scheme is over-funded benefits are increased by more than the full revaluation rate. CDC is widespread in the Netherlands, but not currently legal in the UK. The Dutch have industry-wide CDC schemes, and so most Dutch CDC schemes are large multi-employer CARE schemes.

CDC schemes have a mixture of the attributes of DB and DC schemes. In a CDC scheme the sponsor pays a fixed contribution rate, as in a DC scheme,

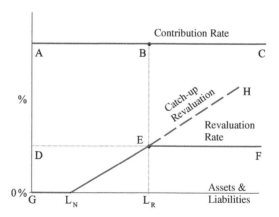

Fig. 2.4 Collective DC scheme

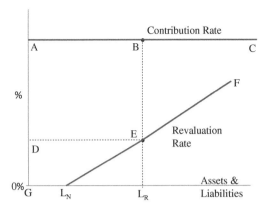

Fig. 2.5 CDC—alternative definition

and faces no risk. The members of a CDC scheme pay a fixed contribution rate, and accrue benefits in the same way as in a DB scheme. (In the Netherlands this is usually on a CARE basis.) The payment of these accrued benefits is conditional on the financial health of the scheme. Collectively, the members and pensioners bear all the risks (e.g. investment risk, longevity risk, interest rate risk, inflation risk, salary risk, and so on), like DC. The contributions to a CDC scheme are invested in a pooled manner by the trustees of the CDC scheme like DB, and if the scheme is in deficit the revaluation of benefits is reduced for members, and the indexation of pensions in payment is also reduced. So, unlike DB and DC schemes, pensioners can have their pensions in payment reduced. In extreme situations, once revaluation has been reduced to zero, benefits may be cut or the members' contribution rate increased. Conversely, if there is a large surplus, bonus revaluation can be paid. As for DB schemes, pensions are paid by the scheme, and not via the purchase of annuities.

Example. SSU is a CARE CDC scheme that up-rates accrued benefits and pensions in payment by inflation, subject to conditional indexation (see Table 2.10). Suppose that Gaspard Shingleton was a member of the SSU scheme for these three years. Table 2.11 shows his accrued benefits for this CDC scheme in column B#, and for a traditional CARE scheme in column B. Under the CDC scheme his final average salary is £71,333/3 = £23,778, and under a traditional CARE scheme it is £69,841/3 = £23,280.

CDC Schemes Versus DC Schemes
There are a number of important differences between DC (individual DC) and CDC schemes.

Table 2.10 Example of a CDC scheme—SSU

Year 1	Value of scheme assets	£100 m.
	Value of revalued liabilities[a]	£120 m.
	Value of nominal (un-revalued) liabilities	£80 m.
	Deficit	£20 m.
	Inflation rate	6 %
	Conditional indexation (100–80)/(120–80)6	3 %
Year 2	Value of scheme assets	£120 m.
	Value of revalued liabilities[a]	£130 m.
	Value of nominal (un-revalued) liabilities	£90 m.
	Deficit	£10 m.
	Inflation rate	4 %
	Conditional indexation (120–90)/(130–90)4	3 %
Year 3	Value of scheme assets	£150 m.
	Value of revalued liabilities[a]	£130 m.
	Value of nominal (un-revalued) liabilities	£100 m.
	Surplus	£20 m.
	Inflation rate	6 %
	Conditional indexation (150–100)/(130–100)6	10 %

[a]The liabilities are increased to incorporate conditional revaluation, i.e. the accrued benefits are increased to allow for inflation

Table 2.11 Example of a CDC scheme—Gaspard Shingleton

Year	Salary	Inflation (%)	Revaluation (%)	A#	B#	A	B
1	20,000	6	3	£20,000	£20,600	£20,000	£21,200
2	21,000	4	3	£41,600	£42,848	£42,200	£43,888
3	22,000	6	10	£64,848	£71,333	£65,888	£69,841

A# = Salary + (Total conditionally revalued salary for previous years i.e. B# for the previous year)
B# = Closing total conditionally revalued salary [A# × (1 + Inflation)]
A = Salary + (Total revalued salary for previous years i.e. B for the previous year)
B = Closing total revalued salary [A × (1 + Inflation)]

1. No Annuities. Since the CDC scheme provides the pension, there is no need to incur the costs and timing risks of buying an annuity, as is required by DC schemes. It also avoids the need to burden individual members with making an annuity purchase decision, which they dislike and may perform badly. This absence of annuities leads to higher pensions for CDC schemes (Westbroom et al. 2013) than for DC schemes.

2. Risk Sharing. CDC pensions are less risky for members than (individual) DC schemes as the risks (investment, inflation, salary, interest rate, longevity etc.) are shared with the other members of the scheme—both the same cohort, and across cohorts. This is accomplished by a pooled investment fund, conditional indexation and an absence of annuities. Successful

risk sharing requires a large number of scheme members amongst whom the risks can be shared, so CDC schemes need to be large.

3. Compulsion. Inter-generational risk sharing means that young members of a CDC scheme may be required to help bail out an under-funded scheme, and so might refuse to join unless this is made compulsory. This issue does not apply to DC schemes.

4. Shrinking Population. If the number of scheme members becomes small (possibly due to the scheme being closed), the risk sharing benefits diminish, and a stand-alone CDC scheme may no longer make sense. Inter-generational risk sharing also means that, if the membership shrinks over time, the costs are spread across a progressively smaller and smaller number of members, which may place a disproportionate burden on young members. DC schemes are not subject to this problem.

5. Sponsor Risk. As for a DC scheme, the sponsor has no risk with a CDC scheme. However, some sponsors fear that a future government could require CDC schemes to become DB schemes (AON Hewitt 2013).

6. Pension Volatility. Members can forecast their CDC pension with greater accuracy than is possible with a DC scheme due to the risk sharing and the absence of annuities (Hewitt 2013).

7. Economies of Scale. Because there are no individual pots of money, a CDC scheme can benefit from economies of scale, leading to lower investment and administration costs than for a DC scheme. This results in CDC schemes achieving higher returns for a given level of risk.

8. Professional Investment Management. Pooled investment decisions made by investment professionals for a CDC scheme will generally lead to better outcomes than individual investment decisions made by the individual members of a DC scheme.

9. Riskier Asset Allocation. Because the risks are shared, there is no need to move the asset allocation to less risky assets or more liquid assets as a member approaches retirement. The entire pension fund, including that required to pay pensions in payment, can remain invested in risky assets. This allows CDC schemes to maintain a more aggressive investment policy than DC schemes, leading to higher returns for CDC schemes.

10. Decision Making. The risk sharing means that the way decisions are made by a CDC scheme is very important to the members, and the agreed rules by which the scheme responds to the funding ratio is sometimes called a 'policy ladder'. This is not an issue for DC schemes.

11. Common Asset Allocation. The pooled investment by CDC schemes means that members cannot make their own individual investment decisions, as is the case for DC schemes. Since the young tend to have substantial

human capital and little financial wealth, and the old have the opposite wealth proportions, the individually desired investment allocations of these two groups may be different. In addition, a number of members may not want their pension pot invested in some types of company, and many DC investment menus offer ethical equity investments and the choice of a portfolio of only government debt.
12. Transfers. It is more difficult to value the pension pot of a member of a CDC scheme who wishes to transfer to another scheme.

Higher Pension
For the same level of contributions and risk, a CDC scheme should produce a pension that is substantially higher than the corresponding DC pension. Five UK studies have estimated the percentage increase in CDC pensions, relative to a DC pension, for three of the advantages available to CDC schemes—economies of scale, riskier asset allocation and an absence of annuities. These studies suggest that switching from a DC scheme to a CDC scheme can lead to a large increase in pensions:-

1	Department for Work and Pensions (2009)	39 % increase in CDC pension
2	Pitt-Watson and Mann (2012)	37 % increase in CDC pension
3	Pitt-Watson (2013), AON Hewitt (2013)	33 % increase in CDC pension
4	Department for Work and Pensions (2013)	19 % increase in CDC pension
5	Popat et al. (2015)	61 % increase in CDC pension

The three advantages of economies of scale, riskier asset allocation and the absence of annuities also apply to DB pensions, relative to DC pensions. Almeida and Fornia (2008) have estimated that, for the same contributions and risk, a US DB pension is on average 46 % higher than the corresponding DC pension, while Van der Lecq and Van der Wurff (2011) have estimated the corresponding figure for the Netherlands at 145 %.

iv. Notional Defined Contribution (NDC)
This is also called a non-financial DC scheme. For NDC schemes a specified proportion of each person's wages are paid by the sponsor and member into the NDC scheme, Williamson (2004). The start dates and total contribution rates for six countries with state NDC schemes appear in Table 2.12. This creates a notional pension pot for every individual. The contributions received are used for paying current pensioners (Pay-As-You-Go or PAYG) or other purposes by the government concerned, and so the scheme is unfunded. Each year these notional pots are increased by a notional rate of return, based on the growth in wages or the growth in GDP.

Table 2.12 NDC schemes

	Start year	NDC contribution rate (%)
Italy	1995	20–33
Latvia	1996	14.00
Kyrgyz Republic	1996	29.00
Sweden	1999	16.00
Poland	1999	12.22
Mongolia	2000	15.00

v. Mixed Pension Schemes

It is possible that workers are allowed to join several pension schemes provided by their employer. For example workers may be allowed to join both a DB scheme with a low accrual rate, and also a DC scheme. Alternatively workers may be offered a DC scheme for an initial period (e.g. 3 years), and then the opportunity to switch to a DB scheme. Another possibility is that pay below some limit (e.g. £55,000) is eligible for a DB pension, and pay above this level is eligible for a DC scheme (e.g. USS from April 2016).

vi. Many Possible Pension Scheme Designs

There are many aspects to the design of a pension scheme, and so a very large number of designs is possible. So far as risk bearing is concerned, there are five main types of participant who bear some or all of the risks involved in occupational pensions, and for each of these participants the main risks they bear are listed below.

1. Sponsors—Single sponsor—DB risk; Multi-employer sponsor—DB risk
2. Members—Individual members—DC risk; Cohorts of members—collective DC risk; All members—collective DC risk
3. Insurance companies—Annuities (see Chap. 5), buy-outs, buy-ins, longevity swaps, bulk annuities; collective self-insurance—Pension Protection Fund and default risk
4. Financial markets—Hedging using financial instruments, such as index linked bonds; Mortality bonds etc.—longevity risk
5. Government—To some extent, the government effectively under-writes, the occupational pension system (e.g. via the welfare state.

Any design of an occupational pension system distributes pension risks and rewards between these five participants in some way. Rather than allocate all the risks to one particular class of participant (e.g. DB allocates almost all the risks to the sponsor, while DC allocates the risks to the individual members, and then the annuity providers), the risks can be shared between a number of participants. In addition, each of the various types of risk (longevity, investment, inflation, interest rate, salary growth and regulation) can be shared between the participants in different ways. The extent and way the risks are shared can be varied, leading to a very large number of potential occupational pension system designs. For example, for DB pensions the retirement age for a particular cohort of members can be increased using a life expectancy adjustment factor (LEAF) so that the age cohort of members bears cohort longevity risk until they retire. Insurance companies can bear longevity risk after retirement for DB schemes, possibly via longevity swaps. Inflation and interest rate risk can be hedged using the financial markets, while investment, regulatory and salary growth risk can be born by the cohort of members, as in collective DC schemes. The government can under-write DB sponsor default risk, leaving DB members with no substantive risk. Given imperfect and incomplete markets, there is no 'optimal' pension scheme design—it depends on circumstances and preferences, although some designs are generally superior to others.

b. Two Pension Fund Separation

Their pension forms part of each member's portfolio of assets and liabilities, and so pensions can be viewed in a portfolio context. Given their other assets and liabilities, including their human capital, scheme members may prefer to take some risk in exchange for a higher expected pension. James Tobin's two-fund separation result has been applied to pension schemes by Modigliani and Muralidhar (2004) to get two pension fund separation. The axes of Fig. 2.6 are the probability of not achieving a replacement rate (i.e. risk) and the expected replacement rate (the expected return). In Fig. 2.6 R_F is a risk-free pension which can be an inflation indexed DB pension where the sponsor has a strong covenant, or a DC pension pot fully invested in inflation indexed gilts. M corresponds to an investment in the market portfolio (e.g. an all-equity DC scheme invested in the market portfolio. After allowing for their other assets and liabilities; by varying the proportions of their pension funds in the riskless (e.g. DB) and risky (e.g. DC) schemes (or other investments) each member can achieve their own preferred risk-return trade-off (e.g. point A. While members can choose the asset allocation of their DC pension, a DB pension with a strong covenant is similar to an inflation-indexed gilt which cannot be traded. This suggests that offering a mixture of DB and DC pensions may be beneficial to some members of DB schemes. If most of a member's wealth is in their DB pension and so highly illiquid, they may prefer to invest a greater proportion of their non-pension wealth in risky assets, or to put some of their pension wealth into a DC scheme invested in risky assets.

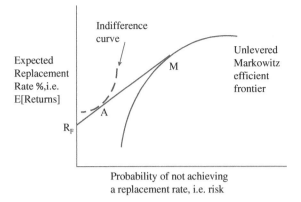

Fig. 2.6 Two pension fund separation

2.10 Age and Uniform Contribution and Accrual Rates

It is common for the members' contribution and accrual rates for DB schemes to be uniform across all members, rather than differing by age or salary. Pensioners and deferred pensioners also face uniform revaluation or indexation rates. However there are reasons why the contribution rate for DB schemes should be higher, or the accrual rate lower, for older active members (see Boeijen et al. 2007; Bonenkamp 2009; Aarssen and Kuipers 2007). Of course, if young members remain in the scheme until retirement, any inequity tends to even out—they lose when young, and gain when old. But since many people leave a scheme when young, or join a scheme when old, uniform contribution and accrual rates cause inequity.

The reasons for the inequity of uniform contribution rates between young and old members are:- (a) Longevity. Young people have a lower expected age at death than old people. For example, some 20 year olds will die before they reach the age of 65, while none of today's 65 year olds have died before the age of 65. Therefore there is a greater chance that today's 20 year olds will not live to receive a pension. This effect may be offset to some extent by cohort-wide improvements in longevity over time, so that today's 20 year olds will draw their pension for a longer period than will today's old people. (b) Life Insurance. On death in service, members receive a tax-free lump sum dependent on their current salary, but independent of their accrued years. So, in effect, part of their annual contributions are buying life insurance for that year. Since expected mortality per year is lower for young people, they are getting less benefit for the same level of contribution. (c) Career Progression and

Final Salary. For final salary schemes, pay rises mean that all accrued benefits are uprated. This benefits the old as they have more accrued benefits to uprate. (d) Accrued Benefit Changes. When benefits per accrued year are improved, there is a one-off gain that is smaller for the young (with few accrued years) and larger for the old (with many accrued years). Therefore when benefits are improved the old get a better deal than the young. It is illegal to reduce accrued benefits, and so the reverse does not apply. (e) Deferred Pension. The young are more likely than the old to have a career break or to become deferred pensioners. A DB scheme will probably uprate deferred pensioners at a lower rate than is the case for the accrued benefits of active members, and this favours the old over the young. (f) Discount Rate. The benefits accrued by younger members are discounted over a longer period than those of older people, but unless the discount rate is expected to change over time, this has no effect on the gains and losses to being young or old. However, if the yield curve slopes up, the benefits to the young will be discounted at a higher average rate than those for the old, and the present value of the benefits they accrue each year will be smaller than for the old.

A couple of reasons for the inequity of uniform contribution rates between the young and old have been proposed that are *not* valid:- (a) Time Diversification. It is claimed that long-term investors (e.g. pension funds with a 40 years plus time horizon) are subject to lower risk than short-term investors (e.g. those with a one year horizon) because, over time, above average returns tend to be offset by below average returns, i.e. time diversification. In consequence, long term investors are more willing than short term investors to hold equities, rather than bonds, enabling them to enjoy higher expected returns. Time diversification implies there is long run mean reversion (or negative serial correlation) in portfolio asset returns, but there is no strong evidence for this. (If mean reversion does exist, the myopic application of one-period portfolio theory ceases to be valid as returns are not independently identically distributed, or i.i.d.) If time diversification exists, the pension contributions of the young could be invested with less risk than those of the old; which implies higher returns for the same level of risk. But there is no firm evidence that long term investors favour risky investments, while short term investors favour low risk investments. (b) Investment. Typically, liabilities are discounted at a fairly low rate, while the assets are expected to grow at a substantially higher rate, given a substantial investment in equities. This difference is argued to represent a gain to the scheme, and is larger for money invested for a longer period. Hence the young are claimed to be more beneficial to the scheme than the old. But while equities have a higher expected return, they also have a higher risk. If the market is in CAPM equilibrium, the risk-adjusted return is equivalent to the riskless rate. The appropriate discount rate is probably just a bit higher than the riskless rate (see Sect. 1.6b), and so the riskless present value of the assets is more or less the same for the contributions of both young and old members.

While a uniform contribution rate means young members get less benefit from their pension contributions than do older members, if the cost of sponsor pension contributions was lower for the young it would give them a competitive advantage over older workers in the labour market. If only the contribution rates of members are age-related, this unwelcome labour market effect largely disappears because the sponsor contribution rate is the same for all age groups. Similarly a higher accrual rate for the young would disadvantage them in the labour market, as for the same contribution rate they would accrue higher benefits than the old, which would increase the scheme's accrued liabilities.

a. Cost-Benefit Ratios for Contributions by the Young and Old

For simplicity the analysis in this sub-section ignores the effects of the above six reasons for the young losing out. It explores the effects of the relationship between the investment return (r) and the rate for revaluing benefits (u) on the cost-benefit ratios for contributions by the young and old. The value at retirement (TV_t) of a contribution made now (salary (S_t) times contribution rate (c)) is $TV_t = cS_t(1 + r)^t$ where r is the annual rate of return on the money (assumed constant), and t is the number of years to retirement. The value at retirement (BA_t) of the pension accrued by a contribution this year is $BA_t = S_t(1 + u)^t/a$, where u is the rate at which accrued benefits are uprated each year (assumed constant), and a is the accrual rate. The cost-benefit ratio TV_t/BA_t (denoted by R_t) gives the relationship between contributions made and benefits accrued in a particular year.

$$R_t = \frac{TV_t}{BA_t} = \frac{cS_t(1+r)^t a}{S_t(1+u)^t} = ac\left(\frac{(1+r)}{(1+u)}\right)^t = acZ^t \quad \text{where } Z = [(1+r)/(1+u)]$$

Since c and a are assumed constant, the value of the cost benefit ratio (R_t) is determined by the relative sizes of r (the rate of return until retirement on investments), and u (the rate at which accrued benefits will be uprated until retirement (e.g. salary growth in a final salary scheme, and the chosen revaluation rate for a CARE scheme). Depending on the value of Z, there are three possible situations, and the first two are illustrated in Fig. 2.7.

i. r > u, or Z > 1

For early contributions the value of R_t (the cost-benefit ratio) is higher than for late contributions, and so early contributions represent poorer value for

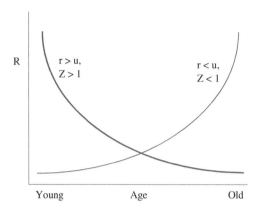

Fig. 2.7   Cost-benefit ratio of pension contributions

money to the member. Actuaries often assume that in the long run the rate of salary increase is 1 % greater than inflation, so this condition will be satisfied for final salary schemes if the real riskless rate is greater than 1 % plus promotional increases. For CARE schemes the chosen revaluation rate is often inflation, and so $Z > 1$ if the riskless rate of interest exceeds inflation.

ii. $r < u$, or $Z < 1$
For early contributions the value of R_t (the cost-benefit ratio) is lower than for late contributions, and so early contributions are better value for the member than late contributions.

iii. $r = u$, or $Z = 1$
There is no difference between early and late contributions, and so the relationship between age and R_t is flat. This possibility is not shown in Fig. 2.7.

b. Importance of Early Contributions in Generating a DC Pension Pot
Contributions made in the first years of membership have a much bigger effect on the value of the final pot than do late contributions due to the power of compound interest, and this will now be illustrated by two examples.

Example. Suppose two identical twins—Bill and Ben—start work at the age of 20. Between the ages of 20 and 35 Bill contributes £3000 per year to his DC pension, and then makes no further contributions. Ben does not contribute anything to his DC pension until he reaches the age of 35, and then contributes £6000 per year until he is 65. Both twins retire at the age of 65. Assuming their DC investments earn 7 % per year, the final value of their

Table 2.13 Example of the power of compounding

	Bill	Ben	Difference
Annual contribution	£3000	£6000	Ben's annual contribution is double Bill's
No. of years of contributions	15	30	Ben contributes for twice as long as Bill
Total contributions	£45,000	£180,000	Ben's contributions are quadruple Bill's
Final value of the pot	£614,036	£606,438	Bill final pension pot is larger than Ben's

pension pots are shown in Table 2.13 Despite contributing at half the rate and for half the time of Ben, Bill's final pension pot is still larger than that of Ben. This is due to the power of compounding.

Example. Suppose that at the age of 20 Felix Summerbee joins a DC pension scheme with constant accrual and contribution rates, and stays in the scheme until he retires 50 years later at the age of 70. At the start of each year Felix contributes £1 to his DC pension which earns a constant rate of return of 8 % per year. Since Felix does not receive any pay rises, he is assumed to contribute the same amount of money each year. How many years (N) does it take before Felix's contribution generate half of the terminal value of his pension pot? The value of N is given by the formula (Philips 2010):-

$$N = \frac{\ln 2 - \ln[1 + 1/1 + (1+r)^L]}{\ln(1+r)}$$

Letting L = 50 and r = 0.08, then N = 8.73 years. So, between the ages of 20 and 28.73 years his contributions generate half of the terminal value of his pension pot. The subsequent 41.27 years of contributions generate the other half of his pension pot, i.e. the first 17.5 % of his contributions generate 50 % of his terminal pension pot. There is also an approximation for the above exact formula, and this is $N \approx 72/100r$. For this example the approximation formula gives N = 9 years.

c. The Back-Loading of Final Salary Pensions

For a DB scheme with uniform accrual and contribution rates it was shown above that contributions by the young represent worse value than for the old when the investment rate of return (r) exceeds the rate of revaluation of accrued benefits (u) (and vice versa). In addition, six additional reasons were given above why the young get worse value for their contributions than do the old. This situation means that pensions are often back-loaded, i.e. the benefits per £1 of contributions are greater for the old than for the young. Therefore there is a cross-subsidy from the young to the old, with some of the contributions of the young used to pay the pensions of the old.

If no-one leaves the scheme early there is no redistribution between individuals, as the same person loses when young, but gains when old. However, early leavers lose out and late joiners benefit. Given back-loading, the viability of a scheme depends on a steady inflow of young members, i.e. an element of pay-as-you-go. If the scheme is closed to new members (soft frozen) this cross-subsidy from new young members ceases, and the contribution rate computed using the projected value of final salaries and the expected value of assets at retirement, has to be increased, the accrual rate decreased, or the benefits reduced. Therefore there is a tendency for the funding ratio of closed schemes to worsen over time. If the scheme is closed to further accruals (hard frozen) not only is this cross-subsidy lost, but it is not possible to increase the contribution rate, reduce the accrual rate or reduce accrued benefits to deal with a declining finding ratio.

Back-loading is greater for CARE schemes than for final salary schemes. In a CARE scheme accrued benefits are uprated by a revaluation factor such as inflation, while in a final salary they are uprated by the member's salary increases including promotional increases which is usually above inflation. Therefore, in terms of the above analysis, u, the rate at which accrued benefits are uprated each year for CARE schemes, is smaller than for final salary schemes. So r, the rate of return until retirement on investments, will generally exceed u by a larger amount than is the case for a final salary scheme. Boeijen et al. (2007) have estimated that the back-loading in PGGM (a very large Dutch DB scheme) is equivalent to roughly 15 % of its liabilities.

2.11 Compulsory Occupational Pension Scheme Membership

For both DB and DC schemes compulsory pension scheme membership has two advantages. It overcomes the myopic behaviour of many people who do not see the need to save to finance their retirement, and the related moral hazard that some people will spend their money and then rely on the welfare state. Compulsion also lowers the costs of providing pensions due to the greater economies of scale from having more members, and the absence of a need to recruit new employees to join the scheme. In addition, for DB schemes compulsory membership enables risk sharing both within age cohorts and between age cohorts. If members can avoid sharing the risks of negative shocks by leaving or not joining a scheme, risk sharing is severely compromised. There may also be adverse selection due to the those with a shorter life expectancy choosing not to join DB schemes. For these reasons the membership of occupational pension schemes is compulsory in many countries (e.g. Denmark, the Netherlands, Sweden, Switzerland, Australia and Chile (Chen and Beetsma 2015). In the UK membership of occupational pension schemes was compulsory until 1988, when it became voluntary. There is a mid-way between voluntary and compulsory membership which is auto-enrollment, and a reliance on the apathy of members not to leave the scheme. The recent introduction of auto-enrolment in the UK, where employees are automatically enrolled but then have the right to opt out, has led to a big increase in the membership of UK occupational pensions.

2.12 Redistribution by Pension Schemes

Pension wealth is unevenly distributed in the UK. The median private pension wealth of the richest 10 % of the households in 2012–14 was £749,000, while the corresponding figure for the bottom 50 % of households was only £2800 (ONS, 2015d). For the richest 10 %, their private pension wealth was valued in 2012–14 at a total of £2.145 trillion, equivalent to 48 % of the private pension wealth of all households, which was £4.459 trillion. This £2.145 trillion represented 43 % of the total wealth of the richest 10 % in 2012–14 making pensions the largest single asset of the wealthy.

Only DB schemes give rise to redistribution between scheme members, as with DC schemes every contribution gives rise to a matching pension entitlement for the member concerned. So redistribution between members is of no importance in DC schemes. But with DB schemes each pension contribution does not give rise to a matching pension entitlement, and redistribution is an important issue for DB schemes. Redistribution in DB schemes is caused, in part, by contribution rates and accrual rates that are uniform across ages and types of member, see Sect. 2.10.

Differences in life expectancy between various groups based on gender, occupation, location, and socio-economic circumstances were described in Sect. 1.8, and such differences result in substantially greater total pension payments being received by the longer lived group. Those who have a life-shortening illness or life-style also receive their pension for a shorter period, and so lose out relative to the long-lived. Unlike DC schemes where members can buy enhanced or impaired life annuities, members with a life-shortening condition do not receive any special consideration in DB schemes. Using data on 3.5 million England and Wales DB pensioners, Evans et al. (2014) find that these gaps in life expectancy have narrowed in the last decade, so redistribution due to differences in longevity have decreased.

As well as redistribution by occupation, socio-economic group, health and location, redistribution occurs: from low to high fliers as final salary schemes reward those with large pay rises near retirement; from single to married members as married members benefit from spouse's pensions, but all DB members face the same contribution and accrual rates; from men to women as women live longer, but face the same contribution and accrual rates as men; and from those who only accrue years when young to those who stay in the scheme for life. The data suggests that the typical loser is an uneducated non-white woman who experiences career breaks, works part time, and leaves the scheme early. The typical winner is an educated white man who does not have career breaks, works full time with fixed hours and who does not leave early. There is also evidence of inter-generational redistribution. In the twenty-first century an increasing proportion of UK productivity growth has been used to fund DB scheme deficits, rather than granting wage increases (Whittaker 2015). This implies that the non-wage compensation of the older generation (i.e. DB pensions) is being funded by holding down the wages of the younger generation.

2.13 Economies of Scale

In 2013 the UK had 35,640 trust-based DC schemes with between two and eleven members (DWP 2014). There are about 160,000 contract-based DC schemes in the UK and approximately 11,000 DB schemes (Harrison et al. 2012), most of which are very small, which raises the question of whether very small schemes suffer from a lack of economies of scale. The costs of running a pension scheme can be divided into two main groups—the costs of investing the money, and the administrative costs of running the scheme. The investment costs cover such items as fund manager fees and bonuses, performance measurement costs, custody fees, transactions costs incurred when buying and selling investments, investment research costs, and legal fees in connection with buying and selling assets. The administrative costs comprise the costs of managing the payment of pensions and the receipt of contributions, together with a wide range of other administrative tasks. For many of these administrative items the costs rise at a lower rate as the volume of activity increases. For example, there are considerable fixed costs in setting up a computer system to handle record-keeping for members, deferred pensioners and pensioners and to make monthly payments to pensioners. Additional members and pensioners can be added at very little additional administrative cost, leading to economies of scale. Similarly, the cost of researching a potential investment is the same whether a large or small sum of money is invested. Ultimately the presence of economies of scale is an empirical issue, and empirical studies have been undertaken of both the administrative and investment costs of running a pension scheme.

When investing the money, large pension funds can benefit from direct access to some asset classes such as private equity, infrastructure and property, and this leads to lower costs, greater diversification and higher returns (Dyck and Pomorski 2011; MacIntosh and Scheibelhut 2012). This may explain why Chemla (2004) found that large US and Canadian DB pension schemes invest a substantially larger proportion of their assets in private equity than do small pension schemes. Large schemes can also negotiate bespoke derivatives trades and proportionately lower fund management fees. As well getting access to additional asset classes, and paying proportionately lower management fees, larger schemes are more likely to manage their funds in-house, and this leads to substantially lower costs (Dyck and Pomorski 2011). However, as funds become larger the price impact of their trades increases, and they may be too big to implement derivatives trades for the whole scheme, leading to decreasing returns to scale. The empirical studies of returns to scale for administrative and investment costs, and then total costs will now be summarised.

a. Administration Expenses

The empirical studies consistently find economies of scale in administration costs. For 119 multi-employer schemes of US construction companies Caswell (1976) found evidence of substantial economies of scale in administration costs with respect to the number of participants. Mitchell and Andrews (1981) studied 745 US DB multi-employer schemes and discovered powerful economies of scale in administrative costs with respect to both the number of scheme participants and total scheme assets. Hsin and Mitchell (1997) looked at US public sector schemes and also found large economies of scale in administration costs with respect to both the number of participants and total assets. Hustead (1998) found economies of scale in administrative costs for both American DB and DC schemes. For 90 large schemes in the USA, Netherlands, and Australia, Bikker et al. (2012b) found strong economics of scale in administration costs. Using data for all Dutch pension schemes Bikker (2013) found substantial economies of scale for administrative costs with respect to the number of participants in the pension scheme, with no upper limit to these economies. For DB and DC schemes in South Africa, Mama et al. (2011) show that as the number of scheme members increases, administrative costs per member drop. In a study of 284 Australian DC and hybrid schemes Cummings (forthcoming) discovered substantial economies of scale in administrative costs. Barrientos and Boussofiane (2005) conducted a data envelopment analysis of the administrative costs of Chilean pension funds. They showed that these funds are highly inefficient, since in aggregate they could have produced the same output with between 58 and 20 % fewer resources, and that the larger funds were more efficient, indicating positive economies of scale. These empirical results for the USA, Netherlands, Australia and South Africa provide clear evidence of economies of scale in administrative costs with respect to the number of members. There is also evidence that administrative costs are lower in countries with a well-developed pension system. Tuesta (2014) conducted a cross section study of the administrative costs of private sector pension schemes in 44 countries. He found that countries with a large stock market capitalization and pension assets relative to GDP, and with a long established private pension system have lower administrative costs. The highest administrative costs were 15.3 % for El Salvador, while for Norway administration costs were well under 0.2 %.

b. Investment Costs

The evidence for economies of scale in investment costs is weaker than for administration costs, with some evidence of diseconomies of scale for very large funds. Using data on 842 schemes from a wide range of countries, Dyck and Pomorski (2011) showed that there are substantial economies of scale in investment. But Bikker (2013) found that the economies of scale in investment costs with respect to total assets for all Dutch schemes were modest, and beyond about £600 million there was no further reduction in costs. In a study of 225 Dutch schemes, Broeders et al. (2015) found that, as assets under management increase, proportionate investment cost drops. These economies of scale are mainly due to savings in the management costs for investment in fixed income, equities and commodities. There was no difference in the economies of scale for DB and DC schemes, and no evidence of diminishing returns to scale. Barros and Garcia (2006, 2007) used data on 12 Portuguese pension fund managers to find that they exhibit returns to scale, although in some cases these are negative. Selman and Wright (2014) investigated the savings from combining the £180 billion of pension assets managed by the 89 separate UK local authority pension funds into a single common passive investment vehicle. They estimated this would save a total of £660 million per year in investment fees and transactions costs (£230 million in lower management costs, £190 million in lower transaction costs, and £240 million from investing in alternative assets via a common fund). Using data on 284 Australian DC and hybrid schemes, Cummings (forthcoming) found no evidence of diseconomies of scale in investment costs. These results indicate the presence of economies of scale in investment, although for very large schemes there may be diseconomies of scale in investment.

c. Total Costs

The clear evidence of economies of scale in administrative costs, and the weaker evidence of economies of scale in investment costs, implies there are economies of scale in total costs. Bateman and Mitchell (2004) studied total costs (i.e. administrative plus investment costs) for 1920 Australian DB and DC schemes, and found evidence of strong economies of scale with respect to both total assets and the number of participants. Basu and Andrews (2014) found similar results for a sample of 130 Australian superannuation funds. For 1421 US schemes Ghilarducci and Terry (1999) also showed that total costs exhibit strong economies of scale with respect to the number of participants and total assets. For all Dutch pension schemes Bikker and De Dreu (2007, 2009) found substantial economies of scale for both administrative and investment costs, with larger economies of scale for administrative costs. Unusually, they also found that administrative costs exhibit an optimal scale, while investment costs do not. Table 2.14 shows the annual average administrative and investment costs per member from a survey of 294 UK DB schemes by IFF Research (2014). These results show that average total costs of UK DB schemes decrease by a substantial amount as scheme size increases, i.e. economies of scale in total costs. So overall schemes generally benefit from economies of scale in both their administrative and investment costs, and since some occupational pension schemes are very large (e.g. ABP of the Netherlands had assets of €416 billion in 2013, these economies can be considerable.

The presence of economies of scale creates an important motive for the merger of schemes (see Sect. 4.5a). In some cases, rather than a full merger, schemes agree to pool their investments to benefit from the economies of scale in investment, while remaining separate schemes (e.g. the recent agreements

Table 2.14 Average administrative and investment costs per UK DB member (IFF Research 2014)

Scheme size	No. of members	Sample size	Average cost
Very large DB schemes	5000+ members	24	£182
Large DB schemes	1000–4999 members	75	£281
Medium DB schemes	100–999 members	106	£505
Small DB schemes	12–99 members	89	£1054

between some UK local government schemes. Another way for small schemes to reduce costs is to outsource the administration of the scheme and its investment activities to an external provider.

Chinese Pensions

Developing countries, such as China and India, face the great challenge of providing for the retired members of their rapidly aging populations. These countries need a massive expansion of their under-developed pension systems, with China facing a greater pension challenge than any other nation. Its pension system will be described in this sub-section as a case study of the problems facing these countries.

China has a very large and rapidly aging population, and this will lead to hundreds of millions of old people. However in 2012 pension assets in China were equivalent to about 1 % of GDP (see Table 1.6), so there is enormous potential for growth in pension provision. What follows is a description of the steps taken by China in recent years to create a modern pension system, and this illustrates some of the problems facing developing countries in undertaking such a task. In the 1990s China sought to create a national three pillar pension system. However much local autonomy remains, and the way the system is implemented differs from region to region, with many local variations (Frazier 2010). In addition, the 40 million public sector workers have an unfunded pension scheme that is separate from the three pillar national system. Except where specified, this section is based on Salditt et al. (2008).

a. The Three Pillars in China

China has separate pension schemes for urban workers, rural workers, civil servants, public servants and the military forces (Leckie 2011). Following the reforms of 2006 the structure for urban workers can be described as a three pillar system.

The first pillar (the state pension) is called the compulsory basic scheme— has two parts:- (a) Social Pool. The employer pays 20 % of wages into an unfunded DB (PAYG) scheme. These pensions only vest, i.e. the date when members get an absolute right to their pension even if they leave, after 15 years of contributions. (b) Individual Accounts. Employees pay 8 % of their wages into a funded DC scheme. Local governments receive the mandatory contributions for employees (i.e. pillar 1B), and some local governments have used this pension money for other purposes, such as meeting the pensions promised under the previous pension system. As a result these individual accounts are seriously under-funded (so called 'empty accounts'), with Hu (2014) reporting that in 2010 these accounts had a funding level of only 11 %. These individual accounts are more similar to unfunded PAYG schemes, than to funded schemes. The returns credited to these empty accounts are notional, and so the individual accounts are effectively a notional defined contribution (NDC) scheme (see Sect. 2.9a(iv)). By 2012 there were 304 million members of the compulsory basic scheme (Lu et al. 2014). The specified retirement ages for the compulsory basic scheme in China are 60 for men and 55 for women. However in 2005 the actual retirement age averaged 51.2 years.

The second pillar (the occupational pension) consists of voluntary occupational DC schemes (called enterprise annuities). The employer and employee pay into a funded DC scheme, with contribution rates varying from scheme to scheme. Employees cannot select the asset allocation of their occupational DC pension pot. In January 2008 there were 45,000 such schemes with 15 million members and assets totalling $55 billion (IPE 2012), and by 2012 the number of members had risen to 18.47 million (Pozen 2013). Enterprise annuities are run by independent trusts who buy-in the services they need, such as administration, custody and fund management.

The third pillar (private pensions) comprises voluntary personal DC schemes, where employees can choose to pay into a funded DC scheme.

In China employer pension contributions are tax deductible, but employee contributions are not. Since social pool pensions only vest after 15 years, workers moving to another region within this period can only take their first pillar individual accounts with them. This encourages workers to evade joining the mandatory first pillar, as well as restricting labour mobility between regions. In 2005 31 % of the Chinese urban population were in a pension scheme, while in rural areas this percentage was very much lower. As a result, the pension coverage for the Chinese population in 2005 was only 13.4 %. In 2009 China rolled out a new programme of rural pensions, and this led to an additional 240 million people joining a pension scheme, making 326 million in total in rural schemes (Economist 2012). By the end of 2012 membership of the rural scheme had risen to 460 million people (Pozen 2013).

Since urban workers are wealthier than rural workers, live longer, and are more likely to be members of a pension scheme, the pension system primarily benefits urban workers. Wang et al. (2014a) examined the pension schemes available to urban, rural, public and enterprise workers, as well as civil servants; and found considerable unfairness as between these five groups. For example, Hu (2014) reports that the average replacement rate for civil servants is 80 %, while for workers in private enterprises it is only 40 %. Lu et al. (2014) report that the average urban pension is 28 times larger than the average rural pension, and express concern that this results in rural poverty.

They propose the introduction of a social pension that is non-contributory and available to rural residents and to those in urban areas who do not receive a contributory pension. This social pension would pay the poverty level, and cost an estimated 0.7 % of GDP per year.

Over the period from 2001 to 2010 China's pension assets grew very quickly at an annual rate of 33.6 %. However in 2012 China's pension assets were only 1.2 % of GDP (see Table 1.6) of GDP. Table 2.15 shows a breakdown of China's pension assets in 2011. By 2020 total assets are forecast to be 28,000 billion yuan, an annual growth rate of 16 % (Z-Ben Advisors 2012). However, Wang et al. (2014b) have estimated that the annual gap between the receipts and payments of the Chinese pension system was 153 billion yuan ($24.6 billion) in 2013, and this funding gap will rise to 2876 billion yuan ($461.6 billion) per year in 2050. This under-funding is expected to be met by the Chinese government.

There are various restrictions on the asset proportions of Chinese pension funds. Mandatory contributions by employees, i.e. first pillar individual accounts, can only invested in bank deposits and government bonds, and members do not decide their own asset allocation. At least 20 % of voluntary contributions by employers and employees must be invested in government bonds, and not more than 30 % of voluntary contributions can be invested in equities.

b. Chinese Longevity

There has been a dramatic increase in Chinese longevity. A Chinese female born in 2005 had a life expectancy of 75 years at birth, while a female born in 1950 had a life expectancy of only 42 years at birth: an improvement of 33 years, or 80 %. In 2005 7.6 % (100 million people) of the Chinese population were aged over 65 years. By 2050 23.6 % (330 million people) will be aged over 65, i.e. more than three times larger. Between 2005 and 2050 the average age of the Chinese population will rise from 32.6 years to 44.8 years, an increase of 37 %. Table 2.16 compares the median ages of the Chinese

Table 2.15 China's total pension assets in 2011—billion yuan (Z-Ben Advisors 2012)

Public pension funds	2050 bn. yuan
National security social fund	920 bn. yuan
Private insurance schemes	4080 bn. yuan
Enterprise annuities	310 bn. yuan
Total	7360 bn. yuan ($1.2 trillion)

Table 2.16 Median population age in years for China and the USA (United Nations 2011)

Year	China	USA	Diff.	Year	China	USA	Diff.
1970	19.7	28.2	−8.5	2020	38.1	37.9	0.2
1975	20.7	28.8	−8.1	2025	40.1	38.6	1.5
1980	22.4	30.0	−7.6	2030	42.5	39.1	3.4
1985	23.9	31.4	−7.5	2035	44.7	39.6	5.1
1990	25.1	32.9	−7.8	2040	46.4	39.6	6.8
1995	27.3	34.1	−6.8	2045	47.7	39.8	7.9
2000	29.7	35.3	−5.6	2050	48.7	40.0	8.7
2005	32.2	36.2	−4.0	2055	49.1	40.2	8.9
2010	34.5	36.9	−2.4	2060	49.4	40.4	9.0
2015	36.2	37.3	−1.1	Increase	29.7	12.2	17.5

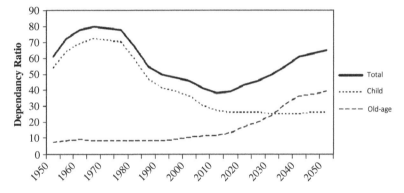

Fig. 2.8 Chinese dependency ratio

and American populations. In 1970 the median Chinese age was 8.5 years less than for the USA (i.e. 30 % less). However shortly after 2020 the median age of the Chinese population is forecast to surpass that of the USA. By 2060 China's median age will be 9 years greater than for the USA (i.e. 22 % greater).

c. Chinese Dependency Ratio

The Chinese working population (15–65 years) have to support two non-working groups:- pensioners (65 years +), and children (0–15 years) and the dependency ratio is: (Non-workers/Workers). Figure 2.8 shows the dependency ratio for China from 1950 to 2050 and also its disaggregation into children and pensioners (Salditt et al. 2007). In 1960 100 Chinese people in the working age range had to support about 71 children and 9 pensioners (80 people). Currently 100 Chinese people in the working age range support about 27 children and 11 pensioners (38 people), a decrease of 52 % from

1960. By 2050, 100 Chinese people in the working age range will have to support about 25 children, and 39 pensioners (64 people), an increase of 68 % from now. There are wide variations in the dependency ratio between regions. For example in Guangdong the number of workers per pensioner in 2005 was 6.77, while in Shanghai it was only 1.85 workers per pensioner.

This brief analysis of China has revealed a wide range of substantial problems in the creation of a viable pension system, which include rapidly increasing longevity, a legacy of minimal pension assets, an urban-rural divide and the problem of inadequate coverage, creating a uniform system in a vast country, unfairness between different groups, and investing the pension assets, Zuo (2014).

References

Aarssen, K., & Kuipers, B. J. (2007). Everyone gains, but some more than others. In O. W. Steenbeek & S. G. Van Der Lecq (Eds.), *Costs and benefits of collective pension systems* (pp. 137–156). New York: Springer.

AitSahlia, F., Doellman, T., & Sardarli, S. (2015). *Efficiency, spanning and the Fiduciary in 401(k) plans* (Working paper). University of Florida, 31 pages.

Allen, S. G., & Clark, R. L. (1987). Pensions and firm performance. In M. M. Kleiner, R. N. Block, M. Roomkin, & S. W. Salsburg (Eds.), *Human resources and the performance of the firm* (pp. 195–242). Madison: Industrial Relations Research Association.

Allen, S. G., Clark, R. L., & Sumner, D. A. (1986). Post retirement adjustments of pension benefits. *Journal of Human Resources, 21*(1), 118–137.

Almeida, B., & Fornia, W. B. (2008). *A better bang for the buck: The economic efficiencies of defined benefit plans.* Washington, DC: National Institute on Retirement Security.

Amir, E., Guan, Y., & Oswald, D. (2010). The effect of pension accounting on corporate pension asset allocation. *Review of Accounting Studies, 15*(2), 345–366.

Angus, J., Brown, W. O., Smith, J. K., & Smith, R. (2007). What's in your 403(b)? Academic retirement plans and the costs of underdiversification. *Financial Management, 36*(2), 87–124.

AON Hewitt. (2013). Collective defined contribution plans: A new opportunity for UK pensions? AON Hewitt, 8 pages.

Atanasova, C., & Hrazdil, K. (2010). Why do healthy freeze their defined benefit pension plans? *Global Finance Journal, 21*(3), 293–303.

Ayres, I., & Curtis, Q. (2015). Beyond diversification: The pervasive problem of excessive fees and "dominated funds" in 401(k) plans. *Yale Law Journal, 124*(5), 1476–1552.

Bank of England. (2012). *The distributional effects of asset purchases.* London: Bank of England, 12 July.

Barrientos, A., & Boussofiane, A. (2005). How efficient are pension fund managers in Chile? *Rivista de Economia Contemporanea, 9*(2), 289–311.

Barros, C. P., & Garcia, M. T. M. (2006). Performance evaluation of pension funds management companies with data envelopment analysis. *Risk Management and Insurance Review, 9*(2), 165–188.

Barros, C. P., & Garcia, M. T. M. (2007). Analysing the performance of the pension fund industry with a stochastic frontier model: A case study for Portugal. *The Geneva Papers on Risk and Insurance, 32*(2), 190–210.

Basu, A., & Andrews, S. (2014). Asset allocation policy, returns and expenses of superannuation funds: Recent evidence based on default options. *Australian Economic Review, 47*(1), 63–77.

Bateman, H., & Mitchell, O. S. (2004). New evidence on pension plan design and administrative expenses: The Australian experience. *Journal of Pension Economics and Finance, 3*(1), 63–76.

Beaudoin, C., Chandar, N., & Werner, E. (2010). Are potential effects of SFAS 158 associated with firms' decisions to freeze their defined benefit pension plans? *Review of Accounting and Finance, 9*(4), 424–451.

Beshears, J., Choi, J. J., Laibson, D., & Madrian, B. C. (2010). The impact of employer matching on savings plan participation under automatic enrollment. In D. A. Wise (Ed.), *Research findings in the economics of aging* (pp. 311–335). Chicago: University of Chicago Press.

Besley, T., & Prat, A. (2005). Credible pensions. *Fiscal Studies, 26*(1), 119–135.

Bikker, J. (2013). *Is there an optimal pension fund size? A scale economy analysis of administrative and investment costs* (DNB Working Paper No. 376). De Nederlandsche Bank, 35 pages.

Bikker, J. A., & De Dreu, J. (2007). Operating costs of pension funds. In O. W. Steenbeek & S. G. Van der Lecq (Eds.), *Costs and benefits of collective pension systems* (pp. 51–74). Berlin: Springer.

Bikker, J. A., & De Dreu, J. (2009). Operating costs of pension funds: The impact of scale, governance and plan design. *Journal of Pension Economics and Finance, 8*(1), 63–89.

Bikker, J., Steenbeek, F., & Torracchi, F. (2012b). The impact of scale, complexity and service quality on the administrative costs of pension funds: A cross-country comparison. *Journal of Risk and Insurance, 79*(2), 477–514.

Bikker, J. A., Knapp, T., & Romp, W. E. (2014). Measuring and explaining implicit risk sharing in defined benefit pension funds. *Applied Economics, 46*(17), 1996–2009.

Blake, D. (2006a). *Pension finance.* New York: Wiley.

Blake, D. (2006b). *Pension economics.* New York: Wiley.

Blake, D., Cairns, A., Coughlan, G., Dowd, K., & MacMinn, R. (2013a). The new life market. *Journal of Risk and Insurance, 80*(3), 501–557.

Boeijen, T. A. H., Jansen, C., Kortleve, C. E., & Tamerus, J. H. (2007). Inter-generational solidarity in the uniform contribution and accrual system. In O. W. Steenbeek & S. G. Van Der Lecq (Eds.), *Costs and benefits of collective pension systems* (pp. 119–136). New York: Springer.

Bonenkamp, J. (2009). Measuring lifetime redistribution in Dutch occupational pensions. *De Economist, 157*(1), 49–77.

Bovenberg, L., & Van Ewijk, C. (2012). Designing the pension system: Conceptual framework. In L. Bovenberg, C. Van Ewijk, & E. Westerhout (Eds.), *The future of multi-pillar pensions* (pp. 142–183). Cambridge: Cambridge University Press.

Boyer, M. M., Mejza, J., & Stentoft, L. (2014). Measuring longevity risk: An application to the Royal Canadian mounted police pension plan. *Risk Management and Insurance Review, 17*(1), 37–59.

Brander, J. A., & Finucane, S. (2007). *Pensions and corporate performance: Effects of the shift from defined benefit to defined contribution pension plans* (Working paper).

Bridgen, P., & Meyer, T. (2005). When do benevolent capitalists change their mind? Explaining the retrenchment of defined benefit pensions in Britain. *Social Policy and Administration, 39*(7), 764–785.

Broeders, D., Van Oord, A., & Rijsbergen, D. (2015). *Scale economies in pension fund investments: A dissection of investment costs across asset classes* (Working paper 474). De Nederlandsche Bank, 50 pages.

Brown, J. R., & Weisbenner, S. J. (2009). Who chooses defined contribution plans? In J. R. Brown, J. Liebman, & D. A. Wise (Eds.), *Social security policy in a changing environment* (pp. 131–165). Chicago: University of Chicago Press.

Brown, J. R., & Weisbenner, S. J. (2014). Why do individuals choose defined contribution plans? Evidence from participants in a large public plan. *Journal of Public Economics, 116*, 35–46.

Brown, J. R., Farrell, A. M., & Weisbenner, S. J. (2015a). *Decision-making approaches and the propensity to default: Evidence and implications* (Working paper). University of Illinois, 41 pages.

Bulow, J., & Landsman, W. (1985). The relationship between wages and benefits. In D. A. Wise (Ed.), *Pensions, labour and individual choice* (pp. 379–397). Chicago: University of Chicago Press.

Burtless, G. (2009a). Financial market turbulence and social security reform. In M. A. Orenstein (Ed.), *Pensions, social security and the privatization of risk* (pp. 72–85). New York: Columbia University Press.

Burtless, G. (2009b). Lessons of the financial crisis for the design of national pension systems. *CESifo Economic Studies, 56*(3), 323–349.

Bush, D., Whitney, L., & Wesbroom, K. (2014). *Escrow White Paper – Reconciling stability and surplus*. AON-Hewitt, September, 21 pages.

Butt, A. (2011). Management of closed defined benefit superannuation schemes – An investigation using simulations. *Australian Actuarial Journal, 17*(1), 27–86.

Butt, A. (2013). Effects of scheme default insurance on decisions and financial outcomes in defined benefit pension schemes. *Annals of Actuarial Science, 7*(2), 288–305.

Campbell, A. C., Grimley, D. C., Pallister, J. K., Stoker, A. M., Walton, A. R., & Yiasoumi, C. A. (2006). Lessons from closure: An analysis and comparison of the issues facing closed life funds and closed pension schemes. *British Actuarial Journal, 12*(3), 639–711.

Cannon, E., & Tonks, I. (2004). UK Annuity Price Series 1957–2002, *Financial History Review,* vol. 11, no. 2, October, pp. 165–196.

Carnes, B. A., & Olshansky, S. J. (2007). A realist view of aging, mortality and future longevity. *Population and Development Review, 33*(2), 367–381.

Caswell, J. W. (1976). Economic efficiency in pension plan administration: A study of the construction industry. *Journal of Risk and Insurance, 43*(2), 257–273.

Cazalet Consulting. (2014). *When I'm sixty-four.* London: Cazalet Consulting.

Chemla, G. (2004). Pension fund investment in private equity and venture capital in the US and Canada. *Journal of Private Equity, 7*(2), 64–71.

Chen, D. H. J., & Beetsma, R. M. W. J. (2015). Mandatory participation in occupational pension schemes in the Netherlands and other countries: An update. Netspar, October, 10/2015-032.

Chingos, M. M., & West, M. R. (2015). Which teachers choose a defined contribution pension plan? Evidence from the Florida retirement system. *Education Finance and Policy, 10*(2), 193–222.

Choi, J. J. (2015). Contributions to defined contribution pension plans. *Annual Review of Financial Economics, 7,* 161–178.

Choi, J. J., Laibson, D., & Madrian, B. C. (2007). $100 bills on the sidewalk: Suboptimal investment in 401(k) plans. *Review of Economics and Statistics, 93*(3), 748–763.

Choi, J. J., Laibson, D., & Madrian, B. C. (2011). $100 Bills on the Sidewalk: Suboptimal Investment in 401(k) Plans, *Review of Economics and Statistics,* vol. 93, no. 3, August, pp. 748–763.

Choy, H., Lin, J., & Officer, M. S. (2014). Does freezing a defined benefit pension plan affect firm risk? *Journal of Accounting and Economics, 57*(1), 1–21.

Clark, R. L., & McDermed, A. A. (1986). Earnings and pension compensation: The effect of eligibility. *Quarterly Journal of Economics, 101*(2), 341–361.

Clark, R. L., Ghent, L. S., & McDermed, A. A. (2006b). Pension plan choice among university faculty. *Southern Economic Journal, 72*(3), 560–577.

Clark, R. L., Hanson, E., & Mitchell, O. S. (2015). *Lessons for public pensions from Utah's move to pension choice* (Pension Research Council Working Paper WP2015-05), 43 pages.

Clarke, M. G. (2013). *Modelling risk-based pension insurance premiums* (Pension Research Council Working Paper WP2013-14), 32 pages.

Comprix, J., & Muller, K. A. (2011). Pension plan accounting estimates and the freezing of defined benefit pension plans. *Journal of Accounting and Economics, 51*(1–2), 115–133.

Confederation of British Industry. (2015, October). A view from the top – CBI/Mercer pensions survey 2015. CBI, 44 pages.

Cotter, J., Blake, D., & Dowd, K. (2012). *What should be done about the underfunding of defined benefit pension schemes? A case study of Ireland* (Working paper). University College Dublin, 42 pages.

Crossley, T., & Jametti, M. (2013). Pension benefit insurance and pension plan portfolio choice. *Review of Economics and Statistics, 95*(1), 337–341.

Cui, J. (2008, September). *DC pension plan defaults and individual welfare* (Discussion paper 09/2008-034). Netspar, 47 pages.

Cummings, J. R. (forthcoming). Effect of fund size on the performance of Australian superannuation funds. *Accounting and Finance*.

De Grip, A., Lindeboom, M., & Montizaan, R. (2012). Shattered dreams: The effects of changing the pension system late in the game. *Economic Journal, 122*(559), 1–15.

De Haan, L. (2015). *Recovery measures of underfunded pension funds: Contribution increase, no indexation, or pension cut?* (Working paper). De Nederlandsche Bank, 34 pages.

Department for Work and Pensions. (2009). *Modelling collective defined contribution schemes.* London: Department for Work and Pensions.

Department for Work and Pensions. (2013). *Reshaping workplace pensions for future generations.* London: Department for Work and Pensions, Cm 8710, November.

Department for Work and Pensions. (2014). *Better workplace pensions: Further measures for savers.* London: Department for Work and Pensions, Cm 8840, March.

Disney, R., Emmerson, C., & Tetlow, G. (2009). What is a public sector pension worth? *Economic Journal, 119*(541), 517–534.

Dixon, A. D., & Monk, A. H. B. (2009). The power of finance: Accounting harmonization's effect on pension provision. *Journal of Economic Geography, 9*(5), 619–639.

Dorsey, S., Cornwell, C. M., & MacPherson, D. A. (1998). *Pensions and productivity.* Kalamazoo: W.E. Upjohn Institute.

Dowd, K., Blake, D., & Cairns, A. J. G. (2011). A computationally efficient algorithm for estimating the distribution of future annuity values under interest rate and longevity risks. *North American Actuarial Journal, 15*(2), 237–247.

Dyck, A., & Pomorski, L. (2011). *Is bigger better? Size and performance in pension plan management* (Working paper). University of Toronto, 59 pages.

Economist. (2012). Pensions: Fulfilling promises. *The Economist, 404*(8797), 37–38.

Ehrenberg, R. G. (1980). Retirement system characteristics and compensating wage differentials in the public sector. *Industrial and Labour Relations Review, 33*(4), 470–483.

Ehrenberg, R. G., & Smith, R. S. (1981). A framework for evaluating state and local government pension reform. In P. Mieszkowski & G. E. Peterson (Eds.), *Public sector labour markets* (pp. 103–128). Washington, DC: The Urban Institute Press.

Elton, E., Gruber, M., & Blake, C. (2006). The adequacy of investment choices offered by 401(k) plans. *Journal of Public Economics, 90*(6–7), 1299–1314.

Evans, H., Gordon, T., Khan, K., & Tetlow, G. (2014). *The NAPF longevity model.* National Association of Pension Funds and ClubVita.

Even, W. E., & MacPherson, D. A. (1990). The gender gap in pensions and wages. *Review of Economics and Statistics, 72*(2), 259–265.

Financial Conduct Authority. (2014). Thematic review of annuities, Financial Conduct Authority, TR14/2.

Financial Conduct Authority. (2015). FCA pension freedoms data collection exercise: Analysis and findings. Financial Conduct Authority, Ref. 005138, September, 31 pages.

Frazier, M. W. (2010). *Socialist insecurity: Pensions and the politics of uneven development in China*. Ithaca: Cornell University Press.

Freeman, R. B. (1985). Unions, pensions and union pension funds. In D. A. Wise (Ed.), *Pensions, labour and individual choice* (pp. 89–121). Chicago: University of Chicago Press.

Gardner, J., Pang, G., & Zou, Q. (2014a). How does the stock market react to the closure of a pension plan in the UK?, Towers Watson Perspectives, June, 10 pages.

Gerakos, J. (2010). Chief executive officers and the pay-pension tradeoff. *Journal of Pension Economics and Finance, 9*(2), 303–319.

Gerrans, P., & Clark, G. L. (2013). Pension plan participant choice: Evidence on defined benefit and defined contribution preferences. *Journal of Pension Economics and Finance, 12*(4), 351–378.

Ghilarducci, T., & Terry, K. (1999). Scale economies in union pension plan administration: 1981–1993. *Industrial Relations, 38*(1), 11–17.

Goldhaber, D., & Grout, C. (2016). Which plan to choose? The determinants of pension system choice for public school teachers. *Journal of Pension Economics and Finance, 15*(1), January, 30–54.

Goldreich, D., & Halaburda, H. (2013). When smaller menus are better: Variability in menu-setting ability. *Management Science, 59*(11), 2518–2535.

Gunderson, M., Hyatt, D., & Pesando, J. E. (1992). Wage-pension trade-offs in collective agreements. *Industrial and Labour Relations Review, 46*(1), 146–160.

Gustman, A. L., & Steinmeier, T. L. (1993). Pension portability and labour mobility; Evidence from the survey of income and programme participation. *Journal of Public Economics, 50*(3), 299–323.

Gustman, A. L., & Steinmeier, T. L. (1995). *Pension incentives and job mobility.* Kalamazoo: W.E. Upjohn Institute for Employment Research.

Harrison, D., Blake, D., & Dowd, K. (2012). *Caveat venditor: The brave new world of auto-enrolment should be governed by the principle of seller not buyer beware.* The Pensions Institute, October 2012.

Haynes, J. B., & Sessions, J. G. (2013). Work now, pay later? An empirical analysis of the pension-pay trade off. *Economic Modelling, 30*, 835–843.

Hoevenaars, R. P. M. M., & Ponds, E. H. M. (2008). Valuation of inter-generational transfers in funded collective pension schemes. *Insurance, Mathematics and Economics, 42*(2), 578–593.

House of Commons Work and Pensions Committee. (2013). *Improving governance and best practice in workplace pensions.* Sixth report of session 2012–13, HC 768–1, volume II, Ev 241–249.

Hsin, P. L., & Mitchell, O. S. (1997). Public pension plan efficiency. In M. S. Gordon, O. S. Mitchell, & M. M. Twinney (Eds.), *Positioning pensions for the twenty-first century* (pp. 187–205). Philadelphia: University of Pennsylvania Press.

Hu, Y. (2014). Diffusing the ticking time bomb: China's pension system. In *Strategic priorities: China's reform and the reshaping of the global order* (pp. 109–142). Singapore: Enrich Professional Publishing.

Hustead, E. C. (1998). Trends in retirement income plan administrative expenses. In O. S. Mitchell & S. J. Schieber (Eds.), *Living with defined contribution pensions: Remaking responsibility for retirement* (pp. 166–176). Philadelphia: University of Pennsylvania Press.

Hymans Robertson. (2013). Managing pension scheme risk – Buy-outs, buy-ins and longevity hedging Q4 2012.

IFF Research. (2014). Defined Benefit (DB) scheme running cost research – A data report on the costs of running DB pension schemes (Quantitative Survey). The Pensions Regulator, 56 pages.

Independent Project Board. (2014). Defined contribution workplace pensions: The audit of charges and benefits in legacy schemes. Independent Project Board, December, 102 pages.

Inkmann, J. (2006). *Compensating wage differentials for defined benefit and defined contribution occupational pension scheme benefits* (Working paper). Department of Finance, Tilburg University.

IPE. (2012). China plans pension tax delay to spur investment. *Investment and Pensions Europe*, 4 July.

Ippolito, R. A. (1995). Toward explaining the growth of defined contribution plans. *Industrial Relations, 34*(1), 1–20.

Ippolito, R. A. (1997). *Pension plans and employee performance: Evidence, analysis, and policy*. Chicago: University of Chicago Press.

Ippolito, R. A. (2000). The new pension economics: Defined contribution plans and sorting. In D. L. Salisbury (Ed.), *The future of private retirement plans* (pp. 77–91). Washington, DC: EBRI.

Johnson, M. (2014a). Retirement saving incentives: The end of tax relief and a new beginning. Centre for Policy Studies, April, 22 pages,

Johnson, S. (2014b). Longevity swaps market shows signs of life. *The Financial Times*, 9th February.

Kisser, M., Kiff, J., Oppers, E. S., & Soto, M. (2012). *The impact of longevity improvements on US corporate defined benefit pension plans* (IMF Working Paper WP/12/170).

LCP. (2014). LCP accounting for pensions 2014, Lane, Clark and Peacock, August, 66 pages.

LCP. (2015a). LCP accounting for pensions 2015, Lane, Clark and Peacock, August, 44 pages.

Leckie, S. H. (2011). Civil service and military service pensions in China. In N. Takayama (Ed.), *Reforming pensions for civil and military servants* (pp. 55–71). Tokyo: Maruzen Publishing.

Lu, J. (2015). Summary – Longevity Modelling, *Longevity Bulletin*, no. 7, November, pp. 4–5.

Lu, J. L. C., Wong, W., & Bajekal, M. (2014b). Mortality improvement by socio economic circumstances in England (1982 to 2006). *British Actuarial Journal, 19* (1), 1–35.

MacDonald, B. J., & Cairns, A. J. G. (2007). The impact of DC pension systems on population dynamics. *North American Actuarial Journal, 11*(1), 17–48.

MacIntosh, J., & Scheibelhut, T. (2012). How large pension funds organise themselves: Findings from a unique 19-fund survey. *Rotman International Journal of Pension Management, 5*(1), 34–40.

MacKenzie, G. A. (2010). *The decline of the traditional pension: A comparative study of threats to retirement security.* Cambridge: Cambridge University Press.

Madsen, C., & Tans, M. (2011). *Longevity and pensions: Protecting company pensions against increasing longevity.* Aegon Global Pensions.

Madsen, C., & Tans, M. (2012a). Personal longevity risk: Defined contribution pensions and the introduction of an 'equilibrium retirement age'. *Pensions: An International Journal, 17*(3), 169–176.

Madsen, C., & Tans, M. (2012b). Corrigendum – Personal longevity risk: Defined contribution pensions and the introduction of an 'equilibrium retirement age'. *Pensions: An International Journal, 17*(4), 349–350.

Mama, A. T., Pillay, N., & Fedderke, J. W. (2011, April). *Economies of scale and pension fund plans: Evidence from South Africa* (Working paper, no. 214). University of Cape Town, 18 pages.

McCarthy, D. (2005). *The optimal allocation of pension risks in employment contracts.* Department of Work and Pensions, Research Report 272.

McCarthy, D. (2006). The rationale for occupational pensions. *Oxford Review of Economic Policy, 22*(1), 57–65.

McFarland, B., & Warshawsky, M. J. (2010). Balances and retirement income from individual accounts: US historical simulations. *Benefits Quarterly, 26*(2), 36–40.

McFarland, B., Pang, G., & Warshawsky, M. (2009). Does freezing a defined benefit pension plan increase company value? *Empirical Evidence, Financial Analysts Journal, 65*(4), 47–59.

Merton, R. C. (2008). The future of retirement planning. In Z. Bodie, D. McLeavey, & L. B. Siegel (Eds.), *The future of life-cycle saving and investing* (pp. 5–18). Charlottesville: Research Foundation of the CFA Institute.

Merton, R. C. (2014). The crisis in retirement planning. *Harvard Business Review, 92*(7&8), 43–50.

Michaelson, A., & Mulholland, J. (2014). Strategy for increasing the global capacity for longevity risk transfer. *North American Actuarial Journal, 17*(1), 18–27.

Milevsky, M. A., & Song, K. (2010). Do markets like frozen defined benefit pensions? An event study. *Journal of Risk and Insurance, 77*(4), 893–909.

Mitchell, O. S., & Andrews, E. S. (1981). Scale economies in private multi-employer pension systems. *Industrial and Labour Relations Review, 34*(4), 522–530.

Modigliani, F., & Muralidhar, A. (2004). *Rethinking pensions reform.* Cambridge: Cambridge University Press.

Montgomery, E., & Shaw, K. (1997). Pensions and wage premia. *Economic Inquiry, 35*(3), 510–521.

Montgomery, E., Shaw, K., & Benedict, M. E. (1992). Pensions and wages: An hedonic price theory approach. *International Economic Review, 33*(1), 111–128.

Montizaan, R., Cörvers, F., De Grip, A., & Dohmen, T. (2016). Negative reciprocity and retrenched pension rights. *Management Science, 62*(3), March, 668–681.

Moore, R. L. (1987). Are male–female earnings differentials related to life-expectancy-caused pension cost differences? *Economic Inquiry, 25*(3), 389–401.

Morris, P., & Palmer, A. (2011). *You're on your own: How policy produced Britain's pensions crisis.* London: Civitas.

Munnell, A. H., & Soto, M. (2007). *Why are companies freezing their pensions?* (Working paper no. 2007–22). Centre for Retirement Research at Boston College.

Munnell, A. H., Sunden, A., & Taylor, C. (2001–2). What determines 401(k) participation and contributions? *Social Security Bulletin, 64*(3), 64–75.

Office for Budget Responsibility. (2014). *Policy measures database.* London: Office for Budget Responsibility.

Office for National Statistics. (2012). *Occupational pension schemes survey, 2011.* London: ONS.

Office for National Statistics. (2013b). *Occupational pension schemes survey, 2012.* London: ONS.

Office for National Statistics. (2014b). *Occupational pension schemes survey, 2013.* London: ONS, 40 pages.

Office for National Statistics. (2014c). *Pension trends,* Chapter 7, Private Pension Scheme Membership, 2014 Edition. London: ONS.

Office for National Statistics. (2015a). *Occupational pension schemes survey, 2014.* London: ONS, 40 pages.

Office for National Statistics. (2015d). Wealth in Great Britain wave 4, 2012 to 2014. ONS, December.

Office of Fair Trading. (2013). *Defined contribution workplace pension market study.* Office of Fair Trading.

Ostaszewski, K. M. (2001). Macroeconomic aspects of private retirement programs. *North American Actuarial Journal, 5*(3), 52–64.

Papke, L. E. (2004b). Pension plan choice in the public sector: The case of Michigan State employees. *National Tax Journal, 57*(2, part 1), 329–339.

Pension Protection Fund. (2015a). *Annual report and accounts 2014/15.* Pension Protection Fund.

Pension Protection Fund. (2015b). *The purple book, DB pensions universe risk profile 2015.* PPF and TPR.

Pensions Policy Institute. (2014). Increasing pension saving in the UK, PPI Briefing Note No. 68, September, 8 pages.

Pesando, J. E. (1984). Employee evaluation of pension claims and the impact of indexing initiatives. *Economic Inquiry, 22*(1), 1–17.

Philips, T. K. (2010). The rule of 72 for lifetime savings. *Journal of Investment Management, 8*(4), 54–57.

Pitt-Watson, D. (2013). *Collective pensions in the UK II.* London: Royal Society of Arts.

Pitt-Watson, D., & Mann, H. (2012). *Collective pensions in the UK.* London: Royal Society of Arts.

Ponds, E. H. M., & Van Riel, B. (2009). Sharing risk: The Netherlands' new approach to pensions. *Journal of Pension Economics and Finance, 8*(1), 91–105.

Popat, S., Curry, C., Pike, T., & Ellis, C. (2015). *Modelling collective defined contribution schemes*. Pensions Policy Institute, November, 51 pages.

Pozen, R. C. (2013). Tackling the Chinese pension system. Paulson Policy Memorandum, The Paulson Institute.

Rauh, J. D., Stefanescu, I., & Zeldes, S. P. (2013, June). *Cost shifting and the freezing of corporate pension plans* (Working paper). Stanford University, 53 pages.

Richards, S., & Jones, G. (2004, October). *Financial aspects of longevity risk*. Paper presented to the Staples Inn Actuarial Society.

Rosenfeld, S. (2009). *Life settlements: Signposts to a principal asset class* (Working paper, no. 09–20). Financial Institutions Centre, University of Pennsylvania.

Rubin, J. (2007). *The impact of pension freezes on firm value* (Working paper). Pension Research Council, PRC WP2007-11.

Salditt, F., Whiteford, P., & Adema, W. (2007). Pension reform in China – Progress and prospects. OECD Social Employment and Migration Working Papers no. 53.

Salditt, F., Whiteford, P., & Adema, W. (2008). Pension reform in China. *International Social Security Review, 61*(3), 47–71.

Salt, H. (2012). *The future of defined benefit pensions provision*. London: Trades Union Congress.

Schieber, S. J. (2012). *The predictable surprise: The unravelling of the U.S. retirement system*. Oxford: Oxford University Press.

Schiller, B. R., & Weiss, R. D. (1980). Pensions and wages: A test for equalizing differences. *Review of Economics and Statistics, 62*(4), 529–538.

Selman, L., & Wright, J. (2014). LGPS structure analysis: December 2013. Department for Communities and Local Government, March, 104 pages.

Sethi-Iyengar, S., Huberman, G., & Jiang, W. (2004). How much choice is too much? Contributions to 401(k) retirement plans. In O. S. Mitchell & S. P. Utkus (Eds.), *Pension design and structure: New lessons from behavioural finance* (pp. 83–95). Oxford: Oxford University Press.

Smith, R. S. (1981). Compensating differentials for pensions and underfunding in the public sector. *Review of Economics and Statistics, 63*(3), 463–468.

Smith, R. S., & Ehrenberg, R. G. (1983). Estimating wage-fringe trade-offs: Some data problems. In J. E. Triplett (Ed.), *The measurement of labour cost* (pp. 347–369). Chicago: University of Chicago Press.

Sutcliffe, C. M. S. (2010b). Should defined benefit pension schemes be career average or final salary? In M. Bertocchi, S. Schwartz, & W. Ziemba (Eds.), *Optimizing the ageing, retirement and pensions dilemma* (pp. 227–257). Hoboken: Wiley.

Sutcliffe, C. M. S. (2015). Trading death: The implications of annuity replication for the annuity puzzle, arbitrage, speculation and portfolios. *International Review of Financial Analysis, 38*, 163–174.

Tang, N. (2008). *The more the better? Characteristics and efficiency of 401(k) investment menus* (Working paper). Population Aging Research Centre, University of Pennsylvania.

Tang, N., Mitchell, O. S., Mottola, G. R., & Utkus, S. P. (2010). The efficiency of sponsor and participant portfolio choices in 401(k) plans. *Journal of Public Economics, 94*(11&12), 1073–1085.

Tuesta, D. (2014). Factors behind the administrative fees of private pension systems: An international analysis. *Journal of Pension Economics and Finance, 13*(1), 88–111.

United Nations. (2011). *World population prospects: The 2010 revision.*

Van der Lecq, S. G., & Van der Wurff, A. W. I. M. (2011). The price of pension risks. *Journal of Risk, 13*(3), 83–92.

Wang, L., Béland, D., & Zhang, S. (2014a). Pension fairness in China. *China Economic Review, 28*, 25–36.

Wang, L., Béland, D., & Zhang, S. (2014b). Pension financing in China: Is there a looming crisis. *China Economic Review, 30*, 143–154.

Westbroom, K., Hardern, D., Arends, M., & Harding, A. (2013, November). *The case for collective DC – A new opportunity for UK pensions* (Aon Hewitt White Paper), 81 pages.

Whittaker, M. (2015). A recovery for all? The evolution of the relationship between economic growth and pay before, during and since the financial crisis. Resolution Foundation Briefing, 13 pages.

Williamson, J. B. (2004). Assessing the pension reform potential of a notional defined contribution pillar. *International Social Security Review, 57*(1), 47–64.

Wood, A., Amantani, L., McDougall, D., & Baker, N. (2014). Landscape and charges survey 2013: Charges and quality in defined contribution pension schemes. Department for Work and Pensions, February, Research Report no. 859, 189 pages.

Yoshida, K., & Horiba, Y. (2003). Japanese corporate pension plans and the impact on stock prices. *Journal of Risk and Insurance, 70*(2), 249–268.

Z-Ben Advisors. (2012). China pension system: Demographic pressure cooker, April, 8 pages.

Zuo, X. (2014). Reforming pensions to ensure equitable and adequate retirement incomes in China. In B. Clements, F. Eich, & S. Gupta (Eds.), *Equitable and sustainable pensions: Challenges and experience* (pp. 293–312). Washington, DC: IMF.

3

Investment by Pension Funds

Pension schemes are major institutional investors, and investment performance has important consequences for pension schemes. In 2014 the assets under management of the largest 300 pension schemes in the world were $15.4 trillion, or an average of $51.3 billion for each scheme (Towers Watson 2015). There are also many tens of thousands of smaller pension schemes, and in 2014 they had assets of roughly $20.7 trillion (Towers Watson 2015). In 2012 pension schemes in the OECD countries had assets worth $32.1 trillion, representing 41 % of the assets held by institutional investors (OECD 2013b). Table 3.1 lists the 45 largest occupational pension schemes in 2014, and shows that 27 of these schemes are American and five are Dutch. Over half of these 45 schemes are for public sector workers, and only a quarter are large corporate schemes.

Table 3.2 lists the UK's largest 20 pension schemes in 2014 together with their assets. Corporate sponsors are strongly represented in this list, particularly the big banks. There are three local authority schemes and the sponsors of a number of denationalised industries such as coal, telecommunications, railways, airways, steel and the electricity grid.

While there has been a big move from defined benefit (DB) to defined contribution (DC) schemes, the legacy DB schemes still hold a large amount of assets to fund their accrued DB benefits, and in 2014 the NAPF 40th Annual Survey found that UK DB schemes held 94 % of pension scheme assets. In 2012 across the OECD DB pension schemes accounted for two thirds of pension fund assets, while DC schemes held only one third of pension fund assets (see Table 3.3). Some countries still have the vast majority of their assets in DB, rather than DC, schemes, for example the Netherlands 95 %, Canada 96 % and Japan 97 % (Towers Watson 2015).

© The Author(s) 2016
C. Sutcliffe, *Finance and Occupational Pensions*,
DOI 10.1057/978-1-349-94863-5_3

Table 3.1　Largest 45 pension funds by assets (excluding sovereign pension funds) end of 2014, $ billion

	Pension scheme	Country	$billion
1	Federal Retirement Thrift	USA	422
2	ABP	Netherlands	419
3	California Public Employees (CalPERS)	USA	297
4	PFZW	Netherlands	215
5	Local Government Officials	Japan	195
6	California State Teachers (CalSTRS)	USA	187
7	New York State Common	USA	178
8	New York City Retirement	USA	159
9	Florida State Board	USA	155
10	Ontario Teachers	Canada	133
11	Texas Teachers	USA	129
12	ATP	Denmark	122
13	Boeing	USA	106
14	New York State Teachers	USA	104
15	IBM	USA	102
16	Wisconsin Investment Board	USA	100
17	Pension Fund Association	Japan	98
18	North Carolina	USA	97
19	Ohio Public Employees	USA	91
20	AT&T	USA	89
21	Alecta	Sweden	88
22	General Motors	USA	86
23	Washington State Board	USA	85
24	New Jersey	USA	82
25	Bayerische Versorgungskammer	Germany	75
26	General Electric	USA	75
27	Royal Dutch Shell	Netherlands	74
28	Ohio State Teachers	USA	73
29	Oregon Public Employees	USA	72
30	California University	USA	72
31	Metaal Tech Bedrijven	Netherlands	71
32	Australian Super	Australia	69
33	BT Group	UK	68
34	Virginia Retirement	USA	68
35	National Public Service	Japan	68
36	Minnesota State Board Scheme	USA	67
37	Michigan Retirement	USA	67
38	Georgia Teachers	USA	67
39	Lockheed Martin	USA	65
40	Bouwnijverheid	Netherlands	65
41	Universities Superannuation Scheme	UK	65
42	PFA Pension	Denmark	65
43	Previ	Brazil	63
44	Ontario Municipal Employees	Canada	62
45	Massachusetts PRIM	USA	60

Source: P&I/TW 300 Analysis, Towers Watson, September 2015

Table 3.2 UK pension schemes assets under management 2015 (Investment & Pensions Europe September 2015)

	Sponsor	€ million
1	BT	52,572
2	USS	52,176
3	Lloyds Bank	51,984
4	Barclays Bank	34,541
5	Royal Bank of Scotland	31,797
6	Railways Pension Trustee Co.	28,431
7	Pension Protection Fund	28,254
8	HSBC Bank	27,969
9	Coal Pension Trustees	26,889
10	BP	26,383
11	BAE Systems	25,970
12	British Airways	23,385
13	National Grid	22,110
14	Shell UK	19,843
15	Aviva	18,969
16	Co-operative Group	17,740
17	Strathclyde (Local Gov.)	17,129
18	Greater Manchester (Local Gov.)	16,210
19	Rolls Royce Group	15,890
20	West Midlands (Local Gov.)	15,840

Table 3.3 DB vs. DC pension fund assets as a percentage of total pension assets[a] (OECD 2012)

Year	DB/hybrid	DC
2001	69.7 %	30.3 %
2011	65.0 %	35.0 %

[a]For selected OECD countries: Canada, Czech Republic, Denmark, Estonia, Finland, Germany, Hungary, Israel, Italy, Mexico, New Zealand, Norway, Poland, Portugal, Slovak Republic, Switzerland and the United States

Table 3.4 compares the net returns on large US DB and DC schemes over a 14-year period. The asset allocation of the DB schemes gave a higher weight than DC schemes to high return assets, with the result that DB returns were 1.18 % higher than for DC schemes. DB schemes had higher investment costs and slightly lower administration costs, and so the net returns for DB schemes were 1.07 % higher than for DC schemes.

3.1   DC Schemes

Both funded DB and DC schemes require the money to be invested until it is required to pay the pensions, but this investment is organised in quite different ways. In DC schemes each member has a separate pension pot, and

Table 3.4 Annual returns and costs of large US DB and DC schemes (1997–2010) (Ambachtsheer 2012)

	DB schemes (%)		DC schemes (%)		Difference (%)
Total return		8.26		7.08	1.18
Investment costs	0.45		0.31		0.14
Administration costs	0.07		0.10		−0.03
Less Total costs		0.52		0.41	0.11
Net return		7.74		6.67	1.07

can decide on the asset allocation of their own pot, leading to the need to make this asset allocation decision. There is also the related issue of whether to investment in the shares of the sponsor, particularly in the USA where the sponsor's pension contribution may be made in the form of its own shares.

a. DC Asset Allocation

Usually DC scheme members are given the opportunity to select the asset allocation of their pension pot. DC schemes generally offer a menu of different assets (external investment funds), for example: a bond portfolio, an index fund and so on, and in 2008 96 % of UK DC schemes offered members an investment choice. While some DC schemes offer a menu of only about 5–10 choices, others offer hundreds of alternatives, and the size of the menu offered to members may have behavioural effects on the investment choices made by members. Iyengar and Kamencia (2010) studied the relationship between the investment choices made by 580,000 members of 638 US 401(k) schemes, and the number of assets in the investment menu. They found that, as the size of the menu increases, members increasingly choose to invest in cash and bonds, and avoid equities.

The main determinant of the investment performance of UK and US pension funds has been shown to be asset allocation, rather than stock selection, so this decision is important. The external funds offered to DC members are usually highly liquid assets because members are continually investing and withdrawing money due to additional contributions, re-balancing their investments, retirements, deaths and transfers in or out. This restriction to liquid investments limits the type of assets in which DC members can invest, and this tends to reduce both the returns and diversification that can be achieved by a member's pensions pot (Spence Johnson 2013) (see Sect. 2.4d).

The empirical evidence on the asset allocation decisions made by members is that many members make poor choices. An analysis of the asset allocations of 986,949 401(k) scheme members showed that poor asset allocation by members resulted in an average reduction of 18 % in the value of their pension pots at retirement, (Tang et al. 2010). Yamaguchi et al. (2007) analysed the trading activity of 1,015,557 members of 401(k) schemes. They found that investing in the life-cycle or balanced funds and not trading generated annual additional risk-adjusted returns that were 0.84 % higher than for those members who actively rebalanced their portfolio; while trading generated zero excess return, relative to not trading. These results suggest that DC members should be encouraged to select life-cycle or balanced funds, and discouraged from trading, even if the transactions costs of trading are borne by all the members of a 401(k) scheme. Ahmed et al. (2013) used simulation to compare the asset allocation decisions of US workers with a simple benchmark of 60 % in equities and 40 % in bonds. They found that member allocations led to increased income inequality and a greater risk of low pensions, and recommend restricting the choice of asset allocations. When DC members are allowed to choose their asset allocation, this freedom affects their choice of member contribution rate. Papke (2004a) found that if US DC scheme members are allowed to choose the asset allocation of their pension pot, they tend to choose a higher member contribution rate, and to invest more in equities (Papke 2004a).

When allocating the assets in their DC scheme, members should consider their other assets and liabilities. For example, if a member owns an electronics business, they should probably be under-weight in electronics companies in their DC fund. Since their DC fund is tax exempt, members may also wish to hold their more highly taxed investments inside, rather than outside their DC fund. There is some evidence that members do take account of the interaction between their pension and their other assets. Salamanca et al. (2013) studied data on about 2000 Dutch households, and found that as the funding ratio of their DB pension scheme dropped, increasing the risk of either default or a cut in benefits, they reduced their household's investment in equities. There is also evidence that the personal circumstances of members tend to affect their asset allocations. In study of the 401(k) asset allocations of 2763 Americans, Clark et al. (2014) discovered that the allocation to equities is higher for young males with high financial literacy and wealth, and more years of service. Bekaert et al. (2014) analysed the 401(k) asset allocations of 3.8 million Americans and found that international diversification is increased for those who are young, educated, financially literate, well paid, foreign born and who work in a state with a high level of exports.

Over time scheme members age, their personal circumstances change, and their asset allocation is altered by movements in relative asset prices. Theory suggests that DC scheme members should rebalance their portfolio in response to these changes, but the empirical evidence shows they do not. Keim and Mitchell (2015) investigated a situation where in 2012 a large firm reduced its DC scheme's menu of investment choices from 88 to 40 funds, which meant that those invested in the 38 deleted funds had to reallocate their money. Those who failed to make a choice were defaulted into the appropriate age-related target date fund. The result of this reallocation was that member portfolios were invested in fewer funds, with a smaller investment in equities, and in funds with lower expenses. After the deletions, transfers of money between funds were lower than before, as members exhibited inertia and did not rebalance their portfolios to restore their former equity proportions.

b. DC Default Funds

Members show little interest in the asset allocation decision, with the vast majority failing to make a decision and ending up in the default fund. In 2008, where a default fund was offered, 82 % of members were assigned to the default fund. Over 99 % of those who have been automatically enrolled into the National Employment Savings Trust (NEST) (see Sect. 1.9) have ended up in one of its 47 target date default funds (Sandbrook and Gosling 2014). A similar unwillingness to select investments applies in other countries. In April 2003, 92 % of new members of the Swedish national DC scheme, which offers the choice of over 700 funds, wound up in the default fund.

Default funds in the UK typically have a high equity content. In 2009, 71 % of UK default funds were invested entirely in equities, while the average equity allocation of default funds was 91 %, and this generates considerable risk and variation in outcomes between different cohorts of members. Recently life-cycle (lifestyle or target date) funds have been introduced and can be specified as the default fund. They automatically and gradually change the asset allocation from risky investments to low-risk investments as the member approaches their retirement date. This adjustment of the asset allocation over time from risky to low-risk assets is called the glide path. Lifestyle funds usually follow a predetermined glide path mechanistically, while target date funds are actively managed around a risk reduction glide path (Cazalet Consulting 2014). In the USA most scheme members do not intend to buy an annuity on retirement and wish to keep their funds in drawdown after they reach their target date. To accommodate these members most US target date funds can be categorised as 'through' funds. These funds aim to have a relatively high risk exposure at their target date, while 'to' funds have a very low risk exposure at their target date to enable them to be converted into cash. The removal in April 2015 of the requirement for UK pensioners with DC pots to annuitise means the need to move into low-risk assets by the retirement date no longer applies to those who intend to move into drawdown on retirement, rather than annuitise or spend their pension pot. Therefore the glide paths of lifestyle and target date funds may no longer be appropriate for these members.

Using a theoretical model, Tang and Lin (2015) computed the optimal stock selection and asset allocation (glide path) for nine different types of member, and compared these with the asset allocation and stock selection offered by 36 US target date fund series. (A series of target date funds is a set of target date funds that differ according to their specified target retirement date.) They found that two thirds of the welfare loss by members was due to the use of an inappropriate glide path, with only one third due to poor stock selection. This implies that the choice of glide path (i.e. the asset allocation decision) is much more important than the stock selection decision. In a cross-section study of 106 Australian DC default funds, Inkmann and Shi (forthcoming) found that, as the average age of scheme members increases, the single default fund contains a lower proportion of risky assets. This is consistent with schemes choosing a default fund which conforms with the life-cycle model, where the proportion of financial wealth held by individuals in risky assets declines with age. Since the risk exposure of default funds matches that appropriate for members of average age, default funds are too risky for older members, and not risky enough for younger members. Therefore, members whose age differs from the average age should be less likely to allow themselves to end up in the default fund, and this is what Inkmann and Shi (forthcoming) find.

In Sweden, mandatory state DC scheme members can choose to invest in up to five of the 779 available funds. Of those who make a choice and do not end up in the default fund, there is strong evidence of investor inertia; i.e. they do not subsequently change their asset allocation (Dahlquist and Martinez 2015). In aggregate, subsequent pension contributions flow into the initially chosen funds, regardless of these funds' investment performance. This leads to poor investment performance, and these members may well have been better off in the default fund.

c. Investment in the Shares of the Sponsor

In the USA members of DC schemes are often encouraged to invest their 401(k) contributions in the shares of their employer. In addition, the employer may make pension contributions to 401(k) pension pots in the form of their own company's stock. This can result in members holding a very large proportion of their 401(k) investments in the shares of their employer. Poterba (2003) found that, for 20 large US companies in 2001, on average their DC schemes had invested 44.2 % of the assets in the shares of the sponsor. Table 3.5 indicates that the pension pots of members working for some large US companies had very high proportions of their pension pots invested in the shares of the

Table 3.5 Investment in the shares of the sponsor in 2001 (*Economist* 15 December 2001)

Employer	Percentage of employees 401(k)s invested in shares of their employer
Proctor & Gamble	95
Pfizer	86
Coca Cola	82
General Electric	77
Texas Instruments	76
McDonalds	74
Enron	58
Ford	57
Qwest	53
AOL Time Warner	52

sponsor. For example, 95 % of the DC pension pots of Proctor and Gamble workers were invested in Proctor and Gamble shares, and the corresponding figure for Enron was 58 %. With the bankruptcy of Enron in December 2001, Gregg Lancaster, a 43 year old father of two, lost both $100,000 in his 401(k) scheme and his job at Enron. In the period before the collapse, Enron had prevented the sale of Enron shares in 401(k) accounts. '*A lot of companies do this, and it stinks*' stated Steven Sass (*Economist* 15 December 2001). For 705 US DC schemes Duan et al. (2015) found that the number of shares in the sponsor held within member pots does not change as the financial distress of the sponsor approaches, leading to large reductions in the value of these pots. They also found that, for a sample of 318 US DB schemes whose sponsor defaulted, as the sponsor approaches financial distress, scheme under-funding increases due to a drop in sponsor contributions.

Substantial investment in the shares of the sponsor is the very opposite of diversification, with members bearing substantial unsystematic risk for no reward. Even and Macpherson (2007) estimated the costs of not diversifying DC pension pots for 5558 US DC schemes. They found that, if a member's 401(k) pot was fully invested in the shares of the sponsor, expected returns could have been increased by 23.9 % if the pot had instead been invested in a well-diversified portfolio with the same risk (see Fig. 3.1). A later study by Even and Macpherson (2009) simulated the performance of investing half the 401(k) pot in the shares of the sponsor, and found that this results in substantial efficiency losses, particularly for those who are risk averse and have little non-pension wealth. Meulbroek (2005) estimated that a member with a quarter of their 401(k) pot invested in company shares for 10 years effectively sacrifices 42 % of the stock market value of this particular investment to compensate for the extra risk they are bearing.

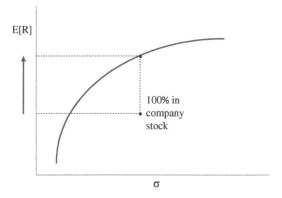

Fig. 3.1 Company stock and return reduction

As well as bearing unrewarded risk, there is the risk that when their employer has difficulties, members will both lose both their job and suffer a reduction in the value of their pension pot, as did Gregg Lancaster at Enron. This raises the question of why members of 401(k) schemes hold such undiversified portfolios, and why sponsors promote such outcomes, (Mitchell and Utkus 2003). Benartzi et al. (2007) considered this question using survey data. Members might choose to concentrate their 401(k) pension pots in the shares of their employer because they (a) receive tax benefits from owning company stock, (b) may possess private information about their employer, (c) will pay lower transactions costs when holding company stock and (d) may derive non-monetary benefits such as demonstrating loyalty to their employer. However Benartzi et al. (2007) found members are largely unaware of the tax benefits, and there is little evidence for non-monetary benefits and the use of private information. So this study cannot explain why some members choose to concentrate their pension pot in the shares of the sponsor. In a study of 28,809 active members of a large 401(k) scheme, Agnew (2002) concluded that the group most likely to invest in the shares of the sponsor are low salary males, particularly after a period of high returns on the sponsor's equity.

There are benefits to the sponsor from contributing their own stock. Sponsors might benefit from (a) increased motivation and productivity by scheme members, (b) tax benefits, (c) reduced risk of a hostile takeover, (d) the retention of cash within the business, (e) a greater willingness by scheme members to accept pay cuts and (f) financial reporting benefits. However, while Rauh (2006a) found empirical support for the view that investing 401(k) pots in the sponsor's stock reduces the risks of a hostile takeover, these benefits to the sponsor were argued to be modest by Benartzi et al. (2007).

They conclude that, as the costs are substantial while the benefits are slight, the large investments in company shares by DC scheme members are due to ignorance and excessive optimism. Duan et al. (2015) suggest that the protection from hostile takeovers afforded by investment in the employer may lead to lower operational efficiency of the sponsor and a higher probability of financial distress. Self-investment by DB schemes can also have consequences for the sponsor. Eaton et al. (2014) found that, if a significant proportion of a US DB scheme's assets are invested in the shares of the sponsor, institutional ownership of the sponsor's shares is reduced.

UK DC schemes do not have substantial investments in the sponsor. The default fund and the menu of investments offered to members typically offer only diversified funds, and do not contain individual shares, leading to very low indirect investment in the sponsor. UK DB schemes are not allowed to invest more than 5 % of the pension fund's assets in the sponsor, while the corresponding figure for the USA is 10 %. UK DB schemes are also prohibited from buying sponsor-related loans. However if the scheme has a big deficit, this is economically equivalent to the DB scheme making a large loan to the sponsor, and is not caught by the 5 % self-investment rule, even if it represents more than 5 % of the scheme's assets (see Sect. 4.8b).

3.2   DB Schemes

The investment decisions of DB schemes are made by the trustees, or their delegated agents, for the entire fund on a pooled basis; and so are different from DC asset allocation decisions. To help to make the operation and investment activity of a DB pension scheme more concrete, the operation of a very large UK scheme (USS) will be used as a case study.

a. Example of USS
USS Ltd is the corporate trustee of the Universities Superannuation Scheme (USS). USS began in 1974, and in 2015 had 322,779 active members, deferred pensioners and pensioners. USS is a hybrid scheme (CARE and DC). It covers UK academic staff at almost all UK universities and related institutions, and so USS is a multi-employer scheme with 419 separate employers (or institutions) in 2015. In October 2011 USS introduced a career average revalued earnings (CARE) section for new members, and soft froze the final salary section. Then in April 2016 the final salary section was hard frozen, with those in the final section offered membership of the CARE section, and a DC scheme introduced for earnings over £55,000 per annum. In 2015 the

members and institutions contributed 26 % of gross salaries to USS. This has created a pension fund valued in 2015 at about £50 billion, the second largest in the UK after BT, and the 38th largest in the world. USS is regulated by three different organizations: the Pensions Regulator (TPR), the Financial Conduct Authority (FCA) and the Prudential Regulation Authority (PRA).

USS has a management committee which runs the entire scheme, and an investment committee that manages the investment of the fund. The USS investment committee consists of seven USS directors and three co-opted experts. USS has a wholly-owned subsidiary, USS Investment Management (USSIM), that acts as internal fund managers of most of the funds. USS also employs a compliance officer who deals with FCA and PRA compliance, and a responsible investment team. The investment committee is advised by an investment consultant from Mercers (who are part of Marsh & McLennan). USS also employs six external fund managers: BlueBay Asset Management, Legal & General Inv. Mgt., Royal London Asset Management, Credit Suisse, Investec and Pictet. The assets are held not by USS, but by two custodians, Northern Trust and JP Morgan Chase, and investment performance is measured by HSBC and Investment Property Databank Ltd. (IPD). Advice on investing in property is supplied by Jones Lang LaSalle (retail, leisure and industrial) and DTZ Inv. Mgt. (offices and international indirects); while management of the property owned by USS is sub-contracted to Workman & Partners, DTZ, Savills and Munroe K Asset Mgt., with property valuation conducted by CB Richard Ellis. USS employs DLA Piper LLP as their solicitors, Barclays Bank PLC as their bankers and Grant Thornton UK LLP as their auditors. As this list shows, many external organisations are highly involved in the functioning of USS.

b. Unusual Features of the Investment Problem

When making investments, DB pension schemes are in a different position than other institutional investors such as mutual funds, investment trusts, unit trusts and so on. Pension schemes have liabilities with unhedgeable risks, lack investment expertise, are often small, have a very long time horizon, face regulatory constraints on their funding ratio, and have highly predictable cash flows. These special features of DB pension scheme investment will now be considered.

i. Liabilities

The aim of a DB pension scheme is to generate sufficient money to fund a specified liability – the pensions promise, not to make as much money as possible. For a scheme that is initially fully funded, provided the values of the assets and liabilities move up and down together, the scheme has a fully hedged position and can guarantee payment of pensions whatever the changes in asset and liability values. This is called liability matching; and portfolio theory can be extended to include the liabilities in the Markowitz model to construct a hedged, or risk minimising, portfolio (see Sect. 3.2e).

The importance of the distinction between matching the liabilities and making a lot of money is demonstrated in Fig. 3.2. This figure shows the cumulative return on a pension scheme's assets, liabilities and an asset performance benchmark. Initially both the assets and liabilities have negative returns, while the benchmark has a positive return. Therefore the assets have negative returns and have under-performed the benchmark by the distance A, while the assets have out-performed the liabilities by the distance B. So far as the scheme is concerned, they have achieved a surplus measured by the distance B, even though asset performance has been negative and substantially less than the benchmark by the distance A. Subsequently, both the liabilities and assets show a positive cumulative return, while the benchmark has a negative cumulative return. As a result the assets have under-performed liabilities by the distance C, while the assets have out-performed the benchmark by the distance D. Even though the assets have a positive return and have out-performed the benchmark by the distance D, the scheme now has a deficit given by the distance C. Figure 3.2 shows that measuring asset returns relative to the liabilities can give the opposite indication of success or failure, relative to the indication given by an asset benchmark. It is asset performance relative to the liabilities that matters to a pension scheme, and not asset performance relative to some benchmark.

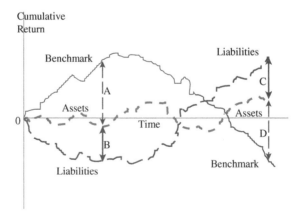

Fig. 3.2 Assets, liabilities and benchmarks

ii. Unhedgeable Risks

Some aspects of pension liability risk cannot be hedged as there are no satis-factory hedging instruments. There are five main risks which pension schemes need to hedge – inflation, interest rates, salaries, longevity and regulations. (a) Investment risk can be avoided by not holding risky assets, rather than by hedging. (Hedging the currency risk of foreign investments will be considered in Sect. 3.2c(iv)). (b) Inflation risk can be hedged using index linked bonds, but the gross nominal value of UK index linked gilts in March 2014 was £380 billion (Debt Management Office 2014), which is well short of the amount required by UK pension funds and insurance companies; so they use over-the-counter (OTC) swaps. For example, in July 2015 USS entered a retail price index (RPI) inflation swap until 2063 for £130 million with Yorkshire Water. However this results in counter-party risk. The recent shift from RPI to consumer price indexation (CPI) in the UK for many DB schemes presents the additional problem of basis risk, as the gilts and swaps are based on RPI, while the liabilities are now largely linked to CPI. (c) Short-term interest rate risk can be hedged using the futures and options markets, while interest rate swaps can hedge long-term interest rate risk. (d) Although a wide range of financial instruments have been proposed for hedging mortality or longevity risk – mortality bonds, longevity futures, longevity options, longevity bonds, longevity swaps, and longevity buyins; it is still hard to hedge (see Sect. 2.7). (e) Pensions depend on risky future salary levels, particularly for a final salary scheme, and this risk cannot be hedged. (f) Regulatory risk cannot be hedged. Rather than seek to hedge these five risks, a different approach is to redesign the pension scheme to reduce exposure to these risks, for example introduce LEAF to reduce longevity risk, LPI to reduce inflation risk, and cap increases in pensionable salary to reduce final salary risk.

iii. Expertise

Pension schemes are usually small units attached to companies producing unrelated goods and services. The sponsor and the pension scheme trustees are not usually experts in investing money as this is outside the core business of the sponsor. So they need to hire such expertise, and this can take various forms – independent trustees who are investment experts, fiduciary manage-ment (see Sect. 3.2c(xii)), external fund managers, internal fund managers and so on (see Sect. 3.2c(vi)).

iv. Size

Relative to mainstream institutional investors, many pension funds are small investors, and some are very small. Hence they lack economies of scale in investment (see Sect. 2.13) leading to higher costs, and an inability to under-take some types of investment.

v. Time Horizon

A new scheme member aged (say) 23 may not start drawing their pension for another 42 years, and then continue drawing their pension for another 22 years after retirement. This gives a very long time horizon to the investment of the money (e.g. 64 years). If this member leaves a young widow who receives a widow's pension, this gap can be substantially longer. However, the investment industry is heavily focused on the short term (e.g. three months, one year), and this lack of long-term investment is a persistent problem for pension schemes.

vi. Funding Constraints

The funding ratio is assets divided by liabilities, and there are regulations governing the funding ratio of pension schemes. It is monitored on an annual basis by The Pensions Regulator (TPR), and if the funding ratio is too low, TPR will require the scheme to take corrective action via the production of a recovery plan. Therefore, it is not sufficient to have ample money in 40 or 60 years to pay the pensions due to high asset returns expected in years 30–40. The scheme must be on track every year to meet its liabilities. So, despite being long-term investors, pension schemes are also concerned about year to year risk. The annual risk of the pension scheme is also a concern for the annual company accounts.

vii. Cash Flows

The net cash flows of pension schemes are highly predictable. The pension contributions are a known proportion of salaries, the magnitude of pensions in payment is known with considerable precision, and income (dividends, interest etc.) on the investment fund is also reasonably predictable. New and expanding pension schemes tend to be immature, i.e. have a high proportion of active members paying money into the scheme, relative to pensioners taking money out of the scheme. For example, USS has a net cash inflow of about £1 billion per year. Therefore, USS has no need to sell assets to pay pensions. Rather USS has to continually find a home for the new money. In consequence, the liquidity of investments is not an important consideration, and USS hopes to reap the liquidity premium (i.e. higher risk-adjusted returns) on some of its investments (e.g. infrastructure). Conversely, mature schemes with a high proportion of pensioners (e.g. the Coal Board), or schemes closed to further contributions, have a net cash outflow each year, and so need to keep liquidating their investments. To them the quick and cheap liquidation of investments is important.

c. Decisions That Must Be Made by Pension Schemes

A range of decisions must be taken by the pension scheme trustees (e.g. the USS Investment Committee) in managing the money, and 15 of these decisions will now be considered.

i. Asset Allocation and Risk Exposure

The most important determinant of the rate of return on the pension fund is the allocation of the assets between asset classes, and the following example illustrates the potential rewards from getting the asset allocation right.

Example. Consider an investment of $1 in January 1926 until December 1996 (71 years) with all proceeds reinvested. This money can be invested in one of three ways: US Treasury bills, (zero market timing), S&P500 index basket, (zero market timing) or switching each month between these two investments to that which will give the better performance over the next month (i.e. perfect market timing). Table 3.6 shows the results of each of these investment strategies. During this period the return on the US stock market was 98 times higher than on US treasury bills; and the return for perfect timing was 1.7 million times higher than on the US stock market, and 164 million times higher than for Treasury bills. This indicates the enormous potential gains available from market timing. However, this comparison takes no account of the differences in risk between the various strategies and assumes perfect foresight.

By law UK pension schemes must publicly specify their investment policy in the Statement of Investment Principles (SIP), and as part of the SIP the trustees must draw up a list of permitted investments. The obvious asset classes are: UK and overseas equities, UK and overseas bonds (sovereign and corporate), UK and overseas property, and cash. There are also some less obvious asset classes (often called alternative assets) and these include: private equity, hedge funds, commodities, currencies, infrastructure, small companies, and emerging markets. Some assets fall into several asset classes, for example small companies in emerging markets, leading to a definitional issue.

Table 3.6 Value in 1996 from investing $1 in 1926

Investment strategy	Value in December 1996
US Treasury bills	$14
S&P500 index basket	$1370
Perfect timing	$2,296,183,456

Table 3.7 has the asset allocation in 2012 of pension schemes in the OECD countries, and this reveals very large differences between countries in their average asset allocation. For example, Korea has 57.8 % in cash and deposits, while Denmark has only 0.4 %; the Czech Republic has 84.4 % in bills and bonds and Korea has only 1.6 %; Belgium has 71.4 % in mutual funds, while Australia, Austria, Finland, Japan, Mexico and Turkey have zero investment in mutual funds. Individual pension schemes will have more extreme asset allocations than these country averages.

Table 3.7 Pension fund asset allocation in OECD countries 2012 (OECD 2013b)

Percentages	A	B	C	D	E	F	G	H	I	J
Australia	18.4	9.6	1.0	*46.0*	7.4	0.0	0.0	0.0	0.0	17.6
Austria	9.2	52.1	1.1	29.5	3.5	0.0	0.0	0.0	0.0	4.7
Belgium	3.0	11.4	0.7	8.2	0.8	*71.4*	1.2	0.0	0.0	3.2
Canada	2.7	27.6	0.3	24.6	5.5	34.6	0.0	0.0	0.0	4.7
Chile	0.5	45.5	1.1	12.5	0.0	40.3	0.0	0.0	0.0	0.1
Czech Rep.	9.8	*84.4*	0.0	0.2	0.7	1.2	0.0	0.0	0.0	3.8
Denmark	0.4	66.1	0.1	13.0	1.0	2.3	0.0	0.0	0.0	17.1
Estonia	16.4	25.6	0.0	5.2	0.0	52.5	0.0	0.0	0.0	0.3
Finland	4.2	36.0	4.6	37.1	11.0	0.0	0.0	0.0	0.0	7.1
Germany	1.4	35.7	*18.5*	0.2	2.4	39.2	0.0	0.5	0.3	1.8
Greece	46.4	37.1	0.0	2.5	0.0	12.5	0.0	0.0	0.0	1.6
Hungary	3.9	64.9	0.0	4.7	0.0	23.2	0.0	0.0	0.0	3.2
Iceland	7.2	50.2	8.3	10.3	0.0	15.3	0.0	0.0	*8.7*	0.0
Israel	5.4	76.1	2.6	5.5	0.6	3.3	0.0	0.2	0.1	6.2
Italy	4.2	45.1	0.0	11.2	2.9	10.3	22.9	0.0	0.0	3.4
Japan	5.1	36.3	2.8	9.7	0.0	0.0	0.0	0.0	0.0	*46.1*
Korea	*57.8*	1.6	0.0	0.0	0.0	5.9	*32.4*	0.0	0.0	2.3
Luxembourg	4.5	57.4	0.0	0.0	0.0	36.3	0.0	0.0	0.0	1.7
Mexico	0.5	80.9	0.0	18.2	0.0	0.0	0.0	0.0	0.0	0.4
Netherlands	1.3	24.0	3.8	11.6	0.9	51.9	0.0	0.0	0.0	6.5
Norway	2.7	50.7	1.6	18.1	2.9	23.0	0.0	0.0	0.0	1.1
Poland	8.3	55.8	0.0	34.8	0.0	0.3	0.0	0.0	0.0	0.8
Portugal	13.6	37.4	0.0	8.4	*12.1*	24.5	0.0	0.0	0.0	4.0
Slovakia	22.7	68.5	0.0	0.2	0.0	7.8	0.0	0.0	0.0	0.8
Slovenia	21.0	54.4	2.8	1.1	0.0	20.6	0.0	0.0	0.0	0.1
Spain	14.6	55.7	0.0	9.1	0.2	9.7	10.0	0.0	0.6	0.1
Sweden	2.4	58.1	0.3	9.4	3.0	26.7	0.0	0.0	0.0	0.1
Switzerland	7.3	19.9	3.3	13.0	9.7	42.8	0.0	*2.4*	1.2	0.4
Turkey	8.9	58.1	0.0	16.0	0.0	0.0	0.0	0.0	0.0	17.1
USA	0.8	16.3	0.3	38.2	1.7	22.0	3.3	0.0	0.0	17.4

A – cash and deposits, B – bills and bonds, C – loans, D – equities, E – land and buildings, F – mutual funds, G – unallocated insurance contracts, H – hedge funds, I – private equity funds, J – other investments

Table 3.8 Average asset allocation of total assets by UK DB schemes 2006 and 2015 (PPF 2015b)

	2006 (%)	2015 (%)	Change (%)
Equities	61.1	33.0	−28.1
Fixed interest	28.3	47.7	+19.4
Insurance policies	0.9	0.1	−0.8
Cash	2.3	3.5	+1.2
Property	4.3	4.9	+0.6
Hedge funds	–	6.1	+6.1
Others	3.1	4.7	+1.6
Total	100.0	100.0	0

Table 3.8 contains the average asset allocations of UK DB pension schemes in both 2006 and 2015. The main change over this period has been a big drop in the allocation to equities and a switch to fixed income, cash and hedge funds. This shift from equities to fixed income meant that 2012 was the first time since the 1950s that UK DB pension schemes had a larger investment in fixed interest (43.2 %) than in equities (38.5 %). This gap has widened further in subsequent years to 14.7 %.

Table 3.9 shows the USS asset allocation in 2014, and the benchmark asset allocation against which performance was judged. This table also shows the extent to which fund managers were permitted to diverge from the benchmark allocation, and the actual deviation in March 2014. This raises the question of how large should these divergence limits be? Louton et al. (2015) used US data to simulate the effects of varying the divergence limits on the performance of a typical US DB pension fund. For limits of between 1 and 5 %, as might be expected, they found wider limits lead to greater tracking error, which is the standard deviation of returns around the benchmark. Depending on the skill of the fund managers, this increase in tracking error may be accompanied by an increase in the information ratio, which is the average return above the benchmark, divided by the standard deviation of returns around the benchmark. This indicates that setting the divergence limit depends on how tightly the scheme wishes to track its benchmark, and how much skill its fund managers are thought to have.

Since pension funds exist to meet the pension promise, their aim is to match or beat wage increases. In Table 3.10 the average return on UK pension funds over a 49-year period is compared to the rate of UK wage increases over the same period. Pension fund returns exceeded wage increases, leaving a margin of 2.6 % per year to cover promotional increases. Even a gilt portfolio would have out-performed wage increases by 1.3 %. This table also shows that wage increases exceeded RPI by 1.6 % over the period.

Table 3.9 USS asset allocation – March 2014

	Actual (%)	Benchmark (%)	Divergence limits (%)	Actual divergence (%)
Equities				
UK equities	15.4	15.6	{	
N. America	4.8	7.0	{ All equities	
Europe	9.5	9.3	{ −7.5 to	−3.1
Pacific	6.4	7.0	{ + 7.5	
Emerging markets	7.7	8.0	{	
Totals	43.8	46.9		
Alternatives				
Private capital	10.9	10.9	(	
Infrastructure	5.1	5.2	(−10 to +10	−0.1
Absolute return	3.3	3.3	(	
Totals	19.3	19.4		
Fixed income				
Global gov. bonds	16.5	17.0	[	
Liability hedging	6.6	4.5	[−5 to	1.5
Inv. grade credit	2.4	2.5	[+ 5	
Emerging mkt. debt	3.0	3.0	[	
Totals	28.5	27.0		
Others				
Property	6.6	6.6	−5 to +5	0
Tactical asset alloc.	3.2	0	–	+3.2
Cash	−1.2	0.2	Max 10	−1.4
Totals	8.6	6.8		
Grand Totals	100.0	100.0	–	0

Table 3.10 Average annual returns 1963–2012 (UBS 2013)

UK equities	11.8 %
UK pension funds	10.2 %
Gilts	8.9 %
UK wages	7.6 %
UK RPI	6.0 %

There is some empirical evidence on how pension schemes choose their asset allocation. Ang et al. (2014) investigated the effects of past asset returns on the asset allocations of 573 large US pension funds. For four asset classes (domestic and foreign equities, and domestic and foreign fixed income) they found allocations to an asset class increased when returns over the previous three years on the asset class increased, i.e. they are long-term momentum traders. However, the best way for a scheme to address the asset allocation decision, and the related risk-return trade-off, is an asset-liability model (ALM) (see Sect. 3.2.e).

Alternative Assets

In recent years there has been an increasing interest in alternative assets, although investment in such assets is not new. For example, from 1974 to 1980 the British Rail pension fund invested £40.1 million (or 2.9 % of its assets) in works of art. Advised by Sotheby's, they bought 2400 objects and sold most of them by 1989. In total they received over £165 million from the sales (with 63 items unsold), and achieved an annual rate of return of 5.5 % above inflation. Returns above the inflation rate varied considerably as between asset classes, as can be seen in Table 3.11.

Rose and Seligman (2015) studied the effect of legislative changes on the allocations by 126 US public sector schemes to alternative assets. They defined alternative assets as covering hedge funds, private equity and real estate funds, and identified four reasons why schemes invest in these assets: (a) to achieve excess returns, (b) to benefit from diversification, (c) herding (see Sect. 3.3a), and (d) ignorance of the true risk and return performance of these assets due to smoothed returns and hidden transactions costs. The average allocation to alternative assets was 3.62 %, and rising strongly over time. These allocations are reduced by legislative changes, particularly those concerned with asset allocation rules. They are also a negative function of the scheme's funding ratio, and a positive function of the total assets of the fund and the assumed return on alternative assets.

Property

Property is an important type of alternative asset and has been a staple asset in pension fund portfolios for many years. A study of property investment using data for almost 1000 large schemes in the USA, Canada, Europe, Australia and New Zealand covering about 40 % of global DB assets was conducted by Andonov et al. (2013, 2015) and. They identified five different ways of investing in property. Schemes can buy direct property (a) using internal staff without any intermediary, (b) via external managers and (c) via a fund of funds and then external managers. They can also buy listed (or indirect) property

Table 3.11 Returns above inflation (1974–1980)

Impressionists (e.g. Renoir, Monet)	12.9 % p.a.
Chinese antiques	6.5 % p.a.
Silver	6.5 % p.a.
Victorian paintings	6.5 % p.a.
Old masters (e.g. Van Dyke, Goya)	2.5 % p.a.
Books and manuscripts	0.9 % p.a.
Primitive art	Loss

and achieve this (d) via a real estate investment trust (REIT) and (e) via external managers and then REITs. By 2011 about 6.5 % of all scheme assets were invested in property, with about 85 % of these assets being held as direct property, and 15 % in REITs. By 2011 about 80 % of the assets invested in property were invested via external managers, 15 % via internal staff, and 5 % via a fund of funds. Andonov et al. (2013, 2015) found that larger schemes tend to use their own staff to invest directly in property, achieving higher than average net returns and lower costs, while smaller schemes tend to use external managers and fund of funds to invest in direct property.

Infrastructure

Infrastructure is an increasingly popular type of alternative asset that is attractive to pension schemes because it offers stable, low volatility, cash flows with a low correlation to other asset classes. It includes investment in railways, roads, power stations, hospitals, sewers, bridges, airports and so on. It usually has a low level of liquidity, but this is not a problem for many pension schemes. Some schemes are willing to bear the construction risk, while others only want to invest in completed projects. Infrastructure investment is a developing area, and currently involvement in infrastructure consortia is difficult for small and medium sized pension schemes. When investing in infrastructure debt the pension scheme can choose the seniority of their debt within the capital structure, thereby adjusting the risk and return of the investment to suit their preferences. USS has a range if infrastructure investments including a Spanish port and railway lines; tunnels and highways in Andorra, Chile, Mexico and Ireland; Heathrow airport; the rail line to Brisbane airport and UK air traffic control.

Domestic or Foreign Investment

When choosing investments, pension funds have to decide how much to invest in foreign assets, as opposed to domestic assets. Foreign investment may expose the scheme to foreign exchange risk, but is also diversifies the portfolio allowing a superior risk-return trade-off. Over the period from 1992 to 2006 Rubbaniy et al. (2014) found a substantial increase in the proportion of Dutch pension fund assets allocated to foreign investments. This trend was more pronounced among older schemes, and they equated scheme age with experience. Lippi (2016) investigated the investments made by Italian managers of Italian occupational pension funds. These schemes are DC, but the investment decisions are made by fund managers, not the members. Lippi found the Italian managers exhibited home bias (i.e. a preference for investing in domestic securities), with a significantly larger investment in Italian stocks, government debt and corporate bonds than non-Italian managers of these Italian pension funds.

Borrowing
UK pension schemes are allowed to borrow, up to a limit of 50 % of the net assets of the scheme, and in 2015 the Church of England Pensions Board issued a £100 million CPI-linked bond via a special purpose vehicle. Pension schemes can also lever their investments by investing in assets such as a highly levered property company or infrastructure. This increases both their risk and expected return.

ii. Active or Passive Fund Management
In 2004 just 12 % of the equity mandates of 2385 UK pension schemes were passive, (Blake et al. 2013b). Amongst investment professionals there is a universal belief that all markets can be beaten, and they favour active investment with its higher fees and potential for out-performance bonuses. Expecting fund managers (and investment consultants) to deny they can beat the market is like expecting turkeys to vote for Christmas. But there is strong empirical evidence that an ability to consistently beat the market is very rare. Here is a hypothetical example that demonstrates the advantages of passive fund management.

Example. Index tracker funds achieve the *gross* return on the market index, less their transaction costs (0.12 % per year in the USA) (French 2008). Since beating the index is a zero sum game, active investors as a group (who constitute all other investors) must have a *gross* return equal to the index, less their transaction costs (0.79 % per year in the USA) (French 2008). Assume the *net* returns of active investors have a normal distribution, with a mean of –0.79 % per year and a standard deviation of 5 % per year. To out-perform tracker funds an active investor needs to achieve a *net* return of –0.12 % or better (see Fig. 3.3). Assuming a normal distribution for the returns of active investors relative to the markets, the probability of a randomly selected active investor out-performing a tracker is 47 %. In this example passive management mean-variance dominates active management as shown in Table 3.12. Passive management has a higher expected return (–0.12 % > –0.79 %), and a lower standard deviation (0 < 5 %).

The total cost of investing in US equities in 2006 was $101.8 billion, or $330 for every man, woman and child in the USA (French 2008). In a study of 46 US state pension schemes, Hooke and Walters (2013) concluded that they could save $6 billion per year in fees if they used index trackers, while

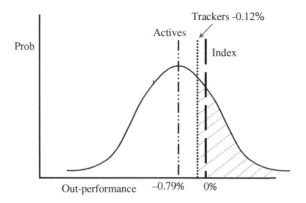

Fig. 3.3 Actives versus trackers

Table 3.12 Pay-offs from active and passive management

	$E[R]$	Std. dev.
Active management	−0.79 %	5 %
Tracker	−0.12 %	Minimal

obtaining similar or better investment returns. A subsequent study by Hooke and Walters (2015) of US states found that passive investment led to higher net returns of 1.62 % per year. Since the total assets of US state schemes in 2014 were over $3700 billion, a move to passive management would increase their assets by $60 billion per year. Clerus (2014) concluded that, for the five years ended in 2013, UK local government pension funds could have increased their value by £17.3 billion, or £3.46 billion per year, if they had used passive, rather than active, fund management.

This leads to the question of why investors engage in active investment. French (2008) has given four reasons why an investor may be active. First, the investor may be ignorant that they or their fund managers are most unlikely to consistently beat the market after allowing for transactions costs. Second, the investor may be overconfident; thinking they can beat the market, when they cannot. Third, active investment provides the opportunity to brag about active investing successes, and keep quiet about the failures. Finally, and most unusually, the investor may have a real ability to beat the market.

Bird et al. (2013) investigated why pension funds choose active management, and suggested the following additional reasons for being active investors. First, investment consultants, advisors and internal investment staff all have a vested interest in promoting active management as their jobs and bonuses largely depend on this activity. Second, pension fund managers need to be seen to be doing something to earn their fees or salary, as passivity is associated with laziness. Third, there appears to be a lack of awareness of the true costs of being active, and the true probability of achieving out-performance. Finally, there is extensive advertising of past out-performance by external fund managers. These out-performance statistics are selected to reflect well on the fund manager. This can be done by carefully choosing items such as the time period and investment fund for which performance is measured, the benchmark used, and the method for computing returns (e.g. time-weighted returns which can over-state performance). Despite the evidence that institutional investors cannot consistently beat the market, there is very little enthusiasm amongst fund managers for tracker funds.

iii. Searching for Alpha in the Wrong Place

Pension schemes allocate their funds between asset classes, possibly by conducting an ALM study (see Sect. 3.2e). The scheme may then appoint a set of specialist fund managers to invest in each of the chosen asset classes. The asset classes to which most of the money is usually allocated are large capitalisation equities (home and overseas) and sovereign bonds. The chosen fund managers are expected to generate alpha (out-performance) by active investment within their asset class (e.g. +2 % for equities). However, alpha is most likely to exist in inefficient markets, and not in large capitalisation equity and sovereign bond markets. Therefore, most of the fund's alpha bets are in highly efficient markets where they are least likely to be successful, and so the scheme (and its fund managers) are searching for alpha in the wrong place. Alpha is more likely to be found in markets where information is limited, access is difficult, liquidity is low, and the individual assets are heterogeneous. Unfortunately the depth of such markets is often small, so that even when a good opportunity is located, only a small sum of money can be invested.

iv. Hedge the Currency Risk?

The liabilities of pension schemes are in their home currency but, like any investor, pension schemes want to hold a well-diversified portfolio, and this necessitates holding a high proportion of overseas assets. This exposes pension schemes to currency risk, as eventually the foreign assets must be converted back to the home currency to pay the pensions. In 2015 USS had about £2 billion in foreign fixed interest securities, and about £15 billion in foreign equities exposing USS to £17 billion of foreign exchange risk. Investing in an overseas country involves both market risk and currency risk, and stock analysts tend to be experts on foreign companies (i.e. market risk), but are not experts in foreign currencies (forex risk). Should schemes such as USS hedge this currency risk, leaving them with just the market risk? The answer to this question partly depends on how exchange rates adjust to differences between countries in purchasing power. There are two main theories – relative purchasing power parity (PPP) and absolute PPP.

In the long run, and pension schemes are very long-term investors, relative PPP should ensure that currency changes wash out differences in inflation rates between countries. Therefore, if relative PPP applies in the long run, the currency risk to which schemes are exposed is just the non-inflation currency risk, and hedging is needed to remove this non-inflation risk. Absolute PPP applies when, in the long run, exchange rates adjust so that similar assets sell for the same price in different countries (the law of one price). If absolute PPP applies in the long run to the financial assets in which pension schemes invest, currency hedging just smooths the time path of their foreign investment returns as in the long run there is no currency risk. It also generates transactions costs as the forex hedges have to be rolled over for many years. Therefore, while hedging may smooth out the effects of short-run currency effects, in the long run it confers no benefit, but incurs costs. However, the empirical evidence in support of absolute PPP is questionable. So, to the extent that absolute PPP applies, the long-term benefits of currency hedging are questionable.

While the long-term risk-reduction benefits of hedging are questionable, there is another rather unexpected reason for forex hedging and in 2006, from being unhedged, USS decided to fully hedge its currency risk using forex forward contracts. The rationale was that, from the point of view of a sterling investor like USS, such hedging has been profitable at a rate of 2–4 % per year. This represents an anomaly and might exist because foreign exchange markets are dominated by non-discretionary traders (e.g. over 90 %). These traders need to convert to or from a foreign currency due to an unrelated transaction (e.g. buying an aircraft, selling oil). They have little discretion over the timing and direction of the trade, and so have a low sensitivity to the exchange rate. A return of 2 % on £17 billion would amount to £340 million per year for USS. If the anomaly disappears, as has been the case for other anomalies, hedging back to sterling should cost on average no more than the transactions costs.

v. Investment Consultants
DB schemes employ an investment consultant to advise on all aspects of investing the money. This includes the selection of external fund managers, where the consultant draws up a short list of fund managers to participate in a 'beauty parade' with the mandate awarded to the chosen manager. They also

offer advice on asset allocation, including asset liability modelling (ALM). For small funds, the investment consultant plays an important role in managing the money, but for very large funds with their own in-house fund management, their value is limited. For example, USS has about 100 in-house investment staff who offer advice and expertise, and three external experts who are co-opted members of the Investment Committee.

Jenkinson et al. (2013) studied the advice provided by US investment consultants to their clients on the choice of active US equity investment managers. They found the main drivers of being recommended by an investment consultant are that the fund manager: (a) has a consistent investment philosophy, (b) employs capable investment professionals, (c) has capable relationship managers, (d) makes effective presentations, and (e) has a good previous investment performance. The most important reasons for recommending a fund manager are the soft factors – investment philosophy and employing capable investment professionals – with past performance being the least important. Clients generally follow the recommendations of their investment consultants, but there is no evidence that this leads to investment out-performance.

vi. Internal or External Fund Management
There are three main types of fund manager. (a) Balanced mangers both allocate the money between the various asset classes, and select particular investments within each asset class. (b) Specialised managers select investments within a specified asset class. (c) Passive managers track a specified index for a chosen asset class. Small funds outsource the day to day investment of the money to one or more external fund managers as there are economies of scale in fund management (see Sect. 2.13). Larger funds may choose to manage some or all of the funds themselves. In 2015 USS employed six external managers to manage about a quarter of the total assets in segregated, rather than pooled, investment accounts (see Table 3.13). Some of these external fund managers are based overseas since fund management is a global business.

In-house management for USS is carried out by USSIM, a wholly owned subsidiary, who only manage funds for USS. In 2015 they managed roughly three quarters of the total USS assets, and invested this is in UK equities, overseas equities, direct property, sovereign and corporate bonds, and alternative assets. USS has varied the proportion of the total fund managed in-house both up and down; and even considered floating off the entire internal fund management operation. This is what the BT Pension Scheme did in 1997 when it created Hermes Fund Managers. This is a separate company which provides fund management services to third parties as well as to BT, and in 2014 managed

Table 3.13 USS's external fund managers in 2014

1. BlueBay Asset Mgt. (UK)	£0.4 billion in euro investment grade credit
2. Legal & General Assurance (UK)	£4.2 billion in multiple asset classes
3. Royal London Asset Mgt. (UK)	£0.4 billion in sterling investment grade credit
4. Credit Suisse (Switzerland)	£0.4 billion in emerging market debt (passive)
5. Investec (UK)	£0.4 billion in emerging market debt (active)
6. Pictet (Switzerland)	£0.4 billion in emerging market debt (active)

£26 billion for a range of clients including BT. In August 2015 the National Grid UK Pension Scheme sold off its in-house fund management company (Aerion Fund Management) which was managing £12.8 billion of assets for its parent at the time of the sale. This sale was due to the increasing complexity of liability-driven investment for a mature scheme.

Large DB schemes have to decide whether to manage their funds in-house, or to employ external fund managers. Often the decision is to use internal managers for the main asset classes, and to supplement this with external managers for assets where the in-house team lack expertise (e.g. infrastructure, private equity). The advantages and disadvantages of in-house fund management are detailed below.

Advantages of In-house Fund Management
MacIntosh and Scheibelhut (2012) used data on over 300 large pension funds from around the world to study the effects of in-house asset management on net returns. They found that, for a 10 % increase in in-house management, there is an increase of 3.6 basis points in net value added. Using a similar dataset, Beath (2015) also found in-house fund management to be beneficial. This superiority of in-house fund management may be due to a number of factors. (a) The costs of external managers are higher than those of in-house managers, provided the funds under management are substantial, because internal managers have no profit margin, no marketing expenditure and less churn, i.e. buys and sells. For example, De Roon and Slager (2012) found that the largest Dutch pension funds held their Dutch equity investments for an average of 3.5 years. (b) The costs of transitioning the money to a new external fund manager are avoided. (c) There are no conflicts of interest between the pension scheme and fund manager, giving more prospects for genuinely long-term investment decisions. (d) The in-house expertise can be used as a source of investment advice by the scheme. (e) In-house managers can vary the asset allocation on a short-term basis as market opportunities arise. For example, in

2015 the PPF announced they were moving to in-house asset management to gain greater control over asset selection, rather than to save costs.

Disadvantages of In-house Management

However, there are some disadvantages from in-house fund management: (a) higher costs for small and medium sized funds due to a lack of economies of scale in investment; (b) potentially less expertise and support than would be available to the employees of a large external fund manager; (c) no diversification of fund managers styles, risks and so on. For example, a single in-house manager may turn out to have a disastrous investment style, or to be corrupt. Having some of the money managed externally spreads these risks.

vii. Multiple Fund Managers

Using data on the investments of 2385 UK occupational pension funds managed by 364 fund managers in segregated accounts, Blake et al. (2013b, 2015) investigated two large linked changes that took place over the 1984–2005 period. These were the shift from balanced to specialist fund managers, and from single to multiple fund managers. Schemes typically started with a single balanced manager and moved to multiple specialist managers. This move from balanced to specialist managers required pension schemes to make the crucial asset allocation decision, i.e. to allocate the total fund between the various specialist managers.

A substantial number of UK DB pension schemes employ more than one fund manager (see Table 3.14), and this has a number of advantages for the scheme. First, having multiple fund managers allows access to specialist expertise in a range of asset classes. Schemes can pursue a pick and mix strategy and select the 'best of breed' for each asset class. However, since the fund's total portfolio is the sum of the portfolios held by the individual managers, if different managers are permitted to invest in the same assets, sometimes one manager may buy (say) bank shares, while another manager is selling bank shares. In this case the pension fund incurs transactions costs for no overall benefit. In addition, if two or more fund managers both decide to go overweight (under-weight) in the same set of companies, the total fund can end up with a poorly diversified portfolio. For example, two fund managers, one with an international equities mandate and another with an emerging markets mandate, may both decide to go overweight in Malaysian shares. More generally, the optimal portfolio computed across all investments differs from the aggregation of a set of separately optimised sub-portfolios, although if each fund manager is passive, there is no problem.

Second, having multiple fund managers allows the scheme to diversify the way its money is managed, for example different styles of management, as well

Table 3.14 Number of fund managers for UK equities used by UK pension schemes 2002 (Cox et al. 2007)

No. of managers	No. of schemes	No. of managers	No. of schemes
1	1334	12	5
2	466	13	0
3	208	14	1
4	128	15	10
5	57	16	4
6	60	17	0
7	17	18	0
8	15	19	2
9	13	20	15
10	4	21	0
11	11	22	3

as protecting against mis-management risk. Third, employing multiple managers for the same asset class creates competition and comparisons between them, which should lead to better performance. Finally, there is empirical evidence that very large institutional investors may experience diseconomies of scale in investment leading to lower gross returns, and so splitting the money between several managers may help to avoid such diseconomies (see Sect. 2.13). However, having multiple fund managers means that the amount of money managed by each manager is reduced, leading to slightly higher management costs, as well as the additional costs of appointing and monitoring multiple fund managers. The giant California Public Employees Retirement System (CalPERS) with $305 billion under management in June 2015 decided to reduce the number of its external fund managers from 212 to 100. In 2014 CalPERS paid $1600 million to external investment managers, and halving their number is expected to reduce both the external management fees and monitoring costs incurred by CalPERS.

Blake et al. (2013b, 2015) found that competition between multiple managers in the same asset class produces better performance, total pension fund return volatility is lower with multiple managers due to diversification across investment skills and styles out-weighing the loss of portfolio diversification benefits, and specialist fund managers out-perform balanced fund managers. Table 3.14 indicates that over 40 % of UK DB schemes use multiple managers, with 55 schemes having 10 or more managers, and 18 employing 20 or more fund managers.

viii. Appointing Fund Managers
When pension schemes appoint external fund managers they usually do so based on advice from investment consultants, after conducting a 'beauty

parade'. Parwada and Faff (2005) examined the determinants of the award of 242 mandates by Australian pension schemes. They found that the probability of being awarded a mandate increases if the manager's gross return exceeded the market return over the previous year, and for managers following an investment style (growth, value, neutral), and is reduced if the manager has a high management expense ratio. The size of the mandate, i.e. the value of the funds they are asked to manage, is larger for managers with more assets under management, who are a top-rated fund manager, who follow a style (growth, value, neutral), and (surprisingly) have higher trading costs. The size of the mandate is reduced the higher the management expense ratio is, and (surprisingly) when the fund has a top quartile ranking for gross returns over the past three years.

Empirical studies have found a strong positive relationship between the past performance of fund managers and the flows to them of new money. This relationship may be due to investors, such as pension funds, expecting past performance to persist, or because past performance can be used to justify the choice of fund manager, even though investors do not think performance persists. Jenkinson et al. (2013) found evidence that, if a fund manager is recommended by an investment consultant, this leads to increased fund flows from pension schemes to that fund manager; and this may be because pension schemes expect recommended fund managers to out-perform, or because they see a consultant's recommendation as a justification for choosing the manager. These two alternative explanations were investigated by Jones and Martinez (2015).

Using data on the expectations of pension schemes and consultants of the future performance of 232 US fund managers, Jones and Martinez (2015) investigated the factors determining the flow of funds to fund managers. They found that expected performance is a positive function of past performance, changes in consultants' recommendations, and some service and soft factors. However actual performance is not a function of these variables, and is unaffected by expected performance and the service and soft factors. Therefore, by basing their expectations of future performance on past performance and service and soft factors, pension schemes appear to be behaving irrationally. Jones and Martinez found that the flow of new funds from pension schemes to fund managers is a positive function of past performance and changes in consultants' recommendations. Expected performance has only a marginal effect on fund flows, implying that funds are allocated to fund managers who did well in the past, rather than those expected by pension schemes to do well in the future. This means that the choice of fund manager is primarily made using factors which can be used to justify the decision, and not because the pension scheme thinks the chosen fund manager will actually produce superior performance.

ix. Dismissing Fund Managers

An important decision that a pension scheme must take is whether to dismiss an external fund manager. In a study of 237 US DB schemes Asthana and Lipka (2002) found that they tend to dismiss a fund manager when the manger's performance in the previous year is below their benchmark. This raises the question of when is the performance by a fund manager bad enough to warrant sacking, and bearing the costs of transitioning the money to a replacement fund manager? The costs of transitioning can be considerable. When USS transitioned about £9.5 billion to new fund managers in February 2004 the cost was estimated to be £50 million but, due to favourable market conditions, was actually about £20 million. Despite the costs of transitioning, USS has parted company with the following fund managers: Goldman Sachs Asset Management (UK equities), Legal and General Assurance (corporate bonds), Henderson Global Investors (enhanced index tracking), Baillie Gifford (balanced manager), Schroders (balanced manager), Wellington (international equities), HSBC (index tracking) and Capital International (international equities).

In a study of 2385 UK pension schemes Blake et al. (2013b) found that, in the year before replacing an equity fund manager, on average they underperformed their benchmark, while in the subsequent year their replacement's performance exceeded the benchmark. This supports the view that short-term under-performance leads to dismissal, and replacing fund managers is beneficial to the scheme in the short run. After the appointment of an additional fund manager Blake et al. (2013b) show that a new manager's share of the total assets of the pension scheme tends to rise over the next 15 years as the scheme learns about the skills of the new manager.

A US study by Goyal and Wahil (2008) investigated the reasons for terminating an external fund manager, and these are summarised in Table 3.15. About three quarters of the terminations were for reasons connected with the behaviour of the fund manager, with only a quarter due to scheme related issues. The most important reason was poor performance, which accounted for over half of terminations; followed by a decision of the sponsor to reallocate the fund across asset classes.

Given market fluctuations, in some periods fund managers will underperform. The difficult question for the pension scheme is how long should a scheme endure under-performance, relative to the specified benchmark, before dismissing a fund manager? A number of periods of poor performance may be just a run of bad luck, or it may signal a lack of ability. At any point in time a pension scheme has a number of observations on the performance of a fund manager, and the length of this time series increases over time. So gradually the pension scheme accumulates more information on the ability

Table 3.15 Reasons given by US pension funds for terminating fund managers (Goyal and Wahil 2008)

Fund manager related:	
Performance	52 %
Staff changes at fund manager	9 %
Regulatory breach by the fund manager	9 %
Merger of the fund manager	4 %
Scheme related:	
Re-allocation across asset classes	20 %
Re-organisation of the sponsor	6 %
Total	100 %

of the fund manager, i.e. the size of the sample increases. This sample can be used to estimate the manager's ability, and the more sample observations are available, the more accurately this can be estimated. Increasing the sample size (n years) reduces the standard deviation of the sample mean (σ_m) according to the formula $\sigma_m = \sigma/\sqrt{n}$, where σ is the standard deviation of the sample returns. This will be illustrated using a hypothetical example.

Assume the standard deviation of the sample observations (σ) is 5 %, returns have a normal distribution, and significance is required at the 5 % level. Figure 3.4 shows that returns have a normal distribution around the fund managers benchmark. A difference of two standard deviations or more from this benchmark is taken to indicate a statistically significant result, i.e. that the fund manager has under- or out-performed their benchmark. Table 3.16 shows that, as the sample size increases, the standard deviation of the sample mean decreases, and so smaller deviations from the benchmark are statistically significant. Figure 3.5 indicates that this relationship is non-linear, with the first few observations leading to the biggest reduction in the required deviation.

Typically, three years' results or less are used to judge a fund manager, which often means there are not enough observations to detect statistically significance under-performance. This use of small samples is driven by the substantial costs that under-performance can cause. If the funds under management are £2.5 billion, three years of 5.78 % under-performance would cost the scheme £460 million. To avoid such losses, funds tend to sack mangers before statistical significance at the 5 % level has been reached. Other criteria for dismissal and appointment include whether the fund manager has a convincing investment decision-making process, whether they are following the conditions of their mandate, and whether they employ good quality staff to manage the portfolio. Schemes such as USS have employed Inalytics to analyse the trading patterns of their fund managers with the aim of answering

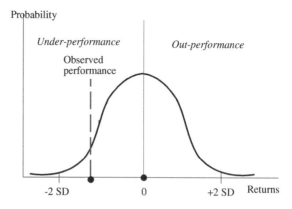

Fig. 3.4   Significant under-performance?

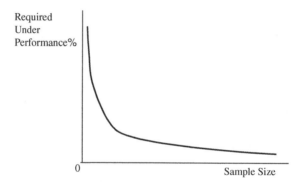

Fig. 3.5   Dismissing fund managers

Table 3.16   Sample size and significance level

Sample size (n)	Std. dev. of the sample mean (σ_m)	5 % sig. level ($2\sigma_m$)
1	$5/\sqrt{1} = 5.00\ \%$	10.00 %
2	$5/\sqrt{2} = 3.54\ \%$	7.08 %
3	$5/\sqrt{3} = 2.89\ \%$	5.78 %
9	$5/\sqrt{9} = 1.67\ \%$	3.34 %
100	$5/\sqrt{100} = 0.50\ \%$	1.00 %

two questions: do the fund managers' over- and under-weight bets pay off, and how does the share price move in the months before and after their purchases and sales? This analysis can reveal trading strengths and weaknesses, and assist in appraising fund managers' performance.

On very rare occasions, not only has a pension scheme terminated a fund manager's contract, but has also sued them for damages caused by poor performance. Carol Galley (known as the ice maiden) was the senior vice-chairman of Mercury Asset Management (MAM), subsequently taken over by Merrill Lynch. MAM managed £4 billion of assets for the Unilever Superannuation Fund. MAM's portfolio manager was Alistair Lennard aged 27, a graduate in accounting and finance from Manchester University. Lennard reduced the Unilever portfolio to just 36 shares. The mandate was to out-perform the FTSE All Share index by 1 %, with a maximum under-performance of 3 %. In fact for 1996–97 MAM under-performed the index by 10.5 %; one of the worst performances of any of the 1600 funds monitored by Wood Mackenzie (WM). In 2001 Wendy Mayall, the chief investment officer of the Unilever Superannuation Fund, issued a writ against MAM for damages of £130 million. She argued that the money managed by MAM for Unilever was insufficiently diversified, and thereby exposed to excessive risk. After two days of the court case, it was settled out of court when MAM agreed to pay Unilever £70 million plus costs (Blake 2003, pp. 538–547).

x. Rewards and Incentives for Fund Managers
Each external fund manager negotiates a mandate, which is a contract that sets out terms under which they manage the money, and this includes the reward system. For example USS pays fund managers a flat fee, supplemented by a performance-related bonus. The bonus is usually based on out-performance of some specified benchmark (e.g. the return on the FTSE 100 +2 % for a UK equity mandate). This situation clearly raises agency problems, as the fund manager may not do what is in the best interests of the pension fund, but what will maximise the fund manager's bonus. Usually a bonus is paid for out-performance, but no penalty is charged for under-performance, so fund managers have an incentive to increase return volatility and therefore the frequency of out-performance events. To deal with the agency problem considerable care needs to be exercised in drawing up such mandates. One way to reduce these agency problems is to pay the bonus retrospectively for out-performance over (say) a five-year period. Introducing penalties (besides termination) for under-performance has also been suggested. In-house fund managers are usually similarly rewarded by a basic salary and a bonus scheme based on out-performance of some benchmark. There are still agency problems, but since these managers are directly employed by the scheme, they are lower.

xi. Paying Active Fees for Passive Management

Fund managers are required to out-perform the benchmark for their asset class (e.g. +2 % for equities). Searching for alpha by engaging in active management is costly, and will usually involve employing staff to collect and analyse data, interview company managers and so on. Fund managers can simply raise the beta value of their portfolio, for example by a derivatives overlay such as a long position in stock index options or futures. This will increase the expected return to the required level at very little cost, although it will also increase the risk. Increasing beta requires no skill or effort by the fund manager, yet the pension scheme is still charged an active management fee for passive fund management. Such behaviour can be discouraged by monitoring the actions of the fund managers, for example are they actively trading or simply using a derivatives overlay. SCM Private (2013) have investigated the extent to which active UK and US retail equity funds are, in fact, closet trackers. The active proportion of a portfolio is defined as the sum of the absolute values of the over- and under-weights, relative to the index, divided by two. The score for exactly tracking the index is 0 %, and the maximum score for a fund that does not hold any shares in the index is 100 % (Cremers and Petajisto 2009). Using an active proportion of 70 % as the cut-off point for active investment, SCM Private found that 76 % of UK active funds are closet trackers, as against only 35 % in the USA. UK investors pay active management fees of roughly three times those of an index fund, and so UK investors are being overcharged by roughly £800 million per year. In a study of 24,492 open ended mutual funds and exchange traded funds from 32 countries, Cremers et al. (2015) found that 20 % had an active share below 60 %, and were classified as closet indexers. They also found evidence that regulatory changes favouring a switch from DB to DC pensions are associated with increases in the active shares of active managers, and a decrease in their fees.

xii. Fiduciary Management

Fiduciary management is a new approach to managing pension fund assets which originated in the USA in 2002. It spread to the Netherlands, and by 2011 about 89 % of Dutch pension assets were subject to fiduciary management, while the corresponding figure for the UK was only 6 % (Shackleton 2011). Fiduciary management may be full or partial, where partial fiduciary management occurs when not all the assets are placed under fiduciary management, or only some functions are delegated. A survey of UK fiduciary managers in 2014 by KPMG found that full fiduciary management applied to 5 % of UK DB schemes, representing 3.4 % of UK DB assets. The total value of the assets under fiduciary management in the UK in 2015 was £114 billion (620 schemes), of which £54 billion (382 schemes) was subject to full fiduciary management (KPMG 2015). Fiduciary management occurs when a pension scheme delegates the management of its pension assets to an external company which provides a one-stop shop for the management of the scheme's assets. Instead of the scheme appointing external fund managers, a custodian, a performance measurement company, and so on, these tasks are performed or sub-contracted to others by the fiduciary manager. The fiduciary manager may also set the performance benchmarks and the long-term asset allocation of the fund. Fiduciary management leads to faster decision making, and to a single composite report to the pension scheme on the management of the pension assets. It can lead to lower costs, as the fiduciary manager drives down the fees of the companies with whom it sub-contracts; but it can also lead to higher fees as the fiduciary manger needs to be rewarded. There is the risk that a bad fiduciary manager can blight the entire asset portfolio, while (say) a single bad external fund manager will have a smaller adverse effect on the total fund. Finally, because the fiduciary manager charges a single fee, it is difficult for pension scheme trustees to access the value for money of the various sub-contracts awarded by the fiduciary manager, i.e. to monitor the performance of the fiduciary manager. KPMG found that in 2015, 13 % of the schemes with a fiduciary manager went to the additional expense of employing independent advisors to monitor their fiduciary manager.

xiii. Corporate Governance and Socially Responsible Investment (SRI)
Concern about how companies are run (corporate governance) and how their actions affect their employees, customers, suppliers and the environment has grown in recent years. Pension schemes are major institutional investors, and UK pension schemes are among the world's leaders on these issues. Because they are shareholders, pension schemes can use their votes to change company policy, red line (or rule out) owning shares in certain companies, or engage with the company's management in private discussions to change corporate behaviour. Most pension schemes delegate corporate governance and SRI to their fund managers (Tilba and McNulty 2013). However, USS is a world leader in corporate governance and SRI and conducts its own corporate governance and SRI.

USS has an in-house team of six staff who deal with all such issues relating to the shares it owns (USS has shares in about 2000 companies). USS prefers engagement with companies in private, rather than not investing or divesting (red lining), or voting for motions critical of current company policy. However, when engagement fails and electoral victory looks possible, USS will use their voting rights to try to change company policy. To successfully change company policy by engagement or voting usually requires action by a substantial proportion of a company's shareholders, and this calls for collective action. To this end, USS staff form and lead many groups of like-minded shareholders in taking co-operative action, e.g. the Enhanced Analytics Initiative which aimed to incorporate corporate governance and SRI into the research provided by stockbrokers, the Institutional Investors Group on Climate Change, the Marathon Club which promoted long-term investment, the Pharmaceutical Shareowners Group, the Long Term Investment Competition which was run in co-operation with the Financial Times and Hewitt Bacon and Woodrow (Bridgeland 2005), US corporate governance, and EU Auditing Standards.

USS is a world leader in corporate governance and SRI because it has some important advantages over many other institutional investors. First, the scheme members (academics) are very keen on these issues. They formed 'Ethics for USS' to pressure USS into taking action to improve its corporate governance and SRI activities. This organisation evolved into 'Fair Pensions' and then into 'ShareAction'. Second, since universities are not commercial organisations, they have little to fear from crossing swords with major corporations by engaging with them and, if necessary, voting against the board. Third, as a large long-term investor (a 'universal' investor in all large companies), USS has a financial interest in ensuring that all companies take sensible long-term decisions. In addition, as trustees it is their fiduciary duty to take such important factors into account when making investment decisions. Finally, USS has employees and trustees who are very keen to develop a leadership role in this area. Some other large UK DB pension schemes are also active in corporate governance and SRI.

xiv. Derivatives

Subject to their SIP, pension schemes are free to use derivatives. For example, USS uses derivatives such as index futures and options, but this is the exception rather than the rule, and until recently the USS SIP stated that derivatives could only be used for hedging, not speculation. Hedging requires that USS hold an offsetting position of at least the size of the derivatives hedge. An increasing number of schemes are using derivatives to hedge interest rate risk, and the use of longevity swaps has also increased in popularity.

xv. Benchmarks

Benchmarks are used to judge investment performance and reward fund managers. The Myners report (Myners 2001) recommended that pension funds shift from using peer group benchmarks to customised scheme specific benchmarks. For example, USS used to benchmark itself against the 50 largest UK

Table 3.17 USS total fund benchmark in 2007

FTSE 100 (equities)	40 %
MSCI Americas (equities)	12 %
MSCI Europe ex UK (equities)	12 %
MSCI Japan (equities)	8 %
MSCI Pacific ex Japan (equities)	8 %
Citi World Government Bonds 10+ years	10 %
IPD index (property)	10 %
Total	100 %

pension funds in the WM universe (the WM50), but switched to a set of asset specific indices weighted by the chosen asset allocation, all hedged back to sterling. While returns on (say) US equities can be directly compared with the MSCI Americas index, exchange rates are needed to compute the total return on all the assets of the fund as they are measured in a range of currencies. For the total fund the weighted benchmark in 2007 appears in Table 3.17.

When a liability driven investment strategy is adopted, the benchmark shifts from beating the market to beating the liabilities. However, as Table 3.17 suggests, it is much easier to benchmark against asset markets than against the liabilities, as the liabilities for each scheme are unique and their value is problematic (see Sect. 1.6b). This can be tackled by setting the asset allocation using an ALM (see Sect. 3.2e) which includes the liabilities. Then the performance of investments within each asset class can be judged against an index for that asset class. There are some difficulties in selecting asset specific benchmarks, as no market data is available for unquoted investments. In addition, when considering the total return on the fund, allowing for derivatives is a problem as no money is invested. To address this problem, the Chartered Financial Analysts' (CFA) Global Investment Performance Standards (GIPS) offer a procedure for including derivatives in performance measurement.

d. Asset Allocation and the 'Cult of the Equity'[1]

Asset allocation involves setting asset proportions for the various asset classes, such as equities (domestic and foreign), bonds (domestic and foreign) and others (property, cash, commodities, hedge funds, currencies, private equity, small companies, infrastructure, emerging markets, etc.). It is much more important than the selection of the investments within each asset class (e.g. nine times more important). The 'cult of the equity' means investing a large proportion of the funds in equities, and UK DB pension funds have historically followed this cult.

---

[1] This section is based on Sutcliffe (2005).

Until after the Second World War UK pension schemes invested very largely in government bonds. In 1947 George Ross Goobey liquidated all the bonds held by the Imperial Tobacco Pension Fund, and invested entirely in equities. His views caused great controversy, and he was barred by the Institute of Actuaries from teaching students about investment. The spread of the cult of the equity was initially restricted because some schemes were banned from investing in equities (e.g. local authority schemes until 1961). However, by 1957 20 % of UK pension funds were invested in equities, and by 1964 this had risen to 37 %. Table 3.18 has the equity proportions for UK pension funds from 1975 to 2002, which peaked in 1994 at 79.5 %. In the mid-1990s UK pension schemes had the highest equity proportion in the world by a considerable margin.

A number of arguments have been advanced to justify the cult of the equity, and the first entails the risk premium. Over the long run equities have a higher expected return than bonds. But this is offset by their higher risks. If risk-adjusted returns on equities exceeded those on bonds it would imply the end of the bond market, as no-one would buy bonds. Some people argue that as pension schemes are long-term investors, over the long run the ups and downs tend to cancel out (mean reversion), and the risks of investing in the equity market are reduced (time diversification). Therefore risks are lower for long-term than for short-term investments, and so the risk premium is higher for long-term investors such as pension schemes. This view encourages them to increase their investment in equities. However, the existence of time

Table 3.18 Equity proportions for UK pension funds

Year	WM All Funds[a]%	Year	WM All Funds[a]%
1975	47.6	1989	67.8
1976	59.7	1990	74.7
1977	52.3	1991	71.9
1978	53.9	1992	77.7
1979	52.8	1993	79.0
1980	49.5	1994	79.5
1981	53.8	1995	76.7
1982	56.2	1996	76.0
1983	58.0	1997	75.2
1984	60.6	1998	72.8
1985	63.0	1999	70.8
1986	65.5	2000	74.5
1987	69.9	2001	71.6
1988	68.4	2002	70.6

[a]The WM All Funds universe accounts for over 75 % of all segregated UK pension fund assets

diversification and different risk premia for short and long-term investors is unproven, and is suspect as a justification for the cult of the equity.

Second, it has been claimed that equity returns match liability returns, so hedging a pension scheme's risks. DB liabilities are subject to four main risks – salary risk, inflation risk, discount rate risk and longevity risk. The empirical evidence that equity returns hedge salary risk is very weak. Equities are a moderately good hedge for long-run inflation, but better instruments are available. If the return on investments is used as the discount rate, equities are an excellent instrument for hedging discount rate risk. But the discount rate should be similar to the return on bonds, and equities are not a good hedging instrument for bond returns (see Sect. 1.6b). Finally, the available evidence indicates that equities have zero correlation with longevity (Rosenfeld 2009).

A third argument used to justify the cult of the equity is that, if a DB pension scheme becomes under-funded, an immature scheme has plenty of time for the sponsor to make higher contributions to the fund to remove this under-funding. Therefore the higher investment risk flowing from the cult falls on the sponsor, not the members and pensioners as the increase in default risk is minimal. However, while it is correct that the sponsor has more time to fund an immature scheme, when the stock market is down, it may also be a bad time for the sponsor to make higher contributions as their profits may also be down.

Fourth, the traditional investment advice offered to individuals who are investing directly or deciding the asset allocation for their own DC scheme is for the young to invest mostly in equities, and for the old to invest mostly in bonds. The principal reason for this advice is that young people have plenty of time to remedy any losses, while those near retirement do not. This strategy can be implemented by life-cycle (or lifestyle or target date) investing, where the asset allocation moves from equities to bonds as the member ages. However this advice for individuals is wrongly applied to pension schemes, to leads to the advice that an immature scheme should invest in equities. DB pension schemes are legal entities not living beings, and have a potentially infinite life. Therefore this simple life-cycle analysis does not apply to pension schemes.

The fifth justification for the cult of the equity is that, until recently, actuaries valued equities and bonds, not at their current market value, but at the present value of the expected dividend stream or coupons. Since dividends are much more stable than share prices, this smoothed the valuation of equities, making them appear less risky than they really are, and encouraging equity investment.

A sixth justification for the cult of the equity is the selection of the discount rate. This is the key choice when valuing the liabilities of a DB pension scheme. Traditionally in the UK and USA the discount rate is the expected rate of return on the assets of the pension fund. Where the fund has a high equity content, this can lead to a high discount rate, and a low valuation of the liabilities. Therefore, a welcome side effect of the cult of the equity, coupled with the use of the expected investment return as the discount rate, is to reduce the value of scheme liabilities. If assets are valued in the traditional way by actuaries, switching assets from bonds to equities increases their value! This contradicts Modigliani and Miller's first proposition which says that the way the money is split between bonds and equities has no effect on the value of the firm (or pension fund). The discount rate ought to be the rate of return on an asset that replicates the risk and return of the liabilities (see Sect. 1.6b). Since the probability of default on the liabilities is low, the appropriate discount rate will usually be just a bit higher than the riskless rate.

Seventh, the cult of the equity may increase the reported earnings of the sponsor, and this is for two reasons. First, investing in equities should, on average, generate the risk premium; leading to higher reported earnings for the sponsor. But the equity risk premium is not a free lunch, as it leads to higher risk. Second, if the expected return on the fund is used as the discount rate, the cult of the equity increases the discount rate used to value the liabilities. This reduces their magnitude, resulting in a stronger-looking balance sheet for the sponsor. However, the introduction of FRS 17 in the UK in 2003 required the use of the corporate bond rate as the discount rate when preparing the published accounts, removing this incentive for the cult of the equity.

Sponsors and fund managers are subject to competitive pressures, and these provide the eighth justification for the cult of the equity. First, if the pension schemes of a firm's competitors are following the cult of the equity, their rivals will, on average, be able to report higher accounting profits than otherwise. This puts pressure on the firm to match the reported profits of its rivals by adopting the cult of the equity. Second, UK pension funds are managed mainly by external fund managers, and this has led to fierce competition between fund managers to win mandates. An important factor when awarding mandates is the previous investment performance of the fund manager (see Sect. 3.2c(viii)), and to improve their performance statistics and win mandates UK fund managers are incentivised to invest in equities with their greater scope for out-performance of the benchmark. Finally, active equity investment also offers higher fund management fees to external fund managers.

The final justification for the cult of the equity is the creation of pension insurance schemes such as the PBGC and the PPF. Where the insurance scheme levy fails to reflect the riskiness of the scheme's investments, it is a heads I win, tails you lose situation (see Sect. 4.5c(i)). This has created a moral hazard which encourages schemes to invest in risky assets, i.e. some of the downside risks are shifted onto the insurer, while the higher expected returns benefit the sponsor.

Pursuit of the cult of the equity has the implication that the pension scheme is speculating on the spread between the returns on equities and debt, i.e. the risk premium. In theory, assuming there are no legal impediments or market imperfections, a fully funded pension scheme with 100 % equities could be modified by: (a) borrowing a sum of money sufficient to buy securities to hedge all the risks of the scheme's liabilities and (b) investing this borrowed money in a liability-matching portfolio, so that the pension scheme's risk is fully hedged. So, in addition to its initial assets and liabilities, the scheme now also has a short position in debt, and a long position of equal value invested in a liability-matching portfolio. Since the scheme liabilities are assumed to be fully hedged by the liability-matching portfolio, the net position of the scheme is the initial long position in equities and the short position in debt (see Table 3.19). This demonstrates that pursuit of the cult of the equity is equivalent to the pension scheme deliberately speculating with what is usually a large sum of money on the spread between the returns on debt and the stock market. This spread ratio will be unity if, as assumed in Table 3.19, the scheme is initially fully funded and the value of the debt equals that of the equities. In effect, the pension fund has become a profit centre, rather than trying to accumulate funds to meet the pension promise, and this is not a sensible strategy. The pension scheme is ancillary to the sponsor's main business, and pension schemes lack the expertise to 'beat the market' as they are not fund managers. If they hire external fund managers, these companies have no incentive to hand over super-normal profits to their customers, and will extract any such profits via fund management fees.

In recent years the cult of the equity has died. The reasons for this change include: (a) the sharp falls in equity prices which automatically reduced the proportionate share of equities in a scheme's total assets, (b) the removal of tax relief on the dividends of UK companies made UK equities less attractive

Table 3.19 Replication of the cult of the equity

	Initial portfolio	Additional portfolio	Final portfolio
Equities	Long	–	Long
Liabilities	Short	–	*Short*
Liability-matching portfolio	–	Long	*Long*
Debt	–	Short	Short

(see Sect. 2.2b.6), (c) the increasing maturity of UK schemes leading to more investment in bonds, (d) a re-evaluation of the risks of equities and (e) doubts about the size of the equity risk premium. In the absence of risk sharing, taxation and default insurance, which are discussed in Sect. 4.6, there is no powerful argument for DB pension schemes to invest in equities. The asset allocation decision requires making a trade-off between risk and return, and a good way of doing this is by using asset liability models (ALM) (see Sect. 3.2e).

e. Asset-Liability Models (ALM)

A DB pension scheme has a portfolio of both assets (the pension fund) and liabilities (the accrued pension benefits), where the liabilities are exogenous so far as the asset allocation decision is concerned. This problem can be viewed as essentially a portfolio problem applied to both the assets and liabilities of the scheme, where the liabilities are fixed. Alternatively this problem can be seen as constructing an asset portfolio which hedges the fixed liability risk. The objective of this hedge is not necessarily risk minimisation, as some pension schemes may be willing to accept a chosen level of risk in order to benefit from the risk premium and a reduction in the sponsor's contributions to the scheme. Recently some DB schemes have been targeting 'self-sufficiency'. Definitions differ, but self-sufficiency usually means there is a very low probability of the sponsor being required to make additional payments beyond the agreed employer's contribution rate. Self-sufficiency could be achieved when there is 100 % funding on a buyout basis (i.e. the valuation an insurance company would use in a buyout), and the pension scheme has minimal investment risk. In this situation there should be only a very small chance of deficits, and the sponsor will only have to make the agreed employer's contribution rate payments to the scheme.

There are many ways of classifying the ALM problem, for example (a) one-period or multi-period models, (b) discrete time or continuous time models, and (c) fixed asset mix or variable asset mix multi-period models. There are also a variety of techniques available for solving ALM problems, and these include: (a) stochastic programming, (b) dynamic stochastic control models, (c) stochastic simulation models, (d) robust optimisation and (e) portfolio theory.

An example of a simple one-period portfolio theory ALM applied to USS is Board and Sutcliffe (2007). This provides an illustration of an ALM approach introduced by Sharpe and Tint (1990), and is easy to formulate and solve because it uses a modified Markowitz portfolio model to compute the efficiency frontier facing the pension scheme. Because the sponsor and its pension scheme are viewed as a single entity (see Sect. 4.1), the portfolio problem should include the assets and liabilities of the sponsor, as well as those of the pension scheme. However, in the case of USS the correlations between the assets and liabilities of the sponsors (UK universities) and those of USS are very low, and are not incorporated in the model.

Board and Sutcliffe divided the liabilities into three categories – active members, deferred pensioners and pensioners and have fixed proportions. The expanded Markowitz portfolio model, including the three different types of liability, is:-

Minimise	$$V_{al} = \sum_{i=1}^{N+B} \sum_{j=1}^{N+B} x_i\, x_j\, V_{ij}$$	(a) Risk (assets and liabilities)
Subject to	$$E_a = \sum_{i=1}^{N} x_i\, E_i$$	(b) Expected return on assets
	$$\sum_{i=1}^{N} x_i = 1$$	(c) Sum to one (assets)
	$x_i \geq 0 \qquad i = 1...N$	(d) Non-negative assets
	$x_i = w_i, \qquad i = N+1...N+B$	(e) Fixed liabilities

Where V_{al} is the variance of the asset-liability portfolio; i and j represent asset or liability classes; N is the number of assets and B the number of liabilities; V_{ij} are covariances of returns between asset or liability classes i and j; E_i and E_a are the expected arithmetic returns on asset or liability class i and the chosen asset portfolio respectively; w_i are the initial portfolio proportions of the B types of scheme liability, which are assumed fixed; and x_i are the investment proportions in each of the $N+B$ asset or liability classes. Thus, for the three types of liability $w_1 = -L_0^1/A_0$ $w_2 = -L_0^2/A_0$, and $w_3 = -L_0^3/A_0$; where: L_0^1 represents the current liability to active members; L_0^2 is the current liability to deferred pensioners; L_0^3 represents the current liability of pensions in payment; and A_0 is the current value of the fund's assets.

Since the liabilities are fixed, the liability returns are not needed, and only the asset returns need be considered in equation (b). Using forecasts of returns, variances and covariances, Board and Sutcliffe employed quadratic programming to derive the efficient frontier for both the ALM including the liabilities, and for the assets only model of USS for the purposes of comparison. These two frontiers are plotted in Fig. 3.6, and the details of the portfolios underlying these frontiers appear in Table 3.20. As can be seen in Fig. 3.6, including the liabilities in the portfolio problem moves the efficient frontier downwards and to the left.

Besides the means and standard deviations, and the asset proportions for the asset-liability portfolios, Table 3.20 also shows the Ederington (1979) measure of hedging effectiveness (*E*). This gives the reduction in the variance of the asset-liability portfolio, relative to the variance of the scheme's liabilities. It shows that the best hedge occurs for portfolios 4 and 5, which offer a 53 % reduction in risk. In contrast, for portfolios 9–11 and the actual portfolio held by USS, the risk of the hedged portfolio exceeds that of the liabilities alone, so that the fund faces extra asset risk, in addition to the risk of its liabilities alone.

The expected return for portfolios 1 and 2 for the assets and liabilities together is negative; a fact obscured if only the asset returns are considered. Figure 3.6 and the results in Table 3.20 also demonstrate the interaction between assets and liabilities in the model, as the asset-liability frontier is not simply a linear transformation of the assets-only frontier (e.g. each point on the asset frontier shifted the same distance to the south west). For example, the risk-minimising portfolio for the asset-liability model is portfolio 4, while for the assets-only portfolio it is portfolio 2. The expected return on the assets in the assets-only risk-minimising portfolio (no. 4) is 4.24 %, which compares with a discount rate of 5.5 % used in computing the actuarial liabilities. The asset-liability results reveal that portfolios 1, 2 and 3 are dominated by the risk-minimising portfolio, while the assets-only results incorrectly suggest that only portfolio 1 is dominated. Similarly, the slopes of the two efficient

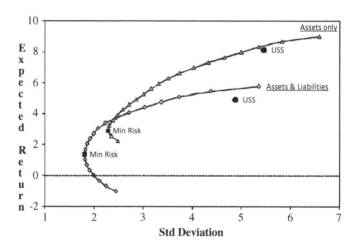

Fig. 3.6 Assets only and assets and liabilities efficient frontiers

Table 3.20 Efficient portfolios – returns, standard deviations and asset proportions

	Assets (%)		Asset-liability (%)			Efficient asset proportions (%)				
	E[R]	SD	E[R]	SD	E	UK equities	Overseas equities	Property	Fixed Interest gilts	Index linked
1	2.20	2.500	-1.03	2.454	15	0.0	0.0	0.0	0.0	100.0
2	2.88	2.335	-0.35	2.112	37	0.0	0.0	2.1	20.7	77.2
3	3.56	2.452	0.33	1.916	48	0.0	0.2	9.4	31.9	58.5
4	4.24	2.676	1.01	1.823	53	0.0	3.2	15.3	39.0	42.6
5	4.92	2.940	1.69	1.828	53	4.4	3.2	20.2	43.8	28.3
6	5.60	3.234	2.37	1.921	48	9.1	3.2	25.1	48.6	14.0
7	6.28	3.550	3.05	2.090	38	13.8	3.2	30.0	53.0	0.0
8	6.96	4.057	3.73	2.452	15	27.8	5.3	31.8	35.1	0.0
9	7.64	4.679	4.41	3.036	-30	41.7	7.5	33.6	17.2	0.0
10	8.32	5.367	5.09	3.742	-97	56.4	9.6	34.0	0.0	0.0
11	9.00	6.599	5.77	5.360	-305	88.9	11.1	0.0	0.0	0.0
USS	8.12	5.462	4.89	4.070	-133	53.1	21.0	11.4	11.8	2.7

frontiers differ, and the correct risk-return trade-off facing the pension scheme for any specified rate of return (or risk) is that provided by the asset-liability results, not the assets only results. This confirms the view that any pension scheme should adopt an asset-liability analysis, rather than attempting to consider the asset allocation separately from the liabilities.

Since pension liabilities are effectively inflation linked annuities, index linked bonds are a good hedging instrument, although final salary and longevity risk remain. However, the low returns on such bonds increases the expected cost of the pension scheme, relative to holding equities, and the pension scheme trustees must decide on their preferred risk-return trade-off.

It is widely accepted that the discount rate for valuing the benefits the members and pensioners are expected to receive is the rate of return on assets with the same risk and expected return (see Sect. 1.6b). Inkmann et al. (forthcoming) have argued that the risk of the liabilities being met depends on the asset allocation of the pension fund, as well as the scheme's funding ratio and the strength of the sponsor's covenant. Since an ALM requires the liabilities to be valued, and this valuation depends on the discount rate, which in turn depends on the scheme's chosen asset allocation, the discount rate should be determined within the ALM, and not pre-specified. Hence the problem is circular, and Inkmann et al. solve this using simulation; assuming that scheme beneficiaries, and therefore the scheme, have a log utility function. As a result, the asset allocation and discount rate are chosen to generate outcomes which suit the beneficiaries. Inkmann et al. ignore the insurance provided by the PBGC because the PBGC itself is also subject to default risk. In addition, default is a situation members wish to avoid, with intervention by the PBGC associated with a reduction in benefits and unemployment.

In 2005 USS employed their investment consultants, Mercers, to conduct an ALM analysis. This study, which relied on stochastic simulation, led to a very substantial change in the USS asset allocation. USS reaffirmed its commitment to a high risk exposure (e.g. 80 % equities), but decided to substitute £5 billion of alternative assets for equity, giving a new long-term target asset allocation of roughly 60 % equities, 20 % alternative investments, 10 % bonds and 10 % property. The rationale was that, while alternative assets had similar risk and return to equities, they provided additional diversification benefits. This change in the asset allocation took many years to achieve as USS assets were slowly moved from equities to a wide range of alternative assets.

There are many other techniques for conducting an ALM, and Platanakis and Sutcliffe (forthcoming) compared the results of applying a variety of one-period portfolio models to USS. These are the Sharpe and Tint model used by Board and Sutcliffe (2007), Bayes-Stein estimation, the Black-Litterman model and robust estimation, and the actual USS investment decisions. The investment selection objective, which provides the risk-return trade-off, was to maximise the Sharpe ratio. Over a 144-month out-of-sample period, robust optimisation was superior to the other three methods and to the actual allocations across 20 performance criteria, with a remarkably stable asset allocation – essentially fix mix.

While most ALM studies are focused on the asset allocation decision, more general models of DB schemes can be built to investigate the likely outcomes of altering the scheme design. Platanakis and Sutcliffe (2016) quantified the redistributive effects of the major rule change by USS in 2011. USS closed its final salary scheme to new members, opened a CARE section, and moved to 'cap and share' contribution rates. Platanakis and Sutcliffe modelled the operation of USS for the next 54 years (e.g. the asset allocation and contribution rate decisions) and the effects on the pensions wealth of different age cohorts of the membership. This was done using a VAR(1,1) model to generate 5000 scenarios of future asset returns, inflation rates and salary increases. The asset allocation was set in one of three ways – risk shifting, risk management and fix mix (see Sect. 4.5c(i)). The pre-2011 USS scheme was not viable in the long run, while the post-2011 scheme was probably viable in the long run, but faced medium-term problems. Future members of USS lost 65 % of their pension wealth (or roughly £100,000 per head), equivalent to a reduction of roughly 11 % in their total compensation, while those aged over 57 years lost almost nothing. The riskiness of the pension wealth of future members increased by a third, while the riskiness of the present value of the sponsor's future contributions reduced by 10 %. Finally, the sponsor's wealth increased by about £32.5 billion, equivalent to a reduction of 26 % in their pension costs.

f. Restrictions on Investment

Some countries place legal restrictions on the asset allocation of pension funds. They may impose maximum weights on investment in particular asset classes, limit investment in the sponsor, rule out short sales, outlaw the use of derivatives and prevent specified levels of risk being exceeded. They may also ban pension schemes from borrowing money. For example, in 2007 Greek pension funds could not invest more than 23 % of their funds in domestic equities, property and mutual funds, while investment outside Greece was not allowed. Poland had an upper limit of 5 % on foreign assets and banned investment in property, Mexico and Korea had a limit of 20 % on foreign assets, and Hungary had a limit of 30 % on foreign assets. Finland restricted investment outside the European Economic Area to 10 %, while Italy limited investment outside the OECD to 5 %, and the Czech Republic and Iceland banned such investments (Hu et al. 2007).

The arguments used to justify such restrictions include pension scheme's lack of experience in fund management, which may lead them to take excessive risks. Limiting risk taking by pension schemes also reduces the moral hazard created by government pension guarantees. Restricting foreign investment stops capital leaving the country, with its potentially adverse effects on the balance of payments, domestic investment and the development of domestic capital markets. But as well as offering benefits, restrictions can have adverse effects. For example, restricting the assets in which pension funds can invest increases the pension funds' share of the markets where they can invest, which increases their market impact. Restrictions may also mean that pension funds cannot invest in their desired portfolio, or that they can only invest in inefficient portfolios. As a result their actual portfolio will probably have a worse return for a given level of risk than would an unconstrained portfolio.

Restrictions on portfolio proportions have a different effect from restrictions on the overall level of risk. Placing an upper bound on the level of portfolio risk may still permit the selection of an efficient portfolio (Berstein and Chumacero 2012). For example in Fig. 3.7 suppose an upper bound of A is placed on risk, then although the AM_2B section of the efficiency frontier is ruled out, the CM_1A section of the efficiency frontier remains available. The optimal portfolio is unaffected if the risk free rate is low and the point of tangency with a ray from the risk free rate is M_1. But if the upper bound on risk is high an optimal solution at a point such as M_2 becomes unavailable. Restricting asset proportions shifts the frontier downwards, as in Fig. 3.8 so that it becomes impossible to select an efficient portfolio for any level of risk or return. Therefore restrictions on the level of portfolio risk are preferable to restrictions on asset proportions as they may leave the optimal portfolio unaffected.

There is a wide range of empirical studies which support the conclusion that investment restrictions harm efficient asset allocation. Angelidis and Tessaromatis (2010) studied the effects of the Greek restrictions on the portfolios of 82 Greek pension schemes, and found that the average equity return dropped substantially due to inefficient diversification. For 26 emerging countries, Pfau (2011) computed the efficient mean-variance portfolios with no restrictions, and then with a ban on foreign investment. The average return dropped by one fifth. For China the returns dropped by more than half, and for India the drop was over a quarter, one sixth for Thailand, and one eighth for Korea. (See Pfau (2009), for results for just Pakistan.) Hu et al. (2007) studied the consequences of relaxing the investment restrictions on Chinese compulsory and voluntary pension contributions, and showed that this would lead to an increase in returns. Berstein and Chumacero (2006) found that the investment restrictions in Chile reduced returns by about 2 % per year, from

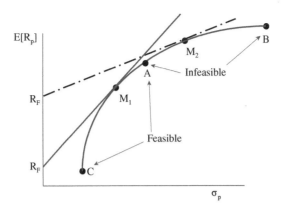

Fig. 3.7 Restricted efficient frontier

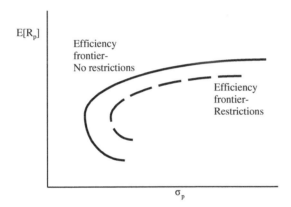

Fig. 3.8 Only inefficient portfolios

roughly 9 % down to 7 %. Davis (2002b) compared the actual asset allocations of pension schemes in 13 countries, with those of unrestricted mean-variance portfolios. He found that returns for the unrestricted portfolios were 2 % higher at 6.6 %, as against 4.4 % for the actual (restricted) portfolios. Finally, Srinivas and Yermo (2002) found that restricting foreign investment worsened the risk-return trade-off for Latin American countries.

g. Investment Performance of Pension Funds

The objective of a pension fund is to provide money to meet the pensions promise, and this involves matching the pension scheme's liabilities. However there have been many studies which have looked at just the investment performance of pension funds and not considered the liability dimension. Two dimensions of the investment performance of pension fund managers have been distinguished by these studies. The first dimension involves studying a fund's performance for a specified asset class (e.g. equities) or studying their performance across all their assets. The second dimension is the average performance of all pension funds, or the persistence of performance of particular funds. Persistent performance by a few fund managers can exist, even though on average there is no out-performance. This classification of the empirical studies appears in Table 3.21, and the empirical evidence concerning each of these four cases will now be considered. The numbers in Table 3.21 refer to the order in which the four combinations are considered.

i. Average Equity Performance
For the USA, UK and Colombia there is no clear evidence of out-performance by the equity investments of pension funds.

USA
Lakonishok et al. (1992b) analysed 769 US pension funds and found their equity investments under-performed the S&P 500 index by 1.3 %. Coggin et al. (1993) investigated 71 US equity pension fund managers, and found positive stock selection skill, but negative market timing ability. Collins and Fabozzi (2000) looked at 36 pension fund managers and found positive stock selection skill, but no market timing ability; with overall performance roughly equal to the market index. Bauer and Frehen (2008) considered 716 US pension funds and concluded that, after transactions costs, their investments in US equities were unable to beat their benchmarks. Busse et al. (2010) analysed 4617 domestic equity pension fund managers in the USA and their average performance was in line with the benchmarks. Coggin and Trzcinka (2000) examined 292 US equity pension funds and showed that, after allowing for style, there was no out-performance, and no evidence of persistence over adja-

Table 3.21 Classification of investment performance

	Single asset class, e.g. equities	Total performance across all asset classes
Average performance across all pension funds	i	ii
Persistence of performance for particular pension funds	iii	iv

cent three-year periods. Bauer et al. (2010) investigated the domestic equity returns of 463 US DB schemes and 248 US DC schemes. For risk-adjusted returns after transactions costs, DB scheme returns out-performed the benchmark by 45 basis points per year, while DC schemes did not out-perform.

UK

Thomas and Tonks (2001) studied 2175 UK pension funds and discovered negative stock selection and market timing skills for their equity investments. Blake et al. (2002) considered 306 UK pension funds and concluded that on average their equity investments under-performed by 0.15 %. Blake and Timmermann (2005) analysed investment by 247 UK pension funds in foreign equities. The average fund under-performed a global benchmark by 0.7 % per year due to poor market timing. Petraki and Zalewska (2013) examined the equity performance of 8255 UK personal pension funds and concluded that the average fund beat their benchmark.

Colombia

Fallón et al. (2010) compared the performance of 30 actively managed Colombian funds administered by private pension companies with that of 30 similar passive Colombian exchange traded funds. They found that the passive investment returns tended to be superior to those of the actively managed pension funds.

ii. Average Total Performance

These studies of total asset performance looked for an ability to beat the market using a combination of stock selection and asset allocation skills. For the USA, UK and Netherlands there is very limited evidence of out-performance across all assets.

USA

Brinson et al. (1986) investigated 91 US pension funds, and discovered total under-performance relative to index tracking of 1.1 % p.a. Brinson et al. (1991) analysed 82 US pension funds, and found no evidence of out-performance. Ippolito and Turner (1987) looked at 1526 US pension funds, and found under-performance of 0.44 % per year. Andonov et al. (2012) studied the total returns of 133 US DB schemes. These schemes achieved average returns that were 89 basis points above their benchmark, but this is not statistically significant. Restricting the analysis to funds with 13 or more observations (75 funds) there is a significantly positive out-performance of

55 basis points per year due to positive asset allocation and market timing decisions, but not to stock selection decisions.

UK
Blake et al. (1999) examined 364 UK pension funds, and concluded that the returns to both stock selection and market timing were negative. Blake et al. (2002) studied 306 UK pension funds and discovered that they under-performed by 0.14 %. Clare et al. (2010) concluded that the average return for 593 UK pooled pension fund managers across a wide range of asset classes was in line with the benchmark.

Netherlands
Huang and Mahieu (2012) studied 57 Dutch pension funds and found that they did not out-perform their benchmarks.

Turkey
Gökçen and Yalçin (2015) could not find any evidence of out-performance by 142 Turkish pension funds.

Many Countries
In a study of around 300 large mostly DB schemes from across the world, Beath (2015) found that they out-performed their benchmarks by 15.5 basis points per year.

iii. Persistent Performance for Equities
While the studies considered above have looked at average performance, other studies have investigated whether there are a few pension fund managers who are able to consistently beat the market (i.e. persistence), even though the average manager does not out-perform the market. The evidence summarised below shows there is some short-term persistence in equity performance by a few pension fund managers in the USA, UK, Spain and Hong Kong.

USA
Christopherson et al. (1998) studied 185 US pension funds, and found persistence in their equity returns, with losers repeating their poor performance. Bauer and Frehen (2008) considered 716 US pension funds and discovered that, with or without allowance for transactions costs, there is no year to year persistence in their domestic equity performance. Busse et al. (2010) analysed 4617 domestic equity pension fund managers in the USA and found no clear evidence of persistence in their performance.

UK
Tonks (2005a, b) used data on 2175 UK pension funds and found persistence for a period of one year in relative abnormal equity performance, with a difference between the top and bottom quintiles of between 0.5 and 1.6 % per year. However, even if the identity of these managers were known, this may not be a profitable opportunity after allowing for management fees, transactions and transition costs, and the delay in publishing a manager's performance for the previous year. Blake et al. (2013b) studied 2385 UK pension schemes and discovered evidence of persistent performance over three year periods for specialist managers of UK equities.

Spain
Ferruz et al. (2007) studied the equity investments of Spanish pension funds and found persistence over annual periods, but little evidence for longer-term persistence. Marti-Ballester (2009) analysed 252 Spanish pension funds, of which 137 were invested in fixed income, and 115 were invested in equities. She found persistence for both six-month and one-year periods.

Hong Kong
Chu (2008) analysed 150 pension funds in Hong Kong and discovered strong evidence of persistence in equity returns.

iv. Persistent Performance for All Assets
There is also evidence of persistence in total performance across all asset classes for the USA, and limited evidence of persistence in total performance for the UK, but none for the Netherlands, Poland and Turkey.

USA
Andonov et al. (2012) found persistence in the market timing and stock selection returns of US DB schemes.

UK
Brown et al. (1997) analysed 232 UK pension funds to see whether the investment performance of particular funds persisted from year to year. They found some support for persistence in performance, which they defined as repeatedly being ranked in the top quartile of fund managers. Blake et al. (1999) also found weak evidence of persistence in the performance of UK pension funds for total assets. Clare et al. (2010) analysed 593 pooled pension fund managers and did not find strong evidence for long-term persistence in total asset returns.

Netherlands

Huang and Mahieu (2012) did not find any persistence in total asset returns for 57 Dutch pension funds.

Poland

Kominek (2012) found no evidence of persistence for 17 Polish pension funds.

Turkey

Gökçen and Yalçin (2015) studied 142 Turkish pension funds, and failed to find any evidence of persistent investment performance.

Overall, the evidence suggests that the average pension fund under-performs the market, and this is probably due to transactions costs dragging down pension fund performance, relative to market indices which do not bear transactions costs. There is some evidence of short-term persistence in relative performance, but this probably does not offer a profitable trading rule due to transactions costs and delays.

v. Corporate Governance and Investment Performance

There has been research for a number of countries on the connection between corporate governance and pension fund investment performance. These studies, which are for the USA, Australia and Poland, find that some aspect of pension scheme corporate governance is correlated with pension fund investment performance, but the aspects of corporate governance correlated positively and negatively with investment performance vary from study to study.

USA

Albrecht and Hingorani (2004) studied 190 US local government schemes and found that abnormal returns were higher when more of the trustees were elected rather than appointed, there were fewer trustees and when the assets of the scheme were larger. A subsequent study by Albrecht et al. (2007) of 81 US local government schemes concluded that the involvement of the trustees in investment decisions leads to lower risk-adjusted returns.

Australia

In Australia DC scheme members decide which superannuation fund receives their contributions, and if they fail to make a choice their money goes into a default fund – MySuper. It is the trustees of these funds, not the members, who decide on their fund's asset allocation. Using data on 100 funds and a very wide range of factors, Liu (2014) examined the connection between the corporate governance of these superannuation funds and their investment performance. He found that the investment performance of funds was better for funds with younger trustees, independent audit and regular self-assessment of compliance, and where the trustees invested their own money in the fund. Therefore the superannuation fund selected by the member matters. However, employing data on 52 Australian superannuation funds, Nguyen et al. (2012) found that corporate governance does not affect a fund's investment performance, although it does affect a fund's fees. As a fund's board size increases, a larger number of consultants and fund managers are hired, leading to higher costs. Tan and Cam (2015) found a similar result for 162 Australian not-for-profit pension funds – larger trustee boards leads to higher investment and administration costs, and more board committees are associated with higher operating costs.

Poland
For 156 Polish DC pension fund management companies Jackowicz and Kowalewski (2012) concluded that corporate governance affects investment performance after finding that, if the supervisory board has an independent chairpedrson, risk-adjusted returns are lower.

3.3   Other Investment Topics

a. Herding
If pension funds tend to hold similar asset allocations, and to change their asset allocations in the same way, this represents 'herding' and this risks creating price bubbles and crashes in asset prices. Institutions such as pension funds are more likely to herd than individual investors because they know more about each other's trades, are evaluated against each other (reputational herding), and tend to receive the same information. Herding can lead to an adverse price impact as many funds try to trade the same assets in the same direction. Such trading can also lead to bubbles and crashes, and create momentum effects in financial markets. Herding may be associated with over-paying for 'active' investment management, as the fund managers are merely following the herd.

The Bank of England (2014) has set out a number of reasons why the asset allocations of DB pension schemes may tend to move together.

(a) DB pension schemes tend to have similar liabilities, with exposure to the same risks with roughly the same maturity. Trustees may also have a broadly similar attitude to the risk-return trade-off. Therefore an ALM will tend to suggest similar asset allocations.

(b) The performance of investment managers is often judged relative to that of their peers. To avoid a poor relative performance, managers may tend to follow the same asset allocation as their peers. This is called 'reputational herding'.

(c) Investment consultants have a substantial influence on asset allocations, and in 2014 the largest three consultants advised 50 % of UK DB pensions, while the largest six consultants advised 70 % of UK DB pension schemes (Bank of England 2014). This concentration in advice may lead to the herding of asset allocations.

(d) The regulatory framework is the same for all DB pension schemes, and this may lead to similar asset allocations.

(e) To the extent that the asset allocation is not rebalanced, relative price changes will change the proportional allocation of all funds in the same way. For example, if the equity market rises, unless funds sell equities, the proportion of their funds invested in equities automatically rises. If funds are following a fix-mix asset allocation, rebalancing as between their asset classes will also exhibit herding.

(f) All schemes face similar asset market expectations, and so may tend to invest in a similar manner.

Few empirical studies have analysed herding by pension schemes, although Table 3.18 shows there have been considerable swings up and down in the aggregate equity allocation of UK pension funds, which is consistent with the presence of herding. Lakonishok et al. (1992a) found no evidence of herding by US pension schemes, although Dennis and Strickland (2002) did detect positive feedback trading by US pension funds; that is on days when the US market rose (fell) by more than 2 %, pension funds bought (sold) shares. Blake et al. (2014) studied 189 UK DB pension funds and found some evidence of short-term herding by subgroups (private sector and public sector schemes), and rebalancing of the asset allocation back to a long-term target. In a study of 142 Turkish pension funds, Gökçen and Yalçin (2015) also found evidence of herding.

Polish pension fund managers are required to provide a minimum guaranteed return based on the average return achieved by all Polish funds. This provides an incentive to avoid under-performing the average fund, which leads to regulatory herding. Kominek (2012) studied all 17 such funds and found evidence of herding, as did Voronkova and Bohl (2005). In June 2007 Colombian regulators increased the margin by which pension fund administrators (PFA) were allowed to under-perform the average PFA performance over the previous three years before being fined. This relaxation reduced the pressure on PFAs to herd to protect themselves from being fined. Acharya and Pedraza (2015) found that this regulatory change reduced PFA herding, excess stock market volatility and excess co-movement in Colombian stock returns.

In Chile PFA compete with each other to receive and invest the pension contributions of workers, and Raddatz and Schmukler (2008) found evidence of herding by these PFA. Da et al. (2014) also looked for herding among pension funds in Chile. For a very small fee investment advisory firms provide advice by email to large numbers of DC scheme members on when to switch their money from an equity fund to a government bond fund, i.e. market timing. Since 30 % of the Chilean equity free float and 30 % of government bonds are held by pension funds, such co-ordinated switching has an effect. It was found to move equity prices by 2.5 %, bonds prices by 30 basis points, and to cause an increase in price volatility.

b. Effects of Pension Schemes on Capital Markets

It has been empirically established that countries with better developed capital markets experience higher rates of economic growth, and funded pension schemes can assist in the development of a country's capital markets. Funded pensions are a form of saving, and they supply long-term finance when the pension money is invested in financial assets. This also increases the demand for the services associated with financial services (e.g. stock markets, stockbrokers, security analysts, fund managers, custodians, performance measurement). A wide range of empirical studies from around the world have found that funded pension schemes have the following beneficial effects:-

- Higher economic growth – Davis and Hu (2008), Bijlsma et al. (2014), Schmidt-Hebbel (1999), Corsetti and Schmidt-Hebbel (1997), Hu (2005), Zandberg and Spierdijk (2013), Murphy and Musalem (2004), Bebczuk and Musalem (2006) and Cagan (1965). However, Samwick (2000) found no effect of pension funding on economic growth.
- Larger stock and corporate bond markets – Niggemann and Rocholl (2010), Hu (2012), Meng and Pfau (2010), Impavido et al. (2003), Hu (2005), Karlsson et al. (2007), Brida and Seijas (2015), Hryckiewicz (2009), Iglesias (1997) and Corbo and Schmidt-Hebbel (2003).
- Higher equity prices – Hu (2006).

- A lower cost of capital for companies – Hu (2006), Walker and Lefort (2002) and Iglesias (1997).
- Higher expenditure on research and development – Davis (2004).
- More financial innovation – Bodie (1990), Vittas (1996) and Iglesias (1997).
- Higher investment in real assets – Schmidt-Hebbel (1999).
- A more developed fund management industry.
- Facilitate privatisation – Vittas (1996).
- Encourage the provision of more price sensitive information.
- More international diversification.
- Higher productivity due to an improved allocation of resources – Corbo and Schmidt-Hebbel (2003).
- Higher saving – Bailliu and Reisen (1998), Poterba et al. (1996), Schmidt-Hebbel (1999), Corsetti and Schmidt-Hebbel (1997), Hu (2005)and Vittas (1996). However, saving in a pension scheme may simply divert money from some other form of saving, so the net change in total saving is zero. Morandé (1998) found that funded pension funds increased savings in Chile, while Holzmann (1997) found they lowered savings in Chile.
- Stronger corporate governance, leading to higher dividends and productivity – Davis (2002a, 2004) and Vittas (1996). However Faccio and Lasfer (2000) found no improvement in dividends or productivity for the UK and Wahal (1996) found that engagement has no long-term effect on the share prices of targeted firms.
- Lower stock and bond market price volatility – Walker and Lefort (2002), Ashok et al. (2013), Thomas et al. (2014), Iglesias (1997) and Bohl et al. (2009). In contrast, some studies have discovered evidence of an increase in volatility. A study of 24 countries by Hu (2006) found higher volatility; and for individual US shares Sias (1996) found that an increase in institutional ownership raised that share's return volatility. Lakonishok et al. (1992a) found no evidence of herding or positive feedback trading by US pension schemes, and no effect on market volatility, while Dennis and Strickland (2002) found evidence of positive feedback trading by US pension funds.

c. Pensions and Business Cycles
Pension schemes are affected by the business cycle as asset values, interest rates, salaries, inflation and employment move up and down. Pension schemes can also amplify or diminish the size of business cycles via mechanisms such as: (a) increasing income and hence consumption; (b) increasing (or decreasing)

wealth and thereby consumption; and (c) increasing (or decreasing) the supply of labour by accelerating or delaying retirement. Ghilarducci et al. (2012) have argued that the effects of pension schemes on the business cycle differ as between DC schemes, and state and DB schemes.

First, the payment of DB and DC pensions directly finances consumption. Second, the value of a member's DC pension pot rises and falls with the economy and stock market. Therefore, to the extent that there is a wealth effect on consumption, DC schemes tend to amplify cycles. This is not the case for DB and state schemes, where the size of the promised pension does not rise or fall with the stock market. Third, during a recession, the fall in the stock market reduces the value of DC pension pots, encouraging members to keep working (or re-enter the labour market, if they have previously retired) to restore the value of their pension pots. This tends to increase the labour supply, increasing unemployment and exerting a downward pressure on wages; exacerbating the recession. During an expansion the opposite effects occur. The rise in the stock market leads to an increase in the value of DC pension pots, encouraging members to retire early, so reducing the size of the labour force and exerting an upward pressure on wages, which tends to amplify the expansion. Thus the dependency ratio fluctuates with the stock market (MacDonald and Cairns 2007). No such effects occurs for DB and state schemes, as the value of the pension is unaffected by the stock market.

Ghilarducci et al. (2012) tested the effects of pensions on the business cycles using data on cash inflows and outflows for US DB, DC and state pension schemes, and the US output gap (the economy's realised minus potential output). Note that this analysis allows for the extra DB pension contributions required during a recession to maintain the funding ratio, and the lower DB pension contributions required during an expansion. Their results show that changes in DC pension cash flows are destabilising, while changes in DB and state pension cash flows are stabilising. Dushi et al. (2013) found that during the recession of 2007–09 contributions to US DC schemes by members dropped or stopped, particularly for those whose earnings decreased. Similarly Butrica and Smith (2016) found that contributions to 401(k) schemes decreased during recent US recessions. Kakes (2008) studied the asset allocation behaviour of 77 Dutch schemes, and found it to be stabilising. When the relative prices of equities and bonds alter, they restore their initial asset allocation by selling the asset whose price has risen, and buying the asset whose price has fallen.

As well as business cycles being affected by pension schemes, DB pension schemes may be affected by business cycles. In a recession the stock market and interest rates tend to drop. This lowers the value of DB pension scheme assets and increases their liabilities, which reduces their funding ratios. Sponsors may then be required to increase their contributions to improve funding ratios. Since there is a recession, the sponsor may be facing difficult economic conditions, and these extra contributions may require the sponsor to divert money from investment, research and development, dividend payments and so on (see Sect. 4.3). During an expansion, when the stock market and interest rates are high, funding ratios will also tend to be high, leading to lower pension contributions, leaving more cash for other purposes. These effects do not apply to DC or unfunded state pensions. Weller and Baker (2005) and Yermo and Severinson (2010) have suggested various ways of changing pension funding rules to remove such cyclical effects on DB contributions, including averaging the discount rate and asset values over 20 years, and allowing higher funding ratios before tax exemption is removed.

d. Sovereign Pension Funds

Sovereign wealth funds are investment funds established by nations who have surplus assets (e.g. from large oil revenues). These funds are invested globally in financial and real assets. Some are stabilisation funds with the objective of smoothing government revenues, despite the volatility in the price of the country's main source of revenue (e.g. oil). Others are savings funds, with the objective of providing funds for future generations (e.g. when the oil runs out). A sovereign wealth fund can be used by a country to help attract asset managers to operate in that country in order to manage part of the fund (Ziemba and Ziemba 2013). To the extent they are invested in domestic assets, sovereign wealth funds can also help develop local capital markets. In some cases the fund is specifically targeted at paying state pensions in future years, and these are classified as sovereign pension funds, and represent a form of inter-generational redistribution in favour of later generations. Details of the largest 20 sovereign pension funds in 2014 appear in Table 3.22. The UK and USA do not have sovereign wealth funds, although in November 2015 it was announced that up to 10 % of the tax revenue from shale gas would go into a UK sovereign wealth fund that would generate up to £1 billion over the next 25 years.

Table 3.22 Largest 20 sovereign pension funds end of 2014 ($ billion)

			$ bn
1	Government Pension Investment Fund	Japan	1144
2	Government Pension Fund – Global	Norway	884
3	National Pension Corporation	South Korea	430
4	National Social Security Fund (NSSF)	China	247
5	Canada Pension Plan	Canada	228
6	Central Provident Fund	Singapore	208
7	Employees Provident Fund	Malaysia	185
8	Government Employees	South Africa	123
9	The Future Fund	Australia	89
10	Employees Provident Fund	India	81
11	National Wealth Fund	Russia	75
12	Labour Pension Fund	Taiwan	65
13	Public Institute for Social Safety	Kuwait	59
14	Fondo de Reserva de la Seguriadad Social	Spain	50
15	Fonds de Reserve pour les Retraites (FRR)	France	45
16	AP Fonden 3	Sweden	41
17	AP Fonden 4	Sweden	37
18	AP Fonden 2	Sweden	37
19	AP Fonden 1	Sweden	36
20	AP Fonden 7	Sweden	29

Source: P&I/TW 300 Analysis, Towers Watson, September 2015

References

Acharya, S., & Pedraza, A. (2015). Asset price effects of peer benchmarking: Evidence from a natural experiment. Federal Bank of New York Staff Reports, no. 727, May, 28 pages.

Agnew, J. (2002). *Inefficient choices in 401(k) plans: Evidence from individual level data* (Working paper). College of William and Mary, 41 pages.

Ahmed, J. I., Barber, B. M., & Odean, T. (2013). *Made poorer by choice: Worker outcomes in social security v. private retirement accounts* (Working paper). Divisions of Research and Statistics and Monetary Affairs, Federal Reserve Board.

Albrecht, W. G., & Hingorani, V. L. (2004). Effects of governance practices and investment strategies on state and local government pension fund financial performance. *International Journal of Public Administration, 27*(8&9), 673–700.

Albrecht, W. G., Shamsub, H., & Giannatasio, N. A. (2007). Public pension fund, governance practices and financial performance. *Journal of Public Budgeting, Accounting and Financial Management, 19*(2), 245–267.

Ambachtsheer, K. (2012). The dysfunctional "DB vs DC" pensions debate: Why and how to move beyond it. *Rotman International Journal of Pension Management, 5*(2), 36–39.

Andonov, A., Bauer, R., & Cremers, M. (2012). *Can large pension funds beat the market? Asset allocation, market timing, security selection and the limits of liquidity* (Netspar discussion paper 10/2012/062).

Andonov, A., Kok, N., & Eichholtz, P. (2013). A global perspective on pension fund investments in real estate. *Journal of Portfolio Management, 39*(4), 32–42.

Andonov, A., Eichholtz, P., & Kok, N. (2015). Intermediated investment management in private markets: Evidence from pension fund investments in real estate. *Journal of Financial Markets, 22*, 73–103.

Ang, A., Goyal, A., & Ilmanen, A. (2014). Asset allocation and bad habits. *Rotman International Journal of Pension Management, 7*(2), 16–27.

Angelidis, T., & Tessaromatis, N. (2010). The efficiency of Greek public pension fund portfolios. *Journal of Banking and Finance, 34*(9), 2158–2167.

Ashok, T., Luca, S., & Nanditha, M. (2013). *Pension funds and stock market volatility: An empirical analysis of OECD countries* (Working paper). University of Pisa.

Asthana, S., & Lipka, R. (2002). Management of defined-benefit pension funds and shareholder value. *Quarterly Journal of Business and Economics, 41*(3–4), 49–69.

Bailliu, J., & Reisen, H. (1998). Do funded pensions contribute to higher aggregate savings? A cross-country analysis. *Review of World Economics, 134*(4), 692–711.

Bank of England. (2014). *Pro-cyclicality and structural trends in investment allocation by insurance companies and pension funds.* London: Bank of England, 52 pages.

Bauer, R. M. M. J., & Frehen, R. (2008). *The performance of US pension funds* (Working paper). Netspar, 2007–045.

Bauer, R. M. M. J., Cremers, K. J. M., & Frehen, R. G. P. (2010). *Pension fund performance and costs: Small is beautiful* (Working paper PI-1010). The Pensions Institute.

Beath, A. D. (2015). *Value added by large institutional investors between 1992–2013.* CEM Benchmarking, 8 pages.

Bebczuk, R. N., & Musalem, A. R. (2006, May). *Pensions and saving: New international panel data evidence* (Working paper no. 61). Universidad Nacional de Le Plata.

Bekaert, G., Hoyem, K., Hu, W. Y., & Ravina, E. (2014). *Who is internationally diversified? Evidence from 296 401(k) plans* (Working paper). Columbia Business School, 64 pages.

Benartzi, S., Thaler, R. H., Utkus, S. P., & Sunstein, C. R. (2007). The law and economics of company stock in 401(k) plans. *Journal of Law and Economics, 50*(1), 45–79.

Berstein, S., & Chumacero, R. A. (2006). Quantifying the costs of investment limits for Chilean funds. *Fiscal Studies, 27*(1), 99–123.

Berstein, S., & Chumacero, R. A. (2012). VaR limits for pension funds: An evaluation. *Quantitative Finance, 12*(9), 1315–1324.

Bijlsma, M., Van Ewijk, C., & Haaijen, F. (2014). *Economic growth and funded pension systems* (Working paper, Netspar, 07/2014-030).

Bird, R., Gray, J., & Scotti, M. (2013). Why do investors favour active management … To the extent they do? *Rotman International Journal of Pension Management, 6*(2), 6–17.

Blake, D. (2003). *Pension schemes and pension funds in the United Kingdom.* Oxford: Oxford University Press.

Blake, D., & Timmermann, A. (2005). Returns from active management in international equity markets: Evidence from a panel of UK pension funds. *Journal of Asset Management, 6*(1), 5–20.

Blake, D. (2006a). *Pension finance.* New York: Wiley.

Blake, D., Lehmann, B. N., & Timmermann, A. (1999). Asset allocation dynamics and pension fund performance. *Journal of Business, 72*(4), 429–461.

Blake, D., Lehmann, B. N., & Timmermann, A. (2002). Performance clustering and incentives in the UK pension fund industry. *Journal of Asset Management, 3*(2), 173–194.

Blake, D., Rossi, A. G., Timmermann, A., Tonks, I., & Wermers, R. (2013b). Decentralized investment management: Evidence from the pension fund industry. *Journal of Finance, 68*(3), 1133–1178.

Blake, D., Sarno, L., & Zinna, G. (2014). *The market for lemmings: Is the investment behaviour of pension funds stabilizing or destabilizing?* (Discussion paper PI-1408). The Pensions Institute, September, 79 pages.

Blake, D., Rossi, A. G., Timmermann, A., Tonks, I., & Wermers, R. (2015). Decentralization in pension fund management. *Journal of Investment Management, 13*(3), 35–56. Third Quarter.

Board, J. L. G., & Sutcliffe, C. M. S. (2007). Joined-up pensions policy in the UK: An asset-liability model for simultaneously determining the asset allocation and contribution rate. In S. A. Zenios & W. T. Ziemba (Eds.), *Handbook of asset and liability management* (North Holland handbooks in finance, Vol. 2, pp. 1029–1067). North Holland: Elsevier Science B.V.

Bodie, Z. (1990). Pension funds and financial innovation. *Financial Management, 19*(3), 11–22.

Bohl, M. T., Brzeszczynski, J., & Wilfling, B. (2009). Institutional investors and stock returns volatility: Empirical evidence from a natural experiment. *Journal of Financial Stability, 5*(2), 170–182.

Brida, J. G., & Seijas, M. N. (2015). *Pension reforms and incentives to domestic capital markets: A global study* (Working paper). Universidad de la Republica.

Bridgeland, S. (2005). Investing pension funds as if the long term really did matter. *Journal of Asset Management, 5*(5), 351–359.

Brinson, G. P., Hood, L. R., & Beebower, G. L. (1986). Determinants of portfolio performance. *Financial Analysts Journal, 42*(4), 39–44.

Brinson, G. P., Singer, B. D., & Beebower, G. L. (1991). Determinants of portfolio performance II: An update. *Financial Analysts Journal, 47*(3), 40–48.

Brown, G., Draper, P., & McKenzie, E. (1997). Consistency of UK pension fund investment performance. *Journal of Business Finance and Accounting, 24*(2), 155–178.

Busse, J. A., Goyal, A., & Wahal, S. (2010). Performance and persistence in institutional investment management. *Journal of Finance, 65*(2), 765–790.

Butrica, B. A., & Smith, K. A. (2016). 401(k) participant behaviour in a volatile economy. *Journal of Pension Economics and Finance*, vol. 15, no. 1, January, pp. 1–29.

Cagan, P. (1965). *The effect of pension plans on aggregate saving: Evidence from a sample survey* (National Bureau of Economic Research Occasional Paper 95).

Cazalet Consulting. (2014). *When I'm sixty-four*. London: Cazalet Consulting.

Christopherson, J. A., Ferson, W. E., & Glassman, D. A. (1998). Conditioning manager alphas on economic information: Another look at the persistence of performance. *Review of Financial Studies, 11*(1), 111–142.

Chu, P. K. K. (2008). Performance persistence of pension fund managers: Evidence from Hong Kong mandatory provident funds. In S. J. Kim & M. D. McKenzie (Eds.), *Asia-Pacific financial markets: Integration, innovation and challenges* (pp. 393–424). Oxford: Elsevier.

Clare, A., Nitzsche, D., & Cuthbertson, K. (2010). An empirical investigation into the performance of UK pension fund managers. *Journal of Pension Economics and Finance, 9*(4), 533–547.

Clare, A., & Wagstaff, C. (2011). *The trustee guide to investment*. Basingstoke: Palgrave Macmillan.

Clark, R. L., Lusardi, A., & Mitchell, O. S. (2014, May). *Financial knowledge and 401(k) investment performance* (GFLEC working paper). George Washington University, 27 pages.

Clerus. (2014). The hidden cost of poor advice: A review of investment decision-making and governance in Local Government Pension Schemes (LGPS) – Part 1. Clerus, 7 pages.

Coggin, T. D., & Trzcinka, C. A. (2000). A panel study of U.S. equity pension fund manager style performance. *Journal of Investing, 9*(2), 6–12.

Coggin, T. D., Fabozzi, F. J., & Rahman, S. (1993). The investment performance of US equity pension fund managers: An empirical investigation. *Journal of Finance, 48*(3), 1039–1055. Reprinted in Z. Bodie, & E. P. Davis (Eds.) (2000). *Foundations of pension finance* (Vol. 1, pp. 349–365). Edward Elgar Publishing.

Collins, B., & Fabozzi, F. (2000). Equity manager selection and performance. *Review of Quantitative Finance and Accounting, 15*(1), 81–97.

Corbo, V., & Schmidt-Hebbel, K. (2003). Macroeconomic effects of pension reform in Chile. In International Federation of Pension Fund Administrators (Ed.), *Pension reform: Results and challenges* (pp. 241–329). Santiago: International Federation of Pension Fund Administrators.

Corsetti, G., & Schmidt-Hebbel, K. (1997). Pension reform and growth. In S. Valdes-Prieto (Ed.), *The economics of pensions: Principles, policies and international experience* (pp. 127–159). Cambridge: Cambridge University Press.

Cox, P., Brammer, S., & Millington, A. (2007). Pension fund manager tournaments and attitudes towards corporate characteristics. *Journal of Business Finance and Accounting, 34*(7), 1307–1326.

Cremers, K. J. M., & Petajisto, A. (2009). How active is your fund manager? A new measure that predicts performance. *Review of Financial Studies, 22*(9), 3329–3365.

Cremers, M., Ferreira, M. A., Matos, P., & Starks, L. (2015). *Indexing and active fund management: International evidence* (Working paper). University of Notre Dame, 71 pages.

Da, Z., Larrain, B., Sialm, C., & Tessada, J. (2014). *Price pressure from co-ordinated noise trading: Evidence from pension fund reallocations* (Working paper). University of Notre Dame, 46 pages.

Dahlquist, M., & Martinez, J. V. (2015). Investor inattention: A hidden cost of choice in pension plans? *European Financial Management, 21*(1), 1–19.

Davis, E. P. (2002a). Institutional investors, corporate governance and the performance of the corporate sector. *Economic Systems, 26*(3), 203–229.

Davis, E. P. (2002b). *Pension fund management and international investment – A global perspective* (Working paper, PI-0206). The Pensions Institute.

Davis, E. P. (2004). Financial development, institutional investors and economic performance. In C. A. E. Goodhart (Ed.), *Financial development and economic growth: Explaining the links* (pp. 149–182). New York: Palgrave-Macmillan.

Davis, E. P., & Hu, Y. W. (2008). Does funding of pensions stimulate economic growth. *Journal of Pension Economics and Finance, 7*(2), 221–249.

De Roon, F., & Slager, A. (2012, November). *The duration and turnover of Dutch equity ownership: A case study of Dutch institutional investors* (Working paper). Eumedion.

Debt Management Office. (2014). *Quarterly Review*, January–March.

Dennis, P., & Strickland, D. (2002). Who blinks in volatile markets: Individuals or institutions? *Journal of Finance, 57*(5), 1923–1949.

Duan, Y., Hotchkiss, E. S., & Jiao, Y. (2015). *Corporate pensions and financial distress* (Working paper). University of Alberta, 39 pages.

Dushi, I., Iams, H. M., & Tamborini, C. R. (2013). Contribution dynamics in defined contribution pension plans during the great recession of 2007–2009. *Social Security Bulletin, 73*(2), 85–102.

Eaton, T. V., Nofsinger, J. R., & Varma, A. (2014). Institutional investor ownership and corporate pension transparency. *Financial Management, 43*(3), 603–630.

Ederington, L. H. (1979). The Hedging Performance of the New Futures Markets, *Journal of Finance, 34*(1), pp. 157–170.

Even, W. E., & Macpherson, D. A. (2007). Pension investments in employer stock. *Journal of Pension Economics and Finance, 7*(1), 67–93.

Even, W. E., & Macpherson, D. A. (2009). Managing risk caused by pension investments in company stock. *National Tax Journal, 62*(3), 439–453.

Faccio, M., & Lasfer, M. A. (2000). Do occupational pension funds monitor companies in which they hold large stakes? *Journal of Corporate Finance, 6*(1), 71–110.

Fallón, E. C., Rojas, T. R. D. S., & Peña, C. R. (2010). Evidence of active management of private voluntary pension funds in Colombia: A performance analysis using proxy ETFs. *Estudios Gerenciales, 26*(115), 13–38.

Ferruz, L., Vincente, L., & Andreu, L. (2007). Performance persistence of Spanish pension funds: The best winners and losers usually repeat. *Geneva Papers on Risk and Insurance: Issues and Practice, 32*(4), 583–594.

French, K.R. (2008)., August Presidential Address: The Cost of Active Investing, *Journal of Finance, 63*(1), vol. 63, no. 1, August, pp. 1537–1573.

Ghilarducci, T., Saad-Lessler, J., & Fisher, E. (2012). The macroeconomic stabilization effects of social security and 401(k) plans. *Cambridge Journal of Economics, 36*(1), 237–251.

Gökçen, U., & Yalçin, A. (2015). The case against active pension funds: Evidence from the Turkish private pension system. *Emerging Markets Review, 23*, 46–67.

Goyal, A., & Wahil, S. (2008). The selection and termination of investment management firms by plan sponsors. *Journal of Finance, 63*(4), 1805–1847.

Holzmann, R. (1997). Pension reform, financial market development and economic growth: Preliminary evidence from Chile. *IMF Staff Papers, 44*(2), 149–178.

Hooke, J., & Walters, J. J. (2013, July). *Wall Street fees, investment returns, Maryland and 49 other state pensions* (Maryland Policy Report, no. 2013–02), 6 pages.

Hooke, J., & Walters, J. J. (2015, July). *Wall Street fees and investment returns for 33 state pension schemes* (Maryland Policy Report, no. 2015–05), 5 pages.

Hryckiewicz, A. (2009). *Pension reform, institutional investors' growth and stock market development in the developing countries: Does it function?* (Working paper). National Bank of Poland, 35 pages.

Hu, Y. W. (2005). *Pension reform, economic growth and financial development – An empirical study* (Working paper). Brune University.

Hu, Y. W. (2006). The impact of pension funds on financial markets. *Financial Market Trends*, (91), 145–167.

Hu, Y. W. (2012, May). Growth of Asian pension assets: Implications for financial and capital markets. Asian Development Bank Institute Working Paper Series, no. 360.

Hu, Y. W., Stewart, F., & Yermo, J. (2007). *Pension fund investment and regulation: An international perspective and implications for China's pension system.* Paris: OECD.

Huang, X., & Mahieu, R. (2012). Performance persistence of Dutch pension funds. *De Economist, 160*(1), 17–34.

Iglesias, A. (1997). Pension system reform and the evolution of capital markets: The Chilean experience. In K. B. Staking (Ed.), *Policy-based finance and market alternatives: East Asian lessons for Latin America and the Caribbean* (pp. 143–158). Washington, DC: Inter-American Development Bank.

Impavido, G., Musalem, A. R., & Tressel, T. (2003, January). *The impact of contractual savings institutions on securities markets* (Policy Research Working paper no. 2948). The World Bank.

Inkmann, J., & Shi, Z. (forthcoming). Life-cycle patterns in the design and adoption of default funds in DC pension plans. *Journal of Pension Economics and Finance.*

Inkmann, J., Blake, D., & Shi, Z. (forthcoming). Managing financially distressed pension plans in the interest of beneficiaries. *Journal of Risk and Insurance.*

IPE. (2015). Top 1000 pension funds 2015. *Investment & Pensions Europe.*

Ippolito, R. A., & Turner, J. A. (1987). Turnover, fees and pension plan performance. *Financial Analysts Journal, 43*(6), 16–26.

Iyengar, S. S., & Kamenica, E. (2010). Choice proliferation, simplicity seeking and asset allocation. *Journal of Public Economics, 94*(7&8), 530–539.

Jackowicz, K., & Kowalewski, O. (2012). Crisis, internal governance mechanisms and pension fund performance: Evidence from Poland. *Emerging Markets Review, 13*(4), 493–515.

Jenkinson, T., Jones, H., & Martinez, J. V. (2013). *Picking winners? Investment consultants' recommendations of fund managers* (Working paper). Oxford University, 47 pages.

Jones, H., & Martinez, J. V. (2015). *Institutional investor expectations, manager performance and fund flows* (Working paper). University of Oxford.

Kakes, J. (2008). Pensions in a perfect storm: Financial behaviour of Dutch pension funds (2002–2005). *Applied Financial Economics Letters, 4*(1), 29–33.

Karlsson, A., Massa, M., & Simonov, A. (2007). Pension portfolio choice and menu exposure. In B. Madrian, O. S. Mitchell, & B. J. Soldo (Eds.), *Redefining retirement: How will boomers fare?* (pp. 248–270). Oxford: Oxford University Press.

Keim, D. B., & Mitchell, O. S. (2015, April). *Simplifying choices in defined contribution retirement plan design* (Working paper). Pension Research Council, 30 pages.

Kominek, Z. (2012). Regulatory induced herding? Evidence from polish pension funds. *Economic Change and Restructuring, 45*(1&2), 97–119.

KPMG. (2015). 2015 KPMG UK fiduciary management market survey. KPMG, December, 4 pages.

Lakonishok, J., Shleifer, A., & Vishny, R. W. (1992a). The impact of institutional trading on stock prices. *Journal of Financial Economics, 32*(1), 23–43.

Lakonishok, J., Shleifer, A., & Vishny, R. W. (1992b). The structure and performance of the money management industry. *Brookings papers on economic activity: Microeconomics* (pp. 339–391). Reprinted in Z. Bodie, & E. P. Davis (Eds.) (2000). *Foundations of pension finance* (Vol. 1, pp. 279–331). Edward Elgar Publishing.

Lippi, A. (2016). (Country) Home bias in Italian occupational pension funds asset allocation choices. *Quarterly Review of Economics and Finance*. Vol. 59, February, pp. 78–82.

Liu, K. (2014). *Governance and performance of private pension funds: Australian evidence* (Working paper). School of Risk and Actuarial Studies, University of New South Wales, 46 pages.

Louton, D., McCarthy, J., Rush, S., Saraoglu, H., & Sosa, O. (2015). *Tactical asset allocation for US pension investors: How tactical should the plan be?* (Working paper). Bryant University, 23 pages.

MacDonald, B. J., & Cairns, A. J. G. (2007). The impact of DC pension systems on population dynamics. *North American Actuarial Journal, 11*(1), 17–48.

MacIntosh, J., & Scheibelhut, T. (2012). How large pension funds organise themselves: Findings from a unique 19-fund survey. *Rotman International Journal of Pension Management, 5*(1), 34–40.

Marti-Ballester, C. P. (2009). Performance persistence of Spanish pension plans. *Pensions: An International Journal, 14*(4), 293–298.

Meng, C., & Pfau, W. D. (2010). The role of pension funds in capital market development (GRIPS Discussion Paper no. 10–17), October.

Meulbroek, L. (2005). Company stock in pension plans: How costly is it? *Journal of Law and Economics, 48*(2), 443–474.

Mitchell, O. S., & Utkus, S. P. (2003). The role of company stock in defined contribution plans. In O. S. Mitchell & K. Smetters (Eds.), *The pension challenge: Risk transfers and retirement income security* (pp. 33–70). Oxford: Oxford University Press.

Morandé, F. G. (1998). Savings in Chile. What went right? *Journal of Development Economics, 57*(1), 201–228.

Murphy, P. L., & Musalem, A. R. (2004, September). *Pension funds and national saving* (Policy Research Working Papers, no. 3210). The World Bank.

Myners, P. (2001). *Institutional investment in the United Kingdom: A review.* London: H.M. Treasury.

Nguyen, T. T. C., Tan, M., & Cam, M. A. (2012). Fund governance, fees and performance in Australian corporate superannuation funds. *Journal of Law and Financial Management, 11*(2), 2–23.

Niggemann, T., & Rocholl, J. (2010). *Pension funding and capital market development* (Working paper). Goethe University.

OECD. (2012). *Pension markets in focus*, no. 9, September,

OECD. (2013b). *Pension markets in focus.* Paris: OECD.

Papke, L. E. (2004a). Individual financial decisions in retirement saving plans: The role of participant-direction. *Journal of Public Economics, 88*(1&2), 39–61.

Parwada, J. T., & Faff, R. F. (2005). Pension plan investment management mandates: An empirical analysis of manager selection. *Journal of Financial Services Research, 27*(1), 77–98.

Pension Protection Fund. (2015b). *The purple book, DB pensions universe risk profile 2015.* PPF and TPR.

Petraki, A., & Zalewska, A. (2013, March). *Jumping over a low hurdle: Personal pension fund performance* (Working paper). University of Bath.

Pfau, W. D. (2009). The role of international diversification in public pension systems: The case of Pakistan. *Economic Issues, 14*(2), 81–105.

Pfau, W. D. (2011). Emerging market pension funds and international diversification. *Journal of Developing Areas, 45*, 1–17.

Platanakis, E., & Sutcliffe, C. (2016). Pension scheme redesign and wealth redistribution between the members and sponsor The USS Rule Change in October 2011: *Insurance: Mathematics and Economics*, vol. 69, July 2016, pp. 14–28.

Platanakis, E., & Sutcliffe, C. (forthcoming). Asset liability modelling and pension schemes: The application of robust optimization to USS. *European Journal of Finance.*

Poterba, J. M. (2003). Employer stock and 401(k) plans. *American Economic Review, 93*(2), 398–404.

Poterba, J. M., Venti, S. F., & Wise, D. A. (1996). How retirement saving programs increase saving. *Journal of Economic Perspectives, 10*(4), 91–112.

Raddatz, C., & Schmukler, S. L. (2008). *Pension funds and capital market development: How much bang for the buck?* (Policy Research Working Paper 4787). The World Bank, 91 pages.

Rauh, J. D. (2006a). Own company stock in defined contribution pension plans: A takeover defence? *Journal of Financial Economics, 81*(3), 379–410.

Rose, P., & Seligman, J. S. (2015). *Are alternative investments prudent? Public sector pension use and fiduciary duty* (Working paper). Ohio State University, 26 pages.

Rosenfeld, S. (2009). *Life settlements: Signposts to a principal asset class* (Working paper, no. 09–20). Financial Institutions Centre, University of Pennsylvania.

Rubbaniy, G., Van Lelyveld, I. P. P., & Verschoor, W. F. C. (2014). Home bias and Dutch pension funds' behaviour. *European Journal of Finance, 20*(11), 978–993.

Salamanca, N., De Grip, A., & Sleijpen, O. (2013). How individuals react to defined benefit pension risk (Netspar Working paper, No 2013–041).

Samwick, A. A. (2000). Is pension reform conducive to higher savings? *Review of Economics and Statistics, 82*(2), 264–272.

Sandbrook, W., & Gosling, T. (2014). Pension reform in the United Kingdom: The unfolding NEST story. *Rotman International Journal of Pension Management, 7*(1), 56–60.

Schmidt-Hebbel, K. (1999, January). *Does pension reform really spur productivity, saving and growth?* (Working paper). Central Bank of Chile.

SCM Private. (2007). Closet indexation: A UK epidemic. SCM Private, 15 pages.

SCM Private (2013). Closet Indexation: A UK Epidemic, SCM Private, London, 15 pages.

Shackleton, K. (2011). Outsourcing investment policy. *Pensions: An International Journal, 16*(4), 266–270.

Sharpe, W. F., & Tint, L. G. (1990). Liabilities – A new approach. *Journal of Portfolio Management, 16*(2), 5–10.

Sias, R. W. (1996). Volatility and the institutional investor. *Financial Analysts Journal, 52*(2), 13–20.

Spence Johnson. (2013). *Mind the gap: The case for a relaxation of daily dealing requirements for DC pension funds.* Defined Contribution Investment Forum.

Srinivas, P. S., & Yermo, J. (2002). Risk management through international diversification: The case of Latin American pension funds. In O. S. Mitchell, Z. Bodie, P. B. Hammond, & S. Zeldes (Eds.), *Innovations in retirement financing* (pp. 282–312). Philadelphia: University of Pennsylvania Press.

Sutcliffe, C. M. S. (2005). The cult of the equity for pension funds: Should it get the boot? *Journal of Pension Economics and Finance, 4*(1), 57–85.

Tan, M., & Cam, M. A. (2015). Does governance structure influence pension fund fees and costs? An examination of Australian not-for-profit superannuation funds. *Australian Journal of Management, 40*(1), 114–134.

Tang, N., & Lin, Y. T. (2015). The efficiency of target-date funds. *Journal of Asset Allocation, 16*(2), 131–148.

Tang, N., Mitchell, O. S., Mottola, G. R., & Utkus, S. P. (2010). The efficiency of sponsor and participant portfolio choices in 401(k) plans. *Journal of Public Economics, 94*(11&12), 1073–1085.

Thomas, A., & Tonks, I. (2001). Equity performance of segregated pension funds in the UK. *Journal of Asset Management, 1*(4), 321–343.

Thomas, A., Spataro, L., & Mathew, N. (2014). Pension funds and stock market volatility: Analysis of OECD countries. *Journal of Financial Stability, 11*, 92–103.

Tilba, A., & McNulty, T. (2013). Engaged versus disengaged ownership: The case of pension funds in the UK. *Corporate Governance: An International Journal, 21*(2), 165–182.

Tonks, I. (2005a). Performance persistence of pension-fund managers. *Journal of Business, 78*(5), 1917–1942.

Tonks, I. (2005b). Performance persistence. *Professional Investor*, April, pp. 12–16.

Towers Watson. (2015). *Global pension assets study 2015*. Towers Watson, February, 39 pages.

Turner, A. (2005). *A new pension settlement for the twenty-first century: The second report of the pensions commission*. London: The Stationary Office.

UBS. (2013). *Pension fund indicators 2013: A long term perspective on pension fund investment*. Union Bank of Switzerland.

Vittas, D. (1996). Pension funds and capital markets: Investment regulation, financial innovation and governance. *Viewpoint*. The World Bank, February, Note no. 71.

Voronkova, S., & Bohl, M. T. (2005). Institutional traders' behaviour in an emerging stock market; Empirical evidence on polish pension fund investors. *Journal of Business Finance and Accounting, 32*(7&8), 1537–1560.

Wahal, S. (1996). Pension fund activism and firm performance. *Journal of Finance and Quantitative Analysis, 31*(1), 1–23.

Walker, E., & Lefort, F. (2002). Pension reform and capital markets: Are there any (hard) links? *Revista Abante, 5*(2), 77–149.

Weller, C., & Baker, D. (2005). Smoothing the waves of pension funding: Could changes in funding rules help avoid cyclical under-funding? *Journal of Policy Reform, 8*(2), 131–151.

Yamaguchi, T., Mitchell, O. S., Mottola, G. R., & Utkus, S. P. (2007). *Winners and losers: 401(k) trading and portfolio performance* (Working paper). Michigan Retirement Research Centre, University of Michigan.

Yermo, J., & Severinson, C. (2010). The impact of the financial crisis on defined benefit plans and the need for counter-cyclical funding regulations, OECD Working Paper on Finance, Insurance and Private Pensions, no. 3, June.

Zandberg, E., & Spierdijk, L. (2013). Funding of pensions and economic growth: Are they really related. *Journal of Pension Economics and Finance, 12*(2), 151–167.

Ziemba, R. E. S., & Ziemba, W. T. (2013). Investing in the modern age. World Scientific, chapter 10, pp. 101–111.

4

Corporate Finance and Pension Schemes

The presence of pensions schemes, particularly defined benefit (DB) pension schemes, creates a range of two-way interactions between the sponsor and the scheme, and these are considered in this chapter. First, it is established that the sponsor and its DB scheme should be analysed as a single economic entity. Next, the effects of sponsoring a DB pension scheme on the firm's leverage are considered, followed by an examination of the liquidity effects on the sponsor of making contributions to the scheme. There is then a discussion of the quantification of the sponsor's asset beta allowing for the risk of the pension scheme, followed by coverage of the effects of having a DB scheme on a wide range of issues. These include mergers and acquisitions, the sponsor's credit risk and share price, and the effects of the sponsor's default risk on the scheme's asset allocation. This is followed by models of the interaction between a scheme's asset allocation, funding ratio and default insurance. Risk sharing between the sponsor and the members is then introduced into these models, followed by an analysis of the scope for tax arbitrage involving DB pension schemes. Finally, models of the effects of default insurance, risk sharing and tax arbitrage on the scheme's asset allocation and funding ratio are presented.

4.1 Consolidation with the Company (Sponsor)

Since the company (sponsor) is responsible for any surplus or deficit on a DB scheme, it is now generally accepted that the assets and liabilities of a company DB pension scheme should be consolidated into the company's overall

© The Author(s) 2016   **191**
C. Sutcliffe, *Finance and Occupational Pensions*,
DOI 10.1057/978-1-349-94863-5_4

Table 4.1 Example of consolidating a pension scheme

	Sponsor	Scheme	Consolidated
Liabilities			
Equity of the sponsor	£100	–	£100
Debt of the sponsor	£800	–	£800
Pension liabilities	–	£1000	£1000
Creditors of the sponsor	£100	–	£100
Total	£1000	£1000	£2000
Assets			
Company assets	£1000	–	£1000
Pension assets	–	£1000	£1000
Total	£1000	£1000	£2000

Unconsolidated leverage = D/A = 800/1000 = 80 %
Consolidated leverage = D/A = 1800/2000 = 90 %

accounts, and not treated as an off-balance sheet item, as is currently the case. Note that define contribution (DC) schemes are not integrated with the sponsoring company as they are always fully funded, and their funding position is unaffected by the status of the sponsor. Security analysts and researchers have tended to ignore DB pensions schemes when analysing companies. This is a big omission, and for some companies it is a huge mistake. In 2002 the pension schemes of both British Airways (BA) and Corus had liabilities more than seven times larger than the market capitalisation of the sponsor, and at one time British Airways pension schemes were nine times bigger than the company market capitalisation. In the USA (1991–2003) the assets in company pension schemes represented, on average, 16 % of the book value of the sponsor's assets, and 62 % of the market value of the sponsor's equity. Across 50 countries Bartram (forthcoming) found that consolidating pension schemes with their sponsor increases average leverage by 32 %. (Leverage can be defined in many different ways, and Bartram used total debt divided by total assets.) Table 4.1 has an example of the way in which consolidating a pension scheme with the sponsor can increase the entity's leverage – in this case from 80 to 90 %.

4.2   Leverage Effects

Pension liabilities are not identical to corporate debt, and this is for five reasons. First, pension liabilities are guaranteed by the Pension Benefit Guaranty Corporation (PBGC) (or Pension Protection Fund (PPF) in the UK), while corporate debt is not guaranteed by an external body. Second, pension contributions offer the sponsor a tax timing option. Since company contributions to the pension scheme are tax deductible, like corporate debt, they provide a tax shield. Since the company has some limited discretion over the size of their annual pension contributions, pensions provide a tax-timing option. This is different to corporate debt, where the company must pay the agreed interest on time. Third, extra contributions to the pension scheme now provide the company with some financial slack whereby they can reduce their future contributions if they need funds for some other purpose. Fourth, pension liabilities do not appear on the company's balance sheet, while debt does. Finally, there is much more discretion in valuing pension liabilities than in valuing corporate debt (see Sect. 1.6b).

Despite these differences, pension liabilities are effectively a form of corporate debt, and so should be included when computing the company's leverage. Shivdasani and Stefanesu (2010) found that a 1 % increase in the ratio of US DB pension liabilities to total assets (company assets plus pension scheme assets) is associated with a 0.36 % decrease in the leverage ratio computed using just the balance sheet debt. Bartram (forthcoming) found that, across 50 countries, a 1 % increase in DB pension liabilities is associated with a decrease of 0.23 % in company debt. These results indicate that companies substitute DB pension liabilities for company debt, although the rate of exchange is less than one for one.

4.3   Liquidity Effects

To ensure that the money in a pension scheme provides security for the members, once the sponsor has paid money into a scheme legal restrictions make it very hard for the sponsor to reclaim it. If the company is facing some form of financial constraint (e.g. debt covenants) raising new capital will be expensive or not possible, and using funds for pension contributions will have an adverse effect on discretionary expenditures by the sponsor. The evidence for the USA and UK is that contributions to a pension scheme by the sponsor are associated with lower capital expenditure, lower dividends and a lower share price.

a. Capital Expenditure

For US companies Rauh (2006b) found that, the higher a sponsor's contributions to its DB pension schemes, the lower its capital expenditure. Similarly, using data for 50 countries, Bartram (forthcoming) discovered that having a DB scheme is associated with a 5 % decrease in capital expenditure, although research and development (R&D) expenditure increased by 12 %.

Phan and Hegde (2013) found that an increase of $100 in US company DB contributions is associated with a $21 drop in the sponsor's capital investment. Campbell et al. (2012) discovered that an increase in DB pension contributions is associated with an increase in the cost of capital for US companies facing financial constraints. They interpret this result as consistent with a drop in capital investment. Using data on 3780 US companies with DB schemes, Chaudhry et al. (2014) found that, for a given level of cash within the sponsor, a higher pension deficit is associated with higher investment in R&D. This may be due to the sponsor using its available cash for R&D, rather than pension contributions.

Kubick et al. (2014) analysed a natural experiment when in 2012 the US unexpectedly and substantially reduced the minimum pension contribution required by sponsors to their DB schemes. For financially constrained sponsors this regulatory relaxation (MAP-21) led to an increase in R&D expenditure, and an increase in capital expenditure the following year, supporting the previous evidence of substitution between capital expenditure and pension contributions. However Dambra (2014) also studied the effects of MAP-21 and found it did not lead to a contemporaneous change in capital expenditure, R&D expenditure or cash acquisitions, but did lead to an increase in stock repurchases and debt payments. Both Kubick et al. (2014) and Dambra (2014) found that when MAP-21 was announced the share price of financially constrained sponsors rose.

b. Dividends

For UK companies Liu and Tonks (2013) and Bunn and Trivedi (2005) found a negative relationship between the sponsor's DB contributions and dividend payments by the sponsor. Cadman and Vincent (2015) studied about 1500 US firms and found that, where a firm CEO is in a DB scheme, this constitutes 15 % of the CEO's total compensation and 23 % of the CEO's firm-related wealth. So US CEOs have a considerable personal interest in the financial health of their company's DB scheme. White (2012) found that for US companies the greater the top executives' compensation leverage, the smaller the dividends paid by the company. Executive compensation leverage is defined as [*Pension*/(*Pension* + *Stocks* + *Options*)]. So a large pension obligation from the company (relative to its equity linked obligations of stocks and options) aligns top executives' interests with the bondholders rather than the shareholders, and they retain cash in the company to increase the resources available to pay debtholders. In a study of 272 large US companies, Eisdorfer et al. (2015) showed that high levels of compensation leverage are associated with lower dividends, and this effect is stronger when the executives' pensions are unfunded. This is consistent with a desire by executives to keep cash in the business to ensure their pensions are paid.

c. Share Price

For US companies subject to financial constraints, DB pension contributions by the sponsor lead to a drop in the share price, Franzoni (2009). For $1 of DB contributions, the value of the company drops by $1.30, and this could be because the company has cut its capital expenditure in order to make this payment. A negative relationship was also obtained by Phan and Hegde (2013), who found that US company value drops by 21 % of the sponsor's DB contribution.

4.4 Betas and Pension Schemes

Equity betas (β_E) give the relationship between returns on a company's shares and returns on the market portfolio. There are also asset and debt betas. A company's asset beta (β_A) is the relationship between returns on the market portfolio and returns on the company's assets, and the company's debt beta (β_D) is the relationship between return on the market portfolio and interest payments on the company's debt. Asset betas are the beta of an ungeared version of the company, and can be used to compute the cost of capital for the ungeared version of the company. Equity betas can be computed using stock market data, but it is more difficult to compute asset betas, and this is usually done indirectly using the weighted sum of the equity and debt betas computed using market data. When computing asset betas the company pension scheme is usually ignored, which generally results in the over-estimation of the asset beta. Table 4.2 presents two alternative balance sheets for a company; the first ignores the pension scheme, and the second includes the pension scheme.

As argued above, a pension scheme should be consolidated with its sponsor, and so for companies sponsoring a DB pension scheme the balance sheet should be, as in the second balance sheet in Table 4.2:

Table 4.2 Balance sheets ignoring and including the pension scheme

Company balance sheet	
Equity (E)	Assets (V)
Debt (D)	–
Consolidated balance sheet	
Equity (E)	Assets (V)
Debt (D)	Pension assets (PA)
Pension liabilities (PL)	–

Assets (V) = Equity (E) + Debt (D) + [Pension Liabilities (PL) – Pension Assets (PA)]

The sponsor's asset beta is the weighted sum of the betas for the sponsor's equity and debt, plus the weighted beta's for the pension scheme's assets and liabilities:

$$\beta_A = \beta_E(E/V) + \beta_D(D/V) + [\beta_{PL}(PL/V) - \beta_{PA}(PA/V)]$$

where β_{PL} is the pension liabilities beta, and β_{PA} is the pension asset beta. Hence the asset beta should include the additional term $[\beta_{PL}(PL/V) - \beta_{PA}(PA/V)]$. In practice β_{PL} tends to zero, while β_{PA} tends to one; and so $\beta_{PL}(PL/V) - \beta_{PA}(PA/V)$ is roughly equal to $-PA/V$. Therefore omission of the pension scheme, and hence of $-PA/V$, leads to the overstatement of β_A. For Boeing, ignoring its pension scheme when estimating its asset beta led to a figure of 0.543, rather than the correct figure of 0.228, an over-estimate of 139 %. This resulted in an estimated cost of capital for Boeing of 8.80 %, rather than the correct number of 6.59 %; an over-estimate of 34 % (Jin et al. 2006).

Opaque and peculiar accounting rules mean that a company's accounts do not present a good picture of the state of its pension scheme. However, for the USA, Jin et al. (2006) found that company equity betas do reflect their pension scheme risk. Similarly for the UK, McKillop and Pogue (2009) used data on 92 FTSE 100 companies and showed that, for those with a higher pension scheme beta, the firm's equity had higher systematic and total risk. These results indicate that the stock market does take account of the pension scheme when valuing the sponsor.

A scheme's funding ratio is commonly used as a measure of pension scheme default risk, but Wang et al. (2013) have shown that the pension beta (i.e. $\beta_{PL}(PL/V) - \beta_{PA}(PA/V)$) is a better measure of pension scheme default risk than the funding ratio. This is because the pension beta includes the risk introduced by a mismatch between the systematic risks of the assets and liabilities.

4.5   Other Effects

Besides the liquidity, leverage and beta value effects discussed above, pension schemes can have a wide range of other effects on the corporate sponsor. They can act as a poison pill to prevent the sponsor being taken over, affect the sponsor's credit rating and share price, alter the risk aversion of the sponsor's management, change the reported profits of the sponsor, help to finance an employee buyout of the sponsor, and encourage the sponsor to engage in tax avoidance. In addition, the sponsor's default risk affects the asset allocation of the scheme, while a sponsor who wishes to merge two schemes needs to consider whether various conditions are met to ensure the merger is fair to the members of both schemes.

a. Mergers and Acquisitions

Pension schemes now play an important part in takeovers and mergers. Takeover bids for WH Smith, Marks and Spencer, Sainsbury's, Uniq, ITV and Beale all failed due to problems with the pension scheme of the target company. Pension scheme issues nearly stopped the takeover of Abbey National by Santander, and Alliance Boots by Kohlberg Kravis Roberts (Brummer 2010), while the takeover of Cooper Tire by Apollo Tyres was threatened by the possible involvement of the UK Pensions Regulator.

In a study of UK companies Cocco and Volpin (2013) found that DB pension liabilities discourage other companies from taking them over (a poison pill effect). Such companies are less likely to be targeted, particularly if they have a large pension deficit, and any bids are less likely to succeed. This is explained by the bidders' lack of detailed knowledge of the pension scheme and the risk that the pension scheme is a 'lemon', i.e. has serious undisclosed problems. However in a study of 712 takeover bids by US companies, Meijdam (2012) discovered that it is just the existence of a DB scheme, and not the size of the liabilities or deficit, that reduces the probability of a takeover bid. Meijdam suggests this is because the stock market is able to successfully impound the disclosed scheme characteristics into the share price, but leaving the 'lemon' problem unpriced.

The evidence is that US acquirers with large pension deficits are less likely to engage in mergers and acquisitions, and when they do, they pay a lower takeover premium and use more cash when paying for a takeover (Chang et al. 2012). These researchers were unable to find any explanations for these results. Sudarsanam and Appadu (2015) analysed 138 UK takeovers involving FTSE 350 companies, and found that where the target has a DB scheme, rather than a DC or no pension scheme, payment is in the shares of the bidder, not cash. If the payment by the bidder is in cash, the leverage of the new consolidated entity is higher than if shares in the bidder are used to buy the target. This is illustrated in Table 4.3 where the leverage of the consolidated entity after the acquisition is 76.7 % when using shares, and 81.0 % if cash is used.

As well as acquisitions, pension schemes can also influence the disposal of parts of a business. In 2015 the chief executive of RSA Insurance, Stephen Hester, said that a strong disincentive to selling parts of the business was that

Table 4.3 Example of consolidation: payment in cash versus shares

	Bidder	Target	Target's DB scheme	Consolidated target	Consolidated-bidder Shares	Consolidated-bidder Cash
Liabilities						
Equity	£100	£80	–	£80	£180	£100
Debt	£800	£50	–	£50	£850	£850
Pension liabilities	–	–	£300	£300	£300	£300
Creditors	£100	£70	–	£70	£170	£170
Total	£1000	£200	£300	£500	£1500	£1420
Assets						
Company assets	£1000	£200	–	£200	£1200	£1120
Pension assets	–	–	£300	£300	£300	£300
	£1000	£200	£300	£500	£1500	£1420

Unconsolidated leverage (target) = D/A = 50/200 = 25 %
Consolidated leverage (target) = D/A = 350/500 = 70.0 %
Unconsolidated leverage (bidder) = D/A = 800/1000 = 80.0 %
Consolidated leverage (bidder) (shares) = D/A = 1150/1500 = 76.7 %
Consolidated leverage (bidder) (cash) = D/A = 1150/1420 = 81.0 %

the trustees of the relevant RSA pension schemes may demand many hundreds of millions of pounds if RSA sold off parts of its operations (*Financial Times* 2 March 2015). In 2013 RSA had sold Ivensys for £1.7 billion, of which £625 million went to the pension scheme. As well as discouraging disposals, pensions schemes can also encourage disposals. It appears that the pension scheme is the reason Mohamed al Fayed sold Harrods to Qatar Holdings on 10 May 2010. At the time al Fayed said: "*We have a pension scheme which it is my duty to subsidise. Come every year, sometime £10 million, £20 million, £30 million I pay from the profits to be sure my pensioners have money to live. But it came just as a surprise that the Government put a body in called pension trustee. I can't take my profit because I have to take a permission of those bloody idiots. For three months I've been trying to get a dividend. They say tomorrow, next week, lawyers … I say Jesus Christ! I say how this can happen? Three months I've been trying to get my finance director and the managing director to clear the dividend. They say yes, the trustee will need this and this and this, coming tomorrow, coming next week. I say is this right? Is this logic? Somebody like me? I run a business and I need to take bloody f****** trustee's permission to take my profit.*' (Mohamed al Fayed, *London Evening Standard* 26 May 2010)

b. Merging DB Pension Schemes

Following a merger or takeover, it is likely the new corporate entity will be the sponsor of two pension schemes, and may wish to merge them to offer the same employment conditions to all the members of its workforce. An underlying issue is the conditions under which the full merger of two DB pension schemes does not disadvantage the members of either scheme. Let companies *A* and *B* merge to form company *C*, and let scheme *A* (the receiving scheme) be the pension scheme to which all of the members of pension scheme *B* (the transferring scheme) transfer, to create the merged scheme, called scheme *C*.

Two requirements will be investigated (Sutcliffe 2006). First, the trustees of scheme *B* do not wish to transfer a surplus into scheme *A*, and scheme *A* does not with to accept a scheme that is in deficit (and vice versa). So schemes *A* and *B* must have a funding ratio of unity. Second, the surplus per member in both schemes should be the same, i.e. no dilution. This is approximated by requiring the same funding ratios for schemes *A* and *B*. While these criteria are unlikely to be met, it may be possible to use side payments and receipts to ensure compliance. Side receipts increase a scheme's funding ratio, and may take the form of a capital sum paid into the scheme by the sponsor before the merger, or an agreement to make higher sponsor contributions for a specified period to scheme *C* in respect of the former members of one of the schemes. Side payments can be a lower sponsor contribution rate to scheme *C* in respect of the former members of one of the schemes, or an increase in accrued benefits for scheme members immediately before the merger.

It is assumed that the funding ratio of each scheme varies positively with the stock market (*M*) in a linear manner. The funding ratios of schemes *A* and *B* can be adjusted by side receipts and side payments, although there are upper and lower limits on their size. The lines A_U and A_L in Fig. 4.1 represent the upper and lower limits to the funding ratio of scheme *A*, and similarly for scheme *B*. To be an acceptable solution, the adjusted funding ratio (AFR) has to meet two conditions:

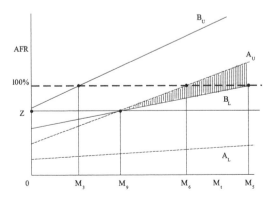

Fig. 4.1 Zero profit or loss and zero dilution: adjusted funding ratio and market

a. Lie between the upper and lower bounds for each scheme, i.e. $A_U \geq AFR_A \geq A_L$ and $B_U \geq AFR_B \geq B_L$
b. Correspond to a 100 % funding ratio for each scheme, i.e. $AFR_A = AFR_B = 100$ %.

For example, provided the value of the market portfolio lies between M_6 and M_5, these two conditions are met. This demonstrates that whether a merger can meet the conditions depends on the current state of the financial markets. It also shows the importance of side payments and receipts in achieving the desired conditions.

c. Asset Allocation of the Pension Fund

A scheme's asset allocation can be affected by many factors. These include the sponsor's default risk, the national mortality rate, the scheme's maturity, the number of external fund managers, stockmarket returns, the familiarity of the sponsor with some types of asset, political bias of the trustees and regulation.

i. Default Risk

Since the sponsor and pension scheme are effectively a single economic entity, the ultimate determinant of scheme default risk is sponsor default risk, i.e. the strength of the covenant. There are two rival views of how the sponsor's default risk affects the scheme's asset allocation between safe and risky assets – risk shifting and risk management.

A. Risk Shifting

Risky investments are expected to generate high returns which will benefit the sponsor's shareholders, as they can reduce their pension contributions. However, if the risky investments generate large losses which cannot be covered by the sponsor, then: (a) the PBGC (or the PPF) will very largely bail out the pension scheme, and (b) the sponsor's shareholders are protected by limited liability. Responding to this situation where they keep the upside, but avoid the consequences of default, shareholders adopt a risk shifting asset allocation strategy, with the equity proportion rising as the sponsor's default risk rises (see Fig. 4.2). The greater the probability of sponsor default, the greater the probability that investment losses by the pension scheme will fall on the default insurance (and members) rather than the sponsor; while the profits from risky investment benefit the sponsor. Hence the incentive to engage in risky investment rises as sponsor default risk increases. When sponsor default risk is very high it is a 'heads I win, tails you lose' situation for the sponsor. If the deficit increases, the loss falls on the insurance company and members; while if the deficit reduces this benefits the sponsor via a reduction in its

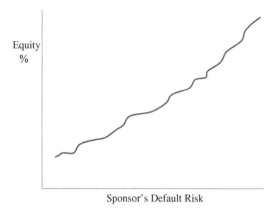

Fig. 4.2 Risk shifting

future contributions. In essence the risk is shifted to the insurance scheme (and members), and this is consistent with the Sharpe (1976) model where the sponsor seeks to maximise the benefit it receives from the under-priced insurance supplied by the PBGC (see Sect. 4.6).

An example of risk shifting occurred in March 2014 when the London Pension Fund Authority (LPFA) sold virtually its entire portfolio of UK gilts and swaps, and invested the money in higher risk assets. The chairman of the LPFA, Edmund Truell, said: '*We are in a position where we do not have enough assets to meet our liabilities. If our rate of return on gilts is 3 % before inflation, probably nothing after inflation, we are not going to be able to pay the pensions. Therefore, we are safely guaranteeing bankruptcy by investing in gilts. I don't consider gilts to be an appropriate investment for an underfunded pension fund.*' Mr. Truell estimated the LPFA funding ratio at only 60 %.

If the expected rate of return on the scheme's investments is used as the discount rate, this provides a different reason for shifting into equities as default risk rises. Investing in equities raises the discount rate, and this lowers the value of the liabilities and the reported deficit, with this incentive to minimise the reported deficit becoming stronger as the deficit rises. There is likely to be a strong positive correlation between the size of the pension deficit and the risk of default, leading to a positive relationship between default risk and the proportion of the scheme's assets invested in equities.

B. Risk Management

Risky investments may lead to losses which are insufficient to cause sponsor default and push the pension scheme into the PBGC (or PPF); and the sponsor is required to inject cash into the pension scheme, reducing the sponsor's liquidity. Such cash injections may crowd out investment and dividend payments by the sponsor (see Sect. 4.3). When sponsor default risk is high, having to make such payments may be particularly damaging to the sponsor, and to prevent such an outcome the pension scheme invests in safe assets, i.e. risk management. For sponsors with a low default risk, losses on pension scheme investments can be more easily borne by the sponsor, allowing the scheme to invest in equities. This relationship is shown in Fig. 4.3.

In addition to the shareholders' motivation to engage in a risk management strategy, senior managers who have accrued large DB pension benefits with the sponsor may not wish to risk sponsor default, with the loss of their job and a pension capital loss on transfer to the PBGC or PPF (see Sect. 4.5f). Therefore, as sponsor default risk rises, they reduce the proportion of equities in the pension fund, i.e. risk management.

C. Empirical Studies

There has been a wide range of empirical studies of risk shifting versus risk management for the USA, and to a lesser extent the UK. Many of these researchers have used the scheme's funding ratio as a (reverse) proxy for default risk; although as Guan and Lui (2014) have shown, the presence of both a low funding ratio and high sponsor default risk may be required. The empirical results on whether schemes favour risk shifting or risk management are mixed.

USA

Rauh (2009) studied 6844 US DB schemes and found that schemes with a low funding ratio tend to invest in safer assets (debt and cash), while schemes with a high funding ratio tend to invest in equities, supporting the risk

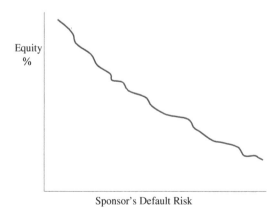

Fig. 4.3 Risk management

management view. Addoum et al. (2010) studied 1885 US DB schemes, and looked at the effect of the direction of change in the funding ratio over the previous year on the asset allocation. After allowing for the automatic effects of price changes on the asset allocation; when the funding ratio drops schemes hold more debt, and when it rises they tend to increase their allocation to equities. This result applies across a wide range of funding ratios and is more supportive of risk management than risk shifting. Friedman (1983) studied 9899 US DB schemes and found that those with the highest sponsor risk tended to invest less in equities, i.e. risk management. Amir and Benartzi (1999) discovered that as the funding ratios of about 150 US schemes dropped to low levels, the percentage of funds invested in equities also dropped, which supports risk management. Petersen (1996) studied 57,000 US schemes (of which 20,000 were DB), and found that as the funding ratio rises, investment in risky assets drops, i.e. risk shifting. Using data on 14,089 US DB pension schemes, Atanasova and Gatev (2013) showed that as the funding ratio increases, funds have riskier investments, i.e. risk management, and that this effect is much larger for quoted than for unquoted companies. They also found that higher contributions lead to a reduction in risky investment for unquoted companies.

Employing data on the DB pension schemes of US quoted companies, Comprix and Muller (2006) analysed the effects of the funding ratio on a scheme's asset allocation. US regulations use the funding standard account (FSA) to compute a scheme's minimum required funding, and even if the scheme is severely under-funded, provided the FSA account has a positive balance, the sponsor need not make additional contributions. Comprix and Muller considered the effects of the FSA on the relationship between the funding ratio and asset allocation. They found that the funding ratio has a positive effect on investment in risky assets, i.e. risk management; and that as the FSA balance increases, investment risk is also increased, especially for schemes that are under-funded. An et al. (2013) studied 1083 US DB schemes, using the pensions beta (i.e. $[\beta_{PL}(PL/V - \beta_{PA}(PA/V)])$ which includes liability as well as asset risk, to measure pension scheme investment risk. They found that funding ratios had a positive effect on pension scheme investment risk, which supports the risk management hypothesis. However, schemes on the verge of bankruptcy or about to be terminated had high pension scheme betas, which supports the risk shifting hypothesis. An et al. (2013) also found some support for the tax arbitrage motive (see Sects. 4.9 and 4.10), and that unionisation of the workforce leads to greater risk taking by pension schemes, possibly because the sponsor is seeking higher returns to cover the higher pensions negotiated by the union.

Anantharaman and Lee (2014) used data on 923 US firms to show that under-funded schemes invest more in equities, i.e. risk shifting. They also found that risk shifting is stronger when the chief financial officer has share options and shares in the sponsor, aligning their interests with those of the shareholders; and weaker when they have a large accrued pension, aligning their interests with those of pension scheme members. For 369 US DB schemes, Bodie et al. (1985, 1987) found that, as the funding ratio increased, investment in risky assets also decreased, i.e. risk shifting. Gallo and Lockwood (1995) analysed 78 US companies and showed that, as the riskiness of the sponsor increases, the DB scheme funding ratio rises, and scheme investment moves towards safer assets. This is consistent with the risk shifting view. Using data on 126 US public sector schemes, Mohan and Zhang (2014) showed that, as the funding ratio declined, the proportionate investment in equities increased, i.e. risk shifting. Since these are public sector schemes they are not covered by the PBGC, and the risk is shifted onto future generations of tax-payer. Coronado et al. (2006) found that, when sponsor bankruptcy risk is high, US sponsors make lower contributions to their schemes. Making a comparison with the UK, which did not have pension insurance at this time, Coronado et al. conclude that these effects are due to the presence of pension insurance in the USA. While this behaviour is consistent with risk shifting, there was only weak evidence that schemes with sponsors close to bankruptcy increase their equity investments.

Guan and Lui (2014) argued that the simultaneous presence of two conditions is necessary for risk shifting: (a) high sponsor bankruptcy risk and (b) severe scheme underfunding, where these two conditions are likely to show a strong positive correlation. From data on 1529 US companies they found that those companies with the highest bankruptcy risk and scheme underfunding invested more of their pension assets in equities. Companies with low bankruptcy risk and well-funded schemes also invested more of their pension assets in equities. These results suggest there is a U-shaped relationship between investment in equities and bankruptcy risk-scheme funding (see Fig. 4.4). This supports risk shifting for high-risk firms with under-funded schemes, and risk management for firms with well-funded schemes and low bankruptcy risk.

UK

Munro and Barrie (2003) looked at 300 UK companies and found that those with the largest deficits invested a higher proportion of their assets in equities, which is consistent with risk shifting. However, this result may be due to reverse causality, as equities had recently suffered large losses, reducing their portfolio weight. McCarthy and Miles (2013) constructed a theoretical model

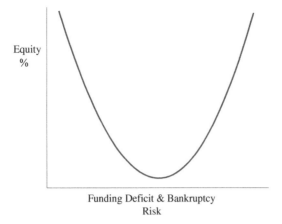

Fig. 4.4 Funding deficit and bankruptcy risk and equity investment (Guan and Lui)

and concluded that there is a negative relationship between the funding ratio and equity investment, i.e. risk shifting. LCP (2014) report that many firms in the FTSE 100 index such as Bunzl and Rexam have specified trigger points, so that when the funding ratio rises above some trigger point the assets are automatically switched from equities to bonds, i.e. risk shifting.

Li (2010) considered 58 UK pension schemes and found the proportion of assets invested in equities increased as the funding ratio increased (as did Rauh 2009), i.e. risk management; but that the equity proportion then decreased as the funding ratio increased further, i.e. risk shifting. In 2006 the PPF priced sponsor bankruptcy risk and scheme under-funding, although not investment risk, in their annual levies. For the period 2003–05 Guan and Lui (2014) found evidence of risk shifting for UK firms with a high bankruptcy risk and severe scheme under-funding. But for 2006 onwards, risk shifting is much reduced, which supports the view that insurance mispricing is an important cause of risk shifting. Bader (quoted in Atanasova and Gatev (2013)) has argued that, if the sponsor aims to minimise the variation in their contributions, the pension fund will have a high equity proportion when the funding ratio is in the middle range. But when the funding ratio is either low (possibly requiring additional contributions), or high (possibly breaching an upper tax limit on funding and requiring a reduction in contributions) the equity proportion will be low, i.e. an inverted U-shaped relationship, as in Fig. 4.5.

Atanasova and Gatev (2013) examined whether changes in the funding ratio 'cause' changes in risky investment, or whether causality runs in the opposite direction. They found that changes in the funding ratio lead changes in the asset allocation, suggesting that changes in the funding ratio 'cause' changes in the asset allocation. But a different hypothesis is that changes in

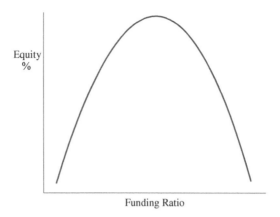

Fig. 4.5 Funding ratio and equity investment (Li)

both the funding ratio and the asset allocation are jointly determined by the presence of pension insurance, tax arbitrage and the desire of the company management for financial slack. It will be shown below in Sects. 4.6, 4.7, 4.8, 4.9 and 4.10 that: (a) pension insurance can lead to under-funding and investment in risky assets (risk shifting), (b) tax arbitrage may result in over-funding and investment in bonds (risk shifting) and (c) a desire for financial slack implies over or under-funding, depending on the liquidity situation of the sponsor.

ii. National Mortality Rate
As longevity increases pension scheme deficits tend to become larger. This can lead to one or other of two opposite outcomes. First, since pension liabilities are effectively liabilities of the sponsor, as argued above, national corporate debt/equity ratios automatically tend to rise. Second, the increase in pension scheme deficits may also lead to pension funds investing a larger proportion of their assets in equities (the risk shifting hypothesis). This will tend to increase equity prices, lower bond prices and encourage companies to issue equities rather than debt, leading to a reduction in corporate debt/equity ratios. Therefore, whether increasing longevity results in an increase or decrease in national corporate debt/equity ratios is an empirical issue. Zhu et al. (2013) used panel data on 30 developed countries and found that for small increases in longevity, national corporate debt/equity ratios increase (as predicted by the automatic increase in the size of sponsor liabilities). As longevity increases further, substantial risk shifting occurs, and national corporate debt/equity ratios decrease to the same level as found with much lower longevity.

iii. Age and Maturity

The maturity of a scheme is the ratio of active members to pensioners. An immature scheme has mostly active members who are paying into the scheme, while a mature scheme is one where there are relatively few active members, and many pensioners taking money out of the scheme. The small inflow of contributions to a mature scheme means that the scheme cannot easily deal with a large deficit by raising the contribution rate (see Sect. 2.9(iii)), and so the scheme's investment strategy becomes more important. Immature schemes tend to favour equity investment as they have the time to recover from a deficit, while mature schemes tend to favour bonds (see Fig. 4.6). Holding bonds (a) hedges the interest rate risk of the pensions, (b) are easy to liquidate to pay the pensions and (c) have low risk. This is borne out by the empirical studies which have found that for the USA and UK more mature schemes invest less in equities. As the average age of the active members increases, the time remaining before they stop making contributions, and the scheme must begin paying their pensions, decreases, and in the Netherlands, Finland and Switzerland schemes with older members also invest less in equities.

USA

For 6844 US DB schemes Rauh (2009) found that mature US DB schemes tend to invest less in equities. Amir and Benartzi (1999) obtained a similar result for about 150 US DB schemes, as did Friedman (1983) for 9899 US DB schemes.

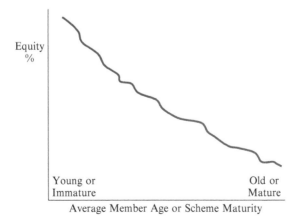

Fig. 4.6   Age or maturity and equity

UK
Munro and Barrie (2003) considered 300 UK schemes and discovered that more mature schemes invest a smaller proportion of their assets in equities.

Netherlands
In a study of 378 Dutch pension schemes, Bikker et al. (2012a) found that their equity allocation decreases as the average age of their active members increases.

Finland
For 44 Finish pension schemes, Alestalo and Puttonen (2006) found that, as the average age of members increases, the equity proportion of the pension fund decreases.

Switzerland
For 2,061 Swiss schemes, Gerber and Weber (2007) found that schemes with older members have a lower proportionate allocation to equities.

iv. Number of Fund Managers
Some pension funds employ a number of fund managers, and this has been interpreted as a competition or tournament, with poor performers being replaced. Cox et al. (2007) analysed the investments in 541 UK companies by fund managers employed by 2353 UK pension schemes, and found that the number of asset managers affects scheme asset allocation. Fund managers with fewer rivals invested more money in companies with a good record of corporate social responsibility and a high beta value, and less in companies with a high total risk. They interpret these results as supporting the view that low tournament intensity (few fund managers) favours long-term investment, while high tournament intensity (many fund managers) encourages short-termism.

v. Stock Market Returns
Bikker et al. (2010) used data on 748 Dutch pension schemes. In the short run out-performance by equities, relative to bonds, automatically causes a rise in the equity proportion of their portfolios. Quarterly portfolio rebalancing then leads to 40 % of the increased equity allocation being liquidated, with 60 % being retained. Therefore, in the longer term, strong equity returns result in a rise in the strategic equity allocation.

vi. Familiarity, Information and Political Bias

Atanasova and Chemia (2013) found that, when the corporate sponsor of a US pension scheme has high R&D expenditure, the pension scheme has a higher investment in private equity. Similarly when the sponsor has a large holding of property, the DB scheme tends to invest a higher proportion of their assets in property. This is argued to be because the pension scheme tends in invest in assets with which the sponsor is familiar. Familiarity should not lead to higher returns on such investments, while superior information ought to result in higher returns. Sinclair (2011) examined four US state pension schemes and concludes that, when the investment performance of the scheme has been poor, this is followed by an increase in their investment in local firms. He also finds local investment leads to higher returns, which is consistent with an information, rather than a familiarity, effect. Brown et al. (2015b) examined the equity investments of 27 US state pension schemes. They found these schemes have over-weight equity investments in companies with headquarters in their state, and that these investments generate excess returns, which again supports information, rather than familiarity. This finding of higher returns for local investments by pension schemes is consistent with other studies of local investment by fund managers, individual investors and hedge funds.

Rather than information, there is evidence which favours political motives for state schemes investing in companies based in the state. This may be due to a desire to be seen to be supporting the local economy, although such a policy reduces diversification and increases the risks to scheme funding. The funding of state pension schemes depends on the financial health of the state government, which in turn depends on the health of the local economy, and over-weighting local companies increases the dependence of the scheme on the local economy. For 16 US state schemes Bradley et al. (forthcoming) confirmed the previous finding of the over-weighting of local companies by state schemes. They also found this over-weighting to be concentrated in a sub-set of local firms. These are local firms making political donations to local politicians (over-weighted by 23 %); and local firms with significant lobbying expenditures (over-weighted by 17 %). State schemes with a larger proportion of politically linked trustees also have an increased over-weighting of local firms. This political bias leads to a negative effect on returns, indicating that the over-weighting of local firms by state schemes is not associated with an improved flow of information to state schemes, contradicting the result of Brown et al. (2015b). Hochberg and Rauh (2013) showed that US public pension schemes over-weight investment in private equity (buyout, venture capital and real estate private equity funds) within their state. This in-state investment in private equity leads to lower returns than their own investments in similar out-of-state investments in private equity, and lower returns than similar investments in their state by out-of-state investors. Therefore this in-state investment is not motivated by access to superior information. Since the over-weighting of private equity is higher in states with more political misconduct convictions, this suggests that political pressure is involved in the over-weighting of in-state private equity.

While there is agreement that US state pension schemes over-weight local firms, there is disagreement about whether this is due to superior information or political bias, and whether it leads to higher or lower returns. If it results in lower returns, coupled with the indications of political bias in such invest-ments, it raises corporate governance concerns.

vii. Regulation

Boon et al. (2014) studied the effects of regulation on the allocation of pen-sion scheme assets to risky assets, and found that regulation has a larger effect on asset allocation than do the characteristics of individual schemes. Each of the seven aspects of regulation that were studied affect the holdings of risky assets by large Dutch, Canadian and American DB pension schemes. Risk-based capital requirements and the balance sheet recognition of unfunded liabilities are the most important influences on the allocation to risky assets.

d. Funding Ratio and Bond Spreads, Credit Ratings or CDS Premia

The empirical evidence is that high pension scheme risk, measured using the funding ratio and other methods, is associated with high bond spreads on the sponsor's debt, poor credit ratings for the sponsor (or non-senior bonds), and high credit default swap (CDS) spreads. These results are in line with the view that a large scheme deficit increases the probability of sponsor default.

i. Credit Spreads

Cardinale (2007) analysed 583 US companies with a DB scheme, and found that as the funding ratio increases, bond spreads for the company's debt decrease. He also analysed 100 UK companies and found a similar negative relationship between the funding ratio and bond spreads. Wang et al. (2013) studies data on 722 US companies and found that their credit spreads rose with their pension beta, although they were unaffected by their funding ratio. Gallagher and McKillop (2010a) studied corporate bonds from over 20 coun-tries and found that pension risk (measured in four different ways) varies positively with the credit spread on the company's bonds.

ii. Credit Ratings
Carroll and Niehaus (1998) studied 253 US companies and discovered that their credit rating improves as the funding ratio of their DB pension schemes increases. Maher (1987) considered 212 US companies and also found that the credit rating of a company's bonds gets better as their funding ratio increases. In a study of US companies with DB schemes, Wang and Zhang (2014) concluded that under-funding of a company's DB scheme reduces the credit rating of its non-senior secured bonds, but not the credit rating of its senior secured bonds. They also found that a 10 % drop in a scheme's funding ratio is associated with a 7.4 % reduction in the probability of non-senior secured bond default and a 3.5 % reduction in the recovery rate, even after controlling for credit ratings. The credit ratings, default probabilities and recovery rates of senior bonds are unaffected by the funding ratio because they have greater security than non-senior bonds. Watson Wyatt (2005) studied 1000 large US companies, and found lower funding ratios were associated with lower credit ratings. For 140 US companies Maher (1996) studied the relationship between the company's credit rating and its pension liabilities, deflated by total assets; and found that a rise in pension liabilities leads to a worse credit rating. Martin and Henderson (1983) applied discriminant analysis to a sample of 129 bonds issued by US companies with DB schemes, and showed that the prediction of bond ratings is improved by the inclusion of nine pensions variables. For the UK McKillop and Pogue (2009) analysed data on 92 firms in the FTSE 100 and found that firms with a high pension risk (measured in three different ways) are more likely to have a low credit rating.

iii. CDS Premia
Gallagher and McKillop (2010b) used the CDS premia for corporate bonds issued by companies in 16 countries, and found that a measure of company pension risk is positively correlated with the CDS premium.

e. Pension Deficits and the Share Price
The evidence for the USA, UK and Japan is that companies with substantially under-funded pension schemes are over-valued by the stock market. This suggests investors are neglecting or misinterpreting information on the status of company pension schemes.

USA
Feldstein and Seligman (1981) and Feldstein and Mørck (1983) showed that US company share prices reflect their unfunded pension liabilities. However, Franzoni and Marin (2006a) found that US companies with the highest pension

deficits (i.e. lowest funding ratios) had the largest over-valuation of their shares (about 10 % per year). This is argued to be due to the stock market ignoring information on the pensions deficits. Chen (2015) has proposed a different explanation for this result. Large pension deficits may be positively correlated with poor financial disclosure by the sponsor as they seek to manipulate their reported earnings, resulting in higher unsystematic risk. This unsystematic risk leads to a drop in the share price, assuming it is not diversified away. Chen studied 5140 US DB schemes and, as he expected, found a positive relationship between pension deficits and unsystematic risk. Castro-Gonzalez (2012) investigated US companies and found that those with the largest drops in their funding ratio were over-priced. Chen et al. (2014) studied analyst forecasts of the earnings of US quoted companies with DB pension schemes. They found that the higher the pension deficit, the greater was the upward bias in the analysts' earnings forecasts, and the lower were subsequent returns on the company's shares. This is consistent with the shares being over-valued. Franzoni and Marin (2006b) show that a trading rule based on the over-valuation of US companies with DB schemes is profitable.

In 2011 the US states of Wisconsin and Ohio were facing budget deficits of $3.6 billion and $8 billion respectively. To deal with these deficits they passed legislation that substantially increased the contribution rates of members to these state pension schemes, and banned unionised workers from negotiating their pension benefits. Cohen et al. (2014) found that events which increased (decreased) the probability of this legislation being passed increased (decreased) the share prices of banks operating in Wisconsin and Ohio. This is argued to be because this legislation reduced the probability of default by these states, so increasing the value of loans to them by these banks.

Japan
Nakajima and Sasaki (2010) looked at Japanese companies, and found that those with the largest pension deficits that were unrecognised in their published accounts, were over-valued by up to 12 % by the stock market.

UK
Liu and Tonks (2010) examined UK data and found that, if a company has a DB pension scheme deficit this leads to a reduction in its stockmarket value, but by less than the size of the deficit. So such companies are over-valued by the stock market.

f. Sponsor Risk

The claims by chief executive officers (CEO) on the companies they run can take two forms: inside debt (e.g. accrued DB pensions plus deferred compensation); and equity claims (e.g. equities and share options). Inside debt aligns the interests of the CEO with the firm's debtholders, while equity claims align their interests with those of the shareholders. The larger is the ratio of the CEO's inside debt to their equity claims the more risk averse they will be, leading them to manage the company in an increasingly risk adverse manner. Wei and Yermack (2011) conducted an event study of the effects of the disclosure of the value of CEO inside debt levels for 299 US companies in 2007. When the company disclosed that the CEO had a high level of inside debt, as expected, the share price fell, the bond price rose and equity and bond price volatility dropped. Liu et al. (2014) found that, as the inside debt of US CEOs increases, they are more concerned about the risk of default. To reduce this effect they favour increased cash holdings by the sponsor to give the CEOs more confidence that their inside debt will be honoured. Lee and Tang (2011) also found empirical support for this proposition. White (2015) studied 272 US companies, and discovered that, if the CEO has substantial compensation leverage (i.e. the ratio of the value of their accrued pension benefits to the sum of their accrued pension benefits, stock options and shares in the employer), and this pension is unfunded, the company has a low default risk. This is because the CEO is managing the company to avoid risks and ensure it remains in business to pay their pension. This reduction in default risk is neutralised if the CEO's pension is funded (e.g. by a Rabbi trust in the US), or if the non-CEO executives have low compensation leverage on average.

Begley et al. (2015) analysed the relationship between the funding level of DB schemes sponsored by about 500 US companies, and the accrued pension benefits of their CEOs. CEOs typically accrue benefits in both a DB scheme and a SERP, where the DB scheme is funded, and the SERP is not. Improving the funding of the DB scheme makes the DB pension more secure, but by taking cash out of the sponsor, it makes payment of the SERP pension less secure. As expected, Begley et al. find that the greater the ratio of the CEO's accrued DB benefits to their accrued SERP benefits, the higher the DB scheme's funding ratio. They also find that CEOs with larger total accrued pension benefits (DB plus SERP) are less likely to implement a hard freeze of the DB scheme.

Anantharaman et al. (2014) analysed the determinants of 1462 loans to 677 US companies, and discovered that the interest rate charged is lower, and the covenant terms less restrictive, when the CEO's relative leverage is lower. Relative leverage is defined as the ratio of the CEO's inside leverage to the company's leverage, where inside leverage is the CEO's accrued benefits in the company's DB and Supplemental Executive Retirement Plan (SERP) schemes plus other deferred compensation, divided by the value of their shares and share options. The more favourable loan terms is attributed to greater inside debt aligning the CEO's interests with those of the debtholders. This effect is mainly due to the SERP component of inside debt, which is unfunded.

g. Supplemental Executive Retirement Plans

The CEOs of some companies have a SERP where their pension is positively related to the firm's financial performance in the years just before their retirement. This gives CEOs an incentive to increase reported profits in these pre-retirement years, possibly at the expense of profits in the years after they retire. In a study of 472 Canadian CEOs, Kalyta (2009a) found a reduction in R&D expenditure during the pre-retirement period for those CEOs whose pensions were positively linked to the sponsor's profits. Similarly, for 1137 US CEOs Kalyta (2009b) found that a positive link between pre-retirement profits and their pension led to a reduction in discretionary accruals, and an increase in reported profits. Stefanescu et al. (2014) analysed the relationship between the bonuses received by top US executives and the hard freezing of their DB pension scheme, or their departure from the company. For top executives their benefits under a SERP are generally many times larger than under the regular DB scheme, and both are usually frozen at the same time. Using data for 1224 US companies they found that, prior to a hard freeze of the DB scheme or the executive's departure, executives received an increase in their bonus (after controlling for other factors affecting the size of the bonus), leading to a big increase in their pension entitlement. These empirical results suggest that SERPs can lead to top managers manipulating the performance of the company they are managing so as to increase their own pension.

h. Employee Buyouts

In the USA excess assets in a DB scheme can be used to help finance an employee buyout, Chaplinsky et al. (1998). The excess pension assets are converted into employee shares in the post-buyout firm, reducing the amount of outside finance required for the buyout, and lowering the leverage of the post-buyout firm.

i. Multi-Employer Liability Spillovers

With multi-employer schemes one of the sponsors may become insolvent and unable to continue contributing to the scheme. The USA operates a last-man-standing rule, which is also used by some UK schemes such as USS, where the failure of one sponsor leads to the remaining sponsors assuming the obligations of the failed sponsor. This process continues until only one sponsor is left shouldering responsibility for all the scheme's obligations – the last-man-standing. Therefore sponsors in such a multi-employer scheme face the risk of insolvency by other sponsors in the same scheme, creating a liability spillover risk. The US has about 1450 multi-employer DB schemes, and their members represent about a quarter of US DB scheme membership. For 75 US multi-employer schemes, Chambers (2014) computed each sponsor's share of the scheme's unfunded scheme liabilities using their share of scheme contributions, excluding the contributions of the insolvent sponsor. The probability of sponsor insolvency was estimated using z-scores, and were assumed to be independent of each other, although it likely they are positively correlated. The expected liability spillover for each sponsor was calculated by multiplying the spillover to them from the insolvency of each of the other sponsors in the scheme by their probability of insolvency, and summing the results. United Parcel Services (UPS) had an expected liability spillover in 2009 of $17.2 million, and the corresponding figure for Safeway was $15.9 million. For the 23 sponsors in the sample with an expected liability spillover in 2009 greater that $1 million, their total expected loss was $405 million. This leads to the question of whether this risk is impounded into the share prices and credit ratings of the sponsors. Chen et al. (2015) investigated the effects of unfunded multi-employer scheme liabilities on the share prices and credit ratings of the sponsors. In each case they found that, as expected, there is a negative effect.

j. Tax Avoidance and the Funding Ratio

If a DB scheme has a deficit this tends to lead to higher pension contributions by the sponsor, which reduces their free cash balances and lowers their reported profits. Therefore sponsors with schemes that have a large deficit are under greater pressure than other firms. One possible response to these twin pressures is to seek ways of reducing the corporate tax bill, thereby increasing net profits and making more cash available to the sponsor. Chaudhry et al. (2015) investigated 3974 US firms with a DB scheme and found that, as the scheme's funding ratio drops, the sponsors engage in more tax avoidance.

4.6   Irrelevance of Scheme Funding and Asset Allocation

Using a consolidated model of the sponsor and DB scheme, this sub-section presents the option-based model of Sharpe (1976), which is then used to consider whether the level of scheme funding and the asset allocation of the pension fund matter, or whether they are irrelevant. Sharpe analysed three cases: (a) no pension scheme default insurance, (b) full pension scheme default insurance and (c) partial pension scheme default insurance, and each of these cases will be considered in turn.

For all three models Sharpe (1976) assumes:

(a) There are no taxes (relaxed in Sect. 4.9).
(b) The sponsor owns any pension scheme surplus (relaxed in Sect. 4.7).
(c) The sponsor is not liable for any pension scheme deficit (relaxed in Sect. 4.7).
(d) The scheme has only active members. If deferred pensioners and pensioners exist this raises the issue of how surpluses and deficits are shared with them. Deferred pensioners and pensioners have minimal bargaining power with the sponsor, making the sponsor's put option (explained below in this sub-section) more valuable than if they were active members.
(e) There are no costs of terminating the scheme (e.g. legal costs).
(f) The model is for one period, although it can be reformulated as a series of periods.
(g) The implicit options embedded in the pension scheme are European style.
(h) Markets are competitive and complete, so that all assets and liabilities are traded at their fair values.

a. No Pension Default Insurance

Given the assumptions above, and adding the assumption of no pension scheme default insurance, the sponsor effectively has a long call option (the pension call) on the assets of the pension fund (A), with a strike price equal to the terminal value of the scheme liabilities (L^*) because it owns any surplus. The members of the scheme effectively have a short put option (the pension put) on the assets of the fund (A), with a strike price equal to L^*, because they will bear any deficit on the pension scheme.

The payoff diagram (Fig. 4.7) shows that:-

$$A = C + L - P \tag{4.1}$$

where C and P are the values of the call and put options respectively. The put option has a negative sign because it is short. Equation (4.1) follows from the European style put-call parity $[C = P+S-K/(1+r)-D]$ where A is the spot price (S), L is the present value of the strike price (K) and there are no dividends

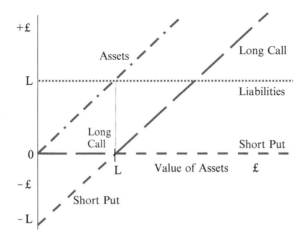

Fig. 4.7 Sharpe – no pension insurance

(*D*). Therefore $C = P + A - L$, which can be re-arranged as $A = C + L - P$. No option premia are shown in Fig. 4.7 as none are paid.

Employees receive compensation in the form of wages with a present value of *W*, and pensions accrued during the period with a present value of *L*. Higher pensions imply an increase in pension liabilities, which leads to an increase in the strike price of the put option, and therefore an increase in the value of the put option (*P*). Since the members have a short position in the put option, an increase in pensions leads to a loss for them as *P* becomes bigger. The total remuneration received by the members (*T*) is wages plus pensions, less the short put, as shown in equation (4.2):

$$T = W + L - P \tag{4.2}$$

It is assumed that *T* is fixed at a constant level (denoted by $\overline{T}$) by negotiations between the sponsor and the members. This relies on the assumption that in competitive and complete markets what matters is total remuneration, and not its components. Using equations (4.1) and (4.2), equation (4.3) gives the total cost to the sponsor:-

$$\overline{T} = W + A - C \qquad (\text{and } \overline{T} = W + L - P) \tag{4.3}$$

The values of the call and put options (*C* and *P*) depend on the values of the underlying assets (*A*), the volatility of this total asset value (*σ*), and the strike price (*L*), i.e. $C = f(A, \sigma, L)$ and $P = f(A, \sigma, L)$. Given the assumptions, equations (4.2) and (4.3) show that the assets of the scheme (A), the asset allocation (which alters both the size (A) and volatility (σ) of the assets), the size of the liabilities (L) and wages (W) are irrelevant and indeterminate because $\bar{T}$ is fixed. Since both equations (4.2) and (4.3) sum to the constant $\bar{T}$, any change in one of the three variables on the right-hand side of equation (4.3) (i.e. W, A and C, or W, L and P) will be accompanied by offsetting changes in the underlying four variables (A, L, W and σ) to ensure $\bar{T}$ remains constant.

b. Full Pension Scheme Default Insurance

The assumptions are the same as for the no default insurance model, except that when there is a deficit it is fully made up by an insurance company which has provided fairly priced default insurance. Now, instead of the members having a short position in a put option, it is the insurance company which has this short position. They do so in exchange for an insurance premium paid by the sponsor. In competitive markets the value of this premium equals that of the put option (P), i.e. the insurance is fairly priced. The total cost to the sponsor increases by P, and the total remuneration received by the members increases by P. Equations (4.2) and (4.3) now become:

$$\bar{T} = W + L \tag{4.4}$$

$$\bar{T} = W + A - C + P \tag{4.5}$$

As before, the assets of the scheme (A), the asset allocation (which alters both the size (A) and volatility of the assets), the size of the liabilities (L) and wages (W) are irrelevant and indeterminate since $\bar{T}$ is constant.

c. Partial Pension Scheme Default Insurance

Most pension insurance schemes (e.g. the PBGC and the PPF) place a cap on the maximum pension paid out under the insurance, and the PPF is estimated to cover about 90 % of the liabilities. Suppose the default insurance covers $x\%$ of any deficit, then the insurance company has a short put (P_1) for $x\%$ of any deficit, while the scheme members have a short put (P_2) covering the remaining deficit $(1 - x)\%$, where $P = P_1 + P_2$. The sponsor pays an insurance premium equal to P_1, and equations (4.4) and (4.5) now become:-

$$\bar{T} = W + L - P_2 \tag{4.6}$$

$$\bar{T} = W + A - C + P_1 \tag{4.7}$$

As before, the assets of the scheme (A), the asset allocation (which alters both the size (A) and volatility of the assets), the size of the liabilities (L) and wages (W) are irrelevant and indeterminate since $\bar{T}$ is fixed.

In reality Sharpe's assumptions are not met, and so for all three models scheme funding and asset allocation do matter in practice, see the empirical evidence in Sect. 4.5.

4.7   Equity Investment and Risk Sharing

The Sharpe (1976) model has been extended to consider sharing the risk of equity investment between the sponsor and the members in the presence of full and fairly priced default insurance (Sutcliffe 2004). The case where T is fixed and there is no risk sharing has already been analysed, which leaves three situations to be considered: (1) the total remuneration of members (T) is *not* fixed and deficits and surpluses are *not* shared, (2) T is *not* fixed, and deficits and surpluses *are* shared and (3) T *is* fixed and deficits and surpluses *are* shared.

1. If T is *not* fixed and deficits and surpluses are *not* shared, the irrelevance result of Sharpe (1976) no longer applies, and changes in W, L, A will not be fully offsetting. If wages or pensions are not increased to fully compensate for an increase in the riskiness of pension fund investments, this will make the members worse off because P has increased, and make the sponsor better off because C has also increased. So the interests of the sponsor and members are diametrically opposed, with the sponsor favouring equity investment, and the members wanting investment in bonds.

2. Suppose T is *not* fixed and deficits and surpluses *are* shared, the situation becomes more complex. Let the sponsor bears a proportion (d) (previously assumed to be zero) of any deficits, and the members receive a proportion ($1 - s$) (previously assumed to be zero) of any surplus. The sponsor shares in any deficits by making extra contributions, either during the life of the scheme or on wind-up, while the members share in any surplus by accruing additional benefits. Equations (4.2) and (4.3 with a variable T) become:

$$T = W + L - P(1 - d) + C(1 - s) \tag{4.8}$$

$$T = W + A + Pd - Cs \tag{4.9}$$

Whether a high equity allocation is beneficial to the sponsor or members depends on how T changes as the volatility of fund returns (σ) changes. Differentiating equation (4.8) with respect to σ gives:

$$\delta T/\delta\sigma = \delta(L+W)/\delta\sigma - (1-d)(\delta P/\delta\sigma) + (1-s)(\delta C/\delta\sigma) \qquad (4.10)$$

where $\delta C/\delta\sigma$ and $\delta P/\delta\sigma$ are vega (ν) from the Black-Scholes model of option pricing. Let $\delta(L+W)/\delta\sigma = z$, which is positive because the members require higher wages plus pensions to compensate them for riskier pension fund investments. This compensation is required by the members because pension obligations typically form a large part of their assets and they are unable to remove this additional pensions risk because pensions cannot be traded on markets, and because this risk is difficult to hedge. Shareholders in the sponsor can probably diversify away the unsystematic default risk of this particular company. Therefore equation (4.10) can be rewritten as:

$$\delta T/\delta\sigma = z + v(d - s) \qquad (4.11)$$

Since $z > 0$ and vega is positive, if $d > s$ then $\delta T/\delta\sigma$ is positive, and increasing the riskiness of pension fund investments increases T to the benefit of the members. If $d < s$ it is possible that $\nu(d - s) + z$ is negative and higher equity investment reduces the total remuneration of members (T). Given the assumptions, the interests of the sponsor and members concerning the equity allocation of the fund are opposed, with the identity of the group favouring a higher equity allocation (sponsor or members) depending of the relative sizes of d and s, and also on z and ν when $d < s$. Who has the power to set the asset allocation (and thereby σ) depends on the rules of each scheme, and in some cases it is solely the sponsor. In the UK over the period 1987–2001 some schemes were forced to reduce their pension scheme surplus for tax reasons. Members received 34.4 % of reductions in the surplus in the form of additional benefits, implying that s is 0.656. For schemes with a strong and successful sponsor, the value of d will be close to one, and so $d > s$ and members will prefer risky investments, while the sponsor will prefer safe investments. But if d is low so that $\nu(d - s) + z < 0$ the sponsor will prefer risky investments, and the members will want low-risk investments, see Table 4.4.

3. Suppose now that deficits and surpluses *are* shared in some way, but that $\overline{T}$ is fixed. In this case the effects of a change in the riskiness of the asset allocation (σ) are offset by a change in W, L or A, so that $\overline{T}$ remains constant. Therefore the irrelevance result of Sharpe (1976) is restored.

Table 4.4 Summary of various combinations of total remuneration and risk sharing

	The Sharpe model and its three variants				
	Sharpe	1	2		3
			2a	2b	
T	Fixed	Variable	Variable	Variable	Fixed
d and s	$d = 0, s = 1$	$d = 0, s = 1$	$d > s$, or $v(d - s) + z > 0$	$v(d - s) + z < 0$	$1 \geq d \geq 0,$ $1 \geq s \geq 0$
Sponsor	Irrelevant	High equity	Low equity	High equity	Irrelevant
Members	Irrelevant	Low equity	High equity	Low equity	Irrelevant

The Sharpe model and the three extensions are summarised in Table 4.4. Only for case 2b, where $d < s$, does determining whether the sponsor or the members have an increased preference for a high equity allocation require valuing z and the value of vega (v), as well as the values of d and s. Table 4.4 shows that when total remuneration is not fixed and the asset allocation and scheme funding are irrelevant, the sponsor and members have opposed preferences. Sometimes the sponsor prefers risky assets and the members prefer safe assets, and sometimes the reverse is true.

4.8   Arguments for Over or Underfunding DB Pension Schemes

a. Arguments for Over-funding
There are a number of reasons why a sponsor may wish to over-fund its DB scheme.

i. Taxation
Tax arbitrage gains are maximised when the scheme is over-funded to the legal maximum allowed as returns on the pension fund are tax exempt (see Sect. 4.9).

ii. Financial Slack
Over-funding the pension scheme provides the sponsor with the ability to reduce their contributions to the scheme whenever they chooses, i.e. this provides the company with liquidity or financial slack. Ballester, Fried and Livnat (2002) used data on 1683 US companies and found that they raise pension contributions when they have positive cash flow, and later use these funds (via lower pension contributions) to fund extra capital expenditure, which supports the financial slack argument. In a study of 208 over-funded US DB schemes, Stone (1987) found that they tend to be terminated when the sponsor

is short of cash, thereby releasing cash to the sponsor. Datta et al. (1996) examined 177 US companies with DB pension schemes and found that, as the equity stake of the managers in the company increases, the funding ratio decreases, as shown in Fig. 4.8. This is consistent with the financial slack argument, as managers with no equity stake have the highest incentive to build up financial slack, and so increase their job security.

iii. Reduce the Risk of Default

Asthana (2009) examined data on 831 US firms and found that those sponsors with a large proportion of highly compensated employees tended to overfund their schemes to reduce the risk of default (see Fig. 4.9). These firms disguise this over-funding by the actuarial choices made when valuing the scheme.

iv. Reduce the PPF Levy

Under-funded UK schemes must pay a higher PPF levy, which provides an incentive to avoid under-funding.

However, despite these reasons for over-funding, in reality most pension schemes are *under*-funded. In January 2015 the PPF 7800 index showed an aggregate deficit of £367.5 billion, and on a buyout valuation most schemes are in deficit most of the time, i.e. under-funded, and the aggregate deficit on a buyout basis in March 2015 for the schemes in the PPF 7800 index was £800.9 billion (PPF 2015b).

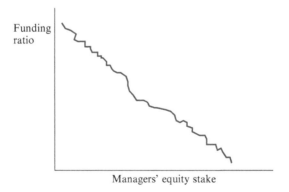

Fig. 4.8 Financial slack

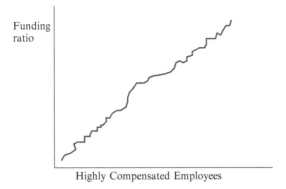

Fig. 4.9 Reduce the risk of default

b. Arguments for Under-Funding

There are also some arguments for sponsors choosing to under-fund their DB pension schemes.

i. Risk Sharing

A risk-averse company may under-fund their scheme to share risk with the members so that if the company defaults on its pensions promise when it is under-funded, the scheme members also lose out (Arnott and Gersovitz 1980). With the introduction of pensions insurance this explanation loses much of its force. However, it can still be beneficial to the sponsor in certain circumstances. In the USA a sponsor can terminate their scheme if they are in severe financial trouble, leaving the PBGC to pay the pensions, which will be reduced by the PBGC caps. Abandoning a scheme to the PBGC has been called 'pension dumping' by Hawthorne (2008). Benmelech et al. (2012) investigated the threat of pension dumping by US airlines when negotiating with their employees to secure wage reductions. They found that, for financially distressed airlines with an under-funded pension scheme where the employee's wages exceeded the PBGC maximum compensation, there were wage reductions of between 9.3 and 11.2 %. This suggests the unions agreed to wage reductions to avoid the losses following from pensions dumping.

ii. Borrowing

If a company is subject to capital market imperfections, such as borrowing restrictions or the cost of borrowing externally exceeds the returns on pension fund investments, it may borrow from its members at a zero rate of interest (Cooper and Ross 2002). This is achieved by under-funding the DB pension scheme. The members agree because it helps the company overcome its borrowing difficulties and retains their jobs.

iii. Bargaining
If the sponsor has invested in specialised equipment and buildings etc. they are vulnerable to a 'holdup loss' by the trade union, where the union threatens industrial action unless the wage rate is increased (Ippolito 1985, 1986, Chaps. 10 and 11; Cherkes and Yaari 1988). To deal with this potential threat the sponsor can deliberately under-fund the DB pension scheme as a way of bonding the workforce not to take industrial action. If the workers do take industrial action, the sponsor can shut down the company and pension scheme. Since the scheme is under-funded the members will lose a substantial amount of their pension, and so the members have a stake in the long-term viability of the company. In essence, as a result of the under-funding they have made a long-term unsecured loan to the company, and this should motivate them to ensure the company's long-term survival. For US public sector pension schemes (which are not covered by the PBGC), Mitchell and Smith (1994) found that unionisation of the workforce led to lower pension funding, which is consistent with bargaining motivation for under-funding. Prior to the introduction of the PBGC, Ippolito (1985) discovered that non-unionised schemes had a funding ratio of 90 %, while unionised schemes had a funding ratio of only 60 %, which is also consistent with bargaining. Ippolito also found that all unionised workers were in DB schemes, as predicted by the theory because, in response to a unionised workforce, the sponsor offers a DB scheme to counter the 'holdup' threat. However, the introduction of pension default insurance in the USA in 1974 and in the UK in 2005 greatly reduced the power of this argument to explain under-funding, as most of any pension default is covered by the insurance.

iv. Pension Default Insurance
The default insurance is under-priced, and so equation (4.5) applies, except that the cost of insurance to the sponsor is too low (P_U). Let $P_U = \alpha P$ where $\alpha < 1$. The remuneration received by workers (T_W) now exceeds the cost to the sponsor (T_S) due to the subsidy provided to the sponsor by the pension insurer, i.e.

$$T_s = T_w - P(1-\alpha)$$

(4.12)

The value of T_S, the total cost to the sponsor, is *not* fixed, and they can benefit from increased insurance under-pricing. In equation (4.12) T_S is minimised when the insurance under-pricing (i.e. $P - P_U$) is maximised. Since $P - P_U = P(1 - \alpha)$ this is achieved by maximising the value of P. P is a function of the assets, liabilities and volatility of the assets, i.e. $P = f(A, L, \sigma)$, and a reduction in scheme assets increases P, while an increase in liabilities increases P. Therefore reducing scheme assets, and/or increasing scheme liabilities (i.e. reducing the funding level) increases P. So the sponsor wishes to under-fund the scheme to maximise the subsidy they receive from the insurance company. The under-funding should not affect members as any deficit is assumed to be fully insured.

v. Over-priced Shares

There is empirical evidence that the stock market tends to ignore part or all of the deficit when valuing the company's shares, (Franzoni and Marin 2006a, b; Castro-Gonzalez 2012; Nakajima and Sasaki 2010; Liu and Tonks 2010) (see Sect. 4.5e). Therefore under-funding a DB pension scheme should increase the sponsor's share price by retaining money within the sponsor.

vi. Deter Takeover Bids

Large pension liabilities, particularly if there is under-funding, may deter another company from launching a takeover bid (see Sect. 4.5a), while over-funding can encourage takeover bids.

vii. Local Authority Schemes

Local authorities run DB schemes for their employees and these are generally under-funded. This has the advantage of reducing the current cost of the local authority workforce, allowing local taxes to be lower, or services better, than otherwise. This pension under-funding will have to be made good in the future, but by then the current residents (local tax payers) may have moved out of the area, or be dead, and so avoid this cost. Therefore, unless the under-funding is capitalised into local property values which may not happen due to the opacity of the size of this pension under-funding, migrants and the deceased avoid paying the under-funded portion of their local services. Even if local tax-payers do not migrate or die and they have to pay higher taxes in the future, under-funding the pension scheme provides a way for them to borrow money now at a low or zero interest rate. The empirical evidence for the US supports this hypothesis. In March 2014 Warren Buffett wrote in his 2013 annual letter to shareholders that '*local and state financial problems are accelerating, in large part because public entities promised pensions they couldn't afford. Citizens and public officials typically under-appreciated the gigantic financial tapeworm that was born when promises were made that conflicted with a willingness to fund them. Unfortunately, pension mathematics today remain a mystery to most Americans*' (Buffett 2014).

In an early study, Inman (1982) analysed 60 US police and fire services and found support for the view that the cost of these services is passed on to future tax-payers by under-funding the pension schemes. Lowenstein (2008) documents how, when threatened by trade unions with industrial action and advise to their members to vote against the incumbents, US local authorities agreed to large pension increases which they failed to fully fund. This avoided the electoral damage of industrial action at little immediate cost, leaving the under-funded pensions to be dealt with by subsequent administrations. Using American data, Jackson (1997) found strong empirical support for this explanation using migration data for 47 states. With data for 67 US cities Leeds (1985) discovered that pension under-funding has no effect on local property values, and this lack of a market price response may be due to knowledge of the pension under-funding not being public. When San Diego City in California unexpectedly revealed a very large pension deficit, this announcement led to a drop in local house prices, suggesting that the deficit had not previously been capitalised (MacKay 2014). Kelley (2014) studied the determinants of the unfunded pension liabilities of 42 US states, and found support for the view that trade union lobbying for higher pension benefits is a major cause. Elder and Wagner (2015) concluded that the self-reported under-funding of 91 US DB state schemes increased with the degree of competition between the political parties in the state, the turnover rate (winning seats from the opposition) in the state's upper house, and the presence of term limits. Bagchi (2013) analysed the pension schemes of 2000 municipal pension schemes in Pennsylvania and found that, where local political competition is stronger, scheme funding ratios are lower, and median pensions and discount rates are higher. These findings are consistent with politicians taking a short-term view of pension scheme funding, and leaving the problem to subsequent administrations.

This situation incentivises local authorities to weight remuneration towards pensions rather than wages, as pensions can be under-funded and so are less costly in the short run. A similar argument can be applied to under-funding the pensions of central government employees, where the subsequently higher taxes, or worse services, at a later date can be avoided by death or migration to another country. In the UK the main government-sponsored pension schemes are unfunded, so the under-funding is 100 %. In Canada Tufts and Fairbanks (2011) report that politicians have been coerced by public sector trade unions into providing higher pension benefits, and running up large public pension scheme deficits, and the authors equate this process to a Ponzi scheme.

c. The Determinants of Sponsor Contributions

Jones (2014) examined the determinants of sponsor contributions to 1606 US DB schemes. She found that sponsor contributions, deflated by total assets, are a positive function of: (a) the age of the sponsor, which may be because older firms tend to have more mature schemes with higher annual accruals per member; (b) the degree of unionisation of the workforce, possibly because a powerful union ensures the maintenance of an expensive pension scheme; (c) the leverage of the sponsor, which may be due to large pension scheme deficits leading to a credit downgrade and the triggering of debt covenants; (d) strong operating cash flows, which enables the sponsor to create financial slack, which accords with the financial slack motive for over-funding; (e) a high marginal tax rate, so that the sponsor obtains greater benefit from the tax deductibility of pension contributions, which consistent with the tax advantage for over-funding; and (f) the pension cost, deflated by total assets. Sponsor contributions, deflated by total assets, were found to be a negative function of: (g) capital expenditure, deflated by total assets, which could be due to the use of limited cash resources for capital expenditure; (h) the size of the pension scheme surplus, deflated by total assets; (i) the return on the pension fund assets; and (j) the change in the number of employees, deflated by total assets, which is an unexpected result that might be due to the cost of a restructuring scheme involving pension enhancements to reduce the workforce. If anything, these results tend to support over-funding, but in reality DB schemes are generally under-funded.

d. The Costs of Under-funding

Under-funding is much more common that over-funding, and so the benefits from under-funding must exceed the costs for sponsors to decide to under-fund their schemes. Under-funding their DB pension scheme has six costs to the sponsor: (a) loss of the tax benefits available on additional contributions to the scheme, (b) the need to pay higher wages to compensate for the higher risk of default on the pension, unless it is fully insured, (c) the loss of some financial slack, (d) wider bond spreads and a lower credit rating, (e) reduced institutional investment in the shares of the sponsor. In a study of US DB schemes, Eaton et al. (2014) found that substantial under-funding of a DB scheme is associated with reduced institutional ownership of the sponsor's shares; and under-funding a DB scheme reduces the value of new projects undertaken by the sponsor to the sponsor's shareholders because some of the profits will go towards eliminating the under-funding (Alderson and Seitz 2013).

4.9　Tax Arbitrage and DB Pension Schemes

Taxation creates a case for the pension fund to invest 100 % in bonds, as did Boots in 2000. In short, if bonds are taxed more heavily than equities, it makes sense to hold the more highly taxed asset (bonds) in a tax-exempt pension scheme. There are two different arguments for all bond investment by a pension fund: (a) Black (1980) (see also Surz 1981; Black and Dewhurst 1981; Frank 2002; Gold and Hudson 2003; Gold 2001); and (b) Tepper (1981) (see also Bader 2003; Frank 2002; Gold and Hudson 2003; Gold 2001).

Assumptions
Both these arguments by Black and Tepper make the following assumptions:

1. The sponsor is liable to pay corporate taxation, and so these arguments do not apply to local authorities, universities, churches, charities, state-owned broadcasters and so on which do not pay corporate taxes. They also do not apply to hard frozen schemes, as the sponsor is no longer contributing to the scheme and so cannot receive tax relief on its pension contributions.
2. The sponsor expects to have taxable income in excess of its expected pension contributions. This assumption ensures the sponsor can obtain tax relief on all its contributions.
3. The pension scheme is viewed as an integral part of the sponsoring company (see Sect. 4.1).
4. Any surplus on the pension scheme is 'owned' by the sponsor and there is no sharing of surpluses.
5. The pension scheme is not expected to default.
6. The tax system is EET (exempt, exempt, taxed).

In addition, both the Black and Tepper arguments require a change in the capital structure of the sponsor, and this may affect its market value. Black assumes the results of Modigliani and Miller (1963) apply, while Tepper assumes that the results of Miller (1977) apply. Tepper also assumes that shareholders in the sponsor are not tax exempt, as otherwise there is no gain, and also that the shareholders in the sponsor can borrow at the bond rate.

Table 4.5 Sponsor and scheme balance sheets

Capital and liabilities			Assets		
		Sponsor balance sheet			
Equity	£10,000	Redeem	Assets	£11,000	
Bonds	£1,000	Issue			
	£11,000			£11,000	
		Pension scheme balance sheet			
Liabilities	£2,000		Equities	£1,000	Sell
			Bonds	£1,000	Buy
	£2,000			£2,000	
Totals	£13,000			£13,000	

a. Black (1980)

This sub-section explains Fischer Black's model of why DB pension schemes should invest 100 % of their funds in bonds. Viewing the sponsor and its pension scheme as a single entity, an example of their combined balance sheet appears in Table 4.5.

The tax advantage occurs because the sponsor's interest payments are tax deductible, while its dividend payments are not. Therefore, by redeeming some of its equity and financing this by issuing bonds, the sponsor reduces its corporate tax bill. Modigliani and Miller (1963) show that it is optimal for a company subject to such corporate taxes to move to 100 % debt. However this increases the leverage of the sponsor, and also the leverage of the consolidated entity of sponsor and pension scheme. To keep the overall risk and return of the consolidated entity unchanged (apart from the tax arbitrage profit), the pension scheme (which is tax exempt) rebalances its assets between debt and equity, i.e. sells equities and uses the proceeds to buy bonds. As shown in Table 4.5, the pension fund sells all its equities and uses the proceeds to buy bonds, while the sponsor issues bonds and uses the proceeds to redeem its equity.

The sponsor's profits are taxed at the rate of t_c, while contributions to the pension scheme are tax exempt. So the net cost to the sponsor of contributing £1 to the scheme is only £1 × $(1 - t_c)$, i.e. the net profits foregone. Therefore, a loss or gain of £1 in pension scheme assets corresponds to a loss or gain of £1 × $(1 - t_c)$ for the sponsor. This means that pension scheme investment risk and return for the consolidated entity are reduced by the proportion $(1 - t_c)$, with the government bearing the remaining t_c proportion. To keep the overall risk and return of the consolidated entity unchanged, for every £1 × $(1 - t_c)$ that the sponsor spends on redeeming equity, the pension fund must liquidate £1 of equity and use the proceeds to purchase bonds (see Fig. 4.10).

The analysis will be split into two parts: (a) the switch of asset allocation by the pension scheme from equities to bonds, and (b) the switch by the sponsor from equity financing to bond financing.

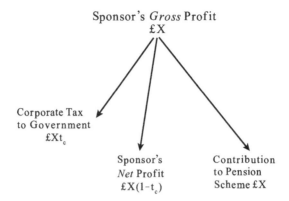

Fig. 4.10   Net cost to the sponsor of contributing £1 to the scheme

i. Switch from Equities to Bonds by the Pension Fund
For simplicity, the pension fund is assumed to be fully invested in equities, all of which it sells; investing the proceeds in bonds. The resulting reduction in the expected *gross* revenue of the pension fund is $F(E[R_b]-E[R_e])$, where F is the value of the equities held by pension fund, $E[R_e]$ is the expected return on these equities, and $E[R_b]$ is the expected return on the bonds purchased by the pension fund. While the pension fund is tax exempt, the sponsor must pay corporate tax at the rate of t_c on earnings, and so the switch from equities to bonds by the pension fund is equivalent to a reduction in the *net* earnings of the sponsor of $A = F(1-t_c)(E[R_b]-E[R_e])$.

ii. Borrowing by the Sponsor to Redeem Equity
The sponsor issues debt to raise the sum $F(1-t_c)$, not F. The interest on this debt has a *gross* cost to the sponsor of $F(1-t_c)(E[R_b])$, where the sponsor's bonds are assumed to pay the same rate of interest as the bonds held by the pension fund (although this assumption can be relaxed a bit).[1] Since the interest paid by the sponsor on its new debt is tax deductible, i.e. it is multiplied by $(1-t_c)$, the *net* cost to the sponsor is $\mu = F(1-t_c)E[R_b](1-t_c)$.

The money raised from issuing this debt, $F(1-t_c)$, is used to buy back an equivalent value of the sponsor's shares. Assuming (a) the sponsor has sufficient equity capital available to be repurchased, and (b) that the sponsor's equity has the same expected rate of return as the equity investments sold by the scheme, this leads to a reduction in the *net* cost of equity capital to the

[1] Even if the sponsor pays a higher rate on the debt it issues (Y) than the fund receives on the bonds in which it invests (R), the strategy is still worthwhile provided $R < Y/(1-t_c)$ (Alexander 2002).

sponsor of $\pi = F(1-t_c)E[R_e]$. Hence the reduction in the *net* cost to the sponsor is $B_B = \pi - \mu = F(1-t_c)\{E[R_e] - E[R_b](1-t_c)\}$.

The overall *net* gain to the sponsor from the Black strategy is $A + B_B = F(1-t_c)(E[R_b] - E[R_e]) + F(1-t_c)\{E[R_e] - E[R_b](1-t_c)\}$ which can be simplified to $A + B_B = Ft_c E[R_b](1-t_c)$.

The present value of a perpetuity (P) is P/r, and so (discounted at the *after-tax* riskless rate of $E[R_b](1 - t_c)$ because it's a *net* gain to the sponsor) the present value of this perpetuity to the sponsor is $PV \sum(A_i + B_{Bi}) = Ft_c$. The present value of this perpetuity to the sponsor's shareholders is $Ft_c(1 - t_s)$, where t_s is the rate of tax on dividends.

Overall, the sponsor and the pension scheme have collectively increased their bond holdings by Ft_c, and reduced their equity holdings by Ft_c as shown in Table 4.6.

Assuming the *gross risk-adjusted* expected rates of return on bonds and equities are equal, as implied by Modigliani and Miller (1963), this change in financial structure will not alter the market value of the sponsor, excluding the tax arbitrage gain (Frank 2002). Therefore the only effect is a tax arbitrage gain.

Example. Table 4.7 has an example of a pension scheme which moves from investing half its assets in bonds to 100 % bonds.

Table 4.6 The Black arbitrage strategy

	Equities		Bonds	
Pension fund	Sell	$-F$	Buy	$+F$
Sponsor	Redeem	$+F(1 - t_c)$	Borrow	$-F(1 - t_c)$
Change		$-Ft_c$		$+Ft_c$

Table 4.7 Example of moving scheme assets to 100 % bonds

		Initial	Change	Final
Sponsor	Equity	£10,000	−£700	£9,300
	Bonds	£1,000	+£700	£1,700
	Assets	£11,000	0	£11,000
Pension Scheme	Liabilities	£2,000	0	£2,000
	Equities	£1,000	−£1,000	0
	Bonds	£1,000	+£1,000	£2,000

The corporate tax rate (t_c) is 30 %, the bond rate $(E[R_b])$ is 5 % and the equity return $(E[R_e])$ is 10 %. $F = £1000$ so $F(1 - t_c) = £700$. Initially the *net* cost of capital to the sponsor is $£10,000(0.10) + £1000(0.05)$ $(1 - 0.3) = £1035$ p.a. After the capital restructuring this *net* cost has dropped to $£9300(0.10) + £1700(0.05)(1 - 0.3) = £989.5$, i.e. a reduction of £45.5 p.a. The initial income of the pension scheme is $£1000(0.10) + £1000(0.0$ $5) = £150$ p.a. After the change to 100 % bonds, its income has dropped to $£2000(0.05) = £100$ p.a., a reduction of £50 p.a. Since the sponsor pays tax at the rate of 30 %, this reduction is equivalent to a reduction in the sponsor's income of $£50(1 - t_c) = £35$. So, overall *net* revenue has risen by £45.5 - £35 = £10.5 p.a., and the present value of this perpetuity is £10.5/ $(0.05 \times 0.7) = £300$. Alternatively $Ft_c = £1000 \times (0.3) = £300$.

b. Tepper (1981)

For Tepper (1981) the sponsor and its pension scheme are again viewed as a single entity. The arbitrage involves the pension scheme and the shareholders of the sponsor, but not the sponsoring company. The pension fund buys bonds and sells equities, and the shareholders in the sponsor sell bonds and buy equities (Table 4.8).

It will be argued below that, so far as the shareholders are concerned, there is no change in the risk and return of their direct and indirect bond and equity holdings, and so the market value of their position is unchanged. The advantage comes from the different tax treatment of dividends and interest payments by shareholders. The shareholders now receive additional dividends, but also pay interest on the money they have borrowed to finance the purchase

Table 4.8 The Tepper strategy

Capital and liabilities			Assets		
			Shareholders balance sheet		
Capital	£11,000		Equities in sponsor	£11,000	
Debt		Issue (borrow)	Equities		Buy
	£11,000			£11,000	
			Pension scheme balance sheet		
Liabilities	£2,000		Equities	£1,000	Sell
			Bonds	£1,000	Buy (lend)
	£2,000			£2,000	
Totals	£13,000			£13,000	

of these equities. If the marginal tax relief on their interest payments exceeds the marginal tax rate the shareholders pay on dividends, they have gained.

i. Switch from Equities to Bonds by the Pension Fund

For simplicity it is assumed that the pension fund is fully invested in equities, which it sells; investing the proceeds in bonds. As for the Black strategy, the switch from equities to bonds by the pension fund is equivalent to a reduction in the *net* earnings of the sponsor of $A = F(1-t_c)(E[R_b]-E[R_e])$. Such a decrease in profits by the sponsor is passed on to the shareholders, who pay tax at the rate t_s on dividends, so that the *net* loss to the shareholders (A_T) is $A_T = F(1-t_c)(E[R_b] - E[R_e])(1-t_s)$.

ii. Borrowing by the Shareholders and Investment in Equities

At the same time as the fund switches from equities to bonds, the shareholders borrow $F(1-t_c)$ at the expected rate $E[R_b]$, which is assumed to be the same rate as that received by the scheme on its bonds; and invest the proceeds in equities with the same expected return of $E[R_e]$ as that of the shares sold by the scheme. The *gross* cost of this borrowing is $F(1 - t_c)E[R_b]$. Assuming that the interest payments by the shareholder are tax deductible at the rate t_b, the *net* interest cost is $\alpha = F(1-t_c)E[R_b](1-t_b)$. The shareholders will have to pay tax on the dividends they receive at the rate of t_s, giving a *net* return on this investment of $\beta = F(1-t_c)E[R_e](1-t_s)$. So the increase in the *net* revenue of the shareholders is $B_T = \beta - \alpha = F(1-t_c)\{E[R_e](1-t_s) - E[R_b](1-t_b)\}$.

The total change in the *net* revenues of shareholders due to the switch from equities to bonds by the pension fund and from the shareholders borrowing to invest in equities is
$$A_T + B_T = F(E[R_b] - E[R_e])(1-t_c)(1-t_s) + F(1-t_c)\{E[R_e](1-t_s) - E[R_b](1-t_b)\},$$
which can be simplified to $A_T + B_T = F(1-t_c)E[R_b](t_b - t_s)$. Provided that $t_b > t_s$, (i.e. the rate of tax relief received by shareholders on the interest payments they make exceeds the tax rate they pay on dividends), the shareholders gain this amount each year in perpetuity. The present value to the shareholders of the profit stream from this tax arbitrage (discounting at the shareholder's *after-tax* bond rate $(1-t_b)E[R_b]$ because this *net* gain is riskless) is $PV \sum(A_{Ti} + B_{Ti}) = F(1-t_c)(t_b - t_s)/(1-t_b)$ If the corporate tax rate equals the tax rate on dividends and $t_b = t_c$, then the gain simplifies to $PV \sum(A_{Ti} + B_{Ti}) = F(t_b - t_s)$ If $t_b < t_s$ the argument is reversed, and the tax arbitrage strategy of Tepper favours all equity investment by the pension fund, so the Tepper argument for 100 % bond investment by the pension fund depends crucially on the relative size of these two tax rates.

The shareholders and the pension scheme have collectively increased their bond holdings by Ft_c, and reduced their equity holdings by Ft_c, as shown in Table 4.9. Assuming the *net risk-adjusted* expected returns on bonds and equities for shareholders are equal making them indifferent between supplying more equity and more debt, as implied by Miller (1977), this change in financial structure will not alter the market value of the sponsor or the wealth of its shareholders, excluding the tax arbitrage gain (Frank 2002). Therefore the only gain is a tax arbitrage gain.

Example. A pension scheme moves from investing half its assets in bonds to 100 % bonds (see Table 4.10). The corporate tax rate (t_c) is 30 %, the bond rate ($E[R_b]$) is 5 % and the equity return ($E[R_e]$) is 10 %. The tax rate paid by shareholders on dividends (t_s) is 20 %, and the rate of tax relief shareholders receive on interest payments they make (t_b) is 30 %, so $t_b > t_s$ and $t_b = t_c$. F = £1000 so $F(1 - t_c)$ = £700. The initial income of the pension scheme is £1000(0.10) + £1000(0.05) = £150 p.a. After the change to 100 % bonds, its income has dropped to £2000(0.05) = £100 p.a., a reduction of £50 per annum. Since the sponsor pays tax at the rate of 30 %, this reduction is equivalent to a drop in the sponsor's net income of £50$(1 - t_c)$ = £35. This is equivalent to an increase in the net income of shareholders of £35$(1 - t_s)$ = £28 p.a. Initially the shareholders are receiving a net income of £10,000(0.10)(1 - 0.20) = £800 p.a. After the capital restructuring they receive a net income of £10,700(0.10) (1 - 0.20) - £700(0.05)(1 - 0.30) = £831.5 p.a., an increase of £31.5 p.a. So, overall the shareholders' net revenue has risen by £31.5 - £28 = £3.5 p.a., and the present value of this perpetuity is £3.5/(0.05 × 0.7) = £100. Alternatively, since $t_b = t_s$, $F(t_b - t_s)$ = £1000(0.30 - 0.20) = £100.

Table 4.9 Tepper arbitrage strategy

	Equities		Bonds	
Pension fund	Sell	$-F$	Buy – lend	$+F$
Shareholders	Buy	$+F(1-t_c)$	Sell – borrow	$-F(1 - t_c)$
Change		$-Ft_c$		$+Ft_c$

Table 4.10 Example of moving scheme assets to 100 % bonds

		Initial	Change	Final
Shareholders	Equities	£10,000	+£700	£10,700
	Bonds	0	+£700	£700
Scheme	Liabilities	£2,000	0	£2,000
	Equities	£1,000	-£1,000	0
	Bonds	£1,000	+£1,000	£2,000

c. Effects of Tax Arbitrage

The bigger F, the bigger the gains from the tax arbitrage, so schemes adopting either the Tepper or Black strategies should also seek to fund their schemes up to the maximum level permitted by the tax authorities, i.e. over-fund the scheme as much as possible. For example, supposing the corporate tax rate is 30 %, the present value of the tax arbitrage gain from the Black strategy for a company that switches £100 million of investment from equities to bonds is Ft_c = 100 × 0.30 = £30 million. Therefore, tax arbitrage can provide a powerful reason for company pension schemes to switch the fund to bonds. This is illustrated by the example of Boots. In 2000 Boots decided to move their £2.3 billion pension fund from an asset allocation of 75 % equities/25 % bonds, to entirely AAA corporate bonds and index-linked gilts. This was for three stated reasons: (a) lower administration costs in managing the investments (£0.25 million p.a., not £10 million p.a.), (b) much less investment risk, as the maturity of the Boots scheme made them less able to tolerate investment risk and (c) the accounting standard FRS 17 meant that volatility in scheme funding fed through to the Boots balance sheet. Surprisingly, tax arbitrage was not mentioned as a motive. As well as switching the pension fund into 100 % bonds, Boots bought back £300 million of their own shares using available cash, which is the tax arbitrage strategy of Black.

Thomas (1988) found empirical evidence for the USA that, if the sponsor's marginal tax rate or expected future taxable income changes over time, this leads to a change in the level of contributions and the funding ratio in order to maximise the tax benefits. In a study of 244 US companies, Frank (2002) found a small positive relationship between the proportion of the fund's assets invested in bonds and the tax benefits from the Black tax arbitrage strategy. There was no relationship for the Tepper arbitrage strategy. Using a sample of 1439 US firms, Bartram (2014) found no evidence for tax arbitrage.

The effects of tax arbitrage are that: (a) it generates a tax gain for the company's shareholders, (b) the pension scheme is now less likely to default because it is fully invested in bonds and so less risky, and is funded to the maximum, (c) the volatility of the pension scheme's funding ratio should be less as bonds are a better hedge for the liabilities than are equities, and (d) it reduces the risk and return of the pension scheme (while increasing the risk and return of the sponsor's shares), so that the *risk-adjusted* return is unaffected by the switch. Given the case for 100 % bonds, why do schemes invest in equities? Here are five possible reasons, although each reason is problematic.

(a) Equities should generate higher returns, reducing the sponsor's expected contributions to the scheme. But equities also lead to higher risk.

(b) The higher expected returns from equities can increase the discount rate used by the scheme actuary in valuing the liabilities, which improves the scheme's funding ratio and increases the sponsor's reported accounting profit. But the scheme should be using a discount rate linked to the liabilities (see Sect. 1.6b).

(c) The higher expected returns from equity investment can be used to offer scheme members increased benefits. But since risk is also higher, there may be lower returns than those on bonds, and benefits might be reduced.

(d) Equities are thought to hedge the scheme's salary and inflation risk. But the evidence is that they are a poor hedge.

(e) The pension scheme is managed as a separate entity from the pension scheme. But it is generally accepted that they are a single economic entity (see Sect. 4.1).

4.10 Tax Arbitrage, Default Insurance and Risk Sharing

The effects of tax arbitrage on the asset allocation and funding level will now be considered, in conjunction with default insurance and risk sharing. There are four possible combinations of tax arbitrage, default insurance and risk sharing. In the absence of any of these three factors, the asset allocation of the pension fund depends on the risk-return preferences of the sponsor and scheme members, as in Sect. 3.2e. If total remuneration (T) is fixed (as in Sect. 4.6a), the outcome is indeterminate. If T is not fixed the preferences of the sponsor and members are opposed, and the asset allocation depends on their collective preferences and bargaining skills. This leaves three possible combinations to be considered.

a. Tax Arbitrage and Default Insurance

Black (1980) and Tepper (1981) argue that tax arbitrage implies 100 % bond investment by the pension fund (and over-funding), while Sharpe (1976) demonstrates that under-priced default insurance leads to a 100 % equity portfolio (and under-funding) (see Sect. 4.6). This is because, if default insurance is under-priced, the sponsor will seek to maximise the difference between the value of the put option and the premium charged. This is achieved by increasing the pension liabilities (L), decreasing the pension fund assets (A) (i.e. under-funding) and increasing the volatility of the pension fund's investments (σ). So these two factors lead to directly opposite conclusions. Whether the tax arbitrage or the under-priced default insurance argument prevails depends on the relative size of the benefits from these two rival strategies.

However in reality pension funds invest in a mixture of equities and bonds (e.g. 40 % bonds and 60 % equities). Bicksler and Chen (1985) explain this fact by an appeal to the costs of terminating a pension scheme (e.g. legal costs), bad will from the workforce, and dealing with the PBGC or PPF and the tax authorities, which make default costly for the sponsor, so discouraging 100 % equities. Investing 100 % in bonds may not be desirable because (using the Black strategy) the sponsor may not have enough taxable income to offset all of the interest it pays on the bonds it has issued. So some equities remain in the pension fund. Public bodies such as local government and tax-exempt organisations like charities such as universities, do not pay corporate taxes, and so have no incentive for 100 % bond investment. In addition, if corporate tax rates are progressive (as in the USA), the tax relief diminishes as the size of the tax exemption increases, so diminishing the marginal benefits from additional investment in bonds. Finally, taking account of all the sponsor's assets and liabilities, the risk minimising portfolio for the pension fund may contain a small proportion of equities. Therefore it is reasonable that the optimal asset allocation is some mixture of equities and bonds.

Chen et al. (2013) examined the determinants of voluntary pension contributions by US scheme sponsors. When the sponsor has a high risk of bankruptcy they make low voluntary contributions, motivated by the insurance provided by the PBGC. When the sponsor has a low bankruptcy risk their voluntary contributions rise with their marginal tax rate, motivated by the tax deductibility of pension contributions and the tax-exempt status of pension schemes.

b. Tax Arbitrage and Risk Sharing

Tax arbitrage indicates an investment of 100 % in bonds for tax-paying sponsors (and over-funding). So far as risk sharing is concerned, when T is fixed the asset allocation is indeterminate, even when the sponsor and members share surpluses and deficits. So the outcome is 100 % bonds.

When T is *not* fixed, the tax arbitrage argument still points towards 100 % bonds, while for risk sharing the values of d, s, v and z determine whether the sponsor or the members prefer equities to bonds. Since the tax arbitrage benefits go to the sponsor and its shareholders, if the members prefer equities the sponsor may be able to use some of the gains from the tax arbitrage to persuade them to accept a higher bond investment than otherwise (e.g. offer higher benefits). Alternatively, a preference by the sponsor for equities due to the risk-sharing motive is reduced by the tax arbitrage gains from investment in bonds. So the final outcome depends on bargaining between the sponsor and members, but may have a bias towards bonds because the members want bonds, and the sponsor's desire for equities is reduced by the tax arbitrage benefits of bonds.

c. Default Insurance and Risk Sharing

Risk sharing when T is fixed and the default insurance is correctly priced is compatible with any asset allocation, as shown by Sharpe (1976). Under-priced default insurance incentivises the sponsor to under-fund the scheme and invest in risky assets as this increases the gain from the under-priced default insurance, thereby benefiting the sponsor (Sharpe 1976). The members remain unaffected, and for them the asset allocation remains indeterminate. So there will be a preference for 100 % equities.

When T is *not* fixed, and the sponsor and members share the risks of deficits and surpluses, the outcome depends on the values of d, s, v and z which determine whether the sponsor or the members favour a high equity allocation. As before, if the default insurance is under-priced, the sponsor will have an additional incentive to under-fund the scheme and invest in risky assets, leading to a bias towards equities.

d. Tax Arbitrage, Default Insurance and Risk Sharing

When all three effects are present the outcome for the asset allocation and funding level are even harder to predict than when any two of these effects are present. Table 4.11 summarises the asset allocations for the various combinations of the three factors, showing a clear result in only two cases. This accords with the reality that DB pension schemes have a very wide range of asset allocations.

Table 4.11 Effect of the three factors on asset allocation

	T is fixed	T is variable
None of the three factors is present	Indeterminate	Indeterminate
Tax arbitrage and default insurance	Indeterminate	Indeterminate
Tax arbitrage and risk shifting	100 % bonds	Indeterminate – bias to bonds
Default insurance and risk shifting	100 % equities	Indeterminate – bias to equities
Tax arbitrage, default insurance and risk shifting	Indeterminate	Indeterminate

References

Addoum, J. M., Van Binsbergen, J. H., & Brandt, M. W. (2010). *Asset allocation and managerial assumptions in corporate pension plans* (Working paper). Duke University.

Alderson, M. J., & Seitz, N. L. (2013). Pension policy and the value of corporate level investment. *Financial Management, 42*(2), 413–440.

Alestalo, N., & Puttonen, V. (2006). Asset allocation in Finnish pension funds. *Journal of Pension Economics and Finance, 5*(1), 27–44.

Alexander, B. (2002). *Gentlemen prefer bonds.* Masters in Finance dissertation. London Business School, 34 pages.

Amir, E., & Benartzi, S. (1999). Accounting recognition and the determinants of pension asset allocation. *Journal of Accounting, Auditing and Finance, 14*(3), 321–343.

An, H., Huang, Z., & Zhang, T. (2013). What determines corporate pension fund risk-taking strategy? *Journal of Banking and Finance, 37*(2), 597–613.

Anantharaman, D., & Lee, Y. G. (2014). Managerial risk taking incentives and corporate pension policy. *Journal of Financial Economics, 111*(2), 328–351.

Anantharaman, D., Fang, V. W., & Gong, G. (2014). Inside debt and the design of corporate debt contracts. *Management Science, 60*(5), 1260–1280.

Arnott, R. J., & Gersovitz, M. (1980). Corporate financial structure and the funding of private pension plans. *Journal of Financial Economics, 13*(2), 231–247.

Asthana, S. C. (2009). Participant mix and management of qualified pension plans. *Accounting and the Public Interest, 9*, 100–128.

Atanasova, C., & Chemia, G. (2013). *Familiarity breeds alternative investment: Evidence from corporate defined benefit pension plans* (Working paper). Simon Fraser University, 46 pages.

Atanasova, C., & Gatev, E. (2013). Pension plan risk-taking: Does it matter if the sponsor is publicly-traded? *Journal of Pension Economics and Finance, 12*(2), 218–249.

Bader, L. N. (2003). The case against stock in corporate pension funds. *Pension Section News, 51*, 17–19.

Bagchi, S. (2013). *The effects of political competition on the funding and generosity of public sector pension plans* (Working paper), 65 pages.

Ballester, M., Fried, D. and Livnat, J. (2002). Pension Plan Contributions, Free Cash Flows and Financial Slack, Working paper, Stern School of Business Administration, New York University.

Bartram, S. M. (2014). *In good times and in bad: Defined benefit pensions and corporate financial policy* (Working paper). Warwick University.

Bartram, S. M. (forthcoming). Post-retirement benefit plans, leverage and real investment. *Management Science* (Working paper). University of Warwick.

Begley, J., Chamberlain, S., Yang, S., & Zhang, J. L. (2015). CEO incentives and the health of defined benefit pension plans. *Review of Accounting Studies, 20*(3), 1013–1058.

Benmelech, E., Bergman, N. K., & Enriquez, R. J. (2012). Negotiating with labour under financial distress. *Review of Corporate Financial Studies, 1*(1), 28–67.

Bicksler, J. L., & Chen, A. H. (1985). The integration of insurance and taxes in corporate pension policy. *Journal of Finance, 40*(3), 943–957.

Bikker, J. A., Broeders, D. W. G. A., & De Dreu, J. (2010). Stock market performance and pension fund investment policy: Rebalancing, free float or market timing? *International Journal of Central Banking, 6*(2), 53–79.

Bikker, J. A., Broeders, D. W. G. A., Hollanders, D. A., & Ponds, E. H. M. (2012a). Pension funds' asset allocation and participant age: A test of the life-cycle model. *Journal of Risk and Insurance, 79*(3), 595–618.

Black, F. (1980). The tax consequences of long run pension policy. *Financial Analysts Journal, 36*(4), 21–28.

Black, F., & Dewhurst, M. P. (1981). A new investment strategy for pension funds. *Journal of Portfolio Management, 7*(4), 26–34.

Blake, D. (2006a). *Pension finance.* New York: Wiley.

Bodie, Z., Light, J. O., Morck, R., & Taggart, R. A. (1985). Corporate pension policy: An empirical investigation. *Financial Analysts Journal, 41*(5), 10–16.

Bodie, Z., Light, J. O., Morck, R., & Taggart, R. A. (1987). Funding and asset allocation in corporate pension plans: An empirical investigation. In Z. Bodie, J. B. Shoven, & D. A. Wise (Eds.), *Issues in pension economics* (pp. 15–47). Chicago: University of Chicago Press.

Boon, L. N., Brière, M., & Rigot, S. (2014). *Does regulation matter? Riskiness and procyclicality in pension asset allocation* (Working paper). Paris Dauphine University, 47 pages.

Bradley, D. J., Pantzalis, C., & Yuan, X. (2016). The influence of political bias in state pension funds. *Journal of Financial Economics*, vol. 119, no. 1, January, pp. 69–91.

Brown, J. P., Pollet, J. J., & Weisbenner, S. J. (2015b). *The in-state equity bias of state pension plans* (Working paper). University of Illinois, 45 pages.

Brummer, A. (2010). *The great pensions robbery: How the politicians betrayed retirement.* London: Random House.

Buffett, W. (2014). *Berkshire Hathaway Inc.* Shareholder Letter 2013.

Bunn, P., & Trivedi, K. (2005). *Corporate expenditures and pension contributions: Evidence from UK company accounts* (Working paper no. 276). Bank of England.

Cadman, B., & Vincent, L. (2015). The role of defined benefit pension plans in executive compensation. *European Accounting Review, 24*(4), 779–800.

Campbell, J. L., Dhaliwal, D. S., & Schwartz, W. C. (2012). Financial constraints and the cost of capital: Evidence from the funding of corporate pension plans. *Review of Financial Studies, 25*, 868–912.

Cardinale, M. (2007). Corporate pension funding and credit spreads. *Financial Analysts Journal, 63*(5), 82–101.

Carroll, T. J., & Niehaus, G. (1998). Pension plan funding and corporate debt ratings. *Journal of Risk and Insurance, 65*(3), 427–441.

Castro-Gonzalez, K. C. (2012). Information content of changes in pension plan funding status and long term debt. *International Journal of Business and Finance Research, 6*(1), 1–14.

Chambers, B. (2014). *Multi-employer defined benefit pension plans' liability spillovers: Important connections in U.S. unionized industries* (Working paper). University of Utah, 76 pages.

Chang, X., Kang, J. K., & Zhang, W. (2012, November). *Corporate pension funding status and the market for corporate control: The disciplinary role of pension deficits in mergers and acquisitions* (Working paper). Nanyang Technological University.

Chaplinsky, S., Niehaus, G., & Van de Gucht, L. (1998). Employee buyouts: Causes, structure and consequence. *Journal of Financial Economics, 48*(3), 283–332.

Chaudhry, N., Yong, H. H. A., & Veld, C. (2014, December). *How does the funding status of defined benefit pension plans affect investment decisions?* (Working paper). Monash University, 42 pages.

Chaudhry, N., Yong, H. H. A., & Veld, C. (2015, March). *Tax avoidance in response to a decline in the funding status of defined benefit pension plans* (Working Paper). Monash University, 44 pages.

Chen, Y. (2015). Funding status of defined benefit pension plans and idiosyncratic return volatility. *Journal of Financial Research, 38*(1), 35–57.

Chen, X., Yu, T., & Zhang, T. (2013). What drives corporate pension plan contributions: Moral hazard or tax benefits? *Financial Analysts Journal, 69*(4), 58–72.

Chen, J., Yao, T., Yu, T., & Zhang, T. (2014). Learning and incentive: A study on analyst response to pension underfunding. *Journal of Banking and Finance, 45*, 26–42.

Chen, T., Martin, X., Mashruwala, C., & Mashruwala, S. (2015). The value and credit relevance of multi-employer pension plan obligations. *Accounting Review, 90*(5), 1907–1938.

Cherkes, M., & Yaari, U. (1988). Unions, default risk and pension underfunding. *Journal of Economics and Business, 40*(3), 239–242.

Cocco, J. F., & Volpin, P. F. (2013). Corporate pension plans as takeover deterrents. *Journal of Financial and Quantitative Analysis, 48*(4), 1119–1144.

Cohen, L., Cornette, M. M., Mehran, H., & Tehranian, H. (2014, June). *The effect of state pension cut legislation on bank values* (Federal Reserve Bank of New York Staff Reports, no. 679), 50 pages.

Comprix, J., & Muller, K. A. (2006). *Pension funding rules and sponsor firms' risk taking with defined benefit pension plan assets* (Working paper). Pennsylvania University.

Cooper, R. W., & Ross, T. W. (2002). Pensions: Theories of under-funding. *Labour Economics, 8*(6), 667–689.

Coronado, J., Liang, N., & Orszag, M. (2006). *Moral Hazard from government pension insurance: Evidence from US and UK firm finances* (Working Paper). Federal Reserve Board, 39 pages.

Cox, P., Brammer, S., & Millington, A. (2007). Pension fund manager tournaments and attitudes towards corporate characteristics. *Journal of Business Finance and Accounting, 34*(7), 1307–1326.

Dambra, M. (2014). *The effect of internal capital shocks on manager behaviour: Evidence from changes in ERISA pension accounting rules* (Working paper). 51 pages.

Datta, S., Iskandar-Datta, M. E., & Zychowicz, E. J. (1996). Managerial self-interest, pension financial slack and corporate pension funding. *The Financial Review, 31*(4), 695–720.

Eaton, T. V., Nofsinger, J. R., & Varma, A. (2014). Institutional investor ownership and corporate pension transparency. *Financial Management, 43*(3), 603–630.

Eisdorfer, A., Giaccotto, C., & White, R. (2015). Do corporate managers skimp on shareholders' dividends to protect their own retirement funds? *Journal of Corporate Finance, 30*(February), 257–277.

Elder, E. M., & Wagner, G. A. (2015). Political effects on pension underfunding. *Economics and Politics, 27*(1), 1–27.

Feldstein, M., & Mørck, R. (1983). Pension funding decisions, interest rate assumptions, and share prices. In Z. Bodie & J. Shoven (Eds.), *Financial aspects of the United States pension system* (pp. 177–210). Chicago: Chicago University Press.

Feldstein, M. and Seligman, S. (1981, September). Pension Funding, Share Prices and National Savings. *Journal of Finance, 36*(4)September, pp. 801–824.

Frank, M. M. (2002). The impact of taxes on corporate defined plan asset allocation. *Journal of Accounting Research, 40*(4), 1163–1190.

Franzoni, F. (2009). Under-investment vs. over-investment: Evidence from price reactions to pension contributions. *Journal of Financial Economics, 92*(3), 491–518.

Franzoni, F., & Marin, J. M. (2006a). Pension plan funding and stock market efficiency. *Journal of Finance, 61*(2), 921–956.

Franzoni, F., & Marin, J. M. (2006b). Portable alphas from pension mispricing. *Journal of Portfolio Management, 32*(4), 44–53.

Friedman, B. M. (1983). Pension funding, pension asset allocation and corporate finance: Evidence from individual company data. In Z. Bodie & J. B. Shoven (Eds.), *Financial aspects of the United States pension system* (pp. 107–152). Chicago: University of Chicago Press.

Gallagher, R., & McKillop, D. (2010a). Unfunded pension liabilities and sponsoring firm credit risk: An international analysis of corporate bond spreads. *European Journal of Finance, 16*(3), 183–200.

Gallagher, R., & McKillop, D. (2010b). Unfunded pension liabilities and the corporate CDS market. *Journal of Fixed Income, 19*(3), 30–46.

Gallo, J. G., & Lockwood, L. J. (1995). Determinants of pension funding and asset allocation decisions. *Journal of Financial Services Research, 9*(2), 143–158.

Gerber, D. S., & Weber, R. (2007). Demography and investment behaviour of pension funds: Evidence for Switzerland. *Journal of Pension Economics and Finance, 6*(3), 313–337.

Gold, J. (2001). Economic design of cash balance pension plans. Cash Balance Symposium Monograph M-RS02-3, Society of Actuaries Spring meeting, Dallas, pp. 1–34.

Gold, J., & Hudson, N. (2003). Creating value in pension plans (or, gentlemen prefer bonds). *Journal of Applied Corporate Finance, 15*(4), 51–57.

Guan, Y., & Lui, D. (2014). *Risk shifting in pension investment* (Working paper). Hong Kong Baptist University, 48 pages.

Hawthorne, F. (2008). *Pension dumping: The reasons, the wreckage, the stakes for wall street*. New York: Bloomberg Press.

Hochberg, Y. V., & Rauh, J. D. (2013). Local overweighting and underperformance: Evidence from limited partner private equity investments. *Review of Financial Studies, 13*(2), 403–451.

Inman, R. P. (1982). Public employee pensions and the local labour budget. *Journal of Public Economics, 19*(1), 49–71.

Ippolito, R. A. (1985). The economic function of unfunded pension plans. *Journal of Law and Economics, 28*(3), 611–651.

Ippolito, R. A. (1986). *Pensions, economics, and public policy*. Homewood: University of Pennsylvania Press.

Jackson, R. W. (1997). Pension underfunding and liberal retirement benefits among state and local government workers. *National Tax Journal, 50*(1), 113–142.

Jin, L., Merton, R. C., & Bodie, Z. (2006). Do a firm's equity returns reflect the risk of its pension plan. *Journal of Financial Economics, 81*(1), 1–26.

Jones, D. A. (2014). When do companies fund their defined benefit pension plans. *Accounting and Taxation, 6*(1), 13–23.

Kalyta, P. (2009a). Compensation transparency and managerial opportunism: A study of supplemental retirement plans. *Strategic Management Journal, 30*(4), 405–423.

Kalyta, P. (2009b). Accounting discretion, horizon problem and CEO retirement benefits. *Accounting Review, 84*(5), 1553–1573.

Kelley, D. G. (2014). The political economy of unfunded public pension liabilities. *Public Choice, 158*(1–2), 21–38.

Kubick, T. R., Lockhart, G. B., & Robinson, J. R. (2014). *Internal capital and investment: Evidence from 2012 pension relief* (Working paper). University of Kansas, 42 pages.

LCP. (2014). LCP accounting for pensions 2014, Lane, Clark and Peacock, August, 66 pages.

Lee, G., & Tang, H. (2011). *CEO pension and defined compensation* (Working paper). Seton Hall University.

Leeds, M. A. (1985). Property values and pension underfunding in the local public sector. *Journal of Urban Economics, 18*(1), 34–46.

Li, Y. (2010). Corporate risk management and pension asset allocation. In M. Micocci, G. N. Gregoriou, & G. B. Masala (Eds.), *Pension fund risk management: Financial and actuarial modelling* (pp. 365–387). New York: Chapman and Hall.

Liu, W., & Tonks, I. (2010). Pension fund deficits and stock market efficiency: Evidence from the United Kingdom. In M. Micocci, G. N. Gregoriou, & G. B. Masala (Eds.), *Pension fund risk management: Financial and actuarial modelling* (pp. 659–688). New York: Chapman and Hall.

Liu, W., & Tonks, I. (2013). Pension funding constraints and corporate expenditures. *Oxford Bulleting of Economics and Statistics, 75*(2), 235–258.

Liu, Y., Mauer, D. C., & Zhang, Y. (2014). Firm cash holdings and CEO inside debt. *Journal of Banking and Finance, 42*, 83–100.

Lowenstein, R. (2008). *While America aged: How pension debts ruined general motors, stopped the NYC subways, bankrupted San Diego, and loom as the next financial crisis.* New York: The Penguin Press.

MacKay, R. C. (2014). Implicit debt capitalization in local housing prices: An example of unfunded pension liabilities. *National Tax Journal, 67*(1), 77–112.

Maher, J. J. (1987). Pension obligations and the bond credit market: An empirical analysis of accounting numbers. *Accounting Review, 62*(4), 785–798.

Maher, J. J. (1996). Perceptions of post-retirement benefit obligations by bond rating analysts. *Review of Quantitative Finance and Accounting, 6*(1), 79–94.

Martin, L. J., & Henderson, G. V. (1983). On bond ratings and pension obligations: A note. *Journal of Financial and Quantitative Analysis, 18*(14), 463–470.

McCarthy, D., & Miles, D. (2013). Optimal portfolio allocation for corporate pension funds. *European Financial Management, 19*(3), 599–629.

McKillop, D., & Pogue, M. (2009). The influence of pension plan risk on equity risk and credit ratings: A study of FTSE100 companies. *Journal of Pension Economics and Finance, 8*(4), 405–428.

Meijdam, W. I. (2012). *Defined benefit pension plans and takeover likelihood.* Master thesis, Tilburg University, 57 pages.

Miller, M. H. (1977). Debt and taxes. *Journal of Finance, 22*(2), 261–275.

Mitchell, O. S., & Smith, R. S. (1994). Pension funding in the public sector. *Review of Economics and Statistics, 70*(2), 278–290.

Modigliani, F., & Miller, M. H. (1958). Corporate income taxes and the cost of capital: A correction. *American Economic Review*, 53(3), 433–443.

Modigliani, F. and Miller, M.H. (1963). Corporate Income Taxes and the Cost of Capital: A Correction, *American Economic Review*, vol. 53, no. 3, June, pp. 433–443.

Mohan, N., & Zhang, T. (2014). An analysis of risk-taking behaviour for public defined benefit pension plans. *Journal of Banking and Finance, 40*, 403–419.

Munro, J., & Barrie, A. (2003). New solutions for pension fund risks: A review of defined benefit investment strategies, Barrie and Hibbert, Pension Fund Strategy Research Report No. 1.

Nakajima, K., & Sasaki, T. (2010). Unfunded pension liabilities and stock returns. *Pacific-Basin Finance Journal, 18*(1), 47–63.

Pension Protection Fund. (2015b). *The purple book, DB pensions universe risk profile 2015.* PPF and TPR.

Petersen, M. A. (1996). Allocating assets and discounting cash flows: Pension plan finance. In P. A. Fernandez, J. A. Turner, & R. P. Hinz (Eds.), *Pensions, savings and capital markets* (pp. 1–26). Washington, DC: US Department of Labour; Pension and Welfare Administration, Office of Research and Economic Analysis.

Phan, H. V., & Hegde, S. P. (2013). Pension contributions and firm performance: Evidence from frozen defined benefit plans. *Financial Management, 42*(2), 373–411.

Rauh, J. D. (2006b). Investment and financing constraints: Evidence from the funding of corporate pension plans. *Journal of Finance, 61*(1), 33–71.

Rauh, J. D. (2009). Risk shifting versus risk management: Investment policy in corporate pension plans. *Review of Financial Studies, 22*(7), 2687–2733.

Sharpe, W. F. (1976). Corporate pension funding policy. *Journal of Financial Economics, 3*(3), 183–193.

Shivdasani, A., & Stefanesu, I. (2010). How do pensions affect corporate capital structure decisions? *Review of Financial Studies, 23*(3), 1287–1323.

Sinclair, J. (2011). *Past performance and changes in local bias* (Working paper). Pennsylvania State University.

Stefanescu, I., Xie, K., & Yang, J. (2014). *Pay me mow (and later): Bonus boosts before pension freezes and executive departures* (Working paper). Indiana University, 46 pages.

Stone, M. (1987). A financial explanation for over-funded pension plan terminations. *Journal of Accounting Research, 25*(2), 317–326.

Sudarsanam, S., & Appadu, N. (2015). *Impact of target company pension liabilities on takeover premium, Bidder's choice of payment currency and shareholder returns* (Working paper). Cass Business School, 41 pages.

Surz, R. J. (1981). Elaborations on the tax consequences of long-run pension policy. *Financial Analysts Journal, 37*(1), 52–54 & 60.

Sutcliffe, C. M. S. (2004). Pension scheme asset allocation with taxation arbitrage, risk sharing and default insurance. *British Actuarial Journal, 10*(5), 1111–1131. Reprinted in G. Gregoriou, G. Masala, & M. Micocci (Eds.) (2010). *Pension fund risk management: Financial and actuarial modelling* (pp. 211–234). Chapman and Hall-CRC, and in (2006). *ICFAI Journal of Risk and Insurance, 3*(1), 32–49.

Sutcliffe, C. M. S. (2006). Merging schemes: An economic analysis of defined benefit pension scheme merger criteria. *Annals of Actuarial Science, 1*(2), 203–220.

Tepper, I. (1981). Taxation and corporate pension policy. *Journal of Finance, 36*(1), 1–13.

Thomas, J. K. (1988). Corporate taxes and defined benefit pension plans. *Journal of Accounting and Economics, 10*(3), 199–237.

Tufts, B., & Fairbanks, L. (2011). *Pension Ponzi: How public sector unions are bankrupting Canada's health care, education and your retirement.* Etobicoke: Wiley.

Wang, F. A., & Zhang, T. (2014). The effect of unfunded pension liabilities on corporate bond ratings, default risk and recovery rate. *Review of Quantitative Finance and Accounting, 43*(4), 781–802.

Wang, J., Wu, C., & Zhang, T. (2013). *An empirical analysis of the effect of corporate pension risk on the cost of debt* (Working paper). University of Dayton.

Watson Wyatt. (2005). *Cashing in: Do aggressive funding policies lead to higher credit ratings?*. Watson Wyatt Insider.

Wei, C., & Yermack, D. (2011). Investor reactions to CEOs' inside debt incentives. *Review of Financial Studies, 24*(11), 3813–3840.

White, R. (2012, May). *Inside debt and firm dividend policy* (Working paper). University of Connecticut.

White, R. (2015, May). *Executive pensions, compensation leverage and firm risk* (Working paper). University of New Mexico, 44 pages.

Zhu, H., Liang, H., & Ding, D. K. (2013). Mortality risk, pension agency problem and a modern Malthusian theory of capital structure (Working paper). Tilburg University.

5

Annuities

An annuity provides a stream of payments until the death of the annuitant (pensioner). The price of annuities is strongly influenced by expectations at the time of purchase of the long-term interest rate on bonds. It also varies with the gender and age of the pensioner, as these determine their expected longevity.

5.1   A Simple Annuity

There are different types of annuity (see Sect. 5.12), but the most common and simplest type of annuity works as follows. The annuitant pays the annuity provider (an insurance company) a sum of money (e.g. £30,000) to buy an annuity. The annuity provider then pays the annuitant a monthly income until they die (e.g. £1800 per year). In this case, after 16.7 years the initial payment has been returned to the annuitant (i.e. the undiscounted payback period is 16.7 years). On the annuitant's death all payments cease. The annuity in this example is: (a) single premium, with a single payment of £30,000 to buy the annuity, (b) level, with an annual payment of £1800 per year that is constant over time, (c) a life annuity, which is an annuity that continues until the annuitant dies, (d) a single life, where the annuity is on the life of the named annuitant, and (e) instantaneous so that the annuity begins paying out the moment it is purchased.

© The Author(s) 2016
C. Sutcliffe, *Finance and Occupational Pensions*,
DOI 10.1057/978-1-349-94863-5_5

5.2   Voluntary and Compulsory Annuities

a. Compulsion

Compulsory annuitisation was introduced in the UK by the Finance Act of 1921, and in 1955 annuitisation was required by the age of 70, extended to 75 in the Finance Act of 1976 (Lloyd 2014). There are a number of reasons for compulsory annuitisation (Horneff et al. 2014):

(a) The presence of a well-developed welfare system creates a moral hazard that some people will spend their pension pot on items such as sports cars and then fall back on the welfare state.

(b) Others may simply underestimate their longevity, spend at too high a rate and then have to rely on the welfare state when they run out of money. The evidence from Australia, where annuitisation is voluntary, is that a quarter of pensioners exhaust their pension pots by the age of 70, and 40 % by the age of 75, equivalent to a drawdown rate of 11.6 % per year (Keohane et al. 2015).

(c) Some people may spend little or nothing from their pension pot, relying on other sources. If there is an EET (exempt-exempt-taxed) taxation system, this delays the payment of tax.

(d) Discretionary withdrawals from a pension pot in drawdown (see Sect. 5.2), rather than the regular payments of an annuity, make the tax flow to the government less predictable.

(e) Compulsion has the advantage that it ensures there is much less adverse selection (see Sect. 5.5b) in the market for compulsory annuities, and this reduces annuity prices.

(f) Compulsion means that government support for pensions via tax relief helps to provide resources for people in retirement, not to create bequests.

(g) Unfunded pension schemes are similar to Ponzi schemes, and depend on an inflow of new members, which is ensured by compulsion.

(h) The recovery of an under-funded CDC scheme is achieved at the expense of all its members, including those who have just joined; and unless membership is compulsory, new members may not join or opt out.

On the other hand, voluntary annuitisation provides pensioners with: (a) freedom of choice; (b) an increased ability to make bequests; (c) greater liquidity; (d) the opportunity to avoid poor annuity rates; and (e) allows pensioners to retain control of their money; (f) encourages the development of new innovative retirement products: (g) may encourage a culture of saving and (h) probably advances the payment of taxation when there is an EET tax system. The introduction of a new UK state pension scheme in 2016 provides a basic income for pensioners, even if they choose not to annuitise any part of their DC pension pot, and it has been claimed this will overcome the moral hazard problem.

Drawdown (also known as self-annuitisation) occurs when a pensioner invests their pension pot in a portfolio of equities, bonds and so on of their choosing, and draws an annual income from this portfolio. In 2006 UK pensioners were allowed to continue in capped drawdown beyond the age of 75 subject to strict limits on the rate of drawdown, and this was called an 'alternatively secured pension', renamed 'capped drawdown' in 2011. In 2011 'flexible drawdown' was introduced which allowed those with a high income to avoid compulsory annuitisation. In 2010 only about 2 % of the UK population met the minimum income requirement needed to be eligible for flexible drawdown (Silcock 2011). Choosing not to buy an annuity and opting for capped or flexible drawdown means pensioners have to invest their pension pot themselves, and for those with reduced mental capacity in their advanced years, this may be a challenge. Figure 5.1 shows that financial literacy declines with age, while confidence in the ability to make financial decisions does not (Finke et al. 2014). So older pensioners may be over-confident of their ability to manage their pension pot in drawdown.

As from April 2015 the requirement for compulsory annuitisation was ended in the UK for all those in DC schemes, with no requirement to enter capped or flexible drawdown. Until April 2015 UK members of DC pension

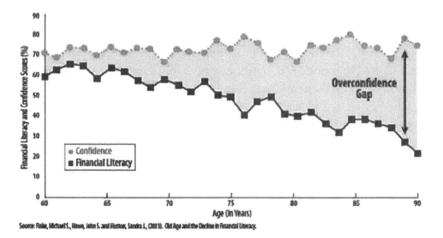

Source: Finke, Michael S., Howe, John S. and Huston, Sandra J., (2013). Old Age and the Decline in Financial Literacy.

Fig. 5.1 Decline in financial literacy with age

schemes had to use at least 75 % of the money in their pension pot to buy an annuity before they were 75, unless they were in capped or flexible drawdown. Emmerson et al. (2014) found that those mainly affected by the abolition of the requirement to annuitise by 75 were males who were better educated, healthier, had a longer life expectancy, higher total wealth and were owner-occupiers. Defined benefit (DB) pensions automatically provide a pension paid by the pension scheme, which is in effect an annuity, and the annuitisation of DB pension benefits remains compulsory. However, those in (non-public sector) DB schemes can transfer their accrued pension to a defined contribution (DC) scheme before they retire via a cash equivalent transfer value (CETV) (see Sect. 2.1.9), and then choose not to buy an annuity on retirement.

b. Voluntary

Whether the annuitisation of DC pension pots is compulsory or voluntary, individuals can always choose to voluntarily buy an annuity using their taxed savings. Until April 2015 less than 5 % of UK annuities were voluntary (Gunawardena et al. 2008). Therefore, until April 2015 95 % of the UK annuity market was compulsory annuities, but since then it has switched to being 100 % voluntary.

5.3   The Importance of Annuities

In 2014 the UK had the largest annuity market in the world (Financial Conduct Authority 2014). In 2012, 420,000 annuities were sold with a total value of £14 billion, and before the abolition of compulsory annuitisation for those in DC schemes, this was forecast to rise to £23 billion per year by 2014–15 (Harrison 2012). The value of the stock of UK annuities in 2013 was estimated at £210 billion (HM Treasury 2014). Over recent years a big switch from DB to DC pension schemes has been underway due to the increased cost and risk of DB schemes (see Sect. 2.3). So, as members of the many new DC schemes retire in increasing numbers, they will have the opportunity to choose to buy annuities. In October 2012 auto-enrolment began operation. This requires sponsors who do not offer a more favourable scheme to automatically enrol their employees in the National Employment Savings Trust (NEST) (see Sect. 1.9) or an equivalent DC scheme. It is expected that by 2018 auto-enrolment will lead to over seven million additional DC members who will eventually have the opportunity to buy an annuity (Harrison 2013). Buyouts of DB schemes (see Sect. 2.5b) are also increasing the number of annuitants. At the moment the future importance of annuities is uncertain.

5.4   A Simple Annuity Pricing Model

The prices of annuities are quoted in two different ways: (a) the initial sum of money paid by the annuitant to purchase an annuity with a specified annuity payment (e.g. paying £100,000 to secure an annual annuity payment of £6000 p.a.); and (b) the annuity rate, which is the initial sum of money paid, divided by the annual annuity payment (e.g. £6000/£100,000 = 6 %). As shown in Fig. 5.2, the relationship between these two ways of expressing the annuity price is negative and non-linear. This can lead to confusion with the statement that 'the annuity price has *risen*' meaning the annuity rate has *fallen* and the cost of buying an annuity with a given income per year has *risen*.

A simple pricing model for a single premium, instantaneous, level, single life annuity is:

$$V_{xA} = \sum_{i=1}^{n} \frac{A.P_{xi}}{(1 + r)^i} \tag{5.1}$$

where V_{xA} is the current cost of the annuity, i is the number of years since the annuity was purchased, r is the rate of interest expected for the life of the annuity (a flat term structure is assumed), A is the annual payment under the annuity, n is a number greater than the remaining years of life of the annuitant, and P_{xi} is the probability that an annuitant aged x when the annuity was purchased survives for at least i years.

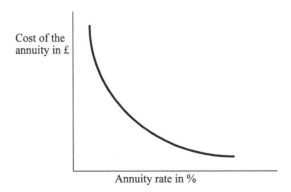

Cost of the
annuity in £

Annuity rate in %

Fig. 5.2   Annuity rate versus cost of an annuity

Example. This simple model values the annuity at the expected present value of the cash flows to the annuitant (see the numerical example in Appendix 3 which has the mortality table for a 65-year-old male living in England). If the discount rate is 5 %, then using equation (5.1), the current fair price for a single premium, instantaneous, level, single life annuity of £10,000 is £111,670.

a. Mortality Table

A key input to this pricing model is a mortality table which supplies survival probabilities. These probabilities depend on the gender, initial age and year of birth (or cohort) of the annuitant. More sophisticated mortality tables would include the annuitant's income or wealth, occupation, education, residential location, size of pot, marital status, lifestyle and health status (Fong 2015; Brown and Scahill 2010; Brown and McDaid 2003). The UK has over 1.75 million post codes, and the census gives access to information on the education, occupation and health of those living in these tiny geographic areas. UK annuity providers have data on the post-codes of their customers, and at least three insurers use them, in conjunction with other information, to price individual annuities (Richards 2008). Using data on 52,824 UK annuitants from 1988 to 1999, Finkelstein and Poterba (2014) found that education, occupation and health improved longevity forecasts. In addition, those who buy guaranteed annuities (see Sect. 5.18) and larger annuities also tend to live longer. Finkelstein and Poterba speculate on why UK annuity providers did not use post-codes in pricing annuities until 2007. In a study of over two million US annuity quotes, Chigodaev et al. (2014) found that the expected longevity implied by these prices has increased by 1.5 months per year. Furthermore, implied longevity expectations increased in a smooth manner, rather than in step changes in response to the occasional release of new mortality data.

b. Discount Rate

This is the rate at which the annuity provider can invest the money received in payment for the annuity. Annuity providers usually invest the money in bonds, particularly sterling corporate bonds; although they also invest in a very wide range of low-risk asset classes including commercial property loans, direct property, infrastructure and equity release (Cazalet Consulting 2014). They may also hold derivatives to reduce risk (e.g. interest rate swaps, currency swaps and CDS). Charupat et al. (forthcoming) studied the speed of response of US annuity prices to changes in interest rates. They found the response takes several weeks, with a larger response to interest rate increases than to interest rate decreases, which means that annuity prices fall quickly, but rise more slowly.

5.5 Other Influences on Annuity Prices

There are a number of variables missing from this simple pricing model. In addition to expected interest rates and longevity, annuity prices are affected by the load factor, adverse selection, mortality risk, credit risk, interest rate risk, regulatory capital, pot size, the degree of competition and the type of annuity being purchased. These additional factors will now be considered.

a. Load Factor

The annuity provider incurs costs, particularly marketing costs, but also administration costs and profit, and the annuity price needs to be increased to cover these costs.

b. Adverse Selection

When there is adverse selection those who subsequently have lives of above average length tend to make decisions which favour the long-lived, and similarly those with a short life expectancy tend to make decisions which favour the short-lived. Annuitants have detailed knowledge of their own health and lifestyle and those of their close relatives which is unknown to the annuity provider, and this creates an information asymmetry between the annuitant and annuity provider. Finkelstein and Poterba (2002) divided adverse selection into active and passive selection. Active selection occurs when annuity purchasing decisions are made using this private health information, while passive selection happens when annuity decisions are affected by some factor correlated with mortality (e.g. wealth). In both the voluntary and compulsory annuity markets adverse selection affects both the type and size of annuity purchased, and in the voluntary market the decision of whether or not to buy an annuity is also affected. In theoretical models this leads to what is called a 'separating equilibrium', where those with different life expectancies buy different products.

In the market for voluntary annuities the long-lived choose to buy annuities, while the short-lived do not. Since those who voluntarily buy annuities have a greater life expectancy than the general population, the suppliers of voluntary annuities increase the price of their product to protect themselves against such adverse selection. These higher prices make voluntary annuities unattractive to those with a shorter than average life expectancy. For example, in the USA where annuity purchase is voluntary, using a sample of 197 older Americans, Payne et al. (2013) found that those who judged themselves more likely to live longer than the median were 50 % more likely to buy an annuity than those with a below median subjective life expectancy.

Dushi and Webb (2006) have proposed an alternative cause of adverse selection in the voluntary market which relies on passive selection, rather than active selection using private health information. For wealthy individuals a lower proportion of their wealth is not already annuitised (e.g. in the form of state and occupational pensions). Therefore the wealthy can choose to devote a greater percentage of their total wealth to voluntary annuities. Since the wealthy also have a larger total wealth, even if they only annuitised the same proportion of their total wealth as the poor, they would invest a larger amount per head in voluntary annuities. Since wealthy people tend to live longer than poor people, this leads to adverse selection. Dushi and Webb (2006) conclude that more than half of US adverse selection is due to active selection using private information, and less than half is explained by passive selection due to pre-annuitised wealth.

These predictions have been investigated by McCarthy and Mitchell (2010) who estimated the effects of adverse selection on the longevity of compulsory and voluntary annuitants in the USA and UK. They calculated the ratio of expected deaths after the age of 65 for annuitants to the expected deaths after the age of 65 for members of the population, which is called the A/E method for comparing mortality tables. Table 5.1 shows that those who buy voluntary annuities have 25 to 35 % fewer deaths that the general population, while those who buy compulsory annuities have only 10 to 20 % fewer deaths.

As well as deciding whether or not to purchase an annuity, in both the voluntary and compulsory markets annuitants have to choose the size and type of annuity to buy (see Sect. 5.12 for descriptions of different types of annuity). Due to adverse selection (active or passive) annuitants tend to buy the type of annuity that favours themselves. Those who expect to live longer than average should tend to buy larger annuities, choose annuities where the payments rise over time (e.g. index-linked annuities and escalating annuities); and to avoid annuities which guarantee a minimum total payment to the annuitant or their estate, as these favour the short-lived. The opposite motivations apply to those with a shorter than average life expectancy, who buy smaller annuities and favour level annuities and annuities with guarantees. An empirical study of 42,054 UK annuities by Finkelstein and Poterba (2004) broadly confirms

Table 5.1 A/E ratios at age 65 in UK and US

	Voluntary annuities		Compulsory annuities	
	UK (%)	US (%)	UK (%)	US (%)
Male	67.5	65.3	82.6	84.0
Female	73.5	73.6	84.9	90.8

these expectations of the type of annuity purchased by different groups of annuitant. They found that, in both the compulsory and voluntary annuity markets, annuitants who buy an index-linked or escalating annuity are longer lived; while in the voluntary market those who are shorter lived tend to buy guaranteed annuities. There is also some evidence that those with a shorter life expectancy tend to favour annuities with guarantees in the compulsory market. In the compulsory market, but not the voluntary market, long-lived annuitants tend to buy larger annuities. These results are summarised in Table 5.2 which shows that the only situation where there is a lack of support for adverse selection is for the size of annuity payments in the voluntary market.

Finkelstein and Poterba (2004) also find that adverse selection affects annuity prices. In both the compulsory and voluntary markets the prices of annuities offering guarantees are lower than otherwise, reflecting the shorter life expectancy of these annuitants, while index-linked annuities have higher prices than otherwise due to the greater longevity of these annuitants. Escalating annuities have higher prices in the compulsory market, but surprisingly have lower prices in the voluntary market. Larger annuity payments also lead to lower prices, despite these annuities being bought by the long-lived, and this result is argued to be due to bulk discounts. These findings are summarised in Table 5.3.

Using a theoretical model Walliser (2000) concluded that adverse selection in the USA leads to an increase in annuity prices of 7–10 %, while Brown and Warshawsky (2004) suggest the price increase due to adverse selection in the USA may be 8–12 %. As Finkelstein and Poterba have argued, adverse selection should affect annuity prices, with higher prices for real and escalating annuities, and lower prices for guaranteed annuities. But these price effects

Table 5.2: Summary of the adverse selection findings of Finkelstein and Poterba (2004)

Type of annuity	Compulsory	Voluntary
Large annuity payments	Long lived	–
Index-linked annuities	Long lived	Long lived
Escalating annuities	Long lived	Long lived
Guaranteed annuities	Short lived?	Short lived?

Table 5.3 Annuity characteristics and prices (Finkelstein and Poterba 2004)

Type of annuity	Compulsory	Voluntary
Large annuity payments	Lower prices!	Lower prices!
Index-linked annuities	Higher prices	Higher prices
Escalating annuities	Higher prices	Lower prices!
Guaranteed annuities	Lower prices	Lower prices

are generally investigated by comparing the money's worth ratios (MWRs) (see Sect. 5.11b) for different types of annuity (e.g. Finkelstein and Poterba (2004)).

Cannon and Tonks (2014) have argued that, due to their greater risk, the cost of supplying real and escalating annuities is greater than for level annuities. This is for a number of reasons:

(a) The cash flows of real annuities are harder to hedge than those of level annuities due to an inadequate supply of suitable inflation-indexed hedging instruments.
(b) Real and escalating annuities make a higher proportion of their payments further into the future than do level annuities, making it more difficult to hedge their risks.
(c) Cohort mortality is harder to forecast in more distant years, which is when real and escalating annuities have a higher proportion of their cash flows, leading to higher risks for these annuities.
(d) The number of real and escalating annuities sold is small, and an insurer may not sell enough annuities to diversify away all the idiosyncratic mortality risk (see Sect. 5.5c(i)).

These factors lead to greater risk for real and escalating annuities than for level annuities. To compensate for this additional risk, annuity providers increase the price of real and escalating annuities. But when computing MWRs, researchers generally ignore the extra risks in supplying real and escalating annuities, and so tend to overstate the resulting MWRs for these types of annuity. For example, until the guarantee period ends guaranteed annuities have certain cash flows, and this risk reduction leads to a lower MWR, even in the absence of adverse selection. Real and escalating annuities may also have higher administrative costs, leading to lower MWRs. The result is that the MWRs for real and escalating annuities appear to be worse than those for level annuities, even if there is no adverse selection. Therefore Cannon and Tonks (2014) conclude that when using MWRs to measure the price effects of adverse selection, it is impossible to distinguish empirically between adverse selection and differences in risk, making the previous studies of adverse selection which have used MWRs open to question.

c. Mortality Risk
There are two types of mortality risk – specific risk and cohort risk – which are analogous to the market or systematic risk and the unsystematic risk of the CAPM.

i. Specific Risk

The pricing model in equation (5.1) assumes the average mortality experienced on the annuities an insurance company has sold corresponds to the mortality table the company used when calculating the prices, and this will only be true if the mortality table is accurate and a large sample of lives is involved (diversification of the longevity risk). Donnelly (2014) investigated the extent to which increasing the number of lives reduces the longevity risk, and she shows that roughly 500 lives are needed to achieve the available diversification benefits; while Aro (2014) finds that only 100 lives diversify away almost all the specific longevity risk. Insurance companies also sell life insurance policies which involve longevity risk. But for life insurance the risk is that the customer dies earlier than expected, while for annuities it is that the customer dies later than expected. Therefore their life assurance business provides insurers with an operational hedge for at least some of their annuity longevity risk, although this involves basis risk. For 542 US insurers Cox and Lin (2007) found that hedging their annuity business with an equivalent value of life insurance business lowered their annuity prices by 2.4 %. However, Zhu and Bauer (2014) found that the hedging effectiveness of life insurance is much reduced when a non-parametric longevity model is used.

ii. Cohort Risk

This is the risk that the average longevity of a cohort of people born in a particular year is higher or lower than expected from the mortality table. Like market risk, it cannot be diversified away, and so annuity prices are increased to cover this mortality table risk.

d. Credit Risk

Annuities can last for three or four decades, and during this period the annuity provider may default on making the annuity payments. This possibility lowers the initial value of an annuity. However, from July 2015 the Financial Services Compensation Scheme (FSCS) increased its compensation from 90 % to 100 %, and there is no upper limit on this compensation. So default risk is effectively insured while the FSCS maintains this policy.

e. Interest Rate Risk

The interest rate for the life of the annuity, which might be 20 to 40 years, is risky; and this investment risk tends to increase the price charged by annuity providers.

f. Regulatory Capital

Annuities are provided by insurance companies who must comply with the prudential regulations in the Financial Conduct Authority (FCA) handbook requiring them to hold capital reserves. Holding this additional regulatory capital increases the cost of annuities, and the introduction of Solvency II by the European Union (CEIOPS, replaced by the European Insurance and Occupational Pensions Authority in 2010) is expected to further increase the costs of providing annuities by requiring a big increase in the regulatory capital needed for annuities. DB pension schemes are not subject to these solvency requirements.

g. Pot Size
Annuity rates vary with the size of the annuitant's pensions pot (Harrison 2013). Annuity providers impose minimum values on the total sum the annuitant pays for an annuity, and in some cases these can be as high as £60,000 (Gunawardena et al. 2008). Since 41 % of annuity pots are smaller than £10,000, there are many annuitants who can only buy an annuity from a restricted range of providers.

h. Competitiveness of the Annuity Market
The UK market for annuities is highly concentrated as the three largest suppliers had 97 % of the UK market in 2012 (Financial Conduct Authority 2014). This has been argued to lead to an uncompetitive market leading to a poor deal for annuitants. In October 2015, after a very long absence, the UK government re-entered the annuity market in a modest way to compete with the private sector annuity suppliers, offering to sell index-linked joint-life annuities of up to £1300 per year at competitive rates to those receiving a state pension in April 2016.

i. Type of Annuity
There are many different types of annuity, and the design of the annuity affects its price. For example, annuities can be joint life, inflation indexed, guaranteed, enhanced, deferred, fixed period and so on (see Sect. 5.12).

While other factors, such as those mentioned above, affect annuity prices, the prime drivers of annuity rates are interest rates and longevity. Lowe (2014) regressed UK annuity rates for a 65-year-old man on the 15 year gilt rate and life expectancy for a 65-year-old man using monthly data for 1991 to 2013. The resulting equation is:

Annuity Rate = Constant + 0.484(Interest Rate) − 0.515(Life Expectancy)

Both parameters were significantly different from zero at the 0.1 % level of significance, as was the equation itself. The R^2 was 97.1 %, indicating that over 97 % of the variation in annuity rates was due to just changes in interest rates and longevity.

5.6 Mortality Discount, Mortality Credit or Mortality Drag

The mortality discount (or mortality credit or mortality drag) is the reduction in the price of an annuity, relative to the cost of purchasing bonds to give the same annual payment. The mortality discount is due to the probability of death each year of the annuitant and the resulting cessation of annuity payments. The higher is the probability of death, the greater is the mortality discount. This relationship between age and the mortality discount (or credit) is shown in Fig. 5.3.

Example. Suppose you have a lump sum of £100,000 to invest for one year. You could invest this money in bonds with a return of 8 % per year, producing £108,000. Alternatively, you could buy a deferred annuity which comes into payment in one year. For simplicity, this annuity is unusual in that it has just one payment, i.e. a fixed term of just one year. Suppose there is a 0.03 probability that you will die during the deferment period, i.e. the next year.

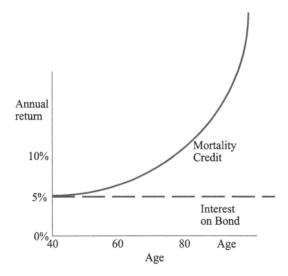

Fig. 5.3 Mortality credit

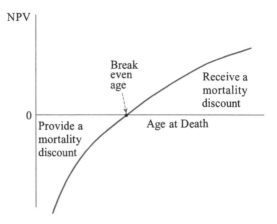

Fig. 5.4 Cross-subsidy

Then solving equation (5.1) for A leads to £100,000 = A(1 − 0.03)/(1.08), and a fairly priced deferred fixed term annuity would pay A = £111,340, conditional on your survival for one year. You have benefited from the mortality discount of (111,340 − 108,000) = £3340. As you get older the likelihood of death increases, and so the mortality discount increases, as shown in Fig. 5.3.

Figure 5.4 shows that, while all annuitants receive their promised annuity until death, those who live longer receive their payments for longer. In this way longevity risk sharing results in a cross-subsidy from those who die unexpectedly young to those who die unexpectedly late.

a. Critical Yield

Suppose that, instead of buying an annuity, an individual decides to invest the money they would have used to buy an annuity to generate the same stream of cash flows as the annuity (e.g. drawdown). The return required on the investment to produce an income equal to that of the annuity is called the critical yield (also known as critical yield A), and is computed in the same way as the internal rate of return (IRR) on an investment. Hence equation (5.2) is solved for R. Note that there are no survival probabilities in equation (5.2).

$$V_{xA} = \sum_{i=1}^{n-j} \frac{A}{(1+R)^i} \qquad (5.2)$$

where V_{xA} is the current price of the annuity, j is the age of the annuitant when purchasing the annuity, R is the critical yield, A is the annual payment under the annuity and n is the maximum age at death.

Example. For a 65-year-old male, letting V_{xA} = £111,670, A = £10,000, n = 101 years, and using the mortality table in Appendix 3, R = 8.5 %. In other words, to offer a better deal than an annuity, non-annuity investment has to outperform the riskless rate of 5 % by 3.5 % p.a. Table 5.4 and Fig. 5.5 show how the critical yield varies with age. As the age of annuitisation (i.e. the age of the annuitant when they purchase the annuity) increases, the critical yield exceeds the riskless rate by an increasingly large margin because the mortality discount increases with age.

b. Implied Longevity Yield

The critical yield does not allow for some important differences between buying an annuity and investing the money via drawdown. Annuities remove longevity risk and have no investment risk, and inflation indexed annuities

Table 5.4 Critical Yield and Age

Age	Cost of an annuity	Critical yield (%)	Risk premium (%)
45	£163,555	5.9	0.9
50	£153,170	6.2	1.2
55	£141,040	6.8	1.8
60	£127,238	7.5	2.5
65	£111,670	8.5	3.5
70	£94,876	10.0	5.0
75	£77,062	12.4	7.4
80	£59,692	16.1	11.1
85	£44,515	21.7	16.7

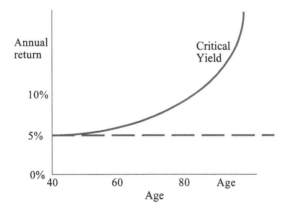

Fig. 5.5 Critical yield and age

also remove inflation risk, while annuities do not permit bequests. Drawdown allows any remaining cash balance to be bequeathed on death, but leads to longevity risk, and may involve investment and inflation risk if the money is not invested in an inflation indexed riskless asset. To partially control for bequests and longevity risks, Milevsky (2005a, 2013) has suggested replacing the critical yield with the 'implied longevity yield'. This is computed by comparing the returns on two different strategies. (1) Buy an immediate inflation indexed annuity for £X, which will produce annual real payments of £a per year until death. (2) Invest £X now, and withdraw £a per year in real terms from this investment until the pensioner reaches the age of (say) 85. The investment and inflation risks are removed if this money is invested in an inflation indexed riskless asset. At the age of (say) 85, buy an immediate annuity of £a per year in real terms at a price of £Y.[1] Neither strategy permits bequests after the age at which the annuity comes into payment, although the drawdown strategy does allow bequests below this age. The rate of return on the investments which equates the payoffs from these two strategies is the 'implied longevity yield'. Shankar (2009) and Haensly and Pai (2014) have conducted empirical investigations of these two strategies using US data, where the money is invested in Treasury Inflation Protected Securities (TIPS) so that the resulting income stream is inflation indexed and very low risk.

Example. Suppose the cost of an immediate annuity of £10,000 per year for a 65-year-old man is £111,670, the price of an immediate annuity of £10,000 per year from the age of 85 is £44,515, and the riskless rate is 5 %. If the drawdown strategy is followed, the implied longevity yield is the IRR on an investment now of £111,670, with payments of £10,000 for 20 years, and then a cash payment of £44,515 for the annuity. The IRR (i.e. the implied longevity yield) of these cash flows is 7.6 %, which is higher than the 5 % risk free rate, i.e. an excess return of 2.6 %. This compares with the critical yield of 8.5 % for a 65-year-old male in Table 5.4, and indicates that controlling for longevity risk reduces the required rate of return on drawdown, making it more attractive.

Aviva (2014) compared buying an annuity with drawdown (self-annuitisation). Three alternative drawdown investments were examined, and the pensioner was assumed to have retired in one of three years. In each case Aviva compared the annuity that could be purchased initially, with the annuity that could be purchased with the remaining drawdown balance in 2014

---

[1] An alternative strategy is to buy a deferred annuity now, which will cost less than £Y due to the mortality discount, and invest the remaining sum.

Table 5.5 Drawdown versus an annuity – annuity income in 2014 (Aviva 2014)

	1999	2004	2009
Annuity	£279.31	£252.97	£240.29
Drawdown – all equity	£16.91	£291.11	£355.63
Drawdown – all fixed income	£119.21	£194.90	£198.37
Drawdown – mixed portfolio	£77.40	£237.64	£260.65

after withdrawing the same income as that provided by the annuity. Table 5.5 shows that sometimes the annuity is superior, and at other times drawdown invested in equities is superior. The annuity rates in Table 5.5 ignore the risk inherent in equity investments and the annuity price risk involved in buying an annuity in 2014. For example, the all-equity drawdown which started in 1999 is only able to buy an annuity of £16.91 in 2014 due to the dramatic drop in annuity rates by 2014, while the income of £279.31 from buying an annuity in 1999 is certain.

5.7   Tontines

Tontines illustrate the mortality discount (or credit) underlying annuities. Lorenzo de Tonti is credited with inventing the tontine in 1653, although similar financial instruments existed earlier. For example in 1581, at the age of 17, William Shakespeare was given a tontine which he enjoyed until his death almost 35 years later (Milevsky 2015). There were state-run tontines in the Netherlands, France, Britain and Germany; and private tontines in Switzerland and the USA (McKeever 2010). In the UK a tontine was used to finance the building of the Covent Garden theatre, and in the USA a tontine financed the building of the Tontine Coffee House, an early home of what became the New York Stock Exchange. In many cases, rather than nominate themselves, tontine subscribers (investors) nominated the lives of other people. For example, in 1789 some investors nominated King George III, who died in 1820 at the age of 81; and Marie Antoinette was nominated in 1777 by investors, but was executed in 1793 at the age of 37 (McKeever 2010). The detailed rules differ between tontines, but the following two examples show a popular model.

Example 1. Ten subscribers choose nominees of a similar age, and each subscriber invests £100 in a tontine run by a promoter (usually the government). The resulting £1000 is invested in bonds at 5 %, producing a total income of £50 per year. This income is divided equally between the subscribers, and so each initially each receives the same income as they would from investing directly in bonds, i.e. 5 % per year. After some years two of the nominees die. The total income of £50 per year is now shared among the eight subscribers with surviving nominees, i.e. a return of 50/8 = 6.25 %. The extra 1.25 % represents a mortality discount (or credit) as the subscribers of the two deceased nominees receive no further payments, and the sum they invested is forfeit. A few years later another two nominees die, and so each subscriber with a surviving nominee now receives 50/6 = 8.33 %. Eventually the last subscriber with a surviving nominee receives a return of 50 % on their initial investment. In most tontines when everyone has died the sum invested in bonds (£1000) reverts to the promoter (usually the government). In a few tontines the subscriber of the last surviving nominee receives the total sum invested.

Example 2. Suppose a 65-year–old man enters a tontine as a nominee and subscriber along with 85,474 other 65-year-old men, their subsequent mortality is given by Appendix 3, and the tontine pays annual interest of 5 % on the initial cost of a share in the tontine (£111,670 per person), i.e. £5583.5 per year. The corresponding annuity pays £10,000 per year. Table 5.6 and Fig. 5.6 show the difference in the present value of the annual income from the tontine and the annuity for a person who survives to the age of 101. This shows that initially the tontine produces a markedly lower expected income, but the longer he survives the better is the relative performance of the tontine. When he reaches the age of 82, the annual income from the tontine is about the same as from the annuity. The breakeven age between the tontine and the annuity is about 93 years, when the present value of all the cash flows to date for both the tontine and annuity are the same. If he makes it to be 101 years old, only 691 men will have survived, and the expected present value of his annual tontine income is £117,488 higher than from an annuity. Given that he survives to be 101, the tontine has a present value that is £375,562 larger than if he had bought the annuity. However, the income from the tontine is risky, due to the uncertain longevity of the nominees. In this example, while those subscribers with nominees who survive into their late 90s do very well, the tontine is not actuarially fair because the promoter retains the capital sum on the death of the last subscriber.

The promoter of a tontine faces a single risk, which is the number of years until the last nominee dies, and this increases with the number of nominees, and decreases as their initial age increases. Until then each year the promoter must pay the same agreed interest on the capital sum, divided between a decreasing number of nominees. The subscribers receive annuity payments whose size increases in a risky way depending on when the nominees die. (The

Table 5.6 Present values of the difference between the annual income from a tontine versus an annuity

Age	Difference	Age	Difference	Age	Difference	Age	Difference
65	−4,417	75	−1,854	85	1,282	95	16,077
66	−4,132	76	−1,610	86	1,804	96	21,390
67	−3,855	77	−1,358	87	2,411	97	28,910
68	−3,588	78	−1,102	88	3,124	98	40,017
69	−3,325	79	−838	89	3,927	99	56,309
70	−3,070	80	−556	90	4,891	100	80,627
71	−2,823	81	−255	91	6,057	101	117,488
72	−2,579	82	73	92	7,603	Total	375,562
73	−2,336	83	430	93	9,682		
74	−2,095	84	826	94	12,425		

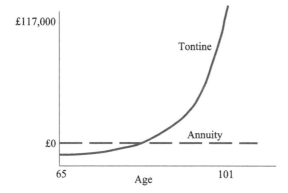

Fig. 5.6 Present values of the difference between the annual income from a tontine versus an annuity

total income of the tontine may also fluctuate with the interest rate on the investment.) In some cases subscribers may receive a risky prize (the total sum invested) when their nominee is the last survivor (a lottery).

With modern annuities, the insurance company estimates the likely size of the mortality discount (or credit) and the rate of return it can achieve on the money invested. These are built into the annuity payments it agrees to make to each annuitant (or subscriber, who is also the nominee). Thus the insurance company bears the mortality and investment risks, and the annuitant receives a certain income stream until death, including the mortality discount (or credit). Providing this guaranteed income means that the insurance company needs to hold capital reserves, and this increases the cost of providing annuities. In addition, to reduce their risks, insurance companies invest in low-risk assets such as bonds, while tontines can invest in riskier securities generating higher expected returns (Newfield 2014). Shu (2013) has argued that tontines appear fairer than annuities. If an annuitant dies shortly after buying an annuity this may be seen as unfair as the insurance company benefits from no longer having to make the annuity payments. Annuitants may not understand that the gains from early deaths are used by the insurer to pay for late deaths. However with a tontine it is transparent that the money that would have been paid to the deceased is now paid to the other subscribers, and is not retained by the promoter.

A modern development where the promoter bears virtually no risk is, what Piggott et al. (2005) have called 'group self-annuitisation', where the annuitants pool the longevity and investment risks. This risk pooling is achieved by varying the level of annuity payments in response to investment returns and mortality experience. The Teachers Insurance and Annuity Association – College Retirement Equities Fund (TIAA–CREF) is a not-for-profit retirement provider for those who work in the academic, research, medical and cultural fields in the USA. They offer CREF variable annuities (or participating annuities) where the annuitants pool investment and longevity risks by varying the annuity payments, i.e. group self-annuitisation.

5.8   Reasons for Buying an Annuity

There are various motivations for individuals to voluntarily buy an annuity:

(a) Each annuitant is insured against longevity risk and the consequences of outliving their resources.
(b) Annuitants benefit from the mortality discount (or credit). Bonds pay the riskless rate, while annuities offer the riskless rate plus the mortality discount (or credit).
(c) Annuitants are guaranteed not to leave unconsumed resources. Therefore, annuitants maximise their consumption without leaving any debts.
(d) Since cognitive ability declines in old age, buying an annuity removes the need for pensioners to make any subsequent investment decisions, such as managing their wealth. A study of retired Americans by Panis (2004) found that, after controlling for differences in income, wealth, health, gender, marital status and age, those with a higher proportion of annuitised wealth were more satisfied.

The benefits of the mortality discount (or credit) to those who live longer than the break-even age are illustrated in the following two examples.

Example 1. Using the example in Appendix 3, if the cost of the annuity (£111,670) is invested at 5 % it will produce £5583 per year, i.e. 44 % less than the £10,000 p.a. from the annuity. To get an income of £10,000 per year forever it is necessary to invest £200,000, i.e. £88,000 more than the cost of the annuity. If the annuitant lives to be 101 years old, he will receive total annuity payments of £360,000, with a present value of £175,469, giving him a NPV from buying the annuity of (£175,469 – £111,670) = £63,799. The break-even age with zero NPV is 79.6 years, while life expectancy at 65 is to live to be 82.8 years, giving an expected profit of £14,395. The break-even age is less than expected life expectancy because the break-even NPV calculation uses the declining time values of money, in addition to the declining survival probabilities. Some of this information can be presented graphically (see Fig. 5.7), and the chances of a positive NPV, i.e. living longer than 79.6 years, are 65 %.

Example 2. The example (Brown 2008, p. 181) in Fig. 5.8 compares the income from four different strategies for an individual with a wealth of £100,000, when the riskless interest rate is 3.52 % p.a.:

1. *Annuitisation* – Buy an annuity and consume £8100 per year until death.
2. *Self-annuitisation* – Invest in bonds at 3.52 %, and consume £8100 per year. The money runs out at age 82.
3. *Amortisation* – Invest in bonds at 3.52 %, and consume an equal amount over the next 35 years (£5000 per year). The money runs out at age 100.
4. *1/(Life Expectancy$_t$)* – Invest in bonds at 3.52 %, and consume *1/LE$_t$* of the current value of the fund each year.

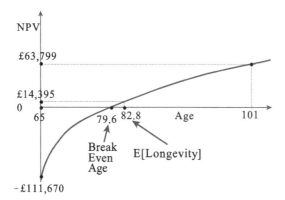

Fig. 5.7 Break even age

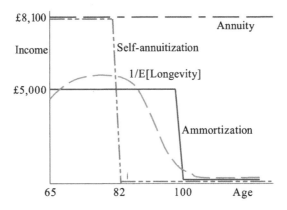

Fig. 5.8 Income from alternative strategies

As shown in Fig. 5.8, annuitisation is the dominant strategy, provided there is no bequest motive, as the other three strategies leave a bequest if the person dies before the money runs out.

A survey of 850 people aged 55 to 70 investigated their views on drawdown (self-annuitisation) versus an annuity, and found that substantial numbers had a mistaken understanding. Over half thought that drawdown would provide them with a guaranteed income; 45 % thought that if they withdrew the same amount as the corresponding annuity would pay, their money would last until they died; and 23 % thought that there are no risks in drawing a regular income from their pension pot (NAPF 2015). However, Mayhew et al. (2015) have argued that drawdown may be preferable to annuitisation for many people. This is due to: low annuity rates, unisex pricing of annuities,[2] loss of flexibility, loss of bequests, small pension pots, loss of means-tested welfare benefits, the small chance of outliving the drawdown pot, the presence of other assets such as a house, and the availability of the welfare state to support anyone who outlives their resources.

5.9   The Annuity Puzzle

Yaari (1965) has shown that consumers can solve the dilemma of ensuring that they exhaust their resources on their last day of life by buying an annuity, with longevity risk passing from themselves to the annuity provider. The purchase of

---

[2] UK annuity and life insurance prices were required to be unisex as from 21 December 2012 by a ruling of the European Court of Justice, making male annuities more expensive. This ruling does not apply to occupational pensions.

an annuity allows higher consumption because: (a) annuitants do not have to undertake precautionary saving to cover unexpected longevity, and (b) annuitants benefit from the presence of the mortality discount (or credit). Yaari (1965) implies that every consumer should voluntarily annuitise their entire wealth because annuitisation makes every consumer better off. Davidoff et al. (2005) derive Yaari's result with less restrictive assumptions, and then go on to consider the case of incomplete markets. They conclude that with incomplete markets substantial, although not complete, annuitisation is likely to be optimal. Therefore, the theory predicts very substantial, although not complete, annuitisation.

However, voluntary annuitisation is uncommon. For example, in the USA in 1999, 2001 and 2003 only 2 % of 401(k) scheme members chose an annuity (Schaus 2005). In Australia only 3.5 % of those who received a lump sum chose to buy an annuity (Cooper et al. 2012); while Cumbo (2014) reports that of the A$70 billion in lump sums received by Australian retirees in 2013, only A$2.2 billion (or 3.14 %) was used to buy an annuity, and in the nine months to September 2009 only 17 annuities were sold in Australia (Mitchell and Piggott 2011; Bateman and Piggott 2011). A UK survey by the *Financial Times* in March 2014 found that only 4.5 % would voluntarily buy an annuity with their lump sum (Eley 2014), while a UK survey by PwC (2014) in April 2014 of 1208 people who were about to retire discovered that only 16 % of pension pots would voluntarily be used to buy an annuity. This leads to the annuity puzzle; which is that the theory predicts individuals will voluntarily annuitise most of their wealth, but in reality this is not the case. In 1986 Modigliani (1986) pointed out this big difference between theory and reality, leading to the search to solve this annuity puzzle.

5.10 Some Partial Explanations for the Annuity Puzzle

Researchers have been trying to explain the annuity puzzle for 30 years, and they have come up with a wide range of potential explanations. Below is a list of 27 of these explanations, divided into 11 that are concerned with the supply of annuities by insurance companies, and 16 that deal with the demand for annuities by pensioners.

a. Supply Factors

Potential annuitants may be deterred because annuities are expensive, illiquid and not designed to deliver the pattern of cash flows annuitants want.

1. Load. The load factor (marketing and administration costs, regulatory capital and profit) leads to low value for money (or money's worth – see Sect. 5.11b).
2. Adverse Selection. The costs of adverse selection make annuities unattractive to those with an average or lower life expectancy (see Sect. 5.5b).
3. Illiquidity. An annuity cannot be sold or redeemed, and so large unanticipated expenses, such as healthcare needs, cannot be met, apart from using the annual annuity payments. However, while annuities cannot be sold or redeemed, an annuity that is not inflation indexed can be offset by borrowing a sum of money now. At the same time the annuitant insures their life for an amount equal to the size of the loan. The interest on the loan and the life insurance premia are paid using the annuity payments. When the annuitant dies the life insurance payout is used to pay off the loan, and so all payments stop (Bernheim 1991; Brown 2001; Yaari 1965; Sutcliffe 2015). Suppose that two years ago Orsino Thruston bought an annuity for £100,008. This yields an annuity payment of £8245 per year until his death. He now wishes to offset this annuity, and so he borrows the current value of the annuity – £93,063 at a fixed rate of 4 %. This requires interest payments of £3723 per year, leaving a net cash inflow of £4522 per year. Orsino uses this £4522 p.a. to pay the annual premiums on a life assurance policy on his life worth £93,063. For simplicity, it is assumed that Orsino dies at the end of the fourth year. So Orsino has effectively sold his annuity now for £93,063, which is the current price of an annuity of £8245 on his life. In 2015 the UK Treasury consulted on creating a secondary annuity market, and so in the future UK annuities may become liquid (HM Treasury 2015a, b).
4. Default. The risk of default by the annuity provider may deter potential annuitants from buying an annuity.
5. Index linking. The unavailability of index linked annuities in the USA means that annuitants are vulnerable to inflation which can greatly reduce the real value of an annuity. Index linked annuities are available in the UK.
6. Low expected returns. If the mortality discount (or credit) is less than the equity risk premium, the consumer may prefer to wait until they are older and this relationship is reversed before buying an annuity, particularly if they have a low level of risk aversion.
7. Small pots. Annuitants with small pension pots (e.g. less than £5000) have difficulty finding an annuity provider willing to sell them an annuity (see Sect. 5.5g).
8. Mortality table risk. The survival probabilities used when valuing annuities are subject to risk, as realised average mortality may differ from those

in the mortality table. Therefore the annuity price includes a risk premium to cover this risk. Stevens (2009) estimated that this risk increases actuarially fair annuity prices by about 7.5 %, making annuities less attractive.

9. Incomplete markets. Consumers are not offered annuity products that meet their preferences (Lloyd 2014) (e.g. an annuity with payments that follow a U-shape by starting high (e.g. to allow travel while health is good), falling, and then rising again (e.g. pay for care) to match the typical consumption pattern of pensioners (MacDonald et al. 2013).

10. Hedging. It is difficult for annuity providers to hedge long-run longevity and inflation risks as suitable instruments are not available in the requisite volume. This increases the risks of providing annuities, leading to higher prices to compensate for the higher risks.

11. Competition. The annuity market is dominated by a small number of large providers, and this has led to a low level of competition and high prices.

b. Demand Factors

Demand for annuities may be reduced by a wide range of factors, including faulty decision making by potential annuitants, the presence of pre-annuitised wealth, a desire for liquidity and a bequest motive.

1. Other pensions. Many people already have other annuities (e.g. state pensions, DB pensions, the welfare state), and so have a reduced need to buy an additional annuity.

2. Housing. The result of Yaari (1965) is that all wealth, including property, should be converted into an annuity. In retirement pensioners need to consume housing services, and owner-occupiers may prefer to continue living in their own house, rather than sell it and use the cash to buy an annuity whose payments can be used to rent another property (Lloyd 2014). Hence housing wealth is not annuitised. Pensioners can convert their existing home into what is effectively an annuity by entering into a reverse mortgage (or lifetime mortgage) with a lender. The lender provides them with a stream of regular payments, or a lump sum loan, until the home owner dies or sells the house. At this time the terminal value of the stream of payments, or the loan plus interest, is repaid from the proceeds of selling the house. Alternatively home owners can sell a proportion of their home to the provider in exchange for a stream of regular payments, or a lump sum paid now. The home owner remains living in the home until their death or the house is sold, at which time the provider

gets the agreed percentage of the sale price, Hanewald et al. (2016) and Bhuyan (2011).

3. Bequest motive. Pensioners may wish to use their wealth to provide an inheritance for their family and others on their death; and using their wealth to buy an annuity means this money cannot be inherited. However, although widespread, this argument is questionable. Pensioners can bequeath any money they save from the annuity payments they receive. More importantly, the purchase of an annuity can increase the certainty that a pre-specified bequest will be made. The pensioner's initial wealth is divided into the amount they wish to bequeath, and this is invested in a safe security until their death, and the remaining sum is used to buy an annuity to support them for the rest of their lives. If no annuity is purchased there is a risk that unexpectedly long-lived pensioners will exhaust their wealth leaving no bequest, and possibly asking their family for financial support in their final years. Joint-life annuities provide an income for the survivor, and guaranteed annuities pay an income for a guaranteed number of years, even if the annuitant has previously died. Using data for Spain, Vidal-Meliá and Lejárraga-García (2006) found no evidence of a bequest motive influencing the demand for annuities by couples.

4. Families. Families provide self-insurance, and so annuities are not needed (Kotlikoff and Spivak 1981). For example, annuitisation is less attractive for couples than for single individuals (Brown and Poterba 2000).

5. Taxation. Taxation may make annuities relatively unattractive.

6. Means tested benefits. The income from an annuity may reduce or eliminate a pensioner's right to claim means tested benefits, while spending their pension pot or giving it away will not (Lloyd 2014).

7. Biased estimates. If consumers make biased estimates they may think that annuities are over-priced and decide not to buy. For example, they may under-estimate future interest rates or inflation, or over-estimate the risk premium, thereby making equity investment appear more attractive. Previtero (2014) studied a sample of 103,000 US lump sum versus annuity decisions. He found a negative relationship between recent equity returns and the decision to annuitise, suggesting that people overweight recent equity returns. In addition he found that women were more likely to annuitise, as were those with a larger pension pot. People may underestimate the risk of outliving their assets (under-estimating both their own life expectancy and the costs of being penniless), and there have been a number of studies which have quantified the degree of the under-estimation of longevity. Crawford and Tetlow (2012) found that, on average, English women under-estimate their life expectancy by four

years, and English men under-estimate their own longevity by two years. A survey of 2028 UK adults by MGM Advantage (2014) found that men under-estimated their longevity by five years, and women under-estimated their longevity by 10 years, while a survey of 5000 people in the UK aged from 55 to 70 years of age discovered that men underestimated their longevity by 4.3 years, and women by 5.9 years (International Longevity Centre-UK 2015). A UK survey of 2000 people in 2014 with an average age of 53 asked them to estimate their longevity at age 65. Their median estimate was between 16–20 years, although the median actuarial estimate was 26 to 30 years, indicating substantial under-estimation by about a decade (Willets 2015). Kutlu-Koc and Kalwij (2013) analysed Dutch data and discovered that women under-estimate their longevity by eight years, and men by one year. Using data for nine European countries, Peracchi and Perotti (2009, 2012) found little under-estimation of longevity by men, but considerable under-estimation by women. For Australia, Wu et al. (2014) showed that people are pessimistic about their survival probabilities, relative to life tables, for ages up to 90 years. Steffen (2009) used data from 7900 Germans, and found that both men and women under-estimate their life expectancy by several years.

8. Longevity prediction. If people think they can accurately estimate their longevity, they do not face any risk of outliving their wealth, and this removes an important motive for buying an annuity.

9. Behavioural biases. There is a range of behavioural factors which may lead people to decide not to buy an annuity: (a) Mental accounting (or framing) – the annuity is viewed as a separate risky gamble, rather than as a way of reducing existing risks (Hu and Scott 2007; Brown et al. 2008, 2009; Gottlieb 2013). Brown et al. (2008, 2009) compared the extent to which US individuals are willing to annuitise under two different frames – a consumption frame where the annuity insures future consumption levels, and an investment frame where investing in an annuity is seen as riskier than a bond due to the possibility of an early death. They found that a consumption frame led to an annuitisation rate three times larger than when an investment frame was used. (b) Endowment effect – whether the default choice is a lump sum with no annuity, or the reverse (Gazzale and Walker 2009). Making an immediate annuity the default choice, rather than a lump sum, can increase annuitisation by over 80 % (Gazzale et al. 2012). Offering a deferred annuity that does not come into payment until an advanced age, rather than an immediate annuity, as the alternative to a lump sum increased annuitisation by over 110 %. (c) Hyperbolic discounting – people undervalue distant cash flows due to

applying a very high personal discount rate, making annuities appear unattractive. In a survey of students in 53 countries, Wang et al. (2016) found that in every country they exhibited hyperbolic discounting. (d) Risk-ordering bias (or loss aversion) – people overweight the risk of dying shortly after buying the annuity (Gazzale and Walker 2009). (e) Regret aversion – people fear entering into an irreversible contract and then discovering they have only a short time to live (Goedde-Menke et al. 2014). (f) Insurance fallacy – buying an annuity involves purchasing insurance against outliving one's resources. But insurance is usually seen as a remedy for negative events, while living longer than expected is a positive event. There is no need to insure against favourable events (Goedde-Menke et al. 2014).

10. Complexity. The purchase of an annuity is a complex, one-off decision. Individuals have bounded rationality and little or no experience of making annuity decisions and so they value annuities with considerable error, and those who undervalue annuities do not purchase. Browning et al. (2012) asked Americans to value an annuity and found massive inaccuracy. Of the sample of 681 subjects, 17 % estimated an annuity value that was, on average, only 30 % of the correct value, while 63 % of the sample estimated a value that was, on average, 2,500 % larger than the correct value. This indicates an enormous inaccuracy in valuing annuities, which was unrelated to the financial sophistication or numeracy of the subjects. Similarly Brown et al. (2013) found that US households undervalued annuities by an average of 18 % of the fair value. There was substantial dispersion in these valuations, with 5 % of the sample willing to accept a discount of 91 %. In 2015 the UK Department for Work and Pensions wrote that *'accurate calculation of the net present value of an annuity is relatively complex and beyond the capability of most consumers'* (DWP 2015a).

11. Control. Individuals have a desire to keep control of their money, which may also increase their negotiating power with their family.

12. Wealth. Very rich people have no chance of outliving their wealth and so have no need to buy an annuity. Analysing the US data in Table 1 of Moore and Mitchell (1997), Neuberger and McCarthy (2003) conclude that as total wealth increases the annuitised proportion drops sharply.

13. Advice. Financial advisors may be incentivised by higher commissions to sell financial products other than annuities. In a survey of US financial consultants, 14 % said low commissions were a reason for not recommending annuities, and in another US survey only 9 % said they had a strong preference for annuities as part of a client's retirement portfolio

(Rotemberg and Gourville 2010).Turner (2014) examined 24 free online retirement planning advisors and, while data which favoured the purchase of an annuity was entered into these online advisors, none recommended the purchase of an annuity.

14. Trust. People mistrust financial institutions, and so are unwilling to trust most or all of their wealth to these institutions: Gardner and Wadsworth (2004), Beshears et al. (2014), Goedde-Menke et al. (2014).

15. Social welfare. Feigenbaum et al. (2013) and Fehr and Habermann (2008) have argued that social welfare would be higher in the long run if there was no annuitisation. Non-annuitisation generates accidental bequests to young people and, given various assumptions, this transfers consumption from the old to the young. This is argued to increase long-run social welfare; although the initial generation of old people are made worse off by not annuitising. Using US data, Auerbach et al. (2001) show that increased annuitisation is associated with reduced saving, which leads to lower wealth. Therefore society as a whole is rational in not annuitising its wealth, although it is not clear why individuals sacrifice their own utility for the common good.

16. Dislike. In a survey of UK adults, Parker (2013) found a strong dislike of choosing an annuity. This was attributed to a lack of knowledge of annuities, coupled with a fear of making a mistake in such an important decision.

A range of empirical evidence is available from the USA, UK, Germany, Italy and Brazil on why people do not annuitise. This evidence comprises: (a) surveys where people are asked for their views on the factors which may be causing them not to buy an annuity, and (b) research that analyses the characteristics of those who choose not to buy an annuity, or who under-annuitise.

A US survey in 1999 investigated why people are reluctant to annuitise and found the following reasons for not annuitising: (a) loss of control of their money 31 %; (b) bequest motive 18 %; (c) low annuity rate 15 %; (d) lack of an inflation adjustment 12 %; (e) not well informed 9 %; and (f) do not need an annuity 5 %. A survey of 1744 people working for a large American university found that 18.7 % would not buy an annuity due to the lack of flexibility (Lown and Robb 2011). This finding is supported by a UK survey of 3511 people aged 50–64 years which found that, of those who said they would never buy an annuity, 74 % said this was because they would lose flexibility. This was the most popular reason for not buying an annuity by a considerable distance (Gardner and Wadsworth 2004). A survey of US financial advisors found that 56 % would not recommend their clients to buy an annuity due to the lack of liquidity (Rotemberg and Gourville 2010). Beshears et al. (2014) conducted a survey of 5130 older US residents. Subjects were asked the importance they attached to various factors in determining their choice between a lump sum and an annuity. Flexibility in the timing of spending was the second most important factor, after making sure of enough income in later life. The third most important factor was a concern about default by the annuity provider. A regression analysis found the percentage of funds annuitised was a positive function of the desire for income in later life, worries about inflation, and the prevention of overspending. Annuitisation was less likely for those concerned about flexibility, possible insurer default, the ability to invest money themselves, a bequest motive and worries about dying early.

The results from the empirical studies which have looked for common characteristics among those who choose not to buy an annuity, or who annuitise a smaller proportion of their wealth, are generally disappointing. They have failed to find a small number of powerful characteristics that are supported by a number of empirical studies. Using US survey data Brown et al. (2007) concluded that the annuity puzzle is not explained by high load factors, a lack of inflation-indexed annuities, pre-existing annuitisation, gender, marital status, income, wealth and the presence of children. Goedde-Menke et al. (2014) surveyed 1546 Germans to test the simultaneous effect of 10 possible explanations for the annuity puzzle. Collectively these 10 factors were only able to explain about 25 % of the variation in annuity purchase, leaving 75 % unexplained. The significant factors they found for not buying an annuity were: (a) viewing an annuity as an investment rather than a gamble, (b) distrust of insurance companies, (c) adverse selection, (d) the bequest motive and (e) low financial literacy. Another five factors had no significant effect: (a) family risk sharing, (b) liquidity, (c) other pensions, (d) the insurance fallacy and (e) regret aversion.

Studies have found significant explanatory factors for annuity demand, but each study usually comes up with a different set of explanatory factors. Using a sample of 8950 Americans aged at least 55 years, Ameriks et al. (2014) investigated the US demand for annuities. They found that the lack of demand for annuities can be explained by a combination of three factors: the bequest motive, the precautionary demand for savings to pay for long-term care, and the availability of means-tested state benefits. As a result, they conclude that there is no annuity puzzle – a view which is not widely shared. The factors determining the intention of 7480 young Italian adults to buy a deferred annuity were analysed by Nosi et al. (2014). They found that women, and those with greater educational attainment and higher income were more inclined to buy an annuity. These results are supported by Guillemette et al. (2016) who surveyed 5074 Americans. Those who are more likely to buy an annuity are younger women with a high income, low wealth and low risk aversion. Vaz et al. (2012) analysed the factors determining whether 14,511 Brazilians chose to convert their pension pot into an annuity. They found the probability of buying an annuity was increased by: (a) being female, (b) having a large pension pot, (c) cheaper annuity prices, (d) being in the pension scheme for a shorter period and (e) leaving the pension scheme at a younger age. Clark and Knox-Hayes (2007) studied the variables associated with the intention to buy an annuity using a survey of 4538 older people in the UK. They found that people in the north of England, Wales and Scotland are less likely to buy an annuity than those living in the rest of the UK, and that a range of seven socio-demographic factors has no effect on annuity purchase intentions. Schreiber and Weber (2013) surveyed 3077 German adults and found that older people tend to choose an annuity rather than a lump sum, as do those who expect a longer life.

DiCenzo et al. (2011) surveyed over one thousand Americans between the ages of 45 and 75, and investigated the effects of supplying them with additional information on the probability of pre-retirees' intentions to buy an annuity. They also collected data on a wide range of other factors which might affect the desire to buy an annuity. They found the following seven factors all lead to a doubling or tripling in the probability of buying an annuity: (a) factual information on annuities, (b) information on behavioural biases that reduce annuity purchases, (c) both factual and behavioural bias information, (d) information on the potential impact of running out of money, (e) concern about their standard of living, (f) concern about their healthcare, and (g) concern about inflation. Life expectancy and knowledge of annuities also has a small positive effect on intentions to buy annuities, while intending to invest retirement assets and being unmarried in a permanent relationship lead to a small reduction in the intention to annuitise. Finally, on the basis of a theoretical model, Laitner et al. (2014) have suggested that the annuity puzzle can be explained by the precautionary demand to meet uninsured health costs, overpriced annuities and the availability of family support.

In summary, a very wide range of possible explanations for the annuity puzzle have been proposed and investigated. However, there is no clear evidence that points to a single explanation, and the available evidence suggests that this puzzle has multiple causes.

5.11 Evaluating Annuity Prices

Annuity prices can be evaluated in three different ways (Mitchell et al.1999): (a) the annuity rate, (b) the money's worth ratio (MWR), and (c) the annuity equivalent wealth (AEW). Each of these approaches will be examined in turn.

a. Annuity Rate

The annuity rate is the simplest method, and is the annual annuity payment (*A*) divided by the sum of money paid by the annuitant for the annuity (or price of the annuity), i.e.:

Annuity Rate = (Annual Annuity Payment) / (Price of the Annuity) (5.3)

This ratio is effectively the price of an annuity, and varies primarily with (a) interest rate expectations, and (b) the expected longevity of the annuitant. In 2015 the annuity rate of a level annuity for a 65-year-old male was about 5.9 %, i.e. for a payment of £10,000, an annuitant receives an annual payment of £590. By recent historical standards this annuity rate is low, and in 1981 it was as high as 17 %. Figure 5.9 from *The Telegraph* 24 September 2014 shows the large decline in UK annuity rates since 1991. While interest rates will rise in the future and this will increase annuity rates, improvements in longevity are likely to continue, tending to depress annuity rates. Using the annuity rate, annuities are currently expensive, but does this mean they are poor value for money?

Sometimes the annuity factor is used to express annuity prices. This is the cost of £1 of annuity income per year, and so is the reciprocal of the annuity rate.

Annuity Factor = (Price of the Annuity) / (Annual Annuity Payment)(5.4)

b. Money's Worth Ratio

The money's worth ratio (MWR) is the present value of the expected stream of annuity payments ($PV\{E[A]\}$), divided by the price of the annuity, or:

MWR = (PV of the Expected Annuity Payments) / (Price of the Annuity)

(5.5)

Ignoring transactions costs, regulatory capital requirements and normal profit, a fairly priced annuity should have a MWR of one. There have been

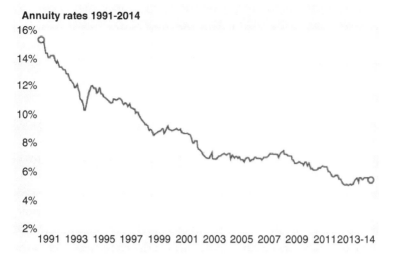

Annuity rates 1991-2014

Fig. 5.9 UK annuity rates 1991–2014

many studies of the MWR of annuities, and (ignoring transactions costs, regulatory capital requirements and normal profit) they usually find a MWR that is a bit below one. This applies both across countries and over time, and suggests that, even though there have been big movements in the annuity rate over time due to changes in expected interest rates and longevity, the MWR is much more stable. This is because the MWR calculation adjusts for expected changes in interest rates and longevity, while the annuity rate does not. In 2015 interest rates were low and longevity expectations were high, leading to a low annuity rate, while the MWR was still about one. In a study for the Financial Conduct Authority, Aquilina et al. (2014) found that UK MWRs were stable over the 2006–14 period with a value of 94 %, even though there was a big reduction during this period in interest rates, along with an increase in longevity. The researchers found that the MWR rises to 99 % for those who use the open market option (OMO) (see Sect. 5.14) to get the best quote, and they conclude that *'an annuity gives good value for money'*, despite the low annuity rate. A related measure is the coefficient of variation of the MWR, i.e. $CV = \text{Std.Dev.}(MWR)/E[MWR]$, which incorporates longevity and interest rate risk (Fong et al. 2014).

c. Annuity Equivalent Wealth

The MWR for some annuities may occasionally be well below one, but consumers may still be better off if they purchase such an annuity. The annuity equivalent wealth (AEW) is computed using the sum of money by which the annuitant's wealth would have to be increased to compensate them for being denied the right to purchase an annuity, and is called their certain monetary equivalent (CME). This is added to the annuitant's initial wealth, and the sum of these two terms is divided by their initial wealth (Mitchell et al. 1999).

$$AEW = (\text{Initial Wealth} + CME) / \text{Initial Wealth} \qquad (5.6)$$

Computation of the CME, and hence the AEW, requires knowledge of the consumer's utility function, and so it varies from person to person. AEWs will usually be greater than one because the present value of the cash flows from an annuity ignores the value of the insurance provided to the annuitant against the risk of running out of money if they live for a very long time, and the risk of leaving unconsumed assets (assuming no bequest motive). Some studies have found AEWs of about 1.3, which means that annuitants would be willing to give up 30 % of their initial wealth for the right to buy an annuity. So, even if the MWR is well below one, buying an annuity may still represent an increase in utility for such annuitants. There is no substantive information on the stability of AEWs over time, although they will have risen with the increasing level of uncertainty over longevity expectations.

5.12 Some Other Types of Annuity

There is a wide variety of types of annuity, and these will now be briefly described.

1. Joint life annuity – e.g. husband and wife. There are two main types of joint life annuity. (a) Contingent survivor pays 100 % while the primary nominee is alive, and x% of the initial annuity payments when only the secondary nominee is alive. (b) Last survivor pays 100 % while both nominees are still alive, and y% of the initial annuity payments to the last survivor. Pricing annuities on joint lives involves some additional factors: (a) the specified fraction of the initial annuity received by the survivor (x% or y%), (b) whether it is a last survivor or a contingent survivor annuity (even if $x = y$ they are still different), and (c) the correlation between the life expectancy distributions of the two lives. This correlation may be affected by the 'broken heart syndrome', which is a temporary heart condition often brought on by stressful situations, such as the death of a loved one. The positive correlation in life expectancy for joint lives has been estimated to reduce joint life annuity prices by 5 % (Frees et al. 1996).

2. Guaranteed annuity – the annuity pays out for a guaranteed period (e.g. five or 10 years), even if the annuitant dies during this period. The pricing formula for an annuity with a guarantee of T years is:

$$V_{xA}^{T} = \sum_{i=1}^{T} \frac{1}{(1+r)^i} + \sum_{i=T+1}^{n-T} \frac{A.P_{xi}}{(1+r)^i} \qquad (5.7)$$

where V_{xA}^{T} is the price of an annuity where the payments are guaranteed for T years. This is equivalent to investing in riskless debt for T years at $r\%$, and buying a deferred annuity which starts in T years (Brown 2008).

3. Value-protected annuity – if the cumulative sum paid out before the annuitant dies is less than X, the difference is paid to his or her estate. So a minimum payout is guaranteed, even if the annuitant dies soon after the annuity comes into payment.

4. Enhanced annuity – for those with a life shortening medical condition, where the evidence can be obtained directly from the annuitant, for example a history of heart attacks, angina or heart surgery, chronic asthma, digestive or bowel complaints, bladder or liver complaints. Because life expectancy is shorter, the annuity payments are higher.

5. Impaired life annuity – for those with a more serious life-shortening medical condition where medical evidence is required, for example cancer, multiple sclerosis, stroke (Burrows 2013).

6. Way of life annuity – for those with a life-shortening lifestyle, for example smoking, obesity, heavy drinking, high cholesterol, high blood pressure, etc., and for joint life annuities where the partner has any such condition. In a survey of UK adults Parker (2013) found that some people think such annuities rewarded an unhealthy lifestyle.

Table 5.7 presents some estimates of the likely increase in annuity income for those with particular medical conditions and lifestyles.

Table 5.7 Medical condition and additional annuity income, Burrows (2013)

Condition	Average additional income (%)
High blood pressure	6.5
Lymph node cancer	11.9
Angina	13.8
Type 2 diabetes	18.2
Smoker (20 per day)	18.8
Angina and smoking	25.5
Chronic pulmonary disease	41.4

7. With-profits annuity – these annuities pay a fixed amount per year, plus an amount varying with the stock market. In theory annuitants can benefit from both the mortality credit and the equity risk premium.
8. Inflation-linked annuity – the annuity payments rise with inflation.
9. Variable annuity – the annuitant receives income from their chosen investments in equities and bonds. If this income drops below some specified level, the deficiency is made good by the annuity provider.
10. Fixed period annuity – the annuity payments end after X years, even if the annuitant is still alive.
11. Deferred annuity – the annuity starts making payments at a later date (e.g. five, 10 or 20 years later. Deferred pensioners in DB schemes have a form of deferred annuity (see Sect. 5.19).
12. Bulk annuities – a buyout by a DB scheme occurs when it buys annuities for some or all of its members, i.e. a bulk annuity (see Sect. 2.5b).

In a standard annuity the worst time to die is immediately after purchasing the annuity. But for guaranteed or value protected annuities, the relationship between the NPV of the cash flows and the annuitant's age exhibits a 'worst time to die' some years into the annuity (see Fig. 5.10). This also increases the break-even age. The NPV pattern during the guarantee period depends on the precise nature of the guarantee. A guaranteed or value-protected annuity can be replicated by investing in debt for the guarantee period, and buying a deferred annuity now that starts paying out when the guarantee period ends (Brown 2008).

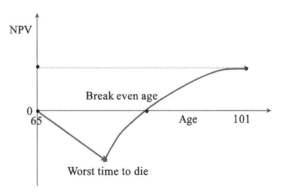

Fig. 5.10 Worst time to die

5.13 Annuity Timing Decision

Until April 2015 DC pensioners in the UK had to annuitise at least 75 % of their pension pot at a time of their choosing between retirement and the age of 75. This gave them an American-style option to delay annuitisation, and this option can be valued using an option pricing model. Even though compulsory annuitisation has been abolished in the UK, pensioners still have the choice of buying an annuity at retirement, or buying an annuity later. This decision has been analysed by Markwat et al. (2015). They conclude that, if the retiree can invest only in bonds, annuities are fairly priced and the retiree has no bequest motive, it is never optimal to delay annuitisation. This is because in these circumstances buying an annuity has an expected NPV of zero, while the retiree loses the mortality discount (or credit) during the delay period. However a delay may be beneficial when the retiree can invest in equities, although this exposes them to risk (see Sect. 5.6). Delay may also be beneficial when the retiree believes interest rates will increase during the delay period. Other reasons for delay include delaying to learn about their post-retirement expenditure and health status. However, as Chigodaev et al. (2014) point out, if expected longevity increases during the delay period, annuity prices will worsen. In the UK, before the abolition of compulsion, 62 % of annuitants bought their annuity on retirement, and only 5 % annuitised in their 70s. Of the 38 % who delayed purchasing an annuity, 39 % gave their lack of need for a pension as their reason for delay, with only 13 % waiting to see if annuity rates improve. This suggests that annuitants were not making rational decisions on when to annuitise, as the main factor driving their decision to delay should be annuity rate expectations.

5.14 The Annuity Decision and the OMO

Annuitants have to choose their annuity provider, as well as when to buy their annuity, and which type of annuity to buy. Since 1978 DC members in the UK have had the right (called the open market option – OMO) to buy their annuity from a supplier other than their pension provider, and about 90 % of annuity buyers are aware of this right (Wells 2014). However, only about half of UK annuitants shop around for a better annuity deal, with just 28 % actually changing their annuity provider (i.e. switching) (see Table 5.8).

Table 5.8 Averages for UK annuity purchase decisions from seven surveys (Wells 2014)

Bought from an external provider	28 %
Bought from the original provider	29 %
Total who shopped around	57 %
Bought from the original provider and did not shop around	43 %
Total	100 %

A UK survey found that the main reasons for annuitants not shopping around when buying an annuity are because of satisfaction with their existing pension provider (37 %), and because the annuity forms only a small part of retirement income (25 %) (Wells 2014). Those who buy their annuity externally have a large proportion of their total wealth in their DC pension pot, and use the internet or have access to email (Crawford and Tetlow 2012). Harrison (2013) also found that those who shop around tend to have larger pension pots. Consistent with this finding, Gunawardena et al. (2008) found that the average size of annuities purchased internally is only half the size of those purchased externally. They conclude that annuitants do not shop around when they will lose a guaranteed annuity rate from an internal purchase, have a small pot and expect little price improvement.

In 2014 the Financial Conduct Authority found that switching annuity provider would lead to a bigger annuity for 80 % of purchasers. In 2009 a comparison of the prices for standard annuities in the UK discovered that a top quartile annuity was 20 % cheaper than a bottom quartile annuity, while Crawford and Tetlow (2012) found a 17 % price improvement for those who purchased externally. Harrison (2013) reports that internal rates in the roll-over market, where a pensioner's DC scheme offers to provide them with an annuity, are up to 30 % worse than the OMO rate. Before the end of compulsory annuitisation the total loss of income to annuitants from not shopping around before buying an annuity was estimated at about £13 million per year (Wells 2014).

The introduction of enhanced or impaired life annuities, i.e. price discrimination on the grounds of health and way of life, means that those with a short life expectancy face lower annuity prices, making the purchase of annuities more attractive. However, while many annuitants have a risky way of life, or some medical condition which means they could qualify for an enhanced or impaired life annuity, they do not buy one. Before the end of compulsory annuitisation, only 2 % of non-advised retirees bought an enhanced or impaired life annuity, although 70 % could have qualified. Since the price of a standard annuity is over 20 % higher than for an enhanced or impaired life annuity, these retirees have chosen a poor deal.

The concept of offering better annuity rates for those with a shorter life expectancy due to their poor health has spread to the bulk annuity market, and in December 2012 the first enhanced bulk buyin occurred in the UK. When a pension scheme transfers the risk of some group of its members and pensioners to an insurance company via a buyin some of them will probably have health conditions leading to a shortened life expectancy. If allowance is made for these health conditions, the cost of a bulk buyin can be roughly 10 % lower (Harrison and Blake 2013). However, while individuals can benefit from buying an enhanced or impaired life annuity, this may not apply when the sponsor initiates a medically underwritten buyout, buyin or longevity swap. This is because insurance companies normally make an allowance for the poor health of some members when pricing such deals. So if a scheme's members turn out to be healthier than expected, seeking a medically underwritten buyout, buyin or longevity swap increases, rather than lowers, the price.

A survey in July 2013 of 2000 people in the UK aged between 45 and 65 revealed substantial misunderstanding of annuity pricing (Partnership 2013). Smoking or being overweight was wrongly believed to result in a worse annuity deal by 27 % of respondents, with only 17 % correctly expecting it to lead to a better deal, and 56 % incorrectly thinking it would have no effect. Similarly, 23 % of respondents wrongly thought that being in ill health would reduce their annuity income, and only 36 % correctly believed it would lead to an increase, while 41 % incorrectly thought it would have no effect. Only 13 % of respondents correctly thought that buying an annuity from their pension provider would lead to a reduction in annuity payments, while 11 % wrongly thought it would result in higher payments, and 76 % wrongly thought it would have no effect. Living in an expensive area was mistakenly expected to increase annuity income by 7 % of respondents, with only 8 % correctly thinking it would lead to a lower annuity income (as wealth is positively correlated with longevity). The remaining 84 % wrongly thought it would have no effect. These results help to explain why few annuitants shop around for a better deal, or seek enhanced and way of life annuities, and are summarised in Table 5.9, where the correct answers appear in italics.

Table 5.9 Survey of the effects of various conditions on annuity pricing (Partnership 2013)

Condition	Higher income (%)	Same income (%)	Less income (%)
Smoker or overweight	*17*	56	27
Ill health/medical condition	*36*	41	23
Buying an annuity from the pension provider	11	76	*13*
Living in an expensive area	7	84	*8*

5.15 Historical Perspective on Mortality Tables

Kopf (1927) claims that the Egyptian prince Hapd'efal purchased an annuity sometime between 1100 BC and 1700 BC. The earliest recorded life annuities were sold by the Greek city state of Miletus in 205 BC, where the initial price was set at 10 times the annual payment, without any use of a mortality table. The word annuity comes from the Latin *annus* meaning year, and the first age-related method for valuing annuities was used by the Romans. From 40 BC Romans were required to leave at least a quarter of their estate to their legal heir. If they had left life annuities (or the use of an asset for life) to others, these were valued using a method which relied on the age of the beneficiary in a very crude way. In about 220 AD Domitius Ulpianus proposed a superior method for valuing such annuities which relied on age in a more sophisticated manner (Kopf 1927). In 1653 Lorenzo de Tonti was the first person to publish a mortality table, but this is not thought to have been based on real world data, and in 1662 John Graunt published the first mortality table based on actual data (for London).

In 1825 Benjamin Gompertz, the chief actuary of the Alliance Assurance Company, discovered that mortality rates at different ages follow a predictable mathematical pattern – each year the probability of death increases by approximately 9 % (Milevsky 2012). Almost two hundred years later, as illustrated in Appendix 4, this rule still applies to UK mortality rates. Gompertz's rule is independent of the level of mortality – it simply specifies the rate of change of mortality. It governs the shape of the longevity distribution, but it does not give the central tendency and dispersion of this distribution, which change over time as life expectancy improves. Figure 5.11 illustrates the positive linear relationship between age and the natural logarithm of the probability of death between just over 20 years to almost 100 years of age. This empirical result means that the probability of death increases by a constant proportion each year (the slope of the line in Fig. 5.11), which in practice is about 9 % per year. In 1890 William Makeham extended the Gompertz model, by adding a constant rate of accidental death that is independent of age, to create the Gompertz-Makeham rule.

As the Roman example proves, even in the absence of data-based mortality tables, age can be allowed for when pricing annuities. For example, annuity prices varied with age in Hanover in 1350, Augsburg in 1373 and Breslau in 1342–1379. However the English government sold life annuities in 1746 without any allowance for age or gender, and UK annuities were sold until 1808 without regard to the age or gender of the person on whose life the

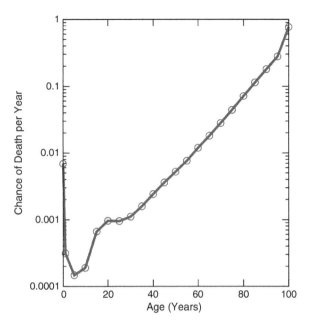

Fig. 5.11 ln[Probability of Death p.a.] and age

annuity was based (the nominee). Since the purchaser of an annuity (the subscriber) in the eighteenth century did not have to be the nominee, nominees tended to be those with the longest life expectancy: for example females aged around five, who had survived or been inoculated against smallpox (Velde and Weir 1992). Until at least 1929 nominees were allowed for UK annuities, and it was also possible for subscribers to sell annuities (Government Annuities Act 1929). However, in more recent times the trading of annuities is not permitted, although in 2015 the UK Treasury consulted on creating a secondary annuity market (HM Treasury 2015a), and in December 2015 it was announced that this market will begin in April 2017 (HM Treasury 2015b).

The failure of annuity suppliers to adjust their price to allow for the age of nominees appears to be irrational when purchasers were aware of the effect of age and gender on the value of annuities. However, it is likely that suppliers of annuities were aware of this behaviour by purchasers, and reacted by adjusting the prices of all annuities to allow for the likelihood that many of the nominees would be female children, rather than adjusting the price of each annuity for the age of the particular nominee. For example, in 1771 the French government sold annuities with a single price, regardless of nominee age. The average age of the nominees was 16.7 years, while the French government anticipated an average nominee age of 17 years. An annuity with a price that is independent of the nominee's age does not require any proof of the age of the nominee, only proof of their continued existence. Until 1558 there was no system of parish registers in the UK by which age could be proved; so basing the price of an annuity on age faced difficulties. However, before dates of birth were formally recorded, ways must have existed for proving age because it was used as a criterion for military service, jury service, inheritance and standing for election.

5.16 Long-Term Care and Adverse Selection

Some people both live a long time and incur lower long-term care costs, while others die early and generate higher long-term care costs, i.e. there is a negative correlation between longevity and long-term care costs. This indicates that an annuity bundled with long-term care insurance will tend to reduce adverse selection and so cost less to supply than the two items sold separately. Very few such bundles are currently traded, although their attractiveness has been advocated during the past two decades: Brown and Warshawsky (2013), Davidoff (2009), Levantesi and Menzietti (2012), Murtaugh et al. (2001), Pla-Porcel et al. (2014), Rickayzen (2007), Spillman et al. (2003), Warshawsky et al. (2002) and Webb (2009).

Such bundles of long-term care and annuities were supplied in medieval times. Corrodies were a type of pension which bundled a pension with long-term care, and were available for purchase in medieval England. Between c.1250–1500 well-off individuals or married couples could purchase corrodies from monasteries and other large religious institutions, such as hospitals. These gave the purchaser the right to live in a religious institution with the monks or nuns and to receive agreed amounts of food, clothing, fuel, accommodation and healthcare until they died. Corrodies were effectively annuities, where the payments were made in pre-specified goods and services, not cash. This pension product was effectively inflation-indexed, although it should be noted that medieval inflation was almost zero. Bell and Sutcliffe (2010a, b) found that corrodies were over-priced, and were used to help finance monasteries. Medieval corrodies provided the bundle of an annuity coupled with long-term care insurance (as well as accommodation) and so offered the monasteries some degree of risk reduction. It shows that medieval financial products were ahead of modern practice in some respects. Learning from this example, modern nursing homes could offer a bundle of long-term care, food and clothing, and accommodation until death for a one-off initial payment – effectively a modern corrody. With many more residents, these nursing homes would be better diversified against specific longevity and long-term care risk than were medieval monasteries.

5.17 Did Joint Life Annuities Indirectly Cause the Credit Crisis?

In 1987 Xiang Lin Li went from China to Canada to be a student at Laval University, and then at Waterloo University (Jones 2009). In 1997 he was awarded a doctorate in actuarial science, and in 1998 began working for the RiskMetrics Group in New York using the name David Li. He published an academic paper in 2000 which used his actuarial knowledge to solve a problem in finance. This was the problem of estimating the probability of a company to whom a bank has lent money going bust, conditional on some other company to whom the bank has also lent money having gone bust previously. He applied his Gaussian copula function analysis of the 'broken heart syndrome' in his PhD to bond defaults (see Sect. 5.12.1). (The word 'copula' comes from Latin and means a 'link' or 'tie'.) On 10 August 2004 Moody's, the credit rating agency, incorporated Li's Gaussian copula default function into its methodology for rating the default risk of collateralised debt obligations (CDOs). A week later Standard & Poor's, the other large credit rating agency, also changed their methodology for rating CDOs to use Gaussian copulas. The result was an explosion of volume in the CDO market – 10 to 20 times larger. By 2006 and 2007 defaults began to snowball, way ahead of the predictions of the Gaussian copula model of David Li. In 2007 David Li moved back to China. His actions join many other reasons that have been proposed for the credit crisis. In reality this credit crisis was caused by a combination of many factors, and David Li's analysis based on an actuarial model of joint lives played a part.

5.18 Guaranteed Annuity Rates (GAR)

Insurance companies offer life insurance policies which pay a lump sum on retirement, which is then used to buy an annuity (i.e. endowment policies). Some insurance companies (e.g. Equitable Life) offered to guarantee that the annuity rate offered when the life insurance policy matured would not be less than X%. This is an option, and valuing it can be complex. These guaranteed rate annuities (GARs) led to very severe financial problems for Equitable Life when the GAR options went deep in the money due to unexpectedly low interest rates (Sullivan 2004; Brummer 2010).

5.19 Deferred Annuities

The purchase of deferred annuities (see below) has been suggested for a variety of reasons:

(a) Benefiting from the mortality discount (or credit). This is bigger than for an immediate annuity because of the time lag before the annuity comes into payment during which the annuitant may die.
(b) Providing longevity insurance to pensioners, for example an advanced life deferred annuity (ALDA) which comes into payment at (say) 85 years of age (Milevsky 2005b; Gong and Webb 2010).
(c) Reducing the cost of adverse selection because the annuitant buys the annuity at a younger, less-informed, age.
(d) If the deferred annuities are purchased in a phased manner this reduces the variance of the cost of an annuity by pound cost averaging.

5.20 A Long-Term Solution? Single Premium Deferred Annuities (SPDA)

Currently sponsors wish to escape the high risks of DB schemes by switching to DC schemes. But DC schemes are unsatisfactory for members, and a superior solution exists which uses annuities. This produces a pension scheme with the advantages of a DC scheme for the sponsor (chiefly no risk) and with the advantages of a DB scheme for the members (again no risk). The risk is borne by insurance companies via the annuity market. The proposal by Sutcliffe (2010a) is to use single premium deferred annuities (SPDAs) to create a scheme that looks like a DC scheme to the sponsor, but a DB scheme to the members. Each year the sponsor and members pay a pension contribution which is some proportion of the members' salaries, as for DB and DC schemes. This sum is used to buy a SPDA from an insurer on behalf of each member. This annuity should offer at least limited price indexation, and preferably provide full indexation. When the member reaches retirement age the payments under these deferred annuities provide their pension. Once a deferred annuity is purchased, the corresponding portion of the ultimate pension is locked in, and the risk transferred to the insurance company.

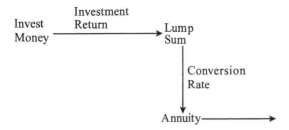

Fig. 5.12 Single premium deferred annuity

These SPDAs involve a specified investment return (which removes investment risk until retirement), followed by a specified rate for converting the lump sum (or final value of the pension pot) into an annuity (i.e. a GAR, which removes longevity risk, inflation risk and interest rate risk) for the annuitant. This is illustrated in Fig. 5.12, which shows that an SPDA locks in a given investment return and annuity rate, with these risks being carried by the insurance company. Although an SPDA-based scheme looks like a DC scheme to the sponsor, to the members it can be made to look like a final salary DB scheme, a CARE DB scheme, or a DC scheme, depending on the revaluation rate for investments (pension contributions) built into the SPDAs.

SPDA-based schemes are highly portable as the SPDA contract is between the member and the insurance company, the default risk is that of the insurance company not their sponsor, and the PCL for early leavers is removed. However sponsors with DB schemes lose the human resource benefits associate with the PCL, as well as the sorting and controlling retirement date benefits. The sponsors of DB schemes also lose the ability to borrow from the pension scheme by under-funding. Insurance companies face a challenge in hedging the risk of SPDAs, and must also meet European Union solvency requirements, which do not currently affect pension schemes.

References

Ameriks, J., Briggs, J., Caplin, A., Shapiro, M. D., & Tonetti, C. (2014, April). *Resolving the annuity puzzle: Estimating life-cycle models without (and with) behavioural data* (Working paper). New York University, 60 pages.

Aquilina, M., Baker, R., & Majer, T. (2014, December). *The value for money of annuities and other retirement income strategies in the UK, Financial Conduct Authority* (Occasional paper no. 5), 95 pages.

Aro, H. (2014). Systematic and nonsystematic mortality risk in pension portfolios. *North American Actuarial Journal, 18*(1), 59–67.

Auerbach, A. J., Gokhale, J., Kotlikoff, L. J., Sabelhaus, J., & Weil, D. N. (2001). The annuitization of Americans' resources: A Cohort analysis. In L. J. Kotlikoff (Ed.), *Essays on saving, bequests, altruism and life-cycle planning* (pp. 93–131). Cambridge, MA: The MIT Press.

Aviva. (2014). Making good retirement choices – An investment special report. Aviva, 15 pages.

Bateman, H., & Piggott, J. (2011). Too much risk to insure? The Australian (non) market for annuities. In O. S. Mitchell, J. Piggott, & N. Takayama (Eds.), *Securing lifelong retirement income: Global annuity markets and policy* (pp. 81–105). Oxford: Oxford University Press.

Bell, A., & Sutcliffe, C. M. S. (2010a). Valuing medieval annuities: Were corrodies underpriced? *Explorations in Economic History, 47*(2), 142–157.

Bell, A., & Sutcliffe, C. M. S. (2010b). Annuities: Lessons from the past and concerns for the future. *The Professional Investor, 19*(4), 26–30. Winter 2009–2010.

Bernheim, B. D. (1991). How strong are bequest motives? Evidence based on estimates of the demand for life insurance and annuities. *Journal of Political Economy, 99*(5), 899–927.

Beshears, J., Choi, J. J., Laibson, D., Madrian, B. C., & Zeldes, S. P. (2014). What makes annuitization more appealing? *Journal of Public Economics, 116*, 2–16.

Bhuyan, V. (2011). *Reverse mortgages and linked securities: The complete guide to risk, pricing and regulation.* Hoboken: Wiley.

Brown, J. R. (2001). Are the elderly really over-annuitized? New evidence on life insurance and bequests. In D. A. Wise (Ed.), *Themes in the economics of aging* (pp. 91–126). Chicago: University of Chicago Press.

Brown, J. R. (2008). Understanding the role of annuities in retirement planning. In A. Lusardi (Ed.), *Overcoming the saving slump: How to increase the effectiveness of financial education and saving programs* (pp. 178–206). Chicago: University of Chicago Press.

Brown, R. L., & McDaid, J. (2003). Factors affecting retirement mortality. *North American Actuarial Journal, 7*(2), 24–43.

Brown, J. R., & Poterba, J. M. (2000). Joint life annuities and annuity demand by married couples. *Journal of Risk and Insurance, 67*(4), 527–554.

Brown, R. L., & Scahill, P. (2010, May). *Issues in the issuance of enhanced annuities* (SEDAP Research Paper no. 265). McMaster University.

Brown, J. R., & Warshawsky, M. J. (2004). Longevity insured retirement distributions from pension plans: Market and regulatory issues. In W. G. Gale, J. B. Shoven, & M. J. Warshawsky (Eds.), *Private pensions and public policies* (pp. 332–382). Washington, DC: Brookings.

Brown, J., & Warshawsky, M. (2013). The life care annuity: A new empirical examination of an insurance innovation that addresses problems in the markets for life annuities and long-term care insurance. *Journal of Risk and Insurance, 80*(3), 677–703.

Brown, J. R., Casey, M. D., & Mitchell, O. S. (2007, December). *Who values the social security annuity? New evidence on the annuity puzzle* (Working paper NBER).

Brown, J. R., Kling, J. R., Mullainathan, S., & Wrobel, M. V. (2008). Why don't people insure late-life consumption? A framing explanation of the under-annuitization puzzle. *American Economic Review, 98*(2), 304–309.

Brown, J. R., Kling, J. R., Mullainathan, S., & Wrobel, M. V. (2009). Framing lifetime income. *Journal of Retirement, 1*(1), 27–37.

Brown, J. R., Kapteyn, A., Luttmer, E. F. P., & Mitchell, O. S. (2013). *Complexity as a barrier to annuitization: Do consumers know how to value annuities?* (Working paper). Pension Research Council, WP2013-01.

Browning, C., Finke, M. S., & Huston, S. J. (2012). Rational choice with complex products: Consumer valuation of annuities. *Journal of Financial Counselling and Planning, 23*(2), 32–45.

Brummer, A. (2010). *The great pensions robbery: How the politicians betrayed retirement.* London: Random House.

Burrows, B. (2013). Healthy choice?, *The Actuary*, 4th April, 2 pages.

Cannon, E., & Tonks, I. (2005). *Survey of annuity pricing* (Department for Work and Pensions, Research Report no. 318).

Cannon, E., & Tonks, I. (2008). *Annuity markets.* Oxford: Oxford University Press.

Cannon, E., & Tonks, I. (2014). *The annuity puzzle: Cohort mortality risk or adverse selection in the annuity market?* (Working paper), 54 pages.

Cazalet Consulting. (2014). *When I'm sixty-four.* London: Cazalet Consulting.

Charupat, N., Kamstra, M. J., & Milevsky, M. A. (forthcoming). The sluggish and asymmetric reaction of life annuity prices to changes in interest rates. *Journal of Risk and Insurance.*

Chigodaev, A., Milevsky, M. A., & Salisbury, T. S. (2014, January). *How long does the market think you will live? Implying longevity from annuity prices* (Discussion Paper). York University.

Clark, G. L., & Knox-Hayes, J. (2007). Mapping UK pension benefits and the intended purchase of annuities in the aftermath of the 1990s stock market bubble. *Transactions of the Institute of British Geographers, 32*(4), 539–555.

Cooper, J., Minney, A., & Sainsbury, P. (2012). *How much super do Australians really have?* Challenger Retirement Income Research, 16 pages.

Cox, S. H., & Lin, Y. (2007). Natural hedging of life and annuity mortality risks. *North American Actuarial Journal, 11*(3), 1–15.

Crawford, R., & Tetlow, G. (2012). *Expectations and experience of retirement in defined contribution pensions: A study of older people in England.* London: Institute for Fiscal Studies.

Cumbo, J. (2014). Australians dismiss fear of pensions profligacy, *The Financial Times*, 21st March.

Davidoff, T. (2009). Housing, health and annuities. *Journal of Risk and Insurance, 76*(1), 31–52.

Davidoff, T., Brown, J. R., & Diamond, P. A. (2005). Annuities and individual welfare. *American Economic Review, 95*(5), 1573–1590.

Department for Work and Pensions. (2015a). *Creating a secondary annuity market.* Department for Work and Pensions, Cm 9046, March, 29 pages.

DiCenzo, J., Shu, S., Hadar, L., & Rieth, C. (2011). *Can annuity purchase intentions be influenced?* Society of Actuaries, 23 pages.

Donnelly, C. (2014). Quantifying mortality risk in small defined benefit pension schemes. *Scandinavian Actuarial Journal, 2014*(1), 41–57.

Dushi, I., & Webb, A. (2006). Rethinking the sources of adverse selection in the annuity markets. In P.A. Chiappori, & C. Gollier (Ed.), *Competitive failures in insurance markets: Theory and policy implications* (pp. 185–212). Cambridge, MA: The MIT Press.

Eley, J. (2014). New Totem for Thatcher's ageing citizens. *The Financial Times*, 20th March.

Emmerson, C., Keynes, S., & Tetlow, G. (2014). *Characteristics of those directly affected by the 2014 budget pension reforms* (IFS Briefing Note BN147). Institute for Fiscal Studies.

Fehr, H., & Habermann, C. (2008). Welfare effects of life annuities: Some clarifications. *Economics Letters, 99*(1), 177–180.

Feigenbaum, J., Gahramanov, E., & Tang, X. (2013). Is it really good to annuitise? *Journal of Economic Behaviour and Organization, 93*, 116–140.

Financial Conduct Authority. (2014). Thematic review of annuities, financial conduct authority, TR14/2.

Finke, M., Howe, J. S., & Huston, S. (2014, August). *Old age and the decline in financial literacy* (Working paper). Texas Tech University, 40 pages.

Finkelstein, A., & Poterba, J. (2002). Selection effects in the United Kingdom individual annuities market. *Economic Journal, 112*(476), 28–50.

Finkelstein, A., & Poterba, J. (2004). Adverse selection in insurance markets: Policyholder evidence from the UK annuity market. *Journal of Political Economy, 112*(1), 183–208.

Finkelstein, A., & Poterba, J. (2014). Testing for asymmetric information using "unused observables" in insurance markets: Evidence from the U.K. annuity market. *Journal of Risk and Insurance, 81*(4), 709–734.

Fong, J. H. Y. (2015). Beyond age and sex: Enhancing annuity pricing. *Geneva Risk and Insurance Review, 40*(2), 133–170.

Fong, J. H. Y., Lemaire, J., & Tse, Y. K. (2014). Improving money's worth ratio calculations: The case of Singapore's pension annuities. *Asia-Pacific Journal of Risk and Insurance, 8*(1), 1–26.

Frees, E. W., Carriere, J., & Valdez, E. (1996). Annuity valuation with dependent mortality. *Journal of Risk and Insurance, 63*(2), 229–261.

Gardner, J., & Wadsworth, M. (2004). Who would buy and annuity? An empirical investigation. Watson Wyatt technical paper series.

Gazzale, R. S., & Walker, L. (2009, March). *Behavioural biases in annuity choice: An experiment* (Working paper). Williams College.

Gazzale, R., Mackenzie, S., & Walker, L. (2012). Do default and longevity annuities improve annuity take-up rates? Results from an experiment, Research Report, AARP Public Policy Institute, 22 pages.

Goedde-Menke, M., Lehmensiek-Starke, M., & Nolte, S. (2014). An empirical test of competing hypothesis for the annuity puzzle. *Journal of Economic Psychology, 43*, 75–91.

Gong, G., & Webb, A. (2010). Evaluating the advanced life deferred annuity – An annuity people might actually buy. *Insurance: Mathematics and Economics, 46*(1), 210–221.

Gottlieb, D. (2013). *Prospect theory, life insurance and annuities* (Working paper). University of Pennsylvania, 52 pages.

Government Annuities Act 1929. (1929). HMSO.

Guillemette, M. A., Martin, T. K., Cummings, B. F., & James, R. N. (2016, January). Determinants of the stated probability of purchase for longevity insurance. *Geneva Papers on Risk and Insurance, 41*(1), 4–23.

Gunawardena, D., Hicks, C., & O'Neill, D. (2008). *Pension annuities: Pension annuities and the open market option* (ABI Research Paper no. 8). Association of British Insurers, 36 pages.

Haensly, P. J., & Pai, K. P. (2014). *A new strategy to guarantee retirement income using TIPS and longevity insurance: A second look* (Working paper). University of Texas of the Permian Basin, 38 pages.

Hanewald, K., Post, T., & Sherris, M. (2016, June). Portfolio choice in retirement – What is the optimal home equity release product?, *Journal of Risk and Insurance, 83*(2), 421–446.

Harrison, D. (2012). Is failure imminent for the United Kingdom's annuity market? *Pensions: An International Journal, 17*(2), 71–79.

Harrison, D. (2013). Annuities and the annuitization process: The consumer perspective. A review of the literature and an overview of the market. Financial Services Consumer Panel, 26 pages.

Harrison, D., & Blake, D. (2013). *A healthier way to de-risk: The introduction of medical underwriting to the defined benefit de-risking market.* London: The Pensions Institute.

Horneff, V., Kaschützke, B., Maurer, R., & Rogalla, R. (2014). Welfare implications of product choice regulation during the payout phase of funded pensions. *Journal of Pension Economics and Finance, 13*(3), 272–296.

Hu, W. Y., & Scott, J. S. (2007). Behavioural obstacles in the annuity market. *Financial Analysts Journal, 63*(6), 71–82.

International Longevity Centre-UK. (2015). Making the system fit for purpose: How consumer appetite for secure retirement income could be supported by the pension reforms. ILC-UK, 24 pages.

Jones, S. (2009). The formula that felled Wall Street. *The Financial Times*, 24 April 2009.

Keohane, N., Evans, K., & Richards, B. (2015). Golden years? What freedom and choice will mean for UK pensioners. Social Market Foundation, 95 pages.

Kopf, E. W. (1927). The early history of the annuity. *Proceedings of the Casualty Actuarial Society, 13*(28), 225–266.

Kotlikoff, L. J., & Spivak, A. (1981). The family as an incomplete annuities market. *Journal of Political Economy, 89*(2), 372–391.

Kutlu-Koc, V., & Kalwij, A. (2013). *Individuals' survival expectations and actual mortality* (Netspar Discussion Paper, DP 05/2013-013), 41 pages.

Laitner, J., Silverman, D., & Stolyarov, D. (2014, September). *Annuitized wealth and post-retirement saving* (Working paper). University of Michigan, 35 pages,

Levantesi, S., & Menzietti, M. (2012). Managing longevity and disability risks in life annuities with long term care. *Insurance: Mathematics and Economics, 50*(3), 391–401.

Lloyd, J. (2014). New annuity era – Understanding retirement choices and the annuity puzzle. Strategic Society Centre, 54 pages.

Lowe, J. (2014). Whither UK annuities? Why lifetime annuities should still be part of good financial advice in the post-pension-liberalization world. International Longevity Centre-UK.

Lown, J. M., & Robb, D. K. (2011). Attitudes toward immediate annuities: Overcoming the annuity puzzle. *Journal of Consumer Education, 28*, 44–60.

MacDonald, B. J., Jones, B., Morrison, R. J., Brown, R. L., & Hardy, M. (2013). Research and reality: A literature review on drawing down retirement financial savings. *North American Actuarial Journal, 17*(3), 181–215.

Markwat, T., Molenaar, R., & Rodriguez, J. C. (2015, February). *Purchasing an annuity: Now or later? The role of interest rates* (Netspar design paper no. 36), 53 pages.

Mayhew, L., Smith, D., & Wright, D. (2015). *Pension pots and how to survive them.* International Longevity Centre, November.

McCarthy, D., & Mitchell, O. S. (2010). International adverse selection in life insurance and annuities. In S. Tuljapurkar, N. Ogawa, & A. H. Gauthier (Eds.), *Ageing in advanced industrial states* (pp. 119–135). New York: Springer.

McKeever, K. (2010). A short history of Tontines. *Fordham Journal of Corporate and Financial Law, 15*(2), 491–521.

MGM Advantage. (2014). *Long life, not according to the wife.* MGM Advantage: Worthing, England

Milevsky, M. A. (2005a). The implied longevity yield: A note on developing an index for life annuities. *Journal of Risk and Insurance, 72*(2), 301–320.

Milevsky, M. A. (2005b). Real longevity insurance with a deductible: Introduction to Advanced Life Delayed Annuities (ALDA). *North American Actuarial Journal, 9*(4), 109–122.

Milevsky, M. A. (2012). *The 7 most important equations for your retirement.* Mississauga: Wiley.

Milevsky, M. A. (2013). *Life annuities: An optimal product for retirement income.* Charlottesville: Research Foundation of the CFA Institute.

Milevsky, M. A. (2015). *King William's Tontine: Why the retirement annuity of the future should resemble its past.* Cambridge: Cambridge University Press.

Mitchell, O. S., & Piggott, J. (2011). Turning wealth into lifetime income: Global annuity markets and policy. In O. S. Mitchell, J. Piggott, & N. Takayama (Eds.), *Securing lifelong retirement income: Global annuity markets and policy* (pp. 1–12). Oxford: Oxford University Press.

Mitchell, O. S., Poterba, J. M., Warshawsky, M. J., & Brown, J. R. (1999). New evidence on the money's worth of individual annuities. *American Economic Review, 89*(5), 1299–1318.

Modigliani, F. (1986). Life cycle, individual thrift and the wealth of nations. *American Economic Review, 76*(3), 297–313.

Moore, J. F., & Mitchell, O. S. (1997). *Projected retirement wealth and savings adequacy in the health and retirement study* (Working paper 6240). National Bureau of Economic Research, 41 pages.

Murtaugh, C. M., Spillman, B. C., & Warshawsky, M. J. (2001). In sickness and in health: An annuity approach to financing long-term care and retirement income. *Journal of Risk and Insurance, 68*(2), 225–254.

NAPF. (2015). *82% positive about pension freedoms but many worried about risks.* National Association of Pension Funds, April.

Neuberger, A., & McCarthy, D. (2003). *Pensions policy: Evidence on aspects of savings behaviour and capital markets.* London: Centre for Economic Policy Research.

Newfield, P. (2014). The Tontine: An improvement on the conventional annuity? *Journal of Retirement, 1*(3), 37–48.

Nosi, C., D'Agostino, A., & Pagliuca, M. M. (2014). Saving for old age: Longevity annuity buying intention of Italian young adults. *Journal of Behavioural and Experimental Economics, 51*, 85–98.

Panis, C. W. A. (2004). Annuities and retirement well-being. In O. S. Mitchell & S. P. Utkus (Eds.), *Pension design and structure: New lessons from behavioural finance* (pp. 259–274). Oxford: Oxford University Press.

Parker, I. (2013). *Defining ambitions – Shaping pension reform around public attitudes.* Institute for Public Policy Research, December, 52 pages.

Partnership. (2013). Almost 80% of people don't realise they could lose out by staying with their existing pension provider says partnership. Press release, August 2013.

Payne, J. W., Sagara, N., Shu, S. B., Appelt, K. C., & Johnson, E. J. (2013). Life expectancy as a constructed belief: Evidence of a live-to or die-by framing effect. *Journal of Risk and Uncertainty, 46*, 27–50.

Peracchi, F., & Perotti, V. (2009). Subjective survival probabilities and life tables: An empirical analysis of Cohort effects. *Genus: Journal of Population Studies, 65*(1), 23–57.

Peracchi, F., & Perotti, V. (2012). *Subjective survival probabilities and life tables: Evidence from Europe* (Working Paper). Einaudi Institute for Economics and Finance, 27 pages.

Piggott, J., Valdez, E. A., & Detzel, B. (2005). The simple analytics of a pooled annuity fund. *Journal of Risk and Insurance, 72*(3), 497–520.

Pla-Porcel, J., Ventura-Marco, M., & Vidal-Melia, C. (2014). *Integrating retirement and long-term care (LTC) annuities using a notional defined contribution (NDC) framework* (Working paper). University of Valencia, 45 pages.

Previtero, A. (2014). Stock market returns and annuitization. *Journal of Financial Economics, 113*(2), 202–214.

PwC. (2014). *UK annuities market could decline by up to 75% as consumers look to alternative retirement products.* Price Waterhouse Coopers.

Richards, S. (2008) Postcode Ratings for Mortality, Momentum Convention, Berlin, 22 pages.

Rickayzen, B. (2007). *An analysis of disability-linked annuities* (Actuarial Research Paper no. 10). Cass Business School, 43 pages.

Rotemberg, J., & Gourville, J. T. (2010). *New York life and immediate annuities.* Harvard Business School, Case 9-510-040.

Schaus, S. L. (2005). Annuities make a comeback. *Journal of Pension Benefits, 12*(4), 34–38.

Schreiber, P., & Weber, M. (2013). *Time inconsistent preferences and the annuitization decision* (Working paper). University of Mannheim, 56 pages.

Shankar, S. G. (2009). A new strategy to guarantee retirement income using TIPS and longevity insurance. *Financial Services Review, 18*(1), 53–68.

Shu, S. B. (2013). *Psychological aspects of decumulation decisions: The case of Tontine insurance* (Working paper). UCLA. 16 pages.

Silcock, D. (2011). What are the restrictions of the UK government's policy to remove the effective requirement to annuitise private pension funds by the age of 75? *Pensions: An International Journal, 16*(4), 277–284.

Spillman, B. C., Murtaugh, C. M., & Warshawsky, M. J. (2003). Policy implications of an annuity approach to integrating long-term care financing and retirement income. *Journal of Aging and Health, 15*(1), 45–73.

Steffen, B. (2009). Formation and updating of subjective life expectancy: Evidence from Germany. MEA Studies 08, May, 144 pages.

Stevens, R. (2009). *Annuity decisions with systematic longevity risk* (Working paper). Tilburg University.

Sullivan, M. (2004). *Understanding pensions.* London: Routledge.

Sutcliffe, C. M. S. (2010a). Back to the future: A long term solution to the occupational pensions crisis. *Insurance Markets and Companies: Analyses and Actuarial Computations, 1*(2), 11–29.

Sutcliffe, C. M. S. (2010b). Should defined benefit pension schemes be career average or final salary? In M. Bertocchi, S. Schwartz, & W. Ziemba (Eds.), *Optimizing the ageing, retirement and pensions dilemma* (pp. 227–257). Hoboken: Wiley.

Sutcliffe, C.M.S. (2015) Trading Death: The Implications of Annuity Replication for the Annuity Puzzle, Arbitrage, Speculation and Portfolios, *International Review of Financial Analysis*, vol. 38, no. March, pp. 163–174.

Treasury (2014). Freedom and Choice in Pensions: Government Response to the Consultation, HM Treasury, July, Cm 8901.

Treasury. (2015a). *Creating a secondary annuity market.* HM Treasury, Cm 9046, March, 28 pages.

Treasury. (2015b). *Creating a secondary annuity market, response to the call for evidence.* HM Treasury, December, 36 pages.

Turner, J. (2014). Why don't people annuitize? The role of advice provided by retirement planning software. *Journal of Retirement, 1*(4), 129–134.

Vaz, T. A., Machado, S. J., & Bortoluzzo, A. B. (2012). Demand for life annuities: A Brazilian perspective. *Brazilian Administration Review, 9*(4), 441–453.

Velde, F. R., & Weir, D. R. (1992). The financial market and government debt policy in France, 1746–1793. *Journal of Economic History, 52*(1), 1–39.

Vidal-Meliá, C., & Lejárraga-García, A. (2006). Demand for life annuities from married couples with a bequest motive. *Journal of Pension Economics and Finance, 5*(2), 197–229.

Walliser, J. (2000). Adverse selection in the annuities market and the impact of privatizing social security. *Scandinavian Journal of Economics, 102*(3), 373–393.

Wang, M., Rieger, M. O., & Hens, T. (2016 February). How time preferences differ: Evidence from 53 countries. *Journal of Economic Psychology, 52*, 115–135.

Warshawsky, M. J., Spillman, B. C., & Murtaugh, C. M. (2002). Integrating life annuities and long-term care insurance: Theory, evidence, practice and policy. In O. S. Mitchell, Z. Bodie, P. B. Hammond, & S. Zeldes (Eds.), *Innovations in retirement financing* (pp. 198–221). Philadelphia: University of Pennsylvania Press.

Webb, D. C. (2009). Asymmetric information, long-term care insurance and annuities: The case for bundled contracts. *Journal of Risk and Insurance, 76*(1), 53–85.

Wells, J. (2014). Pension annuities: A review of consumer behaviour. Financial Conduct Authority.

Willets, R. (2015). The importance of longevity in financial planning, partnership, March. 33 pages.

Wu, S., Stevens, R., & Thorp, S. (2014). *Die young or live long: Modelling subjective survival probabilities* (Working paper). University of New South Wales, 43 pages.

Yaari, M. (1965). Uncertain lifetime, life insurance and the theory of the consumer. *Review of Economic Studies, 32*(2), 137–150.

Zhu, N., & Bauer, D. (2014). A cautionary note on natural hedging of longevity risk. *North American Actuarial Journal, 18*(1), 104–115.

Appendix

Appendix 1: Examples of Asset Backed Funding in the UK Over £50 million

Sponsor	Value	Date	Asset
Marks and Spencer	£1000 m.	2007, 8 &10	Property
Lloyds Bank	£1000 m.	2010	Basket of bonds
John Lewis	£95 m.	2010	Property
GKN	£331 m.	2010	Trademarks and property
Whitbread	£100 m.	2010	Property
Diageo	£430 m.	2010	Maturing whisky
ITV	£174 m.	2010 &11	Digital terrestrial TV licence
Sainsbury's	£757 m.	2010 &11	Property
Kingfisher	£200 m.	2011	Property
Alliance Boots	£146 m.	2011	Property
TUI Travel	£275 m.	2011	Brands
Deloitte	£70 m.	2011	Receipts from debts
Britvic	£105 m.	2012	Drink brands and property
Midlands Co-op	£118 m.	2012	Intra-company loans
Severn Trent	£98 m.	2012	Loan notes
Daily Mail	£150 m.	2012	Loan notes
Canal and River Trust	£125 m.	2012	Property
Centrica	£444 m.	2012 & 13	Intra-company loans
Persimmon	£58 m.	2012	Group assets
Calor Gas	£75 m.	2012	–
Cemex	£300 m.	2012	–
Alliance Boots	£127 m.	2013	–
Scapa	£58 m.	2013	–
Chivas Brothers	£61 m.	2013	–
Taylor Wimpey	£100 m.	2013	–

© The Author(s) 2016
C. Sutcliffe, *Finance and Occupational Pensions*,
DOI 10.1057/978-1-349-94863-5

Sponsor	Value	Date	Asset
Morrisons	£90 m.	2013	Property
Johnson Matthey	£50 m.	2013	Corporate bonds
Allied Irish Bank	£270 m.	2013	Loans
ITV	£50 m.	2014	London TV studios

Source: KPMG Asset-Backed Funding for Pensions, 2010 to 2014

Appendix 2: Some Large Buy-outs, Buy-ins and Longevity Swaps

Buy outs		
Sponsor	Date	Value
Rank	2008	£700 m.
Thorn	2008	£1100 m.
Delta	2008	£451 m.
Leyland DAF	2008	£230 m.
Powell Duffryn	2008	£400 m.
M-Real Corporation	2008	£180 m.
Alliance Boots	2010	£300 m.
London Stock Exchange	2011	£158 m.
Uniq	2011	£830 m.
Law Society	2011	£320 m.
Turner and Newell	2011	£1100 m.
Merchant Navy Officers	2012	£680 m.
Denso Manufacturing	2012	£201 m.
General Motors	2012	£230 m.
InterContinental Hotels	2013	£440 m.
NCR	2013	£670 m.
SR Technics	2013	£200 m.
EMI	2013	£1500 m.
Leaf UK[a]	2013	£35 m.
Western United	2014	£280 m.
Motorola	2014	$3100 m.
Makro	2014	£185 m.
TRW	2014	£2500 m.
Lehman Brothers	2015	£675 m.
Kuwait Petroleum Services[a]	2015	£42 m.
Philips	2015	£2400 m.
Kimberly-Clark	2015	$2500 m.

[a]Medically underwritten

Buy ins		
Sponsor	Date	Value
Weir Group	2007	£240 m.
BBA Aviation	2008	£270 m.
Morgan Crucible	2008	£160 m.
Smiths Group	2008	£500 m.
Friends Provident	2008	£350 m.
Cable and Wireless	2008	£1000 m.
Pensions Trust	2008	£225 m.
OFCOM	2008	£150 m.
Cadbury Schweppes	2009	£500 m.
CDC Group	2009	£370 m.
Dairy Crest	2009	£310 m.
RSA Insurance	2009	£1900 m.
Merchant Navy Officers	2009	£500 m.
British Airways	2010	£1300 m.
Next	2010	£124 m.
GlaxoSmithKline	2010	£892 m.
Aggregate Industries	2010	£203 m.
London Stock Exchange	2011	£203 m.
Meat and Livestock Commission	2011	£150 m.
Home Retail Group	2011	£280 m.
TI Group	2011	£150 m.
Smiths Group	2011	£150 m.
ITB	2011	£153 m.
Trinity Mirror	2011 & 12	£500 m.
West Midlands Integrated Transport Authority	2012	£272 m.
Cookson Group	2012	£320 m.
Tate and Lyle	2012	£347 m.
Western United	2012	£115 m.
Aon Minet	2012	£100 m.
General Motors	2012	$29,000 m.
Verizon Communications	2012	$7500 m.
Gartmore	2012	£160 m.
First Quench	2013	£160 m.
Western United	2013	£115 m.
Tate and Lyle	2013	£347 m.
Cobham	2013	£289 m.
Smith and Nephew	2013	£190 m.
TI Group	2013	£170 m.
Philips	2013	£484 m.
First Quench	2013	£160 m.
Smiths Group	2013	£170 m.
JLT UK	2013 & 14	£205 m.
Church Workers Pension Fund	2014	£100 m.
Institute of Chartered Accountants[a]	2014	£24 m.
ICI	2014	£3900 m.
Interserve	2014	£300 m.
Philips	2014	£610 m.
Total	2014	£1600 m.

Buy ins		
Sponsor	Date	Value
Uniac	2014	£129 m.
Aon Minet	2014	£210 m.
Taylor Wimpey	2014	£205 m.
Northern Bank	2015	£680 m.
Civil Aviation Authority	2015	£1600 m.
ICI	2015	£1800 m.
Wiggins Teape	2015	£400 m.
Aon	2016	£900 m.
ICI	2016	£630 m.
Kingfisher*	2016	£230 m.
Siemens	2016	£300 m.
ICI	2016	£750 m.

[a]Medically underwritten

Longevity swaps			
Sponsor	Insurer	Date	Value
Babcock	Credit Suisse	2009	£1200 m.
RSA Insurance	Goldman Sachs/Rothesay	2009	£1900 m.
Berkshire	Swiss Re	2009	£1000 m.
BMW	Deutsche Bank/Abbey Life	2011	£3000 m.
Pall	JP Morgan	2011	£100 m.
ITV	Credit Suisse	2011	£1700 m.
Rolls Royce	Deutsche Bank/Abbey Life	2011	£3000 m.
British Airways	Goldman Sachs/Rothesay	2011	£1300 m.
Pilkington	Legal and General	2011	£1000 m.
Aegon	Deutsche Bank/Abbey Life	2012	€12,000 m.
Azko Nobel	Swiss Re	2012	£1400 m.
LV=	Swiss Re	2012	£800 m.
Bentley	Deutsche Bank/Abbey Life	2013	£400 m.
BAE Systems	Legal and General	2013	£3200 m.
Carillion	Deutsche Bank	2013	£1000 m.
AstraZeneca	Deutsche Bank	2013	£2500 m.
BAE Systems	Legal and General	2013	£1700 m.
Aviva	Swiss Re, Munich Re and SCOR	2014	£5000 m.
BT	Prudential Ins. Co. of America	2014	£16,000 m.
Phoenix Group	Phoenix Life	2014	£900 m.
Merchant Navy Officers	Pacific Life Re	2015	£1500 m.
Scottish Power	Abbey Life	2015	£2000 m.
AXA	Reinsurance Group	2015	£2800 m.
Scottish and Newcastle	Friends Life	2015	£2400 m.
RAC (2003)	Scor Se	2015	£600 m.
Scottish Power	Abbey Life	2016	£1,000 m.
Pirelli	Zurich Assurance	2016	£600 m.

Source: Hymans Robertson (2013), JLT Pension Capital Strategies (2012), Towers Watson November (2014), and LCP (2011 to 2015)

Appendix 3: Example of the Valuation of a Simple Annuity

Age	No. of survivors of 100,000 births	Probability of survival for at least one year	Present value of an annuity of £10,000 p.a.
65	85,475.2	0.98621	9862.1
66	84,296.1	0.97116	9249.1
67	83,009.9	0.95504	8662.5
68	81,632.0	0.93716	8095.6
69	80,104.2	0.91799	7552.3
70	78,465.0	0.89806	7036.5
71	76,761.6	0.87632	6539.2
72	74,903.5	0.85267	6059.8
73	72,882.0	0.82710	5598.1
74	70,696.2	0.79995	5156.5
75	68,375.6	0.77044	4729.9
76	65,853.8	0.73852	4318.0
77	63,124.8	0.70487	3925.0
78	60,249.1	0.66943	3550.1
79	57,219.7	0.63137	3188.8
80	53,966.2	0.59123	2843.9
81	50,535.7	0.54916	2515.8
82	46,939.6	0.50595	2207.5
83	43,246.6	0.46190	1919.3
84	39,481.1	0.41660	1648.6
85	35,609.3	0.37160	1400.5
86	31,762.9	0.32745	1175.3
87	27,988.5	0.28492	974.0
88	24,353.3	0.24636	802.1
89	21,057.9	0.21020	651.8
90	17,966.9	0.17704	522.8
91	15,132.8	0.14546	409.1
92	12,433.4	0.11643	311.9
93	9952.2	0.09132	232.9
94	7805.3	0.07025	170.7
95	6004.3	0.05215	120.7
96	4457.5	0.03779	83.3
97	3230.0	0.02656	55.7
98	2270.3	0.01826	36.5
99	1560.6	0.01228	23.4
100	1049.5	0.00809	14.7
101+	691.2	?	26.2?
		Sum	111,670.0

The above valuation of a life annuity is for a male aged 65, based on English actuarial tables for 2007–2009 from the Office of National Statistics. This annuity has a flat payment of £10,000 per year until death, and the discount rate is 5%. There are no survivor benefits, or other complications. Its value is £111,670

Appendix 4: Gompertz 9 % Rule – Example for Ages 35–95

Age	No. of survivors per 100,000 births	MR×100	ln[MR×100]	Change in ln[MR×100]
34	98,026.0	0.1102	−2.2057	–
35	97,918.0	0.1244	−2.0843	0.1214
36	97,796.2	0.1208	−2.1139	−0.0296
37	97,678.1	0.1255	−2.0753	0.0386
38	97,555.5	0.1404	−1.9630	0.1123
39	97,418.5	0.1463	−1.9223	0.0408
40	97,276.0	0.1587	−1.8406	0.0817
41	97,121.6	0.1660	−1.7959	0.0447
42	96,960.4	0.1810	−1.7092	0.0867
43	96,784.9	0.1917	−1.6520	0.0572
44	96,599.4	0.2040	−1.5894	0.0626
45	96,402.3	0.2275	−1.4807	0.1088
46	96,183.0	0.2458	−1.4033	0.0774
47	95,946.6	0.2634	−1.3342	0.0691
48	95,693.9	0.2846	−1.2568	0.0773
49	95,421.6	0.3122	−1.1641	0.0927
50	95,123.7	0.3398	−1.0795	0.0846
51	94,800.5	0.3782	−0.9724	0.1071
52	94,442.0	0.4109	−0.8893	0.0831
53	94,053.9	0.4630	−0.7700	0.1194
54	93,618.4	0.5001	−0.6929	0.0770
55	93,150.2	0.5696	−0.5628	0.1301
56	92,619.6	0.6162	−0.4842	0.0786
57	92,048.9	0.6541	−0.4245	0.0597
58	91,446.8	0.7230	−0.3243	0.1002
59	90,785.6	0.7847	−0.2424	0.0818
60	90,073.2	0.8380	−0.1768	0.0657
61	89,318.4	0.9323	−0.0701	0.1066
62	88,485.7	1.0231	0.0228	0.0930
63	87,580.4	1.1517	0.1413	0.1184
64	86,571.7	1.2666	0.2363	0.0950
65	85,475.2	1.3795	0.3217	0.0854
66	84,296.1	1.5258	0.4225	0.1008
67	83,009.9	1.6599	0.5068	0.0842
68	81,632.0	1.8716	0.6268	0.1200
69	80,104.2	2.0463	0.7161	0.0893
70	78,465.0	2.1709	0.7751	0.0591
71	76,761.6	2.4206	0.8840	0.1089
72	74,903.5	2.6988	0.9928	0.1088
73	72,882.0	2.9991	1.0983	0.1055
74	70,696.2	3.2825	1.1886	0.0903
75	68,375.6	3.6882	1.3051	0.1165
76	65,853.8	4.1440	1.4217	0.1165

Age	No. of survivors per 100,000 births	MR×100	ln[MR×100]	Change in ln[MR×100]
77	63,124.8	4.5556	1.5164	0.0947
78	60,249.1	5.0281	1.6150	0.0987
79	57,219.7	5.6860	1.7380	0.1230
80	53,966.2	6.3568	1.8495	0.1115
81	50,535.7	7.1160	1.9623	0.1128
82	46,939.6	7.8676	2.0627	0.1004
83	43,246.6	8.7070	2.1641	0.1014
84	39,481.1	9.8067	2.2831	0.1189
85	35,609.3	10.8017	2.3797	0.0966
86	31,762.9	11.8830	2.4751	0.0954
87	27,988.5	12.9882	2.5640	0.0889
88	24,353.3	13.5316	2.6050	0.0410
89	21,057.9	14.6786	2.6864	0.0814
90	17,966.9	15.7740	2.7584	0.0720
91	15,132.8	17.8381	2.8813	0.1230
92	12,433.4	19.9559	2.9935	0.1122
93	9952.2	21.5721	3.0714	0.0779
94	7805.3	23.0741	3.1387	0.0673
95	6004.3	25.7615	3.2489	0.1102
96	4457.5	–	–	–
Average annual change in the probability of death (ages 35–95)				0.0894

The above computation is based on English actuarial tables for 2007–2009 from the Office of National Statistics for males. MR is the mortality rate which is (the number of survivors in the current year minus the number of survivors in the next year) divided by the number of survivors in the current year. ln[…] is the natural logarithm

References

JLT Pension Capital Strategies. (2012). *Buyout market watch*, July.

LCP (2011 to 2015). LCP Pension Buy-ins, Buy-outs and Longevity Swaps, Lane Clark and Peacock, London.

Hymans Robertson. (2013). Managing pension scheme risk – Buy-outs, buy-ins and longevity hedging Q4 2012.

Towers Watson. (2014). *Pensions and investments/Towers Watson 300 analysis: Year end 2014*. Towers Watson, 46 pages.

Index

CPI Antony Rowe
Chippenham, UK
2016-12-30 21:37